DATE DUE

SNAPSHOT

Carlotta Carlyle Books by Linda Barnes

SNAPSHOT

LINDA BARNES

**Delacorte
Press**

Published by
Delacorte Press
Bantam Doubleday Dell Publishing Group, Inc.
1540 Broadway
New York, New York 10036

"A Dream of Death"
reprinted with permission
of Macmillan Publishing Company
from The Poems of W.B. Yeats: A New Edition,
edited by Richard J. Finneran (New York: Macmillan, 1993).

Library of Congress Cataloging in Publication Data
Barnes, Linda.
    Snapshot : a Carlotta Carlyle novel / Linda Barnes.
      p. cm.
    ISBN 0-385-30612-1 : $19.95
    I. Title.
  PS3552.A682S64   1993
  813'.54—dc20   92-41734
                                         CIP

Manufactured in the United States of America

Published simultaneously in Canada

June 1993

10 9 8 7 6 5 4 3 2 1

BVG

Para mi hermana, Carol

The following friends and family members contributed their time, expertise, and valued opinions during various stages of development and writing: Dr. Steven Appelblatt, Richard Barnes, Brian DeFiore, James Morrow, Gladys Roldan, Alexandra Paul-Simon, R.N., and Dr. Amy Sims. I thank them. I also wish to recognize the valiant efforts of the T-shirt committee, Cynthia Mark-Hummel, John Hummel, and Beth King.

Gina Maccoby continues to do Carlotta proud—and Carlotta joyfully welcomes Carole Baron to her team.

I dreamed that one had died in a strange place
    Near no accustomed hand;
And they had nailed the boards above her face,
    The peasants of that land,
  Wondering to lay her in that solitude,
    And raised above her mound
A cross they had made out of two bits of wood,
    And planted cypress round;
And left her to the indifferent stars above
    Until I carved these words:
She was more beautiful than thy first love,
    But now lies under boards.

—"A Dream of Death"
William Butler Yeats—1891

What goes out of your eyes also gradually leaves
your heart.

—Persian saying

1

Every April my mother used to host her own version of the traditional Passover seder. A mishmash of Hebrew, Yiddish, English, and Russian, it involved all Mom's old union pals—Jews, Christians, Muslims, and pagans—who'd give rapid-fire thanks for the release of the ancient Hebrews from Egyptian bondage, and then launch into pre-chicken-soup tirades against General Motors, J. Edgar Hoover, and the FBI. I grew up thinking they were part of the religion.

I liked the Passover songs best. One of my favorites, "Dayenu," a lively, repetitive reminder that "It would have been enough" had God brought us out of Egypt but not given us the Torah, and "It would have been enough" had God given us the Torah but not given us the land of Israel, must have had about twenty-seven verses. Sung after the ritual consumption of four glasses of wine, sometimes it had forty-three.

Dayenu, I found myself thinking when the whole mess was over. It would have been enough to get the snapshots in the mail.

The first snapshot came on March 20, camouflaged by a sheaf of "urgent" political messages, market circulars, coupon giveaways, and appeals from various charities about to go belly-up unless I forked over twenty-five bucks. My cat and I have an arrangement that allows me to throw most of my mail directly into the wastebasket. It is he, T.C., Thomas C. Carlyle, aka Tom Cat, who subscribes to *Mother Jones* and *The New York Times Book Review*. It is he who fearlessly lists his full name in the phone directory, warding off the heavy-breathers that mere initials invite. When I scoop the mail off the foyer floor, I sort it into two piles, one for me, one for the cat. His stack is always twice as high as mine, but I hold my jealousy in check.

T.C. gets nothing but junk. I used to read it; I know.

Not that the mail with my name on it is such hot stuff. Most of it might as well be addressed to Occupant.

But on March 20 the mail included one hand-addressed envelope, which I suspiciously examined for the telltale return address of a famous person. Some marketing gurus out there genuinely believe I'll rip open a flap just to see what my old buddy Ed McMahon wants to tell me.

My tongue made an abrupt clicking noise, an involuntary response to the lack of a return address on the blue envelope—a shockingly misplaced statement of faith in the U.S. Postal Service as far as I was concerned.

Red Emma, my inherited parakeet, thinking I'd addressed her, began a stream of "pretty birds" and similar pap.

"Stick your head in a water dish," I suggested. I've been trying to rid myself of that bird ever since my aunt Bea died. Or at least teach it to swear.

The envelope was party-invitation size, a bit larger than three by five. Not dime-store stuff either; it had the feel of stationery from a fancy box instead of a banded pack. I allowed myself a brief moment of speculation before slitting the top fold. I don't know a lot of people who issue formal party invitations.

I might as well not have bothered to dredge up the few sociable names. Inside was no invitation, no letter, no card, just a color snapshot of a baby, an anonymous wrinkled raisin of a face swathed in a multicolored pastel thing the name of which I'd forgotten. My aunt used to knit them for the expected grandchildren of her mahjongg ladies. They—the outfits, not the ladies—looked like little bags with zippers down the front and tiny hoods. I flipped the photo over, expecting some kind of birth announcement.

Just KODAK QUALITY PAPER repeated on a series of slanted lines from the upper-left-hand corner to the lower right.

SNAPSHOT

A guessing game: Name that baby. On my desk I keep a magnifying glass, pencils, pens, scissors, and rubber bands in a coffee can. I polished the lens with spit and Kleenex. Under closer scrutiny, the baby's face looked like a wrinkled prune. Turning my attention to the envelope—specifically, to the postmark: Winchester, Massachusetts—I flipped through a mental Rolodex.

I don't know a soul in Winchester.

I slipped the photo under a corner of the blotter and proceeded with the bills. I study the phone statement like a hawk ever since Roz, my third-floor tenant, housecleaner, and sometime assistant, had a late-night vision and dialed a chatty Tibetan monk at my expense.

Exactly one week later, the second photo arrived. The envelope was the same sky-blue. No return address. Postmark: Winchester.

I'm no baby expert, nor do I wish to become one, but I pegged this tot for about a year old. Fair hair, light complexion, with wind-whipped crimson circles of excitement on her cheeks. I say "her" because the baby was wearing a frilly pink dress and tiny black patent Mary Janes so glossy they'd probably never touched the ground. The occasion could have been a first birthday party, although no cake was in evidence.

Nothing, as a matter of fact, was in evidence, just green grass and a couple of leafy elms.

I located last week's photo and got out my trusty magnifying lens. Could have been the same baby, a year older. Could have been another kid altogether.

I was in no mood for games and thought about tossing the snaps in the trash along with T.C.'s Sharper Image catalog and his invitation to use a $6,000 line of credit with Citibank MasterCard.

But I didn't.

The third came on April 3, one week later, right on schedule. I almost expected it. The little girl was wearing bibbed pink overalls and a matching pink-and-white-striped shirt. Same girl as in the second photo; I could see that now. She'd changed, maybe aged

3

another year, but the eyes were the same shape, the mouth had the identical bow.

Same amount of information, too. Zero. I thought about missing kid cases, wondered whether I'd seen the girl on the back of a milk carton.

It was the briefest of thoughts. I shoved the three photos underneath the blotter. I guess I don't feel right about tossing photographs. I keep them around, the way I save leftovers in the refrigerator.

The fourth photo arrived on the tenth of April. My Winchester correspondent had the U.S. mail figured better than I did. When I drop something in the blue box, sometimes it gets delivered the next day. Then I mail a letter from the same place and it takes a full week to make it to the same destination.

Number five, when it appeared, was definitely a birthday photo. A cone-shaped hat was tilted to one side of the girl's head, secured by an elastic band under her chin. Was I going to get a new picture of this child every Friday for the rest of my life?

Kid was a heartbreaker, no doubt about it. It wasn't any one of the features; it wasn't the features at all. The eyes were too close together, the nose small and unformed. It was the grin, a light-up-the-eyes squint that could have melted polar ice caps. Maybe somebody was sending them to cheer me up at the end of each week.

Probably not.

They stayed on my mind, like a measure of half-forgotten music, a melody tantalizingly out of reach. Almost a week later, on Thursday, I spread the photos across my desk and went over the lot with the magnifying lens, speculating about relatives. My mother had no family, except for Aunt Bea, and she was dead. Aunt Bea had never married. I'd lost touch with my father's kin even before his death. He'd never had much use for them. Was some long-lost cousin trying to slowly acquaint me with his or her offspring? Was this the opening salvo of a charity touch?

I do have a little sister, not a blood relation, but a sister from the Big Sisters Organization. Because of a sticky situation with her mom, I haven't seen Paolina for over four months. Could the Big Sisters be trying to soften me up to accept a replacement child?

Forget it.

I put away the magnifying glass with a sigh, sarcastically congratulating myself on some truly momentous discoveries: The child's face had thinned out as she'd turned from baby to toddler to little girl. Her hair had grown. The anonymous photographer had managed well-composed, centered shots with no chairs or lamps growing out of the kid's head.

Brilliant detective work. With the photos laid out like a hand of solitaire, I could watch little raisin-face begin her transformation into a curly-haired, blue-eyed, blond American princess.

Paolina, my little sister, is Colombian, with chocolate eyes and shiny dark hair. Her face is too round for perfection, and will probably stay that way even after her cheeks lose their baby-fat chubbiness.

So who wants perfection?

I gathered the snapshots together like a pack of cards and aimed them at the wastebasket's gaping mouth. At the last minute, I held the shot. Not that I figured they'd lead anywhere, but I found myself more intrigued than irritated by their presence.

After that night, I no longer thought about tossing them. I don't trust anything to the trash.

Not since the attack of the garbage thief.

2

Yes. The garbage thief.

I know it's hard to credit. If I hadn't been leaning out the window, I wouldn't have seen it. If I hadn't seen it—if, say, Roz had reported it to me the next morning—I wouldn't have believed it. And if I'd been wearing any clothes, I'd have stopped it.

"If" is one of my least favorite words.

As it happened, I was bare-ass naked, seated cross-legged on a doubled-up futon that serves as a couch, my elbows propped on the windowsill, my face turned to a flickering sliver of moon. All the lights in my second-floor bedroom were off and my modesty, such as it is, was further protected by some twenty inches of wall separating the low futon and the sill.

A night-chilled breeze brushed my hair. If I closed the window, the screech of badly joined wood would break the silence and send a shiver up my neck. Instead of the deep sky, the barely budding elm tree, the moon, I'd catch a reflection of my sleepy face in the glass. Wide-set hazel eyes that I call green. Pointy chin. A nose broken often enough to acquire either "character" or a bump and a tilt, depending on the relative merits of flattery and honesty.

I left the window open. If I stared hard, I could see the full circle of the moon, the dark part defined by the silver crescent.

I'm an insomniac, a card-carrying member of the club. Since enrollment is secret, I'm the president of my own chapter and I make up the rules. Number one: "Don't lie there. If you can't sleep, get up and do something else."

I recited the other commandments in my head.

"Get plenty of exercise." Well, I sure do. I play killer volleyball three mornings a week. I swim laps at the YWCA pool.

"Eat right." Definitely a failing. I'm a junk-food addict, and the thought of a nice warm glass of milk before bedtime makes me want to puke.

"Always go to sleep at the same time." Sure. I'm a full-time private investigator, but when I can't pay my bills, I drive a cab nights. There is no soothing regularity to my schedule.

"Don't nap." Who has time to nap?

"Cut out the caffeine." Pepsi is a way of life to me.

I did quit smoking. I give myself extra credit for that.

Not for the first time, I considered sleeping pills, the scattering of Dalmanes and Halcions I'd inherited along with Aunt Bea's house. I rejected them, as usual. Live with an addict and you grow wary of medication. Marry and divorce one, you practically convert to Christian Science.

"Exercise." I went back to the second commandment because I thought I'd read somewhere that you shouldn't try any strenuous activity within four hours of going to sleep. I glanced at my bed, shadowy in the moonlight, at the sheet-draped form of Sam Gianelli. Maybe he was my problem. Making love isn't supposed to count as late-night exercise. It relaxes you, right? Makes you sleepy.

Hah. It makes me feel loose, slippery, and warm. But not sleepy.

I considered tossing a pillow at Sam's head. Why should he sleep? Specifically, why should he sleep at my place when he could go back to his Charles River Park apartment? I padded over and kneeled down to reach for my guitar case. I'd ease it out quietly, go downstairs, and practice some finger picking.

The guitar was beyond my reach, centered under the queen-size mattress. Dear God in heaven, Roz must have vacuumed under the bed.

I crawled back to the futon and watched the moon disappear behind a sea of brightening clouds.

The car didn't have its headlights on.

I heard it before I saw it, the closest streetlamp being twenty-five yards away. The motor sputtered to a stop near my driveway. The carburetor needed work.

A car door opened, but the dome light didn't flash. The next sound puzzled me until I realized it was the creak of the trunk. Maybe the driver needed a jack to change a flat tire.

In pitch blackness?

By this time the car had my full attention.

I craned my neck, realized the limitations of my nakedness, and wondered where my clothes were. I felt like yelling "What the hell are you doing down there?" I kept quiet, realizing that the fast-moving moon would soon tell the tale.

It reappeared in a V-shaped break of cloud cover.

A heavyset guy was lifting one of my garbage cans into the gaping trunk of his car. I blinked and shook my head. When I opened my eyes, he was still there.

In my Cambridge neighborhood, barreling is an old and time-honored tradition. The rules are clear. Residents put out big items —old chairs and rickety tables and clunky washing machines—the last Thursday of the month.

It was the third Thursday of April. No one would expect to mine gold in a third Thursday trash collection. And who would rummage for the odd unreturned five-cent-deposit soda can in the middle of the night?

"Stop!" I hollered as loudly as I could. I didn't want the sucker to get away with the trash can. I have only two of them, big wheeled ones that cost $39.95 a piece at the local hardware store. He turned his face and I ducked instinctively. I didn't want to turn the lights on till I found a robe.

I scrabbled around on the floor until I touched cloth. Sam's shirt—hardly long enough, but something to shroud me while I searched more diligently.

I snapped on the light. "Sam!"

"Huh?" He didn't even roll over.

I grabbed my red chenille bathrobe, the one that clashes with my hair, out of the closet. How'd it get in the closet? Roz must have really gone on a cleaning binge.

"Wha'?" I heard Sam mutter as I ran barefoot down the steps.

I have three good locks on my front door. You can't even get *out* of my house without a key for the deadbolt. My purse, with keys inside, was probably on the kitchen counter. Might as well have been on the moon. I ran to the living room and snatched the extra key from the top drawer of my desk. Then I raced back and let myself out in time to see the car two-wheel the corner and disappear.

With both my trash cans.

I stood at the edge of the driveway, in the same spot the cans had occupied a moment before, cursing under my breath, staring at empty darkness but seeing the speeding car, the screeching turn, the mud-smeared license plate. Four. Eight. The last two digits: a four and an eight. Definitely.

My gut reaction: Why me? I'm no rocket scientist. I have nothing to hide. And then I thought, goddammit, yes I do! I have plenty to hide. I don't want anyone to know how much mocha almond ice cream I eat in a week, much less a single detail of my correspondence. I particularly don't want the names of my clients spread around. They hire me for confidential reasons, and, within the law, I do my damnedest to preserve their anonymity.

I did a quick inventory of what I'd been tossing besides the cat's junk mail. Had I received any checks lately? What cases was I still trying to collect on?

A missing husband whose wife should have thrown a farewell party for the bum instead of paying good money to find him living with her stepdaughter. A runaway son-in-law. A habitual bail jumper every private eye in New England has taken a run at . . .

I tried to catalog the trash, but my mind blanked at the scope of the task. And maybe the garbage thief wasn't even after me. Maybe some garbologist was doing a study of Roz's reject artwork. To me, it always looks like Roz frames and attempts to sell every botched endeavor, but what do I know about postpunk art?

Hell. I didn't care if the target was Roz or me. I didn't care if some grad student was doing a thesis on banana-peel disposal in the 02138 zip code. Whoever it was, the garbologist was going to have to research somebody else's garbage.

I wiped my bare feet on the damp grass. Four-eight, four-eight, four-eight, I repeated. With my eyes closed, I teased my memory for details. Color: blue, maybe gray. Rectangular taillights.

I'd have to put a hook near the front door, hang the deadbolt key on it. Should have done it long ago, in case of fire. Of course, with the key hanging there, any burglar who came through a window would be able to open the door and steal the big items—the couch, the bed, the goddamn refrigerator, if he wanted it—as well as the usual small stuff.

I thought about thieves. I thought about garbage. I thought about thieves who steal garbage.

Now, empty trash cans have their uses. Landscapers use them to haul dead leaves and branches. The hawkers who sell soda outside Fenway Park use them to store ice.

But this moron hadn't tried to dump the trash on my front lawn. He'd sped off with Hefty bags full of juice cartons, catfood cans, and old newspapers smeared with parakeet droppings.

If he'd wanted the cans, why steal the garbage? If he'd wanted my garbage, why steal the cans?

3

What with the garbage thief and insomnia, I didn't stir until eleven o'clock the next morning. Sam had long since returned to Charles River Park, complaining that he hardly ever felt rested after a night at my place.

As I groggily crossed the hall, listening to a throbbing hum in my head and hoping the shower would ease it, the day's mail hit the foyer floor with a thud.

Friday. Terrific. Time for another snapshot of little Miss Winchester. Well, she could wait till I'd washed up, eaten breakfast, lunch, or both, depending on the contents of the fridge. She could wait till I'd started my pursuit of the garbage snatcher.

How many light blue, or possible gray, late-model Firebirds had a four and an eight for their final two license-plate numbers? Was I sure it was a Massachusetts plate?

The thought almost drove me back under the covers. Instead I stood in the shower for ten minutes with the temperature at lobster-boil. Then I put in a full two minutes under ice water because somebody told me that cold water is better for rinsing conditioner out of your hair.

Dressed in jeans, sneakers, and a turquoise cotton sweater, I headed downstairs. I pass through the foyer on my way to the kitchen. No harm in stopping to take a peek, I decided. Give me an opportunity to bend over and shake out my wet hair, which I comb as infrequently as possible because it's too thick and too curly and it hurts. I could view the day's photo while chugging orange juice. No time wasted.

I sorted through the pile twice to make sure, but there was no blue envelope. I felt curiously deprived, as if I'd come to the end of a novel borrowed from the library and found the final chapter razored out.

The throb of my headache met its match in the smack of a hammer against a nearby nail.

"You like this here?" The voice came from an unlikely height. Perched on a chair, my tenant, Roz, had gained about a foot in stature. She's short and I'm six-one. Our eyes were now on a level.

I said, "I thought you were going to check with me before you hung any more paintings on my walls." To contrast with her fright-white hair, which she dyes more often than I shampoo, Roz was wearing skin-tight black pants and a redder-than-red T-shirt emblazoned with NINE OUT OF TEN MEN WHO'VE TRIED CAMELS PREFER WOMEN. I read it twice to make sure I'd gotten it right. I don't know where Roz finds her enormous wardrobe of bizarre T-shirts. Maybe secret admirers send them. She has a body, particularly in the T-shirt slogan area, that earns much admiration.

She plucked a nail from between her teeth. "I thought you meant just with offensive stuff."

"This is not offensive?"

"What? You're with the National Endowment for the Arts?"

"Just because it has vegetables in it doesn't make it a still life," I said. "What the hell is that man doing with that carrot?"

"You don't like it?"

"Roz, this is not only my home, it's my office. Clients come here. People who might otherwise consider hiring me."

"Hang it someplace else, huh?"

I nodded my heartfelt agreement.

"Should I yank the other nail out, or try a different painting?"

"Depends on the painting."

"I've got more vegetables. Acrylics really groove with vegetables."

Whenever Roz needs subject matter, her first target is my refrigerator.

The telephone interrupted a promising aesthetic argument.

"Should I answer it?" she asked.

I nodded. "Stall while I get orange juice."

I grabbed the carton from the fridge and raced back in time to hear Roz, in the nasal twang she deems secretarial, report that I was currently taking a foreign call on another line.

"It's okay," I said. "Geneva hung up."

She glared at me. "Ms. Carlyle will be right with you."

"Speaking," I said crisply.

"Hi. Maybe you remember me. I'm the psychiatrist in the brown triple-decker two doors down."

"Sure," I said, "um—"

"Keith Donovan."

Maybe he'd had his trash stolen too. Maybe he wanted me to trace it for him. "What can I do for you?"

"You've been receiving photos in the mail."

"Baby pictures. Kid pictures. Yes."

I could hear him breathing. I wondered what he was waiting for. He exhaled again, inhaled. "I have a patient who's been sending them. I'm sorry. I'd mentioned your name—as someone who wouldn't be, um, a threatening presence, if she decided to investigate a certain matter . . ."

"And?"

"She's having trouble making a decision, and she thought she'd —I don't know—prepare you in some way, in case she decided to seek your counsel."

"Is she in your office now?"

"Yes," he said. "She knows I'm speaking to you."

"Does she want to see me, make an appointment or something?"

"Can you hang on a minute?"

"Sure."

I could hear indistinct muffled voices. I couldn't make out individual words. I tried to remember what he looked like, this Keith Donovan. I remembered the name from some Homeowners Association meeting. Was he the pudgy guy who always complained about

15

the neighborhood dogs? The area I live in, within spitting distance of Harvard Square, is thick with psychiatrists.

"Ms. Carlyle?"

"Yes."

"She—my patient—wonders if you might see her now? I would come along."

"I don't usually have a consulting shrink present."

"Is it out of the question?"

I reviewed my caseload. Tracking down the garbage thief was not going to earn me a fee.

"Come on by," I said.

4

He seemed too young. Perhaps I'd misunderstood. Maybe he was a therapist of some sort or other, but hardly the kind entitled to call himself "doctor." With a haircut fresh off a Marine base and an eager grin, he looked like a big goofy kid. His tweed jacket and muted paisley tie had probably been chosen to make him appear older, and he must have inherited the half-moon reading glasses tucked into his breast pocket. He sure hadn't aged enough to need them.

She was a willow-thin blonde with nervous hands. It took her ten minutes just to remove her raincoat, fingernails clacking against the buttons. She wasn't paying attention to the task; her eyes were darting all over the place, noting the water stains on the ceiling, eyeing the furniture as if she were pricing it for an auction gallery.

I was glad I'd made Roz take the painting down.

I did some appraising of my own. The beige suit, piped in a darker shade, maybe six hundred bucks, and I constantly undervalue due to years of Filene's Basement shopping. Double it to include the shoes, bag, and leather gloves. The raincoat had a plaid lining and a Burberry label. Her slim gold watch and massive solitaire diamond told me she could probably afford both a private eye and a therapist.

The skirt of the fancy suit gapped at the waist and bagged at the hip, as if she'd recently lost weight. Deep purplish-gray shadows tinted the skin under her eyes. A woman who spent megabucks on a precision wedge haircut ought to concentrate more on her makeup, I thought.

Keith Donovan made a ceremony of hanging her raincoat on the coat-tree while she fumbled with her gloves. Clasping her handbag tightly against her chest, she managed the single step down to my living room with an elbow assist from the therapist.

Normally I invite clients to sit in the chair across from my rolltop desk, but I hadn't readied a second chair so I motioned them farther into the room. The woman chose my aunt Bea's favorite rocker, with its needlepoint cushion and faint welcoming creak. Donovan waited for me to take the couch before selecting an easy chair.

The woman absorbed the surroundings with a practiced glance, and I wondered what deceptive conclusions she'd drawn from the antiques and Orientals. The room is exactly as my aunt left it when she died, except for the addition of my desk.

Her eyes fastened on the silver-framed photo centered on the mantelpiece. She mumbled and looked at me expectantly.

"What?"

"Is she your daughter?" she asked in a low urgent tone.

"My little sister."

"Do you have children?"

"No."

"Ms. Carlyle," Keith Donovan said, "I'd like you to meet Mrs. Woodrow, Emily Woodrow."

She twisted her hands, rubbed them along the length of her thighs, clasped them in her lap. Said nothing.

"Would you like a cup of coffee?" I asked.

No response.

"You've been sending me pictures of your daughter?" I made it a question only by inflection.

"She looks like me, doesn't she?" the woman said. On the surface her pale face seemed as passive and calm as an old portrait in an art museum, but I felt uneasy scrutinizing her. She had an odd voice, faint and hoarse.

"She's beautiful," I said. "Your daughter."

The woman lowered her head suddenly. Her hair, falling in wings from a center part, covered her face, so I couldn't tell if tears came with the wrenching sobs. I had a fix on her hoarseness now. Crying jags roughened vocal cords more quickly than Jack Daniel's and cigarettes.

Donovan seemed to be studying his knuckles. I wondered if he was billing my time as one of the woman's treatment sessions.

She did the hand routine again, her fingers rubbing her thighs as if she were searching for something to grasp or tear. Her long fingernails were unpolished and neglected.

"Is there something I can do for you?" I asked.

Color flooded her cheeks. Her chest rose and fell so quickly I thought she might hyperventilate and pass out. I hoped Donovan, young as he was, had some medical experience.

"Doctor," she muttered to him. "I don't know where to—"

"Would you like me to provide some background information?" he asked gently.

"Yes," she said, seizing the words like a lifeline. "But first, I want—I'd like to give her this."

It was a pale blue rectangle. I was going to get my Friday photo after all.

The envelope seemed identical to the ones underneath my blotter, but the enclosed photograph was a formal study, on thicker stock. The child . . . well, the girl wore a hat, but the floppy-brimmed straw was no cover for the fact that she'd lost her bouncy curls. I could practically see bones through her papery skin. She was gamely attempting her angelic smile, but it couldn't make the jump to her sunken eyes.

I swallowed and was glad I hadn't eaten breakfast.

Centered at the bottom, beneath a black border, elaborate calligraphy spelled out: Rebecca Elizabeth Woodrow. 9/12/85–1/6/92. The newborn in the hand-knitted bunting—funny how the word for the damn thing came back to me—the two-year-old in the pink striped shirt and bib overalls, hadn't made it to her seventh birthday.

I glanced up. Emily Woodrow stared at my little sister's photo with an intensity bordering on hunger. I was glad I held her daughter's picture in my hand. It gave me something to look at, besides her face.

"I'm sorry," I said. "She was beautiful."

The woman tried to smile. A mistake. Her lips quivered.

"Mrs. Woodrow has been seeing me since her daughter's death," Keith Donovan volunteered, his voice low and soothing.

"Three months ago," she whispered, as if she were reminding herself. Her hands were working again. The nail on the index finger of her left hand was broken, jagged. "Have you ever had a serious illness?" she asked abruptly.

"No," I said.

"Then you don't know what it's like when a doctor looks at you in that special kindly way, and then he rips your heart out."

I tried to guess how old she was. Forties by the hands. Thirties by the face.

"Do you want to tell me about it?" I shot Donovan a sidelong glance, but if he'd caught me doing my imitation of a therapist, he didn't react.

She lowered her eyes and addressed the carpet in a voice as flat and melancholy as a foghorn. "There's no place to start. No beginning. Becca seemed to get a lot of colds, maybe three times as many as the year before. And the fevers. Scary high fevers, where she'd just go limp, with her face flushed and her hair soaked."

As she spoke, Emily Woodrow lifted a hand to her own hair, as if she were unconsciously feeling for dampness. She left her hand there, forgotten, suspended, and went on.

"One day I kept her home from school, even though she wasn't running a fever. Her father says—said—I babied her. But the listlessness; it wasn't like her. I called our doctor. He said bring her in —no appointment, just bring her in—and I was scared." She swallowed audibly. "For the first time. I was always scared after that. He gave her a quick exam—eyes, ears, throat, heartbeat—and said she seemed okay. She went back to school, but I could tell she wasn't right. She cried a lot, cried for no reason, and she'd never been a complainer. And then she got a bruise on the inside of her leg, big as an apple, but she couldn't remember bumping into anything, and it didn't go away, so I took her back to the doctor—I remember that day. There was such a wind howling; I held her hand. I thought she might blow away. She'd gotten so thin; she'd stopped eating. I bought her whatever she wanted. Pistachio ice cream . . ."

"Go on," said Donovan.

She shrugged and glanced down at her expensive shoes. "Something was wrong with her blood. Platelets. He sent us to a specialist. And another one. They diagnosed Becca with ALL."

"Which is?" I asked.

"Acute lymphoblastic leukemia. It's ninety-five percent curable. That's the cure rate. Ninety-five percent. They kept telling us that, over and over. When she lost her hair, when she couldn't eat, not even applesauce like a baby, when she'd throw up every five minutes, too weak to turn her head, so I was afraid she'd choke on her own vomit, they always came back to that. Ninety-five percent."

I didn't like the way this was going.

"Mrs. Woodrow," I said as gently as I could, my voice barely above a whisper, "I'm sorry. Believe me, I am sorry for your loss and your pain. But five percent die. If the cure rate is ninety-five percent, then five percent die."

Emily Woodrow accorded my observation the same polite interest she might have given if I'd commented on the weather. "At first it didn't matter. Nothing did. My daughter . . . my only child . . . There had to be a funeral and people came and people went and brought food and took food away. Casseroles and covered chafing dishes. Bread. Pots that steamed but never smelled. Nothing smelled, except the flowers. I didn't want any flowers. I hate lilies. The first day, they're beautiful, especially the star lilies, and by the second day, they reek. I remember I couldn't go to her bedroom. I stood in the hall by her door, but I couldn't go inside. I remember that. Her chair is at the kitchen table. I won't let Harold take it away. I want to move, but Harold, my husband—"

Dammit, I ought to keep a box of Kleenex on my desk. She fumbled for tissues in her handbag.

"I was taking pills, medicine. Pills and water, pills and water. Waking and sleeping, waking and sleeping again. I never ate. There's an oak outside my window. I watched its branches rustle. Empty branches. An empty tree. Dead, but living. Why should it be dead, but living? I thought I heard God talking to me. Just the once. He said—or she said—it was a whispery kind of voice: 'If you don't believe in me, it's because you haven't suffered enough.' And I felt almost triumphant, as if I must have found some sort of religion— because I had suffered enough. Not like Becca, but enough."

I glanced at the therapist, tried to send him the silent urgent message that this was his country, not mine.

"The funny thing is," she went on, "I made phone calls and commitments. Friends would ring and say, 'Where were you? Why didn't you meet us for lunch?' And I wouldn't know what they were talking about. I had these perfectly sane conversations, talking about books and gardening, and I made plans, and I don't remember any of it. It was like floating in a fog bank. I never could see or hear anything clearly.

"I spent a lot of time thinking. Brooding. About what I'd done wrong. About why I was being punished. About how I hadn't lis- tened to her when she first said she wasn't feeling well, about how I hadn't taken her to the doctor soon enough, and then about how I must have taken her to the wrong doctor. Keith says I was angry, terribly angry, but I turned my anger inward . . ."

Keith. Not Dr. Donovan. I glanced at his pleasantly earnest, unlined face, and wondered who would choose a shrink so appar- ently unscarred by life.

Mrs. Woodrow seemed to have run out of steam. Even her hands lay idle in her lap.

"I'm sorry," I said, again as gently as I could, forming the words with the care a child takes in trying to blow a large soap bubble, "but I don't know what you want me to do."

"I'm getting to it," she snapped, her voice brittle, her eyes staring deeply into mine. "I can't just tell you cold."

I was sorry I'd interrupted. I'd seen the photos: the baby, the toddler, the child, the beautiful girl. I'd watched her grow.

"I have a picture in my mind," the woman said. "And I can't make it go away."

She sat for a time, a statue frozen in her chair. Lines appeared and disappeared in her narrow face. Sometimes they seemed deeply etched; sometimes a superficial shading of the light. At the right side of her jaw, a tiny muscle twitched.

"You have to remember how hard it was for me," she said finally. "I was taking pills, medicine. Did I say that?"

"Yes."

"It's about the last day, her last day."

"Did she die at home?" She flinched when I said the word.

"At the hospital," she said, staring directly into my eyes, holding them with her gaze. "It was her regular chemotherapy session. The doctors had been, well, noncommittal. But encouraging, very encouraging. She was handling everything well . . ."

"Yes?"

Her eyes were blue, an icy bottomless lake. "I have this picture in my head. The last day. It went wrong so fast. I was sitting near her, in a beige chair, on the right side of the bed, so close I could stroke her forehead. We were in the regular room, the one with the blue wallpaper. Blue wallpaper, with a white lattice pattern and flowers, yellow-and-gold flowers. Zinnias. I used to stare at the wallpaper when I couldn't stand watching the pain in Becca's face. Only for a moment; otherwise, I felt like I was deserting her. But there were times when I'd stare till there were only yellow and blue blotches. It was quiet. The regular nurse was present. She hadn't had any trouble inserting the IV. Everything was ordinary—if horrible things, if your child's pain, can ever be ordinary. And then there was a man in white, a man I hadn't seen before, but he must have

23

been a doctor. Bursting in like that. Yelling. And he pushed me out of the room, shoved me. And through a tiny window, I saw the mask over her face, over Becca's face. He jammed it over her mouth, her nose. The noise she made, I hear it in my sleep—"

"It's okay, Emily," Keith Donovan said quietly. "It's okay. It's okay."

Her silence was more unnerving than her sobs. She sat motionless, staring inward, seeing her child's last moments with the intensity of a fever dream.

"Where was your daughter treated?" I asked.

"JHHI."

The Jonas Hand/Helping Institute, created when the small Jonas Hand Hospital and the even smaller James Helping Institute merged in the late seventies, is housed in a dilapidated building in an area that swings between urban renewal and urban decay, teetering back and forth on the pendulum of local politics, never quite making it into the respectable zone. For years, there've been rumors of JHHI closing, or moving, but they've always proved false. JHHI endures, the major reason the neighborhood never quite succumbs to gang violence, racism, or sheer neglect. Said to be one of the nation's top medical centers, it draws patients from as far away as Cairo and Santiago.

The locals bless the hospital for the police presence it commands. Most of them call the place Helping Hand, and believe it was named for some anonymous Good Samaritan. It's no fly-by-night miracle-cure center, no south-of-the-border laetrile clinic.

Mrs. Woodrow rubbed her temples. "We took her there because of Muir, of course. Because of his reputation."

I didn't respond to the name. She looked at me as if I'd missed a cue.

"Dr. Jerome D. Muir," Emily Woodrow insisted. The name did have a certain familiarity, like a name I might have read once in a newspaper.

"Wouldn't Children's Hospital have been the place to go?" I

inquired. "Better known?" I'd certainly heard more about Children's than I'd read about Muir.

"No. No," Mrs. Woodrow said earnestly. "We checked very carefully. My husband does know doctors. He talked to them. We were afraid of a teaching hospital, of some enormous place where you never know who's actually doing what. I mean, I realize medical students need to learn, and I know they need to learn on living people with real illnesses, but I thought, no, not on my daughter. So we chose JHHI. Because of Dr. Muir."

Donovan said, "He's the best man in the area, maybe in the country." The woman seemed comforted by his assurance.

I asked, "Was Muir your daughter's primary physician?"

"Yes."

"Do you think an error was made in your daughter's medical care?" I asked Mrs. Woodrow.

"I don't know."

"Sounds to me like you want a malpractice attorney."

"I don't," she said vehemently. "I can't and I don't. My husband is an attorney who works closely with doctors, setting up corporations, partnerships, that kind of thing. I can't risk his livelihood by starting up a lawsuit based on shadows. I don't know anything for sure. Maybe I dreamed it. Maybe the drugs I took afterward . . . maybe they altered my perceptions. . . ."

"You must have asked your daughter's doctor what happened."

"He explained. He explains, but it doesn't make sense. He uses words I don't understand, words with twenty syllables, and the next time I ask, after I've looked things up, he uses a different word and says I must have misunderstood him. And lately, he's always out— on rounds or whatever. And the nurses, they don't even bother to hide it anymore. They just whisper to each other. 'It's her again, the crazy woman.' "

A lawyer once told me that more doctors get sued because of rude receptionists than rotten care.

"You lost your daughter," I said. "That's enough to make anyone crazy for a while."

I wondered what Keith Donovan thought about the nontechnical term, *crazy*.

"Becca looked like me, but she wasn't like me," the woman said fiercely. Her jagged nail snagged a beige stocking. She tore it loose, ripping a hole. Didn't notice. "She was matter-of-fact. She accepted what was. Whatever they did to her, whatever those doctors and nurses did to her, she simply assumed they were doing their best. Even when she was so weak she could hardly talk, she never blamed me. She never blamed anyone. She cried when she couldn't go to her friend Jessie's birthday party, but she didn't cry because she had leukemia. She just wanted them to make her well again. So her hair would grow back, and she could jump rope on the playground. And they said they would, and they didn't."

Children died. Parents lived. It broke your heart. Before I could open my mouth to tell her I couldn't help her, she sped on.

"I want you to tell me, assure me, that nothing, absolutely nothing unusual or odd or wrong went on. I owe that much to Becca. To Becca and myself. I need to hear someone say it, before I can go on."

"You want me to talk to her doctor?"

She licked her lips, spoke rapidly, softly. "I need to know that everything that could have been done was done, and done right. That no one could have done more. I don't want to sue anybody. I don't need money. I have money."

"I'm not a whiz at medical terminology," I said.

"I could help with that," Donovan volunteered.

I turned on him. "Do you think this is necessary? Or wise?"

"You mean, do I think it will help Mrs. Woodrow?"

"Yes," I snapped, surprised to find myself angry. I didn't need any psychiatrist to tell me what I meant.

He paused, considering his words. "I think it may help to close off this area, wall up the past. So she can move forward."

"Move forward," Emily Woodrow repeated, shaking her head slowly. She kept moving her head back and forth as if she'd forgotten how to stop.

I sucked in a deep breath, tried to find another way to say what I needed to say. Couldn't. This is what came out: "Mrs. Woodrow, I'm sorry, but I have to say this. Your daughter is dead. What Dr. Donovan means when he says 'move forward,' what he means is that no matter what I discover, no matter what I learn, your daughter will still be dead."

Her eyes closed and she flinched as if I'd hit her. I glanced at Donovan. He inclined his head slightly as if I'd said the right thing, but it didn't make me feel any better.

She wanted to write out a check immediately. I persuaded her to take a day to look over my standard contract, suggest any changes. I assured her that she could mail me the check.

I don't usually go out of my way to avoid prompt payment. Usually I demand it, but there was something about this case— probably the woman's visible pain—that made me want to stall. And what was the hurry? I asked myself. It wasn't like the events had occurred yesterday.

She teetered on her heels when she stood to leave. Since she had her doctor along, I didn't feel required to see her out.

When she reappeared in the doorway, clad in her Burberry, her index finger to her lips, I was surprised. Surefooted now, she glided across the room till she was well within whispering range.

"He thinks I'm looking for my glove," she murmured. "Tell me quickly: Do you own any stocks? Do you speculate?"

"No." I thought she was probably mad but I answered. It was something in her eyes. An intensity, a brilliance.

"Do you work for yourself?"

"Yes."

"For anyone else?"

"I drive a cab."

"What company?"

"Green and White."

"I can check on them. Do you own a gun?"

"Yes."

"Can you use it?"

"Yes."

"Have you?"

"Have I what?"

"Used it. Killed with it."

"Yes."

"Would you do it again?"

"If I had to."

"What does Cee Co mean to you?"

"Seiko? The watch people?"

She handed me a slim envelope. "This is for you. Keep it. And stay here for me. On hold. Don't take any other client. You'll get something in the mail or by messenger. Keep it safe. Keep it for me."

"Wait. Wait just a minute. Hire a safety deposit box."

"No. It has to be this way. Please. You have to." For a moment, her fierce gaze faltered.

"What is Cee Co?" I asked.

She ignored the question.

"Are you in danger?" I asked, louder this time.

"I don't think so."

"Why ask about guns? Do you need protection? Are you afraid?"

"Afraid? Afraid of what? There's nothing to be afraid of now. When you've lost everything, there's nothing left."

She swiveled her head, as if she'd heard a noise, footsteps. All was quiet.

"No," she murmured softly, turning to stare at me again. "No, I take that back. You're right: I am afraid. I'm afraid I'll forget her someday." Her voice was a choked whisper, and the words came faster and faster. "Forget the feel of her hair. Forget the moment I named her. Forget the creases under her eyes when she smiled—"

"Did you find it?" Donovan hovered at the door. Instinctively I slid the slim envelope under my blotter, out of sight.

Emily Woodrow, her gait unsteady, yanked a glove from beneath the rocking chair. I hadn't seen her plant it.

"Here it is," she said automatically, the mask almost back in place. "Sorry to have troubled you."

"I'll be in touch," I said.

She shot me a warning glance. "This is something I won't discuss on the telephone. I cannot discuss it over the phone."

"Still—"

"If you'll do as I've asked," she said mildly, her fierce eyes hooded, "everything will be fine."

Sure, I thought.

"Ms. Carlyle," she said, turning back as she reached the doorway.

"Yes."

"Your little sister—"

"Yes?"

Her voice faltered. She bit her lip and took a deep breath before she could go on. "She's very beautiful."

5

This time I closed and bolted the door behind them. I peered through the peephole as Donovan guided Emily Woodrow down the three steps. Then I hurried back to the living room.

The white envelope, while of lesser quality than the stiff blue ones, was not cheap. I slit it with a letter opener and eased out the contents. Two items: a folded sheet of paper and a powder-blue check. The paper was a photocopy of a death certificate. Rebecca Elizabeth Woodrow's. The date of death was the same as the one on the photograph.

Emily Woodrow's daughter had died. That much of her initial story was true.

The check was big enough to earn an involuntary whistle. And all I had to do to earn it was wait.

I tapped my fingers on my desk. My blunt-cut nails made no noise. Waiting is not what I do best. Nor is it my natural inclination.

I peered into the envelope, dissatisfied with its contents. My eye caught a flash of silver at the bottom. I yanked the sides of the envelope apart and shook until something fell onto my blotter.

I got a stinging paper cut for my effort, and a shiny bit of foil-like paper, about one inch square. When I held it to the light, it seemed to change color. One edge was slightly bent, another looked as if it had been snipped with a nail scissors, separated from a larger item.

What that item might be, I couldn't guess.

My stomach rumbled, so I made breakfast, swallowing the rest of the carton of orange juice, then frying up four slices of bacon and two eggs in a cast-iron skillet.

Ah, the joy of bacon! I'd never tasted its crisp fattiness till I was eighteen: No pig products allowed in my mother's kosher home. As an adult I've found that eating such defiantly *treyf* fare gives me the warm glow of disobedience, as good a fuel as any for trying to pump information out of often-reluctant sources.

I deserted the dishes in the sink, where Roz might or might not notice them, and returned to the living room. Emily Woodrow's check, drawn on a BayBank in Marlborough, had her name and address printed neatly on the upper-left-hand corner. Her own name, not her husband's. I dialed a 1–800 number, asked to speak to Patsy, and sipped my first Pepsi of the day while stuck on hold. Somebody played saccharine-stringed Beatles Muzak in my ear.

Patsy Ronetti's Bronx blare woke me up.

I met her when I was a cop. She's a prize. Took a job right out of high school, a trainee with Equifax, one of those high-profile information-gathering corporations. Spent four years as an insurance investigator, and now she knows it all: data-base access, public-document searches, credit reporting. I send her a bottle of Johnnie Walker Black Label every Christmas. Most of the investigators in town probably do the same. She could run a liquor store on the side, but mostly she reports credit.

I ran Emily Woodrow past her, gave her Harold's name as well, assuming he had the same last name as his wife and child, read her the Winchester address on the check. Then we talked money and time. Her rates are not cheap, but she's fast. I could hear her punching keys on her terminal as we bartered.

I wanted both a credit report and an employment search, and was arguing in favor of a two-for-one deal.

"You hooked yourself a live one," she said.

"Yeah."

"I'm backed up here to Tuesday, Carlotta. Half the country's checking on the other half. I'm not gonna do any rush job on this, understand? But here's a teaser for you. He's a lawyer—"

"I already knew that."

"You also know he pulls down six large? Maybe you can afford the car."

"Huh?"

"You're buying a car, right? Or leasing?"

"Not that I know of," I said while imaginary warning bells pealed in my ears.

"Wait a minute. Carlyle, right?" She spelled it out.

"Yeah."

"I got a call, must be three days ago. Car dealer, I coulda sworn."

"Got the paper on it?"

"Geez, I dunno. I think it was a phone deal."

"Patsy, can you pull my file and see who exactly was doing the asking? Because I'm not buying any car."

"Hang on."

Muzak drowned out the furious clatter of keystrokes.

I gulped Pepsi and brooded. I don't mind using electronic data banks. It's just I hate the thought that somebody else can use one to find out about me.

Her voice was smug. "Stoneham Lincoln-Mercury. What did I tell ya? Memory like a trap."

"Hang on." My phone doesn't feature Muzak on hold. She had to listen to the sound of my lower-left-hand drawer opening and closing. I found the Yellow Pages tucked behind a sheaf of files. I balanced it on my lap, riffled the pages.

"There's no such place," I said.

"Gee, he sounded nice, too," she offered.

"A man."

"Yeah."

"You must have had a phone number or something, so you could tell the guy I was a bum risk."

"Gotta go," Patsy said. "Later."

I was getting used to her abrupt disconnections. Her bosses at E–Z Electronic, a far-smaller outfit than Equifax, didn't know about her free-lance career. Nor would they have approved.

I waited five minutes, but she didn't call back. No telling when she would.

Somebody steals my garbage. Somebody checks my credit. And I hadn't even applied to work for the FBI.

I drummed my fingers on my desk for five more minutes, then I picked up the receiver and dialed Mooney.

When I was a cop, I worked for Mooney, and most of the time he made it seem as though I worked with him, not for him. Green as I was, just out of U.–Mass. and the police academy, I didn't fully appreciate the camaraderie. I thought it was the way all cops worked.

He's a lieutenant now—homicide—and I don't think he'll rise any higher because he's too good at what he does. Too busy closing cases to play politics.

I mentally composed a recorded message because he's out of his office a lot. When he answered on the second ring, I was caught flat-footed.

When Mooney starts sounding good to me, I worry. Not that he doesn't have a nice voice; he does. Not that he's bad-looking. Tall, well-muscled, round-faced—I jokingly tell him he's too white-bread for my taste. He—disapproving of Sam Gianelli—tells me I'm attracted to outlaws, not cops. When Mooney starts sounding good, it makes me wonder how things are really going with Sam and me.

"Moon, hello."

"Hi, there."

"How're you doing?"

"Fine, Carlotta."

"Busy?"

"Usual."

"Somebody's in your office."

"How'd you guess?"

"Intuition." I could have said, "And you haven't asked me out yet," which he usually does right after "hello," but I didn't want to start anything.

"It's a lady," he said. "Somebody who's getting to be a very close friend."

I wasn't sure if he was telling the truth, but I felt a sharp stab of something that felt uncomfortably like jealousy. "You gonna arrest her?"

"Haven't decided yet. What can I do for you?"

"Run a plate?"

Mooney and I keep an ongoing balance sheet in our heads. Anytime I can help him out, I do my best. Private cops need official pals to break bureaucratic logjams.

I said, "I'm looking for a late-model Firebird, light blue, maybe gray."

"Just give me the plate."

"Yeah, look, I'm sorry to bother you at the office. The last two numbers are four, eight."

There was a moment's silence. "Nah," he said, "you gotta have more than that."

"I don't."

"Give the client the money back."

"I would if I could."

"Spent it?"

"It's a personal thing, Mooney. Try it with the Registry, okay?"

"Those clerks hate me already."

"They respect you, Mooney."

"Carlotta, don't even try to butter me up."

"Why not?"

"Might work."

I smiled. "One more thing."

"Where have I heard that before?"

"What does Cee Co mean to you?"

"Huh?"

"Just free-associate, Mooney."

"This a test?"

"Moon, try."

"Short for Coca-Cola?"

I hung up. While I waited for Patsy to call back, I made a list. Seiko. Seeko. See Ko. Ceeko. C. Ko. Somebody Ko. I tried the White Pages and learned that Ko is quite a popular name in the Chinese community. The entries numbered twenty-six and ran from Chi-Fen Ko to Zyuan Ko, with a pedestrian Thomas Ko thrown into the mix.

Patsy didn't call back.

After staring interminably at both the shiny side and the dull side, I carefully placed the foil square back into Emily Woodrow's envelope. Under my magnifying lens, it seemed dotted with a faint crescent-shaped pattern. It didn't look like anything I'd ever seen before.

I sighed. Maybe Roz would have a different take on it. She usually does.

When the doorbell rang, I was relieved.

Waiting is hard.

6

Keith Donovan, hands buried deep in his trouser pockets, was rocking back and forth on my front stoop. Alone. He'd exchanged his jacket and tie for a blue crewneck sweater.

"May I come in?" he asked with a quick on-and-off grin.

"Okay."

He headed to the living room, aiming for the easy chair again. I followed. Last time, he'd kept his feet on the floor, his hands in his lap. This time he leaned back and crossed his legs, relaxed. If he'd been a prospective client, I'd have quoted him top dollar. I go by the shoes.

Give him a break, I scolded myself. He might have a pile of grubby sneakers in the closet. And it's not his fault he looks too young to practice anything more complicated than tying the laces.

His wheat-colored hair would look great when it grew out. He was about my height. Decent build—narrow shoulders, but even narrower hips. He sat high in his chair, evidence of a long torso. Most of my length is in my legs.

"I wanted to thank you for listening to Mrs. Woodrow," he said. "It's quite a painful story."

"Thanks for rustling me up a client. You want a commission?"

The corners of his eyes crinkled, making him look a shade older. "No, really, you were fine. You helped her. Just having somebody listen the way you listen helps."

"Anytime," I said, wondering why we couldn't have exchanged such pleasantries over the phone.

"Look," he said, "this isn't something I usually do. I hope you don't feel like I'm passing the buck."

I recalled the gratifying size of Emily Woodrow's check, and her desire for secrecy, even from her therapist.

"Any bucks I can collect, I'll take," I said lightly.

"No. Really, this step, um, my visit was fairly unorthodox. Psychiatrists aren't exactly known for their activism."

There. He'd said it again. Psychiatrist. How old was he?

"Even in the People's Republic of Cambridge?" I asked.

"You do get a more radical branch of therapy here," he admitted, "but nonetheless, I feel somewhat uneasy about involving you in what will probably turn out to be a waste of your time and Mrs. Woodrow's money."

He seemed to speak in two different voices. One, his shrink voice, used words like *nonetheless* and *somewhat*. The other voice, the easy one, went with the smile. When he used his shrink voice, his forehead wrinkled. I wondered if he practiced in front of a mirror.

"I'm a grown-up," I responded. "I could have said no. Therefore, it's no longer your responsibility, Doctor."

"Keith," he said in the easy voice.

"Keith," I repeated. He had nice brown eyes, a firm but expressive way of moving his hands.

"Mrs. Woodrow's version of reality," he continued in full therapist cry, "may not be entirely responsible."

"Oh?" I said, raising an eyebrow. "What are you trying to tell me, exactly? That she didn't see some guy enter her daughter's hospital room? That she imagined the business with the mask?"

He straightened up and planted his feet on the ground. "You see, when something goes so horribly wrong in a person's life, that person may automatically seek for a reason, a fault, a devil if the individual is of a religious bent, as a way of obtaining some comfort against the horrible randomness of death and disease."

He sounded like he was quoting a textbook, but his gaze was direct and sincere. Too direct and sincere.

"You think she's lying about that last day? Dramatizing?" I admit I was enjoying his academically roundabout way of talking, his frank open gaze. I got the feeling he'd taken a med school course in how to hedge everything he said. If I listened to him long enough, maybe I'd learn.

He lowered his voice conspiratorially. "Hospitals can be enormously confusing places. People come and go; it's all hurry up and rush. And Emily Woodrow clocked a lot of hours at JHHI. She may think she's telling us exactly what she saw, but she may have the time factor off."

"It happened on another day?"

"Possibly."

"I'd think the day her daughter died would be pretty well fixed in her mind."

"She's gone over that day, uh, Carlotta. Over and over it. Rewriting it. Sanitizing it. Making it bearable."

"Fictionalizing it?"

"It's possible that Emily's version is very close to the truth. Whoever was administering the chemo probably saw the child's vital signs failing and called a code."

"A code?"

"Every hospital has a code system. So visitors aren't unduly alarmed by loudspeakers booming 'heart failure in room nineteen.' "

"What would have happened if somebody called a code?"

"All hell would break loose. The place would be flooded with strangers. Someone—a doctor on duty—would grab an emergency cart and rush into Rebecca's room, try to revive her."

"Emily didn't say anything about a crowd or a cart."

"Exactly." He paused, leaned back, and crossed his legs. He seemed to be enjoying himself. "And she didn't tell you that one of her major childhood memories concerns a tonsillectomy that occurred when she was approximately four years old. She doesn't remember much about it. Mainly the mask coming down and covering her face. The smell. The fear."

I didn't like his solved-it-all expression. "You think she's confusing the two episodes in her mind," I said slowly.

His smugness evaporated, and he was all earnest understanding again. "I know the doctor who treated her daughter," he said, "and believe me, if anything irregular went on in that room, Jerome Muir would have been on it like a hawk. He has an international reputation, an impeccable one. He's extremely personable and respectable, and he won't be very pleased to talk to you about this."

"Better me than an attorney," I said. "I don't take depositions."

He sighed deeply, uncrossed and crossed his legs again.

I said, "So what do you do with Mrs. Woodrow? Talk about her childhood, huh? Age four and on?"

"Mainly she talks."

"And you listen."

He took the reading glasses out of his pocket and tapped them thoughtfully on one knee. I wondered if they taught that maneuver at shrink school. "I don't think it would be helpful for this to go on too long," he said slowly. "The therapeutic goal is to get Mrs. Woodrow to pick up the thread of her life. A prolonged investigation would hardly help."

"Quick and dirty?" I inquired.

"Quick, anyway."

I smiled. "Well, I'm sure you didn't mean to come over here and insult me, but you're getting close. If you brought Mrs. Woodrow by for a dose of warm fuzzies, you made a mistake. I'm not a shrink and, frankly, your therapeutic goal does not interest me. If Mrs. Woodrow's imagination is running wild, I'll find that out and close up shop. But she's my client now and you're not. Understand?"

"You're very touchy."

"Am I?"

"I didn't mean to impugn your professionalism."

"Yeah, I'm sure you didn't."

"Do I detect a lack of respect for therapy?"

"Possibly," I admitted.

I went to a therapist once. The cop brass sent me, after I shot and killed a man, right before I left the force. Standard procedure: you off somebody, you see the departmental psychiatrist. I'd hated the departmental psych on sight. A pudgy, balding egomaniac, he'd reminded me of a buzzard circling wounded prey, urging me to tell him all about it, scrounge up every last detail. Please, Detective, when did you first touch the trigger? Please, Carlotta, when was the exact moment you felt you had to fire? Please, tell me, what did you feel when you pressed that trigger? Excitement? Relief? A sense of release? Anything sexual? Oh, please, anything at all sexual? Tell me, and it will be our little secret.

It's not that I didn't react to killing another human. It's not that I don't cry. But I resent being forced.

And I kept wondering what they'd have done to the goddamn felon if it had gone down the other way. Would the same shrink be asking my killer the same questions? And when did you first feel you absolutely had to pull the trigger and shoot the cop?

"A great many people mistrust therapy," Keith Donovan said mildly, "but others are helped by it."

"We all have our ways of dealing with shit," I said.

"Yeah? What do you do when you're angry?"

"Yell. Play volleyball. Smack the ball around."

"Hmmmm," he said.

"And what's that supposed to mean?"

"Just hmmmm. And what do you do when you're down? Depressed?"

I hesitated on that one. "Play guitar."

"What were you going to say? Before you settled for guitar."

Our eyes met and I almost smiled. He grinned, and I thought oh-oh. Whenever I start arguing with a guy for no reason, it's a sure sign the old chemistry's kicking in.

"What kind of guitar?" he asked.

"Blues," I said. "Old-time blues. Mainly Delta, a little city stuff."

He said, "I play drums. Used to, anyway. Rock. Punk."

I have no-fail chemistry. A guy turns me on, he's the wrong one for me.

"Since you're here," I said, bringing the conversation back to a professional level, "maybe you can answer a few questions for me."

"Such as?"

"How does Mrs. Woodrow pay her bills?"

"By check. She's reimbursed by her insurance company."

Nice, I thought. I ought to have that arrangement. Investigation insurance. "And you've been seeing her for three months now? Weekly?"

"I saw her more often right after Becca died."

"Who made the connection? Why you?"

"Why not?"

"You seem, uh, young."

"So do you."

"Are you with Harvard Health or Bay State Medical or anything like that?"

He shrugged. "Another patient may have mentioned me to her."

I temporarily accepted the evasion. "Okay. She mentioned drug blackouts."

"Disorientation," he corrected.

"Right. What's she on?"

"Um. I don't know that I should—"

"I can ask her. You don't have to tell me if it violates any professional standards."

"What's going on here?" he said, his eyes narrowing.

"An investigation."

"You take your work seriously."

"Don't you?"

"I only meant to say that Mrs. Woodrow's suspicions are not uncommon among those who've experienced an unexpected loss."

"You can bring anybody else who wants an unexpected loss investigated over to visit, if you'd like," I said.

"Look, I just felt I should warn you there's a good chance you might be dealing with delusional behavior here. I certainly haven't ruled that out. I think it's highly likely."

42

"What do you mean by delusional?" I asked. Oh, this was fun. I could sit and ask "what do you mean by that?" questions all day.

"Mrs. Woodrow is certainly suspicious and hostile. Something terrible did happen. Her daughter did die. But I have no way of knowing whether Mrs. Woodrow was already suspicious and hostile before this event set her off. I came in on this case as a fireman. I wasn't seeing her before the crisis. I just want you to understand that."

"You toss around words like *suspicious* and *hostile*. How about *paranoid*?" I asked. I once knew a private eye who did regular business with a psychiatrist. Whenever the shrink requested it, the PI would pass his electronic debugging equipment over the dental fillings of extremely paranoid patients. The shrink swore it reassured them tremendously.

Donovan blew out a breath. "*Paranoid* has definite clinical overtones," he said slowly.

"Would you use it to describe Emily Woodrow?"

"Not as a one-word label, no."

"You sound like you regret introducing me to your client," I said into silence.

"My patient," he corrected me. "I only want to reinforce that the patient is seeking closure."

"Or possibly truth."

"Her daughter died of leukemia. That's truth."

"When I was a cop, I got into the habit of treating every death as a suspicious death. Otherwise I found myself tromping all over the evidence before I'd decided to check it out."

"I didn't know you'd been, um, with the police."

"A cop. Would that have kept you away?"

He tried the smile again. "I'd have to think about it. But, no, I don't think so. I find it extremely interesting."

"What?"

He shrugged. "A woman. In your line of work. I hope I don't offend you by mentioning that."

I shrugged in return. "Anything else you'd like to tell me about Mrs. Woodrow?"

"Just this: If you speak to Dr. Muir, I'd prefer you didn't use my name."

"Aha," I said, arching one eyebrow.

"Is that your first clue?"

"Could be helpful. What can you tell me about this Jerome Muir? Aside from his international reputation?"

He thought about the question for a while, opening his mouth to speak, then reconsidering, shifting in his chair, frowning.

"Well?" I prompted.

"I never knew him in his prime."

I wondered what years Donovan considered "prime" ones. Teens? Twenties?

He crossed his arms over his chest and went on. "Muir's a genius. It's that simple and that complicated. The amount he's accomplished, the amount he accomplishes . . . I don't know if he never sleeps, or what. He's the guiding spirit behind Helping Hand, the CEO, the Chief of Staff, and he still manages to see the occasional patient."

"Does he pick and choose patients?"

"If some oil sheikh's kid got leukemia, yeah, Muir would probably see him. But he keeps his hand in, takes a few regular cases. He's part of a practice."

"What practice?"

"The Muir Group."

"And modest, too," I said.

"He is. I mean, if he'd wanted it, they'd probably have named the whole damn hospital after him. He put the deal together that saved the place. You ever hear of MedCare, Inc.? They buy up hospitals—in poor areas, a lot of the time. It's a for-profit chain, mainly in the South, and they can stay there for all I care. If it weren't for Muir, MedCare would have eaten the old Hand place. The merger with the Helping Institute kept it alive and vital, and that combo would never have come together without Jerome Muir.

44

He held MedCare at bay almost single-handedly, and did some smooth financial dealing to arrange funding for the merger. Brought people together, bankers, politicians, doctors, neighborhood activists. As far as the Muir Group goes, the other docs probably begged him to let them use his name."

"So he's a genius," I said.

"He's . . . I don't know how to put it . . . engaging. He has a great manner. He's a force. He gets behind something and it moves, it happens."

"Is he a good doctor?"

"There are doctors who go through the motions, and then there are healers. Genuine committed healers. Muir's a healer." He stuck out his chin defiantly, as if daring me to say something bad about his idol. Defiance sat on him awkwardly, made him look vulnerable.

"Do I sense a bit of hero worship here?" I asked.

"Chalk it up to my youth," he said dryly.

"If you happen to be on staff at Helping Hand, you could tell me things about the place. If you want to cooperate."

"I'm all for cooperation," he said, "provided it's a two-way street."

"Well, I'm taking the case," I said. "Isn't that what you want?"

"If Mrs. Woodrow wants it. If she decides to go ahead."

"Have you met her husband? Harold?"

"No. I've certainly heard about him. But nothing I'd want to share. Anything else?"

"Yeah. Now that you mention it," I said. "I would like to ask another question."

"Shoot."

"How old are you?"

I caught a momentary flash of annoyance in his eyes before the grin reasserted itself. "Thirty," he said. "Why?"

"Honest?"

"Twenty-nine."

"That's kind of young to—"

"I graduated high school at sixteen and then I took an acceler-
ated six-year med school program."

"What was the rush?"

"I don't know. And you?"

"Me?"

"How old are you?"

"Older than you."

"Want to tell me the story of your life?"

"No. But if I wanted to look at your notes on Mrs. Woodrow,
what would you say?"

"My clinical notes?"

"Yeah."

"I'd say that after you check out Emily's story, maybe even talk
with Dr. Muir, we should have a drink."

It seemed like an interesting possibility.

"Maybe," I said.

"I'll let you get back to work," he said.

"Good-bye."

As soon as I heard the door latch, I dialed JHHI and confirmed
my hunch. Dr. Keith Donovan was indeed a member of the staff.

And, I thought, tapping a pencil against the phone, I'd bet good
hard cash that someone at the hospital, possibly even the great Muir
himself, had referred Emily Woodrow.

7

After Donovan departed, I righteously typed, filed, and tied up loose ends, intermittently dialing Patsy until I was informed by a cheerful voice that she'd left for the day. I hoped she hadn't been fired.

Friday afternoon is no time to begin an investigation. Of course, since all I'd been instructed to do was wait, I could honestly say I was fulfilling my end of the deal. My eyes kept veering toward the photo on the mantel as I considered the looming weekend. For the past four years my Saturday mornings have belonged to Paolina. And dammit, there's absolutely no reason they shouldn't still belong to Paolina.

Except her mother.

Marta Fuentes is someone I'd never go out of my way to be-friend, but since she is the mother of my little sister, we have—in the past—been tolerant of each other's behavior. In certain ways I admire her. She had the sense to figure out that her lone girl child might have the need for another female in her life, somebody who wasn't burdened—as Mama was and is—with rheumatoid arthritis, the tendency to take up with rotten men, and three younger kids, all boys. Someone who'd act as a role model, sure, but more important, someone who'd listen to Paolina, care about her.

When I first met my little sister, she was barely seven years old —older than Rebecca Woodrow would ever be—with a hand-shaped bruise splayed across her face where Mom's latest flame had left his imprint. One thing I can never figure about Marta is that she doesn't seem to mind playing punching bag for the current man in her life. On the other hand, she unfailingly protects her kids. The guy who'd smacked Paolina was history before the bruise purpled.

I ran my fingers over the telephone, thought about calling Marta and asking for another chance.

It's too easy to hang up a phone. Too simple to leave it off the hook. So I tidied my desk by shoving all unfinished business into the top drawer, got into my car, and banged the door, imagining that I was slamming it on Marta's stubborn head.

I've tried everything. I've apologized. I've begged. I've attempted bribery.

Time to try again.

Marta lives in a Cambridge project that's not the worst housing in town. Close, but not in the same league as the city-owned high rises. Her development runs to a series of look-alike four-families with scraggly patches of lawn and a concrete playground flanked by a pair of broken, netless basketball hoops.

It's always a struggle to find a nearby parking place, but I persisted and jammed the Toyota into three quarters of a space that other drivers shunned.

The front door to Paolina's building was wedged open by half a cement block. I wondered whether someone was moving in or out, or if the security system had been trashed again. Maybe the door was ajar as shorthand to the neighborhood gangs: nothing left worth stealing.

I buzzed Marta's apartment and hiked up the stairs. Possibly some tenant cursed with a sensitive nose had opened the door to air the stairwell, which smelled like it did double duty as a urinal.

I wondered what Emily Woodrow's Winchester house looked like, if her daughter had been happy in its imagined splendor.

The door to Marta's flat was closed. I knocked once, then again, pressed my ear to the wood, listening for the blare of the TV, usually a constant. Nothing. I knocked louder. I thought I could hear someone fumbling with the lock.

Little Alvaro is only three. I was surprised he could turn the door handle. He looked up at me from under dark curls, gave a shy smile, and ran inside. I said "Hi!" to no one in particular, entered, and closed the door behind me.

Marta's no great housekeeper, but I'd never seen the place so filthy. Dishes were heaped on the table, smelly and coated with food. Bedding lay in piles on the floor, as if the whole family were camping out. Two boys stretched out on their stomachs in front of the TV, which was on, but silent. They stared at the moving images as if they were more real than I was.

"Is your mother home?"

The oldest nodded toward the single bedroom.

"¿Quién es?" The voice was definitely Marta's. "Paolina?"

I leaned in the bedroom doorway.

"I tell them no to open the door," she said. "I tell the boys. Do they listen? No."

"Marta, are you okay?"

"It looks maybe like I'm okay?"

"What's wrong?"

"Nada. Only my stomach. I can't keep the food down. Me duele. It hurts." Her last words came out through clenched teeth.

"You taking your medicine?"

"What there is. No puedo caminar. I no walk to the store like this."

"You can have it delivered."

"Don' you tell me what I do. What you doin' here is what I ask."

"Marta, is the phone working?"

"No. No esta trabajando."

"Why?"

"No es su problema." None of your business. That was clear enough.

"Money?"

She turned her face to the wall.

Her middle boy, asleep on another bed, hadn't stirred during the entire discussion. I placed a cautious hand on his forehead. It seemed cool enough, but I wondered if a four-year-old should be asleep at dinnertime.

I wondered if the kids still ate dinner.

But mostly I wondered where Paolina was. Marta always slept on the fold-out couch in the living room. Why was she resting on Paolina's bed?

I checked the brick-and-board makeshift shelves that lined the room. Paolina's clothes were there, neatly folded, along with her meager collection of books.

Marta kept her face stubbornly to the wall. I went back into the living room.

"Hi."

I couldn't remember the name of Alvaro's oldest brother. It made me feel bad. "How are you?"

"Hungry. You cook?"

I picked up the phone. Dead.

"Can you lock the door and then open it when I knock?" I asked. There's a pay phone on the corner.

"I'm not supposed to."

"I might bring something to eat."

"I'll open it."

The pay phone worked, an unexpected blessing. I hit 411 because there was no phone book, and got the number of the nearest Pizza Delite. I ordered two large—one with cheese, one with the works—hung up, and fumed.

I couldn't remember the name of the social worker assigned to Marta's case. Probably she couldn't remember Marta's name either. Most likely, she was the last person Marta would want me to call, a rule-bound bureaucrat who'd take one look at the place and start talking about moving the boys to a more "child-centered environment."

Roz picked up on the third ring.

"What time are you going out tonight?" Friday nights, I don't bother asking if she's going out. Hell or high water, hair-dye emergency or acrylic inspiration, Roz makes the weekend scene.

"Ten, eleven maybe."

The hours she keeps, you'd think she partied in New Orleans instead of Boston. "Want to earn a few extra?"

"Sure."

"Stop at a store and buy cleaning stuff. Basics. Meet me at Paolina's."

"You didn't say cleaning."

"You didn't ask."

"I'll have to change clothes."

"You can do it. See you soon." I vocally underlined the last word.

The oldest boy was disappointed that I didn't bring goodies, but I assured him help was on the way. Then I sighed deeply, and plunged in.

I hate routine cleaning with a passion, but this was so far from ordinary that there was a certain satisfaction involved, reminiscent of an archeological dig. I could make discoveries, like the true color of a dish, or the actual pattern on the linoleum. I should have asked Roz to bring a friend. Several.

"How long has your mom been sick?" I asked the boys.

"I dunno. Long time."

"You eat lunch today?"

The little one held out an empty cracker box.

I was afraid to open the refrigerator.

I folded bed linens, wondered where the closest Laundromat was located. Where was Roz?

Where was Paolina?

Marta wasn't speaking and the boys just stared at each other solemnly when I inquired. So I scrubbed the countertop near the sink with a pitiful remnant of sponge, and awaited fresh supplies.

When the bell rang, I thought it might be her. It wasn't. I tipped the nervous pizza-delivery boy well. Neither cabbies nor delivery folk adore the prospect of a project destination.

The kids, the freshly awakened four-year-old included, fell on the pizza like starving animals. I found a can of chicken soup without a dent in it, scrubbed a battered pot. No trays, so I balanced the bowl on a plate when I carried it into the bedroom.

"You still here?"

"Can you sit up?"

"Why you do this for me?"

"Because I want to see Paolina again."

She grunted while I shifted the pillows. It hurt her to move, to sit. I made the mistake of waiting for her to grasp the spoon. When she didn't, I glanced down and saw what the arthritis had done to her hands.

I held the spoon while she sipped.

She hesitated, her jaw clenched, then said, "Is okay with me. You and Paolina, I mean."

"Does she want to see me? She never answered my letters."

"I talk to a new social worker. She don' think is right, you an Anglo. She thinks is maybe better I find Paolina a Spanish sister."

"Does Paolina feel like that?"

"She don' answer you because I throw the letters away. Now you get me a glass of water, no?"

I bit back an angry response. "So who's this new social worker? What's her name?"

"Cynthia, the old one, she quit. She say she make more money clerking a grocery store. Why go to college for that? I tell her marry some man. Is better."

Ah, Marta's magic cure-all for women. Marry some man. Is better. She, still wedded to a guy who took off while she was pregnant, was living proof.

I sighed.

"You bring the water?"

"What you need is a doctor."

She seized my wrist and held on with surprising strength. "No doctor," she said. "No social worker. Nobody. Or you never get back with my Paolina."

She turned her face to the wall again and I walked out.

Roz had arrived and was staring at the apartment in horror and amazement. I hadn't heard her knock, but one of the boys must have let her in. I wondered what creation she'd been modeling before she changed. Could she own something more bizarre, less appropriate, than the fringed thigh-high outfit she now wore?

Roz is a karate expert. Dress like that, certain skills come in handy.

The pièce de resistance was her hair.

"Roz?"

"Yeah?"

"You shaved your head." Sometimes I'm compelled to break my vow never to comment on Roz's appearance.

"Less than half. You like it?"

It was more like a quarter of her head, to be honest. A strip extending from just above her right ear to about an inch below where the part might be on anyone so hopelessly conventional as to part her hair on the right. The bald strip had scalloped edging, sculpted and precise as topiary.

She must have reached total hair-dye saturation, I thought, experimented with every available shade. And now, imagine the possibilities—new horizons in hair art.

She'd remembered to bring rubber gloves. They lent a science-fiction touch to the ensemble.

"Whoa. Gross," she marveled, wrinkling her nose. "Is this a crime scene or what?"

The kids had eaten more pizza than I would have believed possible. The middle boy wiped a tomato-stained hand across his mouth and calmly inquired about dessert. Without a pause, Roz whipped a box of Girl Scout cookies from her canvas tote. God knows what else is in there.

"You want milk?" I asked the boys.

"Coke," they demanded. "Root beer."

Maybe Roz had something yummy in her purse. I fetched Marta's water, first washing the glass. The counter on the far side of the sink was so littered with pill bottles it looked like a pharmacy. I read the labels: Naprosyn, Medrol, Nalfon. All empty. Zorprin, full.

Feldene, empty. A warning label said to take this medicine only with or following food.

The warning label was in English.

I opened a window and inhaled a noseful of early spring before going back into the stale bedroom.

"Did you stop taking your pills because you ran out?" I asked while she sipped.

"I have more."

"Are you taking them?"

"*Cuándo el dolor es muy fuerte.*" Only when the pain is real bad. "They make my stomach hurt."

"You have to take them with food."

"*A veces no puedo comer.*" Sometimes I cannot eat. "Then I can no take the pills?"

"You need to eat," I said.

"The boys, they eat?"

"They ate. What about Paolina?"

"You only care for her. The boys are good boys. They help me."

"Where is she? Please."

"Is Friday? She has maybe a date."

"C'mon, Marta. She's a kid."

"You want to ask where is this kid, no? Maybe after you hear, you no want her for your sister."

"Don't worry about that."

"The little girl, the kid, has got herself a man. Twenty-five, maybe thirty years he's a day. I see him walkin' with her. I see them in his car. Lots a times. She says no. She says I'm crazy. Her own mother."

"Paolina? With a guy?"

"You don' believe me, maybe?"

"In his twenties? Has to be a teacher or something."

"Oh, you a stupid lady. Guy like that don't teach no school."

"Guy like what? You know his name?"

"She don' bring no man like that to her house. I throw her out, I see her with a man like that."

I wanted to ask what kind of men she'd expect Paolina to fall for, with such a sterling example of how not to pick 'em for a mother.

Instead I made her another bowl of soup.

"When will Paolina be home?"

"Soon, I think."

Roz beat it to the Laundromat with two giant bags of reeking clothes, leaving me the moldy bathroom to scour.

"Soon," Marta constantly assured me.

When the last light had faded from the sky, I wanted to call the cops. That's when Marta told me not to worry, she'd suddenly remembered: Paolina was staying the night with her aunt Lilia. And no, I couldn't phone the aunt to make sure all was well. Lilia left her receiver off the hook after nine o'clock. Too many wrong numbers. Too many salesmen. Too many perverts.

I drove by the aunt's place. All seemed quiet and dark.

Back home, I played my National steel guitar late into the morning hours, fooling around with an old tune, trying out different bass runs and slides till my calloused fingertips ached.

> Baby, please don't go.
> Baby, please don't go.
> Baby, please don't go down to New Orleans,
> You know I love you so.

I played all the standard verses, borrowed a few from other songs, even made up a couple of my own. I settled on a down-and-dirty bass and a bottleneck slide.

And I worried.

8

By Saturday morning I'd decided to see for myself. Which might be difficult. Marta's hardly my greatest fan, but her sister Lilia—Paolina's only aunt—really despises me. She'd take great delight in spitting in my eye.

The way she sees it, I cost her a job, almost single-handedly shutting down her place of employment. Of course, if she'd taken my advice and applied for immigration amnesty, she could have gotten other work easily. But her distrust of the government is almost as strong as her dislike of me.

Instead, she relies on badly forged papers, and she's been fired twice in the past year.

Paolina's life was endangered during the same case that cost Lilia her job. That's the root cause of our estrangement. It wasn't all my fault. A lot of the blame rests with Marta, which is probably why she's so keen to shift the entire burden to me.

I'm not the one who lied to Paolina about her father.

Anyway, I knew that Lilia would foam at the mouth if my car so much as appeared on her street in daylight, so I decided to use a cab, which makes as good a surveillance vehicle as anything outside a power company van.

Gloria, massive dispatcher and half owner of the Green & White Cab Company, was sitting in her wheelchair behind her battered metal desk, phone to ear, listening, talking, and eating at the same time, a trick perfected only by Gloria and certain politicians on the campaign trail.

I never understand why Green & White's Allston garage hasn't been shut down by some sort of health or public safety bureau.

Payoffs probably, arranged by none other than my lover, Sam Gianelli, the coproprietor of the company.

Maybe that's his main contribution to the business: veep in charge of bribery.

Or maybe he supplies Gloria with junk food.

I glanced at the top of her desk in shock. On a typical visit, I expect to find, within arm's reach, a sampling of America's best, say a box of Bugles, a six-pack of Hershey Bars, a one-pound bag of M&M's, an openmouthed jar of marshmallow fluff, and a can of Planter's peanuts.

There was nothing but a single sack of Orville Redenbacher microwave popcorn, empty and forlorn.

"Dieting?" I asked, my voice layered with disbelief.

"My dumb-ass brothers," she said angrily, hanging up the phone and momentarily ignoring the flashing lights on her console. "My brothers are saying I got to diet, watch what I eat and all. I come in here and they cleaned me out. Nothin' but rabbit food, carrots, and shit."

Gloria's got the three largest brothers imaginable, but you wouldn't call any of them fat. You wouldn't call any of them anything. Former sports stars all, they now earn bucks as bar bouncers, or in less savory trades.

You might call Gloria fat, but not in their hearing.

"You want food?" I asked, hoping she'd say no because who in her right mind wants to oppose the world's biggest brother act?

"Hell, long as they make pizza to go, I ain't gonna starve. And I got stashes they ain't found yet. They let me have this popcorn stuff, but where's the butter?"

"I need a cab," I said. "You got something barely functional?"

"Let me guess. You want a cut-rate lease."

"Ask me, all your junkers ought to be cut-rate."

"You just gonna charm it right outa me."

"Give me a deal and I'll bring you a package of Hostess Cream-filled Cupcakes."

"Make it four packages." She patted one plump dark cheek and let a laugh rumble up from deep inside her. "Chocolate's good for my complexion."

"You drive a hard bargain."

"And you get to drive an old Ford. Keys on the pegboard. How long you gonna keep it out?"

"You'll know when I get back."

"Six packages. And some Twinkies."

She was still outlining her grocery list when I slammed the door.

Lilia lives in Cambridgeport, a slightly slummy part of the University City, on the top floor of a triple-decker. The place is no showpiece with its peeling gray paint, but it's better than her sister's project. Lilia's fifteen years older than Marta and she's got problems of her own, like chronic unemployment. But if Marta had asked, she'd take in Paolina. No doubt about it. For her, family is family.

Only rarely did I wish I had one.

Oh, maybe somebody else's family, some idealized make-believe family. But I certainly felt no longing for the barely masked hostility of my parents' marriage, no nostalgia for my own brief attempt.

It was convenient for sex, my marriage, but life isn't lived in bed.

Thoughts of sex led to images of Sam Gianelli, which segued into fantasies of Keith Donovan. I have strict rules about not getting involved with clients. But then he wasn't technically a client. And I break my own rules all the time.

Sam and I have had an on-again-off-again affair steaming for more years than most marriages last. It will never lead to wedded bliss. I'm not in the market and, by his father's standards, I'm off limits, being both divorced and non-Catholic. Was I using Sam for relatively safe sex in this scary AIDS-ridden time? Hell, was he using me? Yeah. Both. But it wasn't the safety that attracted me; I hadn't met a lot of guys who turned me on the way Sam did.

Donovan was a distinct possibility. Too young, of course, but

LINDA BARNES

that had its good side. He probably wasn't looking for a long-term commitment. Yet.

I'm monogamous in my fashion. One at a time. No marrieds. Was I ready for a total breakup with Sam?

Cradle snatching. That's what a fling with Dr. Donovan would amount to. The mirror image of what this older guy was trying with Paolina. If I believed Marta . . .

I settled back in my car and stared at nothing. On surveillance I can semidoze, almost go into a trance. I don't think of it as patience, just the ability to turn off and turn on when necessary. It used to be one of my best cop traits. What a boring job that was. On the good days.

One Pepsi, two tiny boxes of raisins, and a banana later, I saw them approaching out of the corner of my eye. I didn't move. I'd expected Paolina to be leaving the house, not returning to it. I'd expected her to be with Lilia. Or alone.

He was in his twenties. At least. Marta had been right.

He wasn't holding Paolina's hand, but they were walking close together, and she was smiling up at him in a way that transformed her from a child to a strange and precocious young woman. I realized I was biting down on my bottom lip.

I'd only wanted to see her. To make sure she was safe. To speak to her if she was alone, pass some secret signal if she was with Lilia. Now I felt like a voyeur. The man said something and she rewarded him with a dazzling smile.

He was big, beer-bellied big—a look I associate with bars and motorcycle gangs. Studded belt, leather jacket, frayed jeans slung low on his hips. If I'd been a vice cop, I'd have hauled him in on probable cause.

What the hell did Paolina find attractive in a man almost old enough to be her father?

Bingo. I'd just answered my own question.

I sat like a statue, my mind racing. Should I jump out and confront him? Ask him what the hell he was doing with a girl young enough to define jailbait? How would Paolina react?

60

She was dressed for spring in spite of the chill, wearing tight pink leggings. A long purple shirttail hung out from under her multizippered red jacket. A red beret plastered her bangs to her forehead. She wore earrings. Earrings! When the hell had she started doing that?

He didn't walk her up to Lilia's doorstep. Instead, they loitered on the sidewalk. He shook a cigarette out of a pack, mockingly offered her one, then lit up. They talked three cigarettes' worth. I couldn't see her face.

I cracked the window of the cab, but I was parked too far away to hear anything but mumbling. His voice dominated, deep and husky. He pulled something from the back pocket of his jeans, maybe an envelope, or a card. Paolina shook her head no, but her resistance gradually weakened, and after ten minutes, the item passed from his possession into hers.

I heard a bang, and jumped. Paolina glanced up sharply, but not at me. On the third floor of the gray building, a window had opened. I could hear Lilia's angry voice.

I'd be angry too, my niece littering the sidewalk with trash like that guy.

Paolina blew a defiant kiss at him and raced up the walk. He flipped an upraised middle finger at Lilia, turned and started back down the sidewalk.

I sat till he passed me, till he turned the corner. Then I gunned the engine, banged a U-turn, and followed. If he stayed on foot I might have to abandon my wheels and do the same, especially if he made for any of the Central Square subway entrances. Shadowing a guy solo in the subway is no fun.

Where had she met the creep? Not at school; it was ten years out of his league. Hanging around the projects, more likely. An unemployed loser. Or illegally employed.

He walked two quick blocks in the direction of Central Square while I considered the possibilities. There's no place to leave a cab on Mass. Ave. where it won't get towed or stolen. I could park it now and walk, or trust to providence to find a space. Last time I did that, I wound up retrieving my car from the city lot, paying eighty-five dollars in tow fees, and practically getting eaten by a German shepherd guard dog. I tried to figure how close to Central Square I could safely approach before taking the last available parking space.

They ought to mark them the way they do gas stations: last space before the Mojave Desert.

He was still walking at Pilgrim Street, brisk stride, cigarette in hand. I'd obviously passed the last parking space. The loading zones, even the fireplugs were occupied territory.

He strolled across Mass. Ave., dodging traffic, hung a left, and started toward Prospect Street and the MBTA station. Took a surprise right into the alleyway next to the liquor store that used to be a Greek restaurant. I put on a burst of speed, two-wheeled the next corner. I thought I'd pick him up easily on Bishop Richard Allen Drive.

No sign of him. Two black ladies in full Easter finery strolled toward the church across the street. A tiny Oriental girl balanced a boom-box on her shoulder.

A steel-blue Firebird came barreling out of the parking lot.

The last two numbers on the plate were four-eight.

Paolina's friend was driving. I swung in behind him.

9

He signaled right on Main Street, left on Mass. Ave., tooling along easily in the smelly wake of a bus. I started to radio Gloria with a quick message to call the cops. Then I hesitated. What did I have on this guy? Probable garbage theft? Offering a cigarette to a minor? The cops wouldn't exactly put out an all-points.

He swerved past the bus in front of MIT, sped up, and headed over the Harvard Bridge into Boston, hitting a major pothole so hard I was amazed he didn't lose his engine, much less a hubcap.

Left on Commonwealth. Didn't the jerk ever check his rear-view mirror?

Right on Gloucester. He'd been inching along so slowly that he caught me when he squealed a left on Boylston, catching the very tail of a yellow. If I'd had my own car, I'd have chanced it, but Gloria hates to have the least little dent on one of her fenders.

When I drive for her, I carry a secret repair kit consisting of one bottle each of green and white nail lacquer. Punk fashion has helped me camouflage a couple of nasty scratches.

I watched the Firebird do a tricky little scoot into the Pru Center garage. This guy believed in paying for parking. I don't.

I tapped the steering wheel impatiently. The light took forever to change. Instead of following him into the garage, I decided to ditch the cab in front of the Lenox Hotel. The head bellman knows me, and I was making up a likely story when I saw a junky Renault vacate a space in front of the drugstore. I crossed three lanes of traffic without a qualm. There was time on the meter.

On foot, I sped back across the street and down the ramp into the shadowy garage.

Once past the punch-a-ticket machine, motorists could turn in any one of three directions to seek parking. No humans to pinpoint the trail of the steel-blue Firebird.

I walked the lanes, crisscrossing the green level.

The car was the only way to trace him. I couldn't cover all the pedestrian exits. He could have chosen from two banks of elevators, eight separate staircases. Lost himself in a department store. Entered the Prudential Center Tower, wound his way through the plywood boardwalk of the under-construction shopping mall clear to the Sheraton. Strolled through the glass bridge to Copley Place and descended the escalator into Back Bay Station.

The car was not on the green lower level. Which left the blue.

As I made the upper circuit, I unconsciously started counting the number of Japanese and German imports. As a native Detroiter I have a hard time believing things have come to such a pass. But then, as the driver of a Toyota, I have met the enemy and she is I.

The long and the short of it is I lost him. I couldn't find the damned car. Had he spotted me? Driven straight to an exit with some phony wrong-turn story?

I located a pay phone. Tried Mooney. He was not in the office. Good for him, I thought. Somebody should be enjoying Saturday. I tried his home number and he picked up as if he were waiting for someone to call.

"Good," he said as soon as he heard my voice, not giving me a chance to speak. "Look, I can't get zip from the last two digits of a plate. It's the way the computers are rigged. You've got the first two digits, my guy says, he could give you a print-out—thousands of names, but a print-out anyway. But they're not geared for the last two digits, or the last digit or anything. I'm gonna raise hell. I mean, we get a lot of partials, and if they can find the first two numbers, why the hell shouldn't they be able to find the last two, especially with a make of car—"

"Mooney," I said. "Listen."

"Everybody gets off blaming the Registry. So do I, so I don't mind about you asking, and I'll be glad to—"

"Five-three-six, Mooney," I said. "Five-three-six—zero-four-eight. A Mass. plate. Still a late-model Firebird."

"You got all the numbers?"

"That's what I've been trying to say."

"This guy's hanging around? Hassling you or what?"

"Not exactly," I said hesitantly.

"Wanna give Papa the whole story?"

"You're not old enough."

"Papa loves dirty stories," he said.

"Gonna run the plate?"

"I'll run it," he said after pausing long enough for me to wonder whether he would.

I hung up. I'd put a quarter in the slot for a dime call, because a quarter was all I had. I wondered about change, but decided not to risk sticking my finger in the coin return. Kids put used chewing gum in them. Worse.

Since I'd found such a great parking place, I decided to take advantage of it. At the Pru Star Market, I stocked up for Gloria. I bought junk, but I tried to sneak in a little nutrition on the side—oranges, a couple apples. I asked the check-out clerk to bag it separately, the unembarrassing stuff in one plastic sack, Twinkies and cupcakes in the other. I'd tote in the wholesome bag first, disappointing Gloria, but decoying any brother who might be hanging around in between bone-cracking sessions for a local loan shark.

Gloria and I dined together, with me sticking to a minimal portion of Kraft Macaroni and Cheese, while she downed the rest, along with multiple Tootsie Rolls, Mars Bars, and a large box of chocolate-covered graham crackers. I spent the whole meal scared her brothers would show up.

At least I knew Paolina was okay, alive.

Sunday was a bust. No progress on the plate. No messages from Emily Woodrow. No mail at all.

10

By Monday morning I'd had it with waiting.

As soon as I got back from the Cambridge Y, still sweaty from volleyball, I tackled New England Telephone, rising higher and higher in the supervisory ranks till I reached someone who took my threat of dire legal repercussions seriously enough to promise to reconnect Marta's phone. Flushed with victory, I dialed Patsy Ronetti.

"Sorry," she murmured in what, for her, were dulcet tones. I held the receiver an inch away from my ear instead of the customary five. "I got hung up on a trace."

"You got what I need?" I asked, pencil poised.

"Yeah."

"Shoot."

"Harold Winthrop Woodrow. Age: forty-eight," she began. She rattled through his social security number and date of birth. "Harvard University. Rutgers Law. *Law Review.*" She gave me a list of firms where he'd been employed, and I envisioned how much easier life would be once I joined the computer set. Electronic mail was the only way to go, I thought while scribbling at breakneck pace. Otherwise I'd have to learn shorthand. Spelling.

"Currently a partner at Irwin, Woodrow, and Place," she continued, naming an influential local firm at which I had absolutely no contacts. I know lots of lawyers; I mainly work for them. But IWP boasts such a blue-blooded clientele that they rarely do business with investigators. Or if they do, they keep it quiet.

"So he's that Woodrow," I said.

"Fancy taxes are his speciality."

"Her?"

"Inherited major money."

"From his name, sounds like he did, too." Nobody in my family has a middle name like Winthrop.

"Nope. He made it the old-fashioned way. Married it. She's a Ruhly. The department-store Ruhlys."

"She pay the bills?"

"No need. Hers sits in investment accounts. Okay? You know where to send the check, right?"

"Wait. What about her?"

"I told you. Rich."

"Employment history. She work?"

"No."

"Never?"

"I didn't check on her. Just him."

"Kind of a sexist assumption," I said.

"Classist. Why should she work?"

"Classist, sexist, whatever, if I'm paying for an employment check, I want both of them."

"Okay."

"Hey, anything turn up on that guy who was asking questions about me?"

"Sorry," she murmured softly. Then she hung up. Dammit, I was going to have to cultivate somebody who did less apologizing and more conventional farewells.

I chewed my fingernails till the mailman brought my usual pile of bills and political pleas. Maybe Emily Woodrow, unwilling to break the weekly rhythm, would time her mysterious, vital, and probably cuckoo information to arrive this Friday, or next Friday, or the Friday after that.

The hell with waiting. I'd deposited her check. At least I could meet the players.

I reviewed my notes. Jerome Muir, Becca's doctor, the man with the impeccable international rep, the "genius," according to Keith Donovan, seemed the logical place to start.

SNAPSHOT

After some deliberation, I selected a card from my ever-growing phony business-card file, took a few duplicates as well. Upstairs I tried to dress to match my new identity. I might, someday, if this investigation ever blossomed, wish to meet Dr. Muir as myself. An initial foray called for disguise.

I pity male detectives, I really do. Some may laugh and ask where a six-foot-one redhead's gonna hide, but I have my response down pat: A *female* six-foot-one redhead is as easy to hide as a trip to your local wig shop.

I could do it with hair dye, like Roz—or Roz before she discovered the clippers—but the truth of it is, I like my own particular shade of flame, and I take umbrage when anyone suggests I may have helped nature's hand. So I do wigs. They're not especially comfy, and the cheapies, the kind they foist off on undercover cops, are a guaranteed headache. So I stick to two decent ones, a long straight brunette and a curly blond.

I gazed at the business card's neat type. Sandra Everett. Sandy. Definitely curly blond. Cute is not easy to achieve at six-one, so I decided on earnest. Older than me, maybe thirty-five to forty. Well groomed. Wealthy. Unaccustomed to the word *no*.

I own a single good navy business suit, purchased at a Filene's Basement sale. Paired with a prim white silk blouse, it would see me through. A hat would be good. In one of the many rooms I could rent to Harvard students if I bothered, I keep the few things of Aunt Bea's that I didn't send to charity. I plucked the frivolous silk flowers off a straw boater, pinned it to my wig so it would sit at a properly unbecoming angle.

Pearls would have been nice if I'd owned any.

I found a pair of Italian leather flats that pinched my toes, another Filene's Basement deal. I wear sneakers most of the time, but they wouldn't do for Sandra.

Disguised, I spent some time with the current Yellow Pages. Muir wasn't listed under Physicians, but he was part of a special feature, the GUIDE TO PHYSICIANS AND SURGEONS, ARRANGED BY PRACTICE. Under Oncology at the Jonas Hand/Helping Institute. Tiny letters beneath his name spelled out: Chief of Staff, Pediatric Oncology-Hematology. I cut to the big print: Longwood Avenue. I cross-checked the reference under Hospitals, but the ad for JHHI gave no specifics, not even physicians' names. Just a single all-purpose phone number.

While I ran my finger down the lists of names and places, I tried to imagine how Sandy Everett would sit in her clothes, how she'd move. Since she'd opted for flats rather than heels, I decided she'd try to try to make herself seem shorter. Ducking my head forward and hunching my shoulders, I felt a surge of righteous determination.

I made sure my message machine was operational, grabbed my purse with a more ladylike motion than usual, and left the house.

When I drive a cab, I keep strictly away from the Longwood Medical area, preferring a tricky left turn and a crescent-shaped detour onto the Riverway to avoid the whole of Hospital Row, which boasts—in addition to Helping Hand—Children's Hospital, Beth Israel Hospital, Brigham and Women's, the Deaconess, the Dana-Farber Cancer Institute, and probably a few new health-care havens that have opened since the last time I checked. The traffic is appalling. People late for doctors' appointments, hurrying to give birth, or racing to see loved ones *in extremis* tend to be less than mindful of their turn signals. Add the fact that every intersection in the one-mile stretch has its very own traffic light, and the result is a caliber of gridlock unique even in Boston.

An old yellow Saab decided to turn left in front of me. From the right-hand lane. No signal.

I usually cab nights because I don't have the patience for daytime driving. I'd rather risk midnight muggers than hang out behind a five-mile-an-hour stream of honking commuters. While traffic crawled, I slid Bonnie Raitt's *Collection* into the tape deck, a much-practiced maneuver I can perform blindfolded on an S curve.

Another reason I avoid the Longwood Medical area is that once you hit your destination, there's no place to park. The few metered slots are regulated in scant twenty-minute allotments. There is nothing you can do in a hospital in twenty minutes, right? So the meters are perpetually red-flagged and traffic tickets adorn every windshield. But that doesn't create any more parking spaces, and the garages are incredibly expensive.

Whoa, I said to myself. Incredibly expensive is Emily Woodrow's middle name. And since this visit was on her, I could afford a garage.

I crossed Brookline Avenue after two lights worth of left-turners. Kept up a stop-and-go pace in front of Children's Hospital.

Unlike the rest of the medical outfits, JHHI lies south of Huntington Avenue. I began looking seriously for a garage. The chance of car theft increased dramatically on the wrong side of the streetcar tracks.

JHHI had its own meager parking facility. I yanked the car into the barely marked drive. The ramp spiraled steeply, a two-way job too narrow for more than a mile-an-hour creep. The structure beyond the ramp featured cramped spaces, mostly occupied. Few cars seemed to have parked entirely between the yellow lines. For two bucks a half hour, it was no bargain. I squeezed between a badly parked Mercedes and a battered Plymouth. Signs and arrows directed me to an arched passageway that led to the lobby.

I wondered if the passageway, newer than the garage, had been built to shield the hospital from its surroundings, ushering patients from parking lot to front door without making them confront the boarded-up tenements across the street, the littered playground to one side, the seemingly abandoned factory on the other.

I glanced quickly around. No one in sight, so I gave my wig a quick downward tug with both hands, settled the straw hat on top, and eased through the automatic doors wondering how Marie Antoinette had ever kept her hairdo afloat.

The high-ceilinged lobby was pleasant enough. Both the elegant chandeliers and the ultra-utilitarian reception desk seemed out of place in opposing ways. To the left, a low fountain spilled into a shallow pool. Pennies and silver coins glittered in the shallows. Of course: A body of water in a hospital would soon become a wishing well.

Make my child healthy. Keep me whole.

A dark-skinned woman pulled a contraption halfway between a wagon and a wheelchair around and around the fountain. In its depths, a reclining child, pale as the pillows behind her head, lay tethered to a machine that gurgled and spat. A second machine, attached to her arm, flashed green blips across a screen.

A nurse pushed an IV stand across the wagon's path. It squeaked as it rolled by.

A young mother, impossibly burdened with diaper bags and car seats, tried to bundle her two small children against the chill. A third child, older, possibly four, splashed in the fountain, drenching the sleeves of his navy-blue jacket and giggling. She yelled at him, then glanced furtively around the lobby and bit her lip.

The lobby was hot. Sandra Everett was sure going to sweat in her suit jacket. Perspire. Sandra would perspire.

I sweat.

I approached the information desk.

"Where would I find Dr. Muir?"

The aging attendant looked up at me with instant respect. On her desk was a chart, printed on graph paper. She ran a fingertip down one column, then another. "It's a clinic day. With the construction, let's see, he'll be on Eastman Two. Take the last elevator on the right, or you could just climb these stairs if you want to."

"Thank you."

"You have an appointment with Dr. Muir?"

"Yes."

"He's a wonderful man," she said, looking off in the direction of my right shoulder. "I hope everything works out for the best."

I followed her gaze and found myself staring at a row of portraits, stiff men in formal dress, lined up like ancestors in a family gallery. JONAS HAND read the bronze plaque under one. James Helping, a plump smiling presence, hung next to him. Jerome Muir had already earned a place of honor on the wall.

He was extraordinarily handsome. I would have taken more time to study his likeness, but the receptionist kept her eyes fastened on me, making me feel guilty, as if I were late for a genuine appointment.

I climbed the stairs quickly. Surrounded by all the wheelchairs and wagons, I was grateful I could.

Directly ahead, an area was boarded off, under construction. Hammers pounded and a buzz saw worked. A temporary plaque on a column announced EASTMAN TWO. A signboard listed names and displayed arrows, sending patients to a waiting room on the right or one on the left. I scanned the list and veered right.

Jerome D. Muir, Dr. Renee Talbot, Dr. Simon Piersall, and Dr. Edward Hough worked to the right. Presumably the Muir Group.

The waiting room was nothing much. Blues and grays. Tweedy aged carpet. Landscape prints on pale walls. Magazines overran a square coffee table and sat haphazardly on a couple of the upright blue chairs. Seating for thirty. The place smelled of disinfectant. Or maybe I was just imagining it, confronted by all that white behind the reception counter.

The main room had an adjoining alcove, a children's wing, featuring low furniture in primary colors, stacks of kiddie books, and cabinets full of Raggedy Anns and toy racing cars.

Behind the counter, backed by a wall of tabbed files, two women peered at computer terminals, single-mindedly entering data. The dark-haired, middle-aged one wore glasses that had left red moon-shaped weals on either side of her nose. The other was a knockout: slim, young, and black, with strikingly tilted eyebrows. Neither acknowledged my approach, so I waited. Sometimes if they just notice you standing there, they feel guilty. Not often. But I've conducted a survey, and if you interrupt, they're almost always in foul humor.

The middle-aged woman glanced up first. "Can I help you?" she asked with no hint of apology.

I drew in a deep breath and started the gag.

First I handed over my card and smiled as if I were doing her a favor.

"The *Suffolk News*?" she said.

"Oh, don't let that alarm you," I said easily. "I'm not here in my capacity as a reporter."

"I don't understand."

"Well, of course you don't," I said generously. "I told the advisory board that we should have called first, but they wouldn't hear of it. And since I was going to be in the neighborhood—"

"Miss Everett, I don't—"

"Mrs. Everett, dear. Now if Dr. Muir can't see me right away, I'll absolutely understand. I'm quite willing to wait, but the board insisted that I deliver the invitation personally."

"Invitation," she repeated.

"Yes. Invitation. I'm the current vice-president of the local Silver Crescent chapter. We're a charitable organization, and each year we honor an individual who's made a major contribution to our community. Dr. Muir is an overwhelmingly popular selection, and the consensus of the nominating committee was that I approach him in person."

"He's extremely busy." It was a line she was so used to dishing out, she probably didn't even hear herself say it.

"It's just eleven fifteen, and I've brought lots of busy-work," I said. "I can catch up on the minutes of the last meeting, work on the phrasing of the press announcement. I only need a few moments of his time, and I know he'll be pleased. The Silver Crescent isn't in the Shriners' league, dear, but we do what we can."

The middle-aged woman exchanged a quick glance with her young co-worker. Which one had called Emily Woodrow crazy? I wondered.

The black receptionist shrugged and bent over her typing. She might as well have announced that she was the less senior of the two. The older one would have to flip the coin and make the call. I pressed a little harder.

"Look," I said, with a smile glued to my face, determination shining through, "I know it might have been preferable, from your angle, to arrange matters formally with the public relations department. But there'll be plenty of time for that. Right now, the ladies of the Silver Crescent are waiting for my report, waiting to hear how Dr. Jerome Muir reacts when he learns that he's been named our very special speaker of the year. I'm willing to wait. It's a waiting room, isn't it? And sooner or later, I'm certain he'll find time to see me." I put more warmth in my smile and added, "I'm really in no hurry, Barbara."

I sure would hate to wear a name tag to work, especially one that gave only my first name.

"Dr. Muir is extremely busy," she repeated, wavering.

"He must be a wonderful man to work for."

She inserted her tongue between her teeth. She'd made a mistake and she knew it. She should have implied that he was out, on hospital rounds.

I quickly retreated to a chair and busily shuffled through my handbag. If that didn't get me into the presence I didn't know what would. I'd used the key words: charity, contribution, Shriners, honor. No receptionist would want to be tagged as the obstacle who'd blocked a hefty donation.

I'd taken a chance using the reporter's card rather than an ordinary calling card, but I wanted an excuse to question. This way, any apparent lack of tact could be attributed to journalistic habit.

I surveyed the waiting room's inhabitants—a young woman staring into space, a couple holding hands, a tiny black teenager wearing a turban—trying to make eye contact, develop likely sources of gossip. No one took any notice of Sandra Everett.

Two wan children, one about five, the other eight, sat listlessly nearby, ignoring the toys.

"It could be some time," the receptionist warned.

"I can wait," I said. And I did.

11

The staring woman jerked back to reality when a nurse called her name. Leading the eight-year-old, she hurried past the reception counter and down a curtained hallway. The young couple never exchanged a word, but they never stopped holding hands either. The five-year-old made airplane noises and drummed his feet.

I entertained myself by trying to remember my mother's favorite Yiddish maxims concerning doctors. She had quite a few, all passed down to her by my grandmother, an awe-inspiring woman by all accounts, union firebrand and scab nemesis extraordinaire.

The only one I could remember was: *"Far der tsayt ken afile a dokter a mentshn nit avek'hargenen."* Or, "If your time hasn't come yet, even a doctor can't kill you."

I'd folded and stuffed a sheet of typing paper into an envelope before leaving my house. Under the watchful gaze of the receptionist, I carefully inscribed a few sentences. Too bad Roz hadn't been home. She could have fixed me up with something fancy, even parchmentlike. This phony testimonial business cried out for her artistic touch.

A man wearing a white smock over khaki overalls passed by with a brisk step. His keys jingled as he opened a metal lockbox next to a column. He withdrew wrapped test tubes, stashed them in a pouch, and disappeared with a nod in the direction of the desk.

I finished writing, reinserted paper into envelope, shifted my weight, and smiled, self-importantly and pointedly, at Barbara, the receptionist. She returned my stare blankly and I wondered if she'd bothered to inform Muir of my arrival.

The exotic black woman fetched noontime sandwiches for herself and her colleague. She didn't ask if I was hungry.

By one o'clock I was starving, but I didn't want to give up my seat, my silent battle of wills with the receptionist.

One o'clock ticked slowly into two o'clock. I removed my straw hat; the wig was making my scalp sweat. Waiting-room magazines revealed that seafood was potentially hazardous, while beef would definitely kill you—provided the ozone layer held out for another twenty years. Sexual harassment was moving out of the office and into the courtroom, and three out of four movies featured slice-and-dice killers.

I started getting the waiting-room willies. Anytime I'm stuck in a room smelling of antiseptic, I flash back to my father's death. It wasn't like I saw him every day; he and my mom had long since separated. But viewing him so shrunken, so different from his larger-than-life cop self, so diminished by tubes and drains and cotton hospital johnnies . . . The memory still makes me want to snatch cigarettes out of the mouths of teenagers.

The couple disappeared down the hallway shortly after the mom with eight-year-old departed. I waited. More patients were called. More arrived to occupy their vacant chairs.

I kept an eye on my receptionist. Carlotta Carlyle was steaming under the collar, but that was unimportant. How would Sandra Everett handle the situation?

Sandra, I decided, had two kids, was recently divorced. Determined to make a career in journalism, her old college major, she was genuinely puzzled that there weren't more opportunities out there for ladies who'd taken ten years off to raise the kids. The kind of woman who prefaced her sentences with "Well, I'm not a feminist, but—" Maybe a touch of the South in her background. A woman taught to value niceness over just about anything else.

A woman who might use her volunteer work to gather quotes from the wives of community leaders, but who'd never *ever* print anything scandalous.

I fingered my synthetic blond curls. Time for a reminder, I thought. A gentle reminder.

I waited until the black woman was handling the desk alone.

"Has Dr. Muir given you any idea when I might have a few minutes?" I asked.

"I'm sorry," she said. "I just don't know."

"Could you give him a buzz and find out?"

"Not if I want to keep my job."

"Like that?"

"Like that." She gave me a rueful grin that changed as she looked over my shoulder. She bent immediately to her work and I assumed my dragon lady had returned. Instead I heard a man's voice.

"Savannah," he said to the black woman, "you guarding the desk all by yourself? Think you can manage that?"

SAVANNAH was printed plain as day on her badge. But it was evident from his tone that he knew her.

"Barbara will be right back," she said with a faint edge to her voice.

"You ought to do fine," he said coolly. "Ring Jerome and tell him I'll be in his office."

"He's, uh, tied up, Dr. Renzel," Savannah said.

"Where's Barbara?"

"Oh, Dr. Renzel. I didn't see you come in!" The middle-aged receptionist rushed up, smiling and ineffectually patting her hairdo.

"Hey," the doctor said, his deep voice warming with her arrival, "you look great. I see they've got you breaking in another one. You ought to earn extra as chief trainer."

Barbara's plain round face turned blotchy with pleasure. She chuckled while Savannah stretched her lips in a meaningless parody of a smile.

"I'll be waiting in his honor's office. You let him know, okay, Barbara?"

"Well, he is with a patient." She smiled indulgently, negating any reproof.

"What else is new? I've got five minutes." With a broad wink, the man sailed through. Fortyish, medium height, a narrow bony face with knife-blade cheekbones. Thick glasses. He didn't quite live up to his pleasing baritone.

Barbara immediately pressed a button on her phone console.

"While Dr. Muir's on the line," I urged, "please remind him that I'm waiting."

She mentioned only Dr. Renzel, not Sandra Everett, before hanging up.

I glanced at the black woman. She lifted her lovely eyebrows in a weary gesture of resignation. Savannah what? I wondered. A dissatisfied employee can be an information gold mine.

My scalp itched under my wig. "Where's the ladies' room?" I inquired.

Barbara began a complicated string of instructions that would have taken me downstairs through the lobby and halfway to the Himalayas.

"There must be one for the patients," I murmured softly when her phone rang, commanding her attention. "I'll only be a minute."

She didn't see me dodge down the narrow opening into which Renzel and the patients had disappeared. The corridor opened into a chamber decorated with gilt-framed diplomas. The name *Muir* appeared on no less than four. I studied his degrees, reading the parts that weren't in Latin. Harvard. Johns Hopkins. Yale. University of Michigan. Not exactly offshore diploma mills.

I figured Sandra Everett had a fifteen-minute head start before the reception witch came hunting, and the searching-for-a-bathroom ploy is as tried and true as any, so I moseyed down the door-lined hallway.

It irked me that this Dr. Renzel had crashed the secretarial barricades so easily. Maybe I should have posed as a doctor. Sure. Easy. I'd just need to cram for eight years to carry off the impersonation.

There was an open doorway five feet down the corridor. I stepped quickly inside and shut the door behind me.

It was a small examining room, a cot against one wall, a wooden step stool leading up to it. The walls were painted, not papered. No trace of the blue-and-white lattice design Emily Woodrow had described. A scale dominated one corner. A blood-pressure cuff was secured to the wall over the cot. No trace of an oxygen mask.

I wondered where the chemotherapy rooms were located, whether they were equipped, like operating rooms, with wall outlets for oxygen and air. Were oxygen masks wall-mounted as well? I twisted the doorknob slowly, peered out into the empty corridor, and began a search for floral wallpaper. Hospitals rarely paper individual rooms; possibly all the chemo rooms were similarly decorated.

The examining-room doors featured small ledges on which to balance patients' file folders. Rooms without ledges seemed to be offices. None bore so much as a stenciled name or number.

I passed a metal canister labeled MEDICAL WASTE in bright red letters. It had a domed top, a WARNING! label on each of its four sides. A nearby philodendron plant needed watering. A flushing sound came from behind a wooden door marked W.C.

A woman passed and nodded. A child cried and a male voice murmured soothingly.

I heard voices issuing from a room with no door ledge. One was the mellow baritone of Dr. Renzel. I assumed the lower, gruffer voice belonged to Jerome Muir.

Sandra Everett discovered that her panty hose were slipping. She bent to straighten them. I took advantage of her strategic location to eavesdrop.

At first it sounded like Renzel was reciting letters. I shifted closer and got sentences. "One Florida place has been taken over three times in six months. Started with Humana and then went to SurgiCare and then CritiCare. Drove the billing department nuts."

I heard footsteps and swiveled to find the dragon lady in hot pursuit.

"Mrs. Everett," she said firmly, "the restrooms in this area are reserved for patients only. You'll have to go back to the lobby."

Right outside Muir's door seemed as good a place as any to dig in my heels. I made sure my voice was loud enough to penetrate wood.

"Really," I said. "Have you any idea how the ladies of the Silver Crescent might react if I can't make our presentation to Dr. Muir personally? Today? How can we print up the invitations? How can we set the level of contributions? I understand that he's a busy man, but good news is not to be ignored. He is certainly not the only medical man worthy of this honor—"

I could have continued, but I didn't have to. The door swung open on well-oiled hinges.

12

Dr. Renzel appeared, staring at me quizzically. "I was just leaving, Barbara," he said. "Hope I haven't made a hash of your schedule."

"What seems to be the problem?" I heard a gruff voice demand from within.

I sidestepped both Barbara and Renzel, stuck my foot in the door.

"A minute of your time, Dr. Muir," I said.

The gruffness was age, I realized. Much older than his lobby portrait, he sat in a high-backed leather throne behind a slab of mahogany and inclined his head a fraction of an inch in my direction. I felt almost as if I'd been granted a blessing. His crisp white shirt and red speckled bow tie were hardly clerical garb, but I was vividly reminded of an old priest my father, a much-lapsed Catholic, had revered. Jerome Muir's hair had turned beautifully white, without a trace of yellow; his moustache and bushy sideburns were elegant.

"The lady from that charity," Barbara murmured in a low voice, as if she thought I might be hard of hearing. "I'm still checking on her. The newspaper . . ."

The number on my *Suffolk News* business card is hooked into the Green & White Cab Company's fancy phone system, courtesy of Sam Gianelli. It's not just an unlisted number; it's unpublished and pretty close to untraceable. Sam's picked up a few tricks from his mobster dad over the years. The efficient Barbara would have reached an answering machine: "All lines are currently busy. Please hold."

"Checking!" I echoed indignantly. "Surely, Dr. Muir, you've

heard of the Silver Crescent. We're currently seeking affiliation with the Eastern Star."

"Barbara, perhaps I'd better handle this directly." Muir's broad face was slightly florid and crisscrossed with a fine web of lines. His piercing blue eyes rarely blinked. He focused his full attention on me, and it seemed like a gift seldom bestowed, something the speaker needed to earn.

Renzel's casual, "Can I stay?" made it sound as if there were going to be a movie screening, with popcorn and Coke.

I said, "The membership gave me very specific instructions. They wanted me to do it just so."

Renzel said good-naturedly, "Don't let me stop you."

Barbara turned on her sensible heel and departed without a word.

"You've upset her," Renzel said. I wasn't sure if he was talking to me or Muir. Talking about me or Barbara.

"Oh, Jerome, I almost forgot," Renzel went on. "Have you decided on the Portugal conference?"

While the two doctors debated the merits of meeting with colleagues in Lisbon, I inspected the office. Matching bookcases lined two walls. A marble-topped table held an ornate Chinese vase. A collection of creamy, spiraled shells filled two shelves of the right-hand bookcase. A full-rigged frigate in a bottle sailed another. Two oil paintings looked like the real thing, but who knows, what with Polaroid reproductions? Muir had covered the wall behind his desk with framed photographs. Student groups from college days, gowned graduation photos, Muir standing beside a man in flowing Arabian robes, Muir smiling while he clapped a well-known congressman on the back.

A power wall.

In most of the photos he wore a polka-dot bow tie. As he apparently did in real life.

"I'll consider it," Muir said firmly. "Decision by Wednesday. Now, young lady, please sit down." Muir nodded me into a plush blue chair. "I do hope Barbara hasn't made your life difficult. She's extremely protective of my time."

I sat.

"I'm sorry if we seem to have behaved rudely," he continued, "but we were under the impression that you were a reporter. We have strict procedures—"

He'd shifted to the royal *we*, but it didn't seem ludicrous. Didn't even seem inappropriate.

"I'm not here on a story." I withdrew the envelope from my handbag, unfolded my precious sheet of paper. "May I read?"

"Please." Muir carefully stifled a yawn so that only the edges of his nostrils fluttered. I wished I'd spent more time gazing at the painting in the lobby. He must have been incredibly handsome.

My speech was brief, but I spluttered a little and made several mistakes, to make it seem as if I hadn't just written it in the waiting room, as if I were nervous at being in the presence of JHHI's Chief of Staff and CEO.

To my surprise, I was nervous. If I'd known Muir was going to be like this, I thought, I'd have taken more time composing my speech.

"Whereas the ladies of the North Shore Chapter of the Silver Crescent," I intoned, "select each year a person of good character and great achievement, and whereas Dr. Jerome Muir has been duly nominated and considered for this honor, we, the undersigned, hereby name him Silver Crescent Man of the Year with all the honors and benefits traditionally accorded thereunto."

And Mumbo Jumbo, Alakazam, I silently added.

"Charitable donations, bequests, and volunteerism," Muir said after a long pause, "are the lifeblood of the community hospital. On behalf of this institution, and myself, I thank you." Another benediction conferred.

"The presentation copy got delayed at the printers," I offered apologetically. "But we were afraid to wait any longer. The membership has asked me to formally congratulate you on your impressive contributions to the medical well-being of New England, and to request that you honor them by appearing as this year's Silver Crescent Lecturer at our November twenty-fifth banquet. We feel that Thanksgiving is the true start of the giving season, and if you'd like us to direct our fund-raising toward a specific hospital project, we could certainly accommodate any request."

Renzel said, "This is great, Jerome. God knows we've got projects to fund."

The phone buzzed. Muir picked up on the first bleep. His hands hadn't aged as well as the rest of him; they were gnarled, the knuckles scarred and red. "Yes, Barbara, I know. I know. I'm on my way."

"Do you accept?" I asked eagerly. "Can you do it?"

"I'm extremely honored," he said solemnly. "And I'd be delighted. I'll need to check my calendar, make sure I'm available. Hank, do we have any conferences near Thanksgiving?"

"Not that I remember," Renzel said. "Unless that Hoffman-La Roche thing—no. That's December in Hawaii."

Muir smiled warmly. "Mrs. Everett, please extend my gratitude to your membership, and do leave your phone number with Barbara. I'll have her get back to you within the week."

"That would be wonderful. Thank you so much." I took a deep breath and plunged on. "We were worried you'd be all booked up, and after Emily Woodrow recommended you in such glowing terms —well, we did hope you'd accept."

Muir grew very still. "Emily Woodrow?"

"Her daughter was treated for leukemia here."

He examined my face searchingly. "Are you certain it was Mrs. Woodrow who recommended me?"

"Yes, I am."

He smoothed back his carefully combed white hair. "How extraordinarily generous of her. I thought she might have harbored some . . . hard feelings. You know her daughter didn't respond to . . . her daughter died." He seemed genuinely distressed, possibly more upset than a doctor who'd seen death so often ought to be.

"Oh, I'm sorry," I said. "I could be mistaken. But I thought—no, I'm sure it was Emily."

"It doesn't matter," Muir said, almost his regal self again.

"No," I said hesitantly, "I guess it doesn't. Only—well, I suppose I ought to ask. The ladies might think me rude, but please, don't be offended. I feel I have to follow through on this. There isn't any reason why you *wouldn't* wish to be our speaker, is there?"

"I'm not sure I know what you mean."

"You're not expecting any difficulties, uh, nothing of a legal nature, concerning Emily's daughter's death?"

The sparkling eyes froze and I got a glimpse of steel. "Certainly not. Not to my knowledge."

"I'm sorry. It's just I know that Emily's husband's a lawyer, and lawyers do tend to sue anytime things don't work out."

He made a dismissive noise and straightened his perfect tie. "Some people believe there always has to be a happy ending. Perhaps it's the television they watch. I don't know."

"The death of a child is hard to accept," I said.

"Indeed," Muir responded. "For all of us."

The phone buzzed again, two short bleats.

"I really must go now, Mrs. Everett."

"Thank you so much for your time, and for all the good work you do." I stood and offered my hand. He crossed to take it. His handclasp was firm and dry. He was wearing a spicy after-shave that successfully blocked the hospital smell. With his door shut, we could have been in any fancy corporate office.

Dr. Renzel interrupted our farewells. "I could show you a couple of current construction projects, if you're interested," he said.

I turned to him and he flashed a quick smile. I studied his face. Ordinary, except for the prominent cheekbones. Not quite enough chin. His voice was another story. Smooth as a well-bowed cello. Put him to work in telephone sales, he'd have a hell of a future.

"Mrs. Everett, this is Dr. Renzel." Muir made the belated introduction hurriedly, then added, "Mrs. Everett's from a local newspaper," as if Renzel hadn't been hanging on our every word. I wondered if Muir stressed my newspaper affiliation to remind Renzel to discuss only printable matters.

"A newsweekly, really. But I'm here only as a representative of the Silver Crescent," I reminded them.

Renzel smiled enthusiastically. "Well, maybe I can talk you into doing a puff piece for us. Something that will get a few philanthropists to stop sitting on their wallets."

"That's an idea," I said.

"Have you seen any of the newer areas of the hospital?" he asked me.

"No." I patted my phony curls. Maybe blondes do have more fun. And maybe I could talk him into a guided tour of the chemotherapy treatment rooms.

Muir left the room before we did, his back imperially erect. We followed him like sheep, like courtiers.

13

"First of all," Renzel said, leading me briskly into the waiting room, taking a sharp right, then a left toward the elevators, "do you have all our literature? We do a quarterly magazine that details our progress. Scholarly articles. Chitchat. Who's new on the staff."

I fumbled a notebook out of my purse: Sandy Everett, resourceful reporter, always prepared for a story. I doubted I could get him to tell me the *right* story, but maybe I could finesse him into tossing me a lead.

"This is very kind of you," I said, "but first things first. Like who exactly are you?"

He lowered his lashes and gave me a little-boy-lost look. His thick-lensed glasses microscoped his brown eyes.

"Probably most of the people around here know who you are and what you do," I said. "But I've got to start with the basics: who, what, when, where, why."

"Just because people at JHHI may know who I am," Renzel said contritely, "is no reason to come off as a self-important windbag. I'm sorry. I get carried away. My enthusiasm for the hospital takes off."

The legendary Muir, I thought, might rate as a self-important windbag, but so far Renzel, with his great voice and his willing tour-guide offer, certainly hadn't.

"I'm Chief of Pharmacy," Renzel declared. After a brief pause, he added, "Everybody calls me Hank."

"Not Doctor?"

"Oh, that, too. I am a doctor. A Ph.D. doctor. A scientist, not a clinician."

He pressed the elevator call button. "I'm going to show you the new floor," he said, the way a doting father might say "I'm going to show you the new baby."

"And how long have you worked here?" I asked.

"Four years or so. It surprises me I've stayed this long. I'm an academic at heart."

"Chief of Pharmacy certainly sounds impressive," I said. "If Muir can't give the Silver Crescent lecture, maybe you can pinch-hit for him." I was trying to figure how far I could push my reporter ruse. Why had Renzel volunteered so cheerfully to show me around? Was he lonely? Underworked?

"Well, it may sound impressive," he said ruefully, "but it would be a lot more impressive if I held a key chair at a medical school as well. You know what it costs to endow a university chair these days? Two biggies. That's two million dollars."

I whistled. "More than the Silver Crescent could raise."

"And, admit it, your ladies would be disappointed if they had to put up with a relative nobody like me. Around here, Jerome Muir's pretty much the show. Rightfully. He deserves it. I'm more the professorial type. I'm used to people calling me Professor, not Doctor. What are you used to?"

"Huh?"

"I mean, do people call you Mrs. Everett or what?"

I almost confessed to Carlotta. He had a way about him, an engaging bedside manner. "Sandy," I said.

He reached over and formally shook my hand. "Pleased to meet you, Sandy." He was slow to end the handshake. Close up, his bony face seemed interesting rather than homely.

"You seem fond of Dr. Muir," I said. "Do you see him as kind of a role model, a father figure?"

"Why do you ask?" His mouth curved into a smile.

"Oh," I said, "I don't know. I guess it's because I've been seeing a therapist lately. Stuff like that rubs off."

"You've had some troubles?"

"It's nothing," I lied cheerfully. "My divorce."

"That's not nothing, Sandy," he responded earnestly.

The elevator slowly opened its doors. We got in and he brushed his hand against mine. Muir had been wearing after-shave. Renzel's scent was definitely cologne, pungent and sweet.

"So tell me," he said. "Are you dating yet?"

"Not really," I said.

"Well, you ought to be." He edged a little closer.

I took a step back and felt the wall behind me. "Soon, maybe," I said.

The doors closed.

"Um, you mentioned a new floor," I said. "You're expanding up? Why is that? I noticed a lot of vacant buildings nearby."

"The changing ethnic character of the area is a fund-raising problem," he said. "We're confining ourselves to renovation at the moment. We freed up the sixth floor by streamlining our records. Computerizing. Contracting out some of the billing and accounts. Medical technology changes so rapidly, it's all we can do to keep pace. Real expansion would cost more money than we've got. Unless Silver Crescent runs a close second to the Shriners."

"We don't. Sorry." I was starting to feel guilty.

"Well, we have great hopes: a major bequest in the wind."

"Can you tell me more about that?"

"No."

"Well, can I get a little more background?"

"Like what?" he asked.

"Dr. Muir," I said quickly. "How old is he?"

"I thought you were going to ask about me. My job. But everybody's interested in Muir." He sighed deeply and shot me a grin. "Did you ask him how old he was?"

"No."

"Why?"

"I didn't have the nerve. It would have seemed so rude."

"He has that effect, doesn't he? You don't want to discuss anything unpleasant in front of him. And age, well, there's no reason to think he won't go on forever."

The elevator opened its doors. Renzel took my arm and ushered me into an unfinished lobbylike area.

"You're not answering my question," I said.

"You're right." He seemed in no hurry to rush into guided-tour mode. He looked comfortable enough, just standing and talking. Didn't seem to mind that I had a couple inches' height advantage on him. Some guys hate that.

I tried another tack. "His memory, how good is it?"

"He probably has to write down a few more things now than he did when he was twenty, if that's what you mean. But don't worry, he'll do a bang-up lecture for your group."

"It's not that."

"What?"

"I'm surprised he remembered Emily Woodrow's name right off."

"The woman whose daughter died?"

"I think it's sort of touching, him remembering, as busy as he must be."

"It doesn't surprise me," Hank Renzel said resolutely. "I'm sure he loses sleep over every child who doesn't make it."

"Oh, come on," I said. "I'm not writing this down."

"You can write it or not. It won't change. Jerome Muir's a gentleman, an old-fashioned word for an old-fashioned man. I know. I travel with him. Time-zone changes, lost luggage, fouled-up hotel reservations, he sits politely and waits, as if he were a small-town schoolteacher instead of one of the most powerful voices in American medicine."

"That might make a good story," I said. "Sort of a companion piece to the Silver Crescent award. Play up his humble side."

Renzel went on. "We do a lot of traveling together. On business. Mainly abroad, but in the states, too. Do you like to travel? Weekends? Up north? I have a little place in Vermont, just a cabin really, but it's on a hill and the view is astonishing."

"Maybe I can work it into the story," I said pensively, ignoring the dating-bar chat, "about his remembering that little girl, Rebecca Woodrow."

"Did you know her?" Renzel asked.

"No, but the family's socially prominent," I said.

"The kind of name that sells newspapers?" he asked pointedly. "Funny. Jerome remembers the mom's name and you remember the girl's."

Time to abandon newspaper talk, I thought. Even if it meant a brief return to the dating bar. "So tell me about your job," I said.

"Mainly managerial," he responded. "Not enough funds to do the kind of research and development I'm trained to do."

"Which is?"

"It's all biotech, now. Genetic engineering. Never enough space, never enough money. These days, you really need university backing. Here, let me show you around the floor."

He touched my arm again and led me through a corridor, past tarpaulin-covered sawhorses and partially glassed-in chambers. I couldn't see a construction crew, but hammering and hollering told me they weren't far off. The creamy wallboard hadn't been painted yet.

"We're doing amazing things, amazing," the Chief of Pharmacy said. "You can't tell by this, but the whole floor—you can see the blueprints, if you'd like—will be absolutely devoted to patients undergoing bone-marrow transplants. An entire sterile floor, because the immune system becomes so compromised in these patients that the chance of opportunistic infection skyrockets."

I heard more about bone-marrow transplants than I wanted to know. The man was a motor-mouth nonstop Helping Hand booster. They should have hired him as a professional fund-raiser.

"Will the chemotherapy rooms be located up here?" I asked, hoping to stem the tide of information.

"No," he said. "Why?"

"Doesn't chemotherapy lower your resistance to other diseases?"

"To some extent, but conventional sterile methods are generally considered adequate."

I sighed. "I guess I was still thinking about Rebecca Woodrow. How she died."

"We have hundreds of patients who get well. Why not do a story on one of them?"

"Dog bites man, you know, that's the story. This one little girl who didn't make it, in spite of the odds."

"I don't like it," he said, staring down at glossy linoleum, cut and stained to imitate parquet. "I'd skip that one, if I were reading your paper."

"It's human interest," I said with a shrug. "You wouldn't want to help me out on it, would you?"

"How?"

"Well—just off the top of my head—I could start with a peek at the room where she died. Maybe do sort of a mood piece."

He shrugged. "I wouldn't know where it was."

"Probably a lousy idea anyway. My editor's more of an upbeat guy. Loves sports."

"Do you know about our bike race?" Renzel asked eagerly.

"Huh?"

"Bike race. With research costs out of control, and with the government cutting back and insurance rates taking off, we have to rely on charity more and more. We have wonderful organizers here. Every year, there's a cross-country bike race, a balloon race, a carnival, a Las Vegas night. You name it."

"Um," I said. "That's really interesting."

"If your editor's into sports, the bike race is a natural."

"Maybe," I said.

"You don't sound enthusiastic."

"If it's biking, he'll assign one of his buddies to write it. I'll come up with the story idea, and somebody else will get the by-line and the paycheck."

"Too bad."

"Yeah," I agreed wholeheartedly, as we passed another wing of unfinished rooms. "But, you know, I may have another idea."

"What?"

"Well, tell me what you think of this," I said, reaching back to Donovan's story about Emily Woodrow's early memory. "When I was really little, I had my tonsils out."

"They hardly do that anymore," he said. "I'm surprised they took yours out. It couldn't have been fashionable when you were a kid. You're way too young."

He was right. I hadn't adjusted for the age difference between Emily and me. "Mine were infected," I said hastily. "But the main thing I remember is a doctor putting something over my mouth, like a mask, and I guess I passed out after that."

"Anesthesia."

"I mean, there must be a lot of people with the same memory. Maybe I could sell my editor on an update, what they do in a modern place like this. I bet you don't just knock kids out like that anymore, right?"

"Anesthesia's not my area."

"Is there somebody I could talk to? Somebody you'd recommend? I don't mean today. I'd go through regular channels, do it right, get in touch with PR."

"You'd want to make an appointment to see Dr. Hazelton. Or even Dr. Peña."

I scribbled their names in my notebook. "Why do you say 'even' Dr. Peña?"

"Well, he's a new resident. He's here so many hours, he probably sleeps here. He wouldn't thank me for volunteering him for more work."

"I'll try for Hazelton."

"I'd do that. I'm not sure Peña is as up-to-date in his methods."

"I thought you said he was new."

"My understanding is he didn't exactly graduate at the top of his class."

"A place like this, I'd think you could pick and choose."

"We used to," he said, lips pursed disapprovingly. "Tell me, do you do this, uh, reporter work, full-time?"

"No," I said, deciding to turn him off the personal stuff once and for all. "The kids take up most of my time. The twins, especially."

"You must be busy," he said, edging back from the precipice. I pretended not to notice his discomfiture, but I was almost certain he'd been on the verge of asking me out.

He glanced abruptly at his watch. "I'm sorry. I have to get back to my office." It was a definite kiss-off. Little doubt about it; he'd played escort because he needed a date for Saturday night.

I smiled politely. "Well, thank you. And I'll be sure to tell the ladies about the new construction at the next meeting."

"Can I see you out?"

"I think I ought to stop by Dr. Muir's receptionist first. Make sure he's not going to be out of town November twenty-fifth."

"You remember the floor?"

"Two."

"I'm on four. If you decide you want to do a story on the pharmacy. Or if you need an escort for that Silver Crescent bash."

Well, if twins and a two-inch height difference didn't discourage the man, what would?

"I'll keep it in mind," I promised with a genuine smile. Maybe if he wore contact lenses . . .

Looks change, but great voices are great voices.

14

I thought I was in luck. The black woman, Savannah, was in sole possession of the counter. She recognized me and smiled.

"Still here?" she inquired.

"Would you know where I could find a guy named Peña? Anesthesiologist?"

Barbara, the dragon lady, came up behind me and cleared her throat to let me know she was in charge.

"Hi," I managed pleasantly. "An anesthesiologist named Peña, would you know where I might find him?"

"Dr. Peña?" It was more a correction than a question.

"Doctor," I agreed, perhaps with less than the proper reverence.

"I wouldn't know," she said disapprovingly.

The young black woman piped up with, "I saw Pablo about ten minutes ago in the lounge on the fourth floor. Drinking coffee. Big dark-skinned guy, kind of vague-looking."

"Thanks," I said, regretting the dragon lady's untimely return. "Appreciate it." I left without asking the black woman her last name. I figured she was in enough trouble, first-naming a doctor.

Pablo. Pablo Peña. On the whole, I thought his parents should have considered a different choice. On the other hand, they could have christened him Pedro, which would have been worse.

People like me, cursed with alliterative names, think about stuff like that in elevators. Sandra Everett had no such problem. I decided Everett was probably her married name. She was the kind who'd keep it for the kids' sake. I'd never taken my ex-husband's name, even though it would have moved me out of the alliterative ranks.

I roamed the fourth floor in search of something resembling a lounge. I couldn't wander far; JHHI was housed in a tall building, but not a large one. I strolled past another roped-off construction area with a sign that read: PLEASE EXCUSE OUR APPEARANCE. A RENOVATED JHHI TO SERVE YOU BETTER! The pharmacy seemed to take up more than a quarter of the floor space. I wondered at its location. More convenient on the ground level, I'd have thought. But then, old buildings rarely seem designed with human needs in mind. The pharmacy looked busy and efficient. One line of customers stood at a counter to hand in prescriptions and another waited by a register to pay. A stream of white- or green-clad individuals bypassed the civilian queues and went about their business behind the counters, in a warren of rows and shelves and refrigeration units.

Hank Renzel was nowhere in sight, but then I wouldn't expect the Chief of Pharmacy to hold down some front-desk clerical position or count out pills.

As long as I kept up a purposeful stride no one challenged my right to pass. I kept walking, not wishing to endanger my status by asking for directions.

I did a perimeter search, then picked a bisecting hallway.

Four small tables and a collection of vending machines behind a partially closed curtain made up the lounge. It was deserted except for a man who matched Savannah's description. His hospital greens were wrinkled and stained, and a surgical mask drooped below his chin. He rested his elbows on a table, his head in his hands.

"Dr. Peña?" He wasn't that dark. More the color of heavily creamed coffee.

He didn't lift his head. "What?"

"Dr. Muir said I'd find you here." Since I was planning to lie anyway, I thought I might as well start by dropping a name that would carry weight.

"Muir? What's he want?" Peña muttered in hardly the awed tone I'd come to expect. He had no trace of an accent.

"He said you wouldn't mind speaking with me. I won't take much of your time."

He finally glanced up at me and Sandy awarded him her very best smile. He reached to straighten a nonexistent tie. Pure reflex action.

"Time, I've got. Sit down." He stared at his watch. "I'm on for another six."

"Six hours?"

"Thirty down, six to go."

"You want a cup of coffee?"

"Nah. I forget whether I'm tired or not after the first twenty-four. It's better that way."

Sandy giggled. I let her. Me, I never giggle.

"What did Muir send you for? See if my health insurance is paid up?"

"He said you'd give me a good quote. I can see why. You're funny."

"He said that?"

"Not exactly."

"I'm surprised he knew I was on duty."

"I got the impression he took a personal interest in the staff."

"Look, he's great. I'm tired. Way past tired. It's just—"

"Just?"

"I mean, I heard so much about him. Before. I guess nobody could live up to press like that. Greatest doc in the world, you know, and all he does is worry about the building fund. What do you want to talk to me about?"

I handed over another of Sandy's phony business cards. I don't know why, but cards seem to inspire confidence. "I'm writing a story about a little girl who died here."

"You're from a newspaper? And they let you in?"

"I'm a personal friend of Dr. Muir's," I said. I sound much more convincing when I lie than when I tell the truth.

"Oops," he said.

"Oh, I'd never repeat what you just said to Jerome. I mean, no one would trust me if I gossiped, would they?"

"Well, what do you wanna know? A lot of kids die." His voice was flat and uninterested. His words about kids dying—well, he could have been talking about plants wilting or rain falling.

"The girl's name was Rebecca Woodrow. I'm doing a feature story about her last day."

"She spent it here? Too bad. She should have gone to the beach."

"It was January."

"She should have stayed home, then."

"You remember her?"

"You want coffee?"

"If you have a cup, I'll have one."

He patted all his pockets and looked bewildered and vague, and I wound up buying the two plastic foam containers of brown liquid.

A uniform, even just hospital greens, makes it hard to get a fix on somebody. His watch was good, but not flashy. Probably something he needed for work, an accurate watch with a sweep second hand. He wore paper hospital slippers, so I couldn't use his shoes to figure his financial worth or fashion flair. He was a big guy, even sitting down. Maybe six-two or six-three. Twenty pounds overweight. He had a habit of licking his lips.

"You remember Rebecca Woodrow?" I asked when I'd sipped enough coffee to regret buying it.

"It's a big place."

"How big?"

"Two hundred and twelve beds."

"That's not huge."

"I put 'em to sleep and wake 'em up."

"This one didn't wake up."

"I don't remember names."

"A six-year-old girl. In for chemotherapy."

"You're talking to the wrong person. I don't supervise chemo. Nurses handle that." His eyes were almost closed, his speech faintly slurred, as if he couldn't make the effort to be more precise.

"Have you slept lately?"

"Twenty minutes here, half an hour there. I'm fine, really."

"You don't look fine."

"Muir send you to check up on me?"

"No."

"I got less than a year to go and then I'm out in practice."

"You're not a real doctor yet?"

"Of course I'm real. I'm just not paid like I'm real yet, okay?"

"I thought this wasn't a teaching hospital."

"It's private, but even private places take in a few residents. They need to. Time I'm putting in, I'm probably earning a buck an hour. System's built on slave labor."

I drank bad coffee and let him talk.

"Guys collecting the fees and the guys putting in the hours, they're two different sets of people," he complained.

"Paying your dues," I suggested.

"Yeah, and when I'm out of here, you think I'll be able to cash in the chips? Hell, it'll be National Health by then. These old guys, they did a number. Milked the system so bad, the rest of us are gonna pay. If I'd done an MBA, a lousy MBA, I'd be rolling by now. Kids five years younger than me got houses and two BMWs, and I'm working my butt off."

"You're a specialist. Aren't specialists well paid?"

"Oh, yeah, and now the government's coming in to tell me what to do, how to treat a patient, how long a patient can stay in the goddamn hospital, and setting my fee wherever some clerk outa high school thinks it ought to be. It's the damn DRGs."

"DRGs. Is that, like, drugs?"

"DRGs. Diagnostic-related groupings. Fitting a patient into a diagnosis, and getting paid based on which grouping you plug them into, like all people only have one thing wrong with them at a time."

He still hadn't made much eye contact, but his voice wasn't a monotone any longer. "Bunch of legislative lawyers," he went on. "They hate doctors. Screwing the whole system and it's just gonna get worse. Bureaucrats'll take the money, and the patients'll end up worse off than ever. It's not doctors, it's technology. It's tests. It's machines. Own the machines and the technology, you've got it made. Me, if I don't invest, I'm gonna be a wageslave working for some bureaucrat doesn't even respect what I do."

"That bad?" I murmured sympathetically.

"And it's not like there's no money. You see the construction, like we've got to have a new wing and a new garage and a new lab and a helipad on the roof, the whole nine yards. You writing this down? I thought you were a journalist."

"I'm doing a small story, focusing on this little girl, Rebecca Woodrow. Her mother's name is Emily. Acute lymphoblastic leukemia, that's what she had. I understand it can be cured."

"Yeah. Chances are damned good."

"Rebecca died during chemotherapy treatment."

"You know what I always say?"

"What?"

"Sleazebags never die. You get some guy in a hospital, some scumball wanted by cops in thirty states, it's a given: he'll make it. Sweet little kid, apple of her mama's eye, she dies during some routine thing. Never fails."

"This girl was the apple of Mom's eye, all right. Only child. Wealthy folks. Pretty girl."

"None of that counts."

"Would any nurse here be qualified to administer chemotherapy?"

"No, no. Specially trained nurses. Nurse-practitioners."

"Part of my story involves interviewing the last people to see this girl alive. My editor loves that kind of stuff. Human drama."

"Glad I don't have your job," Peña muttered.

"So I need to interview the nurse who handled the chemo. On a little girl who died suddenly. In January."

"January," he repeated.

"Yeah."

"Beginning of January?"

"Yeah."

"I suppose it was Tina," he said as if he were speaking to himself.

"Tina?" I echoed very quietly, not wanting to wake him in case he was talking in his sleep.

"Tina Sukhia. Lovely woman." He added regretfully, "She doesn't work here anymore."

"The dead girl's mother says a doctor rushed into the room at the end and placed a mask over the girl's face." Emily hadn't mentioned whether or not the stranger was *wearing* a surgical mask, like the limp green rectangle dangling around Peña's neck. Surely she would have noted that, a masked man carrying a mask. "Would that doctor have been an anesthesiologist?"

"Might have been. Logical thing to do," Peña said. "First rule: Establish an airway. Somebody's not breathing for herself, you do it for her, with a bag and a mask."

"Do you remember—?"

"Look, lady—I forget your name—"

"Sandy. Sandra."

"Sandra. You think I'm gonna remember what we talked about in ten minutes, you're wrong. I'm zonked, see? I need to sleep. Some of the guys, they can take this, and I'm pretty good at taking it too. But the thing you're talking about happened months ago. I can't remember if I ate breakfast."

"Aren't you worried you're going to make a mistake?"

"No. No, once I'm working, I'm fine. Adrenaline comes to the old rescue. I know my job. You know how people say 'I could do that in my sleep'? Well, I can. I can do my job in my sleep. I just forget other things."

"Like Rebecca Woodrow."

"I don't check on the chemo. That's not what I do."

"The mother says the man with the mask pushed her, shoved her out of the way."

"That I'd remember. It definitely wasn't me. I don't push mothers around."

An overhead speaker came to life, announcing "Code Thirty. Code Thirty." Peña's beeper emitted sharp little bleats. Then it said, quite clearly, "Code Thirty, room four-oh-two. Code Thirty. Four-oh-two."

"I gotta go," Peña said unnecessarily. He was already moving.

I followed, wishing my flats had rubber soles. It was hard to stay silent, but the anesthesiologist was traveling so fast he never glanced behind him.

We shoved through two sets of swinging doors, took two quick turns down featureless corridors. He pushed open a wooden door and entered full tilt.

A glance into the narrow window next to the door, five inches wide, ceiling height, stopped me cold.

The room was crammed, jammed, as crowded as a stateroom in an old Marx Brothers film. Any resemblance to comedy ended there.

I couldn't see the occupant of the bed, only an extended arm here, a leg there. It must have been a child. The limbs were small.

A thing that looked like a tool chest on wheels, studded with drawers, half of them flung open, blocked part of my view. Plastic tubing curled from one drawer. Clear plastic bags of liquid filled another, bottles and jars a third. The top of the cart was dominated by a machine with complex dials and buttons and a computerlike screen. Paddles grew out of the top. I noticed a metal cylinder strapped to the side of the cart.

A man in a white coat held a bag and a mask near the head of the bed. A hose led from the bag to a wall-mounted spigot.

A woman wearing white slacks repeatedly slapped the back of a small hand, tried to insert an IV needle. On the other side of the bed, a second woman strapped a blood-pressure cuff to a limp arm. A man in greens, not Peña, had a hand where the child's midsection must have been. He was speaking, but I couldn't distinguish the words.

There must have been twelve people in the room, not counting the patient. Whatever Emily Woodrow had seen when her daughter died, it couldn't have been this. Not unless she'd passed out after the first stranger arrived.

I was the sole idle onlooker. Everyone in the room moved with intent, carried out a given task, performed the required steps in some secret ballet.

Peña seemed to take charge. There was nothing sleepy about him as he barked orders, moving more quickly than his bulk should have allowed. A woman handed him a syringe.

Someone was sticking patches, like small round Band-Aids, to areas of the patient's bare skin. Peña spoke and a woman scrambled to grab the paddles off the cart.

The resident anesthesiologist glanced up suddenly, and his eyes met mine. His mouth moved. A sharp-featured woman began a march to the door.

I turned quickly and ran. My wig felt too tight. It wasn't until after I'd pressed the down button, after the elevator door had closed behind me, that I recalled the room's wallpaper: blue, with white latticework and gold flowers.

If all the chemotherapy rooms were outfitted the same, then each had a single wall-mounted spigot. Oxygen, most likely. No way to make a mistake with only one source.

If oxygen was readily available in the rooms, I wondered what was kept in the metal cylinder strapped to the cart.

15

In a first-floor bathroom, I breathed deeply, washed my hands, and fluffed my fake hair until two nurses finished arguing and agreed that Isabel had one hell of a nerve dating Danny. I kept glancing at myself in the mirror. I have photo IDs—laminated official-looking badges—for both my blond and my brunette identities. Neither looks much like me, nor did the woman in the mirror.

When the nurses finally left, I hid in a stall and, with overwhelming relief, peeled off the wig, feeling my hair spring back to life. I ran my fingers over my scalp, ruffling my curls and scratching all the pesky itches, then wrapped the blond wig in crumpled tissue paper and stuffed it into my purse.

As a redhead, I returned to the mirror and unfastened the top two buttons on my blouse. Could I make it through one more interview? I placed a hand firmly over my racing heart and wondered if the child on the fourth floor was breathing yet. I exhaled enough air to fog the mirror.

One more interview. I kept my suit jacket on, just in case. My freshly released hair was wild, but a few pins and the straw hat held it down. Sandy's lipstick clashed with my natural coloring, so I dipped a rough paper towel in warm water and scrubbed my lips till they paled.

The water felt so good that I dampened another towel in icy water and pressed it to my cheeks. My heartbeat slowed.

In about a week, with Roz's help, I'd fake a Silver Crescent letterhead and cancel the whole shebang. Maybe my imaginary chapter would go bankrupt, their treasurer accused of embezzlement. Simply shocking.

Tina. Tina Sukhia. I should have asked Peña to spell it. A shaky lead, but my only one, given that my client showed a marked disinclination to talk. No hospital would give up information on an ex-employee. I'd probably have to transfer more of Emily Woodrow's advance to Patsy Ronetti in order to get the necessary address. But first, outside the bathroom, I ducked dutifully into a nearby phone alcove. Never neglect the obvious, Mooney used to preach. And damned if he wasn't right.

Tina Sukhia listed her number in the phone book. The address was on Buswell Street. The nurse-practitioner who might have administered chemotherapy to Rebecca Woodrow had given up a job conveniently close to home.

I fed a coin into the slot. Three rings and a quick pickup. "Hi." The voice was wrong. Male.

"May I speak to Tina, please?"

"Who's this?"

"Is Tina there?"

"She oughtta be home any minute."

I shifted to a more official tone. "That's perfect. I'm calling from JHHI, about Tina's exit interview. We're a little concerned."

"Yeah? Why's that?"

"As you may know, we're required to withhold her last week's salary until we complete the exit-interview process."

"Oh."

"Hang on a minute, please," I said, because real people expect bureaucrats to put them on hold. I counted to twenty-five, slowly, then spoke again. "I'm sorry. Where were we? Oh, yes, listen, this could work out very well. We have someone right in your neighborhood. She could be in and out in five minutes."

"Would she bring the check?"

"Well, no. But I'll be able to drop it in the mail as soon as our rep phones in and tells me the exit interview's complete."

"Okay," the man said. "Good enough. Bye, now."

I emerged from JHHI blinking like I'd spent the day in a darkened movie house, dazzled, disoriented, amazed by the light in the sky and the fresh air. Since I'd already hit the maximum daily rate at the garage—an astounding sum—I temporarily abandoned my car and headed up Longwood, counting crocuses. Even on heavily trafficked Brookline Avenue, a few blossoms challenged the concrete. On the less-traveled cross streets, bright patches of yellow and blue turned city lawns into gardens.

I took deep gulping breaths, gagging on exhaust fumes for my trouble. The hell with formality in the late-afternoon heat, I decided, plucking off the straw hat and shaking my hair loose. I wished I'd stripped off my panty hose in the JHHI ladies' room. I was tired of disguises.

Buswell Street is in Boston University country. B.U. tried to buy most of the area outright a few years ago and might have succeeded if not for a vigilant neighborhood association that saw few benefits in losing more of the city's rarest commodity—taxable property—to an insatiable juggernaut.

B.U. continues to chew away at Kenmore Square, threatening its seedy bars and pizza joints with gentrification, but a few blocks down Beacon Street no new dorms rise high. Just weathered brick four-stories, basking in faded glory.

According to two strips of linotype pasted over the doorbell of 551 Buswell, Tina Sukhia shared apartment 4D with Tony Foley. In Boston, where the O'Reillys tend to stick to the O'Days, and the Cabots to the Forbeses, Sukhia seemed an odd matchup with Foley.

I rang the bell. A metallic squawk issued from the speaker. "Tina? That you? You forget your keys?"

I hollered my real name and no further information since I don't like yelling my business in strange vestibules. A buzzer sounded and I pushed open the heavy oak door.

The vestibule was small, paneled in dark wood. The stairs beckoned. If people are slapping down hard-earned bucks for Stairmaster machines, it must be good exercise, right? My resolve was strengthened by a quick glance at the elevator, a cell with no evidence of a state inspection certificate.

It seemed like a long climb for only four levels. The steps

twisted and spiraled, three steep short flights per floor. I heard a door unlatch, and a deep voice, familiar from the phone, demanded, "Tina, that you?"

I'd beaten her home. I kept climbing. My appearance wiped the welcoming smile off Tony Foley's face. He rearranged it and came up with a grin that managed to be both tentative and flirtatious at the same time.

"Who're you?"

"Carlotta Carlyle. That's what I said at the door," I answered cheerfully, pleased to leave Sandy Everett behind.

"Speaker doesn't work worth shit."

"I'm here to talk to Tina."

"Coulda saved yourself a climb. She ain't in yet." He was lanky and blond, with an accent out of the rural South. As he spoke, he ran a hand through greasy hair that spilled over his forehead. Twenty-five to thirty. With a shampoo and a lot of dental work, he'd be close to handsome.

"But you're expecting her," I said. "Soon."

"You that exit-interview lady?"

"Right."

He stared at me blankly for a minute, then broke into a know-it-all grin. "You're scared she's gonna sue you, right? She tol' me. Anytime she leaves a place, they get all worried 'counta she's a minority, and did she file a complaint with MCAD or some such." He seemed pleased by the prospect, as if a lawsuit would be the punchline of a joke.

MCAD is the Massachusetts Committee Against Discrimination.

"It's nothing like that," I assured him.

He sucked on his ill-spaced teeth and aimed a pointing index finger at me, cocking his thumb for a trigger. "Well, is it, like, if she was laid off, she gets severance?" He seemed like he was earnestly trying to fit together pieces of a jigsaw puzzle.

I was trying to figure something out too, namely this guy who talked like a hayseed, looked like a sheet-carrying Klansman, and lived with a woman who was definitely not an Irish townie.

I blew out a sigh. I'm glad when people surprise me. Sometimes you think you've got it all mapped out, and then whammo.

He hadn't invited me in and he was blocking the door to the apartment. I said, "You think I could have a glass of water?"

"Elevator busted again?"

"Didn't look too reliable."

He snorted. "Come on in." He shifted a good five inches and I brushed past him.

The door opened onto a wall with a row of wooden pegs, heavy with winter jackets and bright-colored filmy scarves. From the hallway, I could see into four tiny rooms: kitchen, living room, bedroom, and bath. The place was bigger than the elevator, but not much. From the bedroom came a pungent smell of incense, smoky and floral, with a hint of something underneath.

Tony nodded me toward the kitchen.

Along one wall, a dinky two-burner range nestled next to a toy refrigerator and a half-size sink. The rest of the room was crowded with a card table, two chairs, and a stack of boxes emblazoned with the logo of a local stereo outlet.

The man rummaged in a high cupboard, found a glass, rinsed and filled it with tepid water.

"Thanks," I said.

My nose and my memory got together: marijuana. How quaint.

"So, she's got money comin' from JHHI?" the man demanded while I drank.

"Are you Tina's husband?"

"You mean, like, you shouldn't discuss stuff with somebody ain't family?"

"Something like that," I replied coolly. Near the sink, peacock feathers fanned out of a purple vase. Someone in the apartment had a taste for exotic colors, and I didn't think it was the man in the white T-shirt and khakis.

"We're engaged. I'm Tony." He offered the name as if anyone

who'd ever encountered Tina, even on paper, would automatically recognize it. "Nothin' wrong in tellin' me."

His brief nervous smile made me wonder if Tina knew about the engagement. "New equipment?" I asked, nodding at the boxes, pretending I hadn't heard his request for information.

His face lit up. A shame about those teeth. "Reason I was hopin' you were Tina. Wanted to show her. It's like her weddin' present to me. She just told me go pick it out, put it on her card."

"Nice," I said, because his enthusiasm demanded some response, and because stereo components are one of the few things I spend money on.

"Terrific," he corrected me. "'Bout time something good happened 'round here."

"Did something good happen?"

"Tina's job."

I removed a notebook from my bag, found a pen, and prepared to take notes like a diligent bureaucrat. "A new job? I'm glad to hear she found work so soon," I said.

"She hadn't had something, she wouldn't have left JHHI—Hey, I'm not gettin' her in any trouble, sayin' that, am I?"

"I'm not here to make trouble. It's just one of those follow-up studies. The institute likes to keep track. We want to make sure we're offering comparable benefits, competitive salaries—"

"Hah!" Tony had quite a line in snorts. "You guys must have your heads stuck in the sand. Competitive!"

"Tina's doing better now?"

"Better! Man, that don't even touch it!"

I waited for him to tell me more, but he didn't, so I pretended to consult a form. "Did she feel her schedule at JHHI was too demanding?"

"I sure did. Hell, I hardly ever saw her. One shift after another. We didn't even eat together, or if we did, we barely had time for takeout."

I made squiggles with my pen. "Would you say she was suffering from professional burnout?"

"She was tired, I know that. New job, she practically sets her own hours. We eat out."

"And what's the nature of her new employment?"

"Well, it's not frontline nursing care. There's no money in that. Some kind of experimental training or research."

I kept my pen poised. "Would you know her new job title?"

"I dunno." He broke into another of his sudden nervous smiles. "Say, you want to see this stuff I just bought? I got to show it off to somebody."

With minimal encouragement, he started opening cartons, eagerly setting equipment on the kitchen table. He'd apparently unsealed the boxes earlier, removing the bubble-wrap and plastic peanuts and bagging them for the trash. What I was watching was more like a ceremonial unveiling with running commentary.

"Look at this CD player! I didn't get the changer, the kind takes six CDs at once. Too much money. Coulda got a changer for the same money, but not this kinda quality."

He had a good two thousand bucks' worth of sound equipment laid out on the table by the time he'd finished. Top-grade stuff: Bose, Nakamichi, Denon. While he was patting it and singing its praises, I leaned out the kitchen door and took a quick inventory of the living room: Pier 1 wicker, potted plants, red-and-orange-patterned cushions. More money invested in the stereo than in anything else in the apartment.

Nurses earned decent salaries. Maybe she drove a good car, had a hefty savings account, helped out her family.

I stretched small talk to the limits, but no Tina. We moved into the living room, sat in two cushioned chairs on either side of a bow window. He offered me a beer.

"You think she might be working late?" I asked, consulting my watch. "I could try her at her new place."

"She didn't say she'd be late, but you know nurses." He leaned forward and lowered his voice. "She comes home and finds me with a pretty gal, you just bet she'll be pissed."

I was glad I'd turned down the beer. There was a framed photo of a young woman on the windowsill. The frill of white lace balanced on her head made her skin seem ebony. She had a heart-shaped face, knowing eyes.

I let Tony see me studying the photo.

"She's beautiful," I said.

"Yeah," he agreed happily. "Sure you won't have a beer?"

"No, thanks."

"You got incredible hair, you know. Super color. Want to take your jacket off, or anythin'?"

"No, thanks. Maybe I ought to try her at work. I wouldn't have, like, any language difficulties, would I?"

He grinned, displaying those awful teeth. "With Tina? 'Cause of her name and the way she looks? Hell, her folks speak English better 'n me, and they're the foreigners. Tina's never even been to Pakistan. I mean, she likes to wear the clothes, the whad-ja-call-it, but she's a hot-dog all-American."

"No problem trying her at work, then?"

"Can't it wait?"

"No," I said.

His eyes narrowed. "Don't get huffy. Hey, you're not one of those Q.A. people, are you? Quality whatever? About taking good care of the patients? 'Cause you know, Tina is one damn fine nurse."

I made a noncommittal noise and lowered my voice confidentially. "Well, you know, we did receive a letter about her," I said, wrinkling my forehead in a concerned frown.

"Don't sound like no card from a grateful patient," he said.

I studied his face. "It was from a Mrs. Woodrow. Did Tina ever mention her, or Rebecca Woodrow, a six-year-old girl? She was Tina's patient—oh, three months ago. She died."

"Look, Tina worked with dyin' kids all the time, and we didn't discuss it over dinner a whole lot. Too depressin', you know? I'm glad she's out of it."

"You think she's happier at her new job?"

His face clouded briefly, then he flashed the nervous smile. "I dunno. I hope so."

SNAPSHOT

"Before I can clear her exit interview, I have to speak to her about this letter," I said. "Thanks for the water. The new place close by?"

He shrugged.

"You know, you never said where she worked. My boss would kill me if I forgot to get that."

"Place called Cee Co."

I kept my voice level, uninterested. "How do you spell that?"

"I dunno."

"Well, just the address then," I said.

"I never been there. I mean, everybody knows where JHHI is, and I went to plenty of parties there with Tina, but she just started this other place. We ever meet at one of them parties, you 'n' me? At JHHI?"

"I don't think so," I said. "I'd have remembered. Is Cee Co. the whole name?"

"Short for somethin' else, I guess. You know, I never get any of that shit straight. DG is Data General and DEC is Digital and that's short for Digital Equipment Corporation—"

"You in computers?"

"No."

"What is it you do?"

"I get by," he said with a quick grin.

"Is Cee Co. with a C or an S? Do you know?"

"C, I think. Some long name."

"And they do medical research?"

"I guess."

I stood up and returned my notebook to my purse. I was fed up with all this Cee Co. hanky-panky. Dammit, I'd call Emily Woodrow tonight, in spite of her instructions, demand a few answers.

In the meantime, I gave Tony Foley my real card, the one with Carlyle Detective Agency on it. "Ask her to call me as soon as she comes in," I said brusquely. "Thanks for your time."

"Tina's never this late. You want to have dinner or somethin'?" he said speculatively, arching an eyebrow.

"Save it," I said.

"Hey, what's this?"

He was finally reading the card. "Detective agency?" he spluttered. "What kind of crap is that?"

I didn't join him for dinner.

16

I hoofed it back to the Longwood garage and paid the ransom for the car. Considering the price, they should have washed and waxed it.

Cee Co. was a business. C-something Company. Emily Woodrow had mentioned it in an urgent whisper, Tina Sukhia worked there, and I'd never heard of it.

Traffic crawled over the B.U. Bridge and inched sluggishly along Memorial Drive. I cut down River Street and started using twisting cabbie shortcuts, turning every two blocks. I'd rather drive miles out of the way than sit still. I punched on a tape and sang along with Chris Smither's "It Ain't Easy," silently agreeing with the lyrics, and trying to avoid thoughts of food. A quick stop for a burger and fries was tempting even after last night's junk-food orgy with Gloria.

I usually don't eat much when I dine with Gloria. Watching her sock away Tootsie Rolls humbles my appetite.

No time for food now. I turned down Flagg Street, made my way to Mount Auburn. The business pages of the *Globe* might identify Cee Co. Maybe Cee Co. was a stock-market abbreviation. I'd hit the tables, the New York Stock Exchange, the American, NASDAQ, the local Boston exchange.

Cars snarled Broadway near Cambridge Rindge and Latin, the high school Paolina would attend one day. I sighed and hit the brake. A stalled car, an accident, maybe. It wasn't the usual place for a rush-hour jam.

Would Paolina, discouraged by her mother's remarks, overwhelmed by home responsibilities, drop out before high school?

What could her friend want with my trash? My mind balked at the word *boyfriend. Friend* was bad enough. What does an eleven-year-old need with a twenty-year-old friend?

I ought to keep food in my car. Trail mix. Beef jerky. Behind me, a man in a blue Chevy had the nerve to honk. I love it when the seventh driver in line decides to honk. I didn't bother giving him the finger. Every other driver on the street beat me to it anyway.

The problem: a stuck traffic light at Cambridge Street. Once past it, I flew, making it home in three minutes only to find a man pacing my front stoop. For a minute I thought it was Mooney with a name to match the garbage thief's license plate, but the shape was all wrong. I didn't know this guy. Maybe he was waiting for Roz.

I revised that opinion on the way up the walk. He was too old for Roz. Too ugly. Roz has a penchant for the male body beautiful— not Schwarzenegger types, but solidly built hunks. This one looked forlorn, unkempt, and a little bit angry.

"Miss Carlyle?" he said accusingly.

I didn't fit the key into the lock, just kept the ring in my pocket, where, almost unconsciously, I'd closed a fist around it. I learned that as a cop: If you need to hit somebody, keys make a great substitute for brass knuckles. "Yeah?"

"I wonder if I might have a word?"

"You got one."

"I'd like to speak with you."

"Who would I be talking to? About what?"

"My name is Harold Woodrow."

I unclenched my fist and worked the key. He followed me into the living room like a docile puppy, sat stiffly in the straight-backed chair next to my desk.

It was his nose, I decided, that made his face unpleasant. Thin, sharp, and long, it made him appear arrogant even before he opened his mouth.

"What can I do for you?" I asked, giving myself points for sounding far more polite than I felt. I was hungry and I desperately wanted to kick off my flats and run cold water on my abused toes.

"You can explain this." He removed a folder from his inside jacket pocket. His speech and manner did nothing to warm the arrogance. His shoes were soft leather with an expensive sheen.

The folder was his wife's check register. He tapped it with a manicured fingernail.

"My wife paid you a thousand dollars. The memo says 'retainer.'"

I pretended to study the entry while trying to read the adjacent lines. She didn't write many checks.

"Why has my wife hired you?"

"Mr. Woodrow, I understand you're an attorney, and you do a considerable amount of financial consulting and advising—to doctors."

"Yes."

"How would you react if I asked you about one of your clients?"

"You haven't asked. I have." He had a light complexion, a thin-lipped mouth made smaller by the prominent nose.

"Ask your wife," I suggested.

His mouth tightened. "My wife told me you were a psychic, and that the amount in question covered several séances and a detailed tarot reading."

Thanks a lot, Emily.

I said, "Everybody's got to earn a living."

"I mentioned Emily's bizarre conduct in consulting you to a fellow attorney who deals in criminal matters. He knew your name. Remembered it. Said you were an investigator."

"What's your friend's name?"

"That's not what I'm here to talk about."

"Talk about what you're here to talk about," I said dryly.

"I want to know what you're doing for my wife."

"Talk some more," I suggested.

"I expect some answers."

I stared at my desk top, glanced around the room, and sighed. I hadn't fed the parakeet in days, and the cat was probably poised to claw me as soon as I stepped into the kitchen.

"Fifteen eighty-eight," I recited. "That's the year of the Spanish Armada. I don't know why I remember that one, but it's up there with 1620 and 1492 as far as answers go."

"You don't take this seriously."

"Ah."

"Young woman," he said, "you are going to take this seriously before I'm finished."

"Oh," I said, "and why is that?"

"If my wife hired you to spy on me, you'll be very sorry. You people are licensed by the state." He hesitated before the word *people,* made it sound like *vermin.*

"My wife is under the care of a psychiatrist," he continued. "She is not a well woman and I won't have her taken advantage of by some rumor-mongering private eye."

He'd lost a child not four months ago, but I found myself having empathy trouble.

"My wife, much as I, uh, love her, is not a completely truthful woman at the best of times. And now, well—you have to understand where she's coming from."

I wasn't about to tell him anything, but if he wanted to confide in me that was a different story. I eased my heels out of my shoes, waggled my toes.

"It's not often you come across a spoiled child of forty," he said, snapping out his words, "but that's my Emily. Up until—up until our disaster—I don't think she ever wanted anything she couldn't have. You've seen her type before, haven't you? Rich, pretty, homecoming queen. And now she's behaving as if she were the only person in the universe to lose a child, the only one to suffer. She acts as if . . . as if she's completely forgotten that Rebecca was my daughter as well.

"Emily's the one who's frozen me out, not the other way around. I'm not an unfeeling man. She may have made it sound like I'm uncaring, but it's not as if she's played the perfect little spouse."

His voice shook, but he pretended to cough and firmed it up. He put a hand to his cheek, rubbed it as if he were checking to see whether or not he'd shaved recently. "Good God," he murmured softly, his voice gaining volume as his chagrin turned to anger, "this is what she's driven me to, babbling in front of a—I beg your pardon, young woman. I shouldn't have come here at all."

"You're probably right about that," I agreed.

"Dammit." He squeezed syllables out from between clenched teeth. "One more chance, all right? What exactly did my wife pay you for? What service do you offer for a thousand dollars?"

I reached over and picked up the telephone.

"What are you doing?"

"Calling your wife," I said, jamming my heels back into my shoes. I was actually punching Roz's upstairs number because it's nice to have a karate expert around when you're going to throw somebody out of your house.

"Stop."

"It's ringing."

"I don't want her to—"

"Don't you think it's time to go?"

He gave me the kind of look actors use to signify that they'll get even someday, and crossed to the hall. I opened the door for him, locked all three locks as soon as he'd departed. Then I leaned against the wall.

Why had I thought of actors? Something about the performance hadn't rung true. Words or emotions? Which?

"My wife, much as I, uh, love her . . ." Had his hesitation spoken of more than Yankee embarrassment at a declaration of affection? Did he love his wife? He'd seemed convinced that I'd been hired to spy on him. Query: When does a wife hire a private eye to follow her husband? Response: When she believes he's having an affair. Less so nowadays, what with divorce-law reform. Still, evidence of infidelity can be a potent weapon in child-custody cases.

Here, there was no longer a child to consider.

I freed my aching toes and padded around the house barefoot, digging through the daily rubble until I found the *Globe* neatly folded on the hall table. Nearby, Roz had hung a glistening portrait of two large onions draped by a bunch of limp parsley.

No good. Monday's paper didn't carry the stock quotes since the exchanges were closed on Sundays. Slovenly housekeeping, however, has its bonuses. I located the Saturday paper under a chair, took it to my desk, and ran a finger down the tiny print of the Stock Exchange listings. CCO, maybe. I found a C COR on NAS-DAQ, but that was corporation, not company. My eyes started to hurt. I gave up the tables and read the entire section, front to back, and all the miscellany in between. A columnist advised me to *Keep My Stock Records Up to Date.* I learned that health-care funds slumped in the first quarter.

Nothing about Cee Co.

T.C. yowled while I yanked the flip-top ring and presented him with a tin of Fancy Feast. I put a big pot of water on to boil for spaghetti. I use sauce straight from the jar, with a dollop of red wine to give the illusion of homemade. It's not great, but it's quick. Eating takes enough time out of life. Who has hours for cooking?

I practiced some tricky guitar riffs from Rory Block's new *Ain't I a Woman* tape, listening for the telephone, the doorbell.

I didn't hear from Tina Sukhia.

I didn't get a package from Emily Woodrow.

My fingers stopped picking in the middle of a song while I considered Tony's assertion that his fiancée was a fine nurse. Had he sounded overly defensive? He'd asked if I was from the Q.A. Department—Quality Something. Quality Analysis? Quality Assurance?

And what about the timing? When exactly had Tina left JHHI?

A death and a departure. No reason for them to be related.

My fingers chose an old Robert Johnson tune:

I got a kindhearted woman, do anything in this world for me,
I got a kindhearted woman, do anything in this world for me,
But these evil-hearted women, man, they will not let me be.

17

I spent the next morning juggling phone books, checking out variants of Cee Co., riling secretaries with useless calls, and finding no trace of the company that employed Tina Sukhia, who, for her part, neither answered her phone nor responded to the messages I left on her answering machine.

When the doorbell rang just after two o'clock, I ran a hand through hair uncombed since volleyball practice and smoothed my ratty gray sweatshirt over black jeans that were ripped at both knees and faded from too many go-rounds in the washer.

I peered out the peephole and saw Mooney, his weight evenly balanced in classic traffic-cop stance. I figured he'd come about the license plate so I started unchaining chains and unbolting bolts. No quick dives into the powder room necessary; Mooney's used to my come-as-you-are appearance.

He wore a beige cotton sweater, chinos, and sneakers. Loose comfy stuff he could run in if he had to. It was nice of him to come by with the plate rundown. He could have called. I grinned when I opened the door. He didn't smile back. "Can I come in?" he said somberly. No sparkle in his eyes. No handshake, no mock-brotherly squeeze.

"Something happen to Paolina?"

"No. I must look pretty grim."

I sighed. "You do. You want a beer?"

"Orange juice?"

"Okay." That meant he was working. Not working, Mooney drinks beer. He followed me into the kitchen and scraped a chair across the linoleum as he pulled it away from the table.

"This guy Paolina's seeing is a known child molester, right?"

"What guy? Sit down," Mooney said. "It's not about Paolina."

I sat.

Mooney drank juice.

"You gonna break it to me gently?"

"You went to visit Tina Sukhia yesterday."

I quickly cast my mind back to the street outside her apartment. Had I strolled into somebody's surveillance? I remembered the stale marijuana smell in the tiny apartment, but I didn't think cops cared about marijuana anymore, not with crack around. Not with heroin, crystal, speed, PCP, and an Uzi in every other high-school locker.

Mooney said, "Her boyfriend gave us your card."

"Why?"

"I guess because of the coincidence—you showing up, her dying."

Dying.

"No," I heard myself say.

"That must mean no, it's not a coincidence—because I just saw the body, and yes, she sure is dead."

"Hell," I said, and then "damn," over and over. It sounded like my voice was coming from far away, working on its own, without the cooperation of my lips or larynx.

"So I need to know why you wanted to talk to her. And you're gonna tell me because it's part of an official police investigation."

"Homicide?" I asked, stalling, knowing Mooney wouldn't be here if it wasn't.

"A definite possibility."

"But not a certainty?"

"Listen when I talk. I said possibility."

"How likely?"

"Likely enough that you ought to answer me instead of playing games."

"Shit."

"So do we talk here?"

"Or what? You gonna haul me down to the station house, use a rubber hose?"

"I'm not in the mood, Carlotta."

"Sorry. Me, I'm in a great mood."

"I coulda sent somebody else. I come all the way over here and you're gonna give me crap?"

"I work for a living, Moon. Same as you. My clients deserve a little discretion."

"Any client who sent you to see Sukhia better not leave the jurisdiction."

"Why don't you tell me how Tina Sukhia—a lady I never met in my life—died? I haven't read the papers yet."

"That's not how this song goes."

"You want to keep the details from me because you think I killed her and then left my business card with the boyfriend—who told me yesterday, by the way, that he was the fiancé."

"Boyfriend, fiancé. They were shacked up, is what."

"You use phrases I haven't heard in ten years. Shacked up."

"You use phrases I don't hear much either," he said. "Except from hookers." Mooney was brought up a strict Catholic. Women did not swear, not even a discreet *hell* or *damn*. They didn't become cops, either.

"The boyfriend-fiancé a suspect?" I asked.

"Seeing as it happened in a hospital, and we can't place him there, no more than anybody else."

"JHHI?"

"Good old Helping Hand," he said.

"She worked there."

"You working for them?"

"Them?"

"The hospital?"

It's not that I mind telling lies, it's that I know it's not smart to lie to Mooney. Withold information, maybe. But he's got an incredibly good mental lie detector.

"And why would the hospital hire me?" I asked.

"Nice try," he said.

"Come on, Mooney."

"It looks very much like the lady overdosed on barbiturates."

"People OD on downers all the time. What's against it being an accident?"

"No evidence she was a user at all."

"When did she die?"

"Body found about six forty-five this morning. That's all I've got till the M.E. talks."

"That's probably all you'll ever get then," I said sympathetically. M.E.'s are pretty useless when it comes to precise time of death. Oh, they can shove thermometers into orifices and plug numbers into equations, but there are too many variables. The more they learn, the less they know.

"It's not even cast in concrete on the six forty-five. Doctors," Mooney said, raising his eyebrows. "Deaths in hospitals—no matter what the circumstances—cops are considered the last resort. Doctors think there's no such thing as a situation they can't handle."

"Doctor find her?"

"Nurse. Anne Reese, R.N. Didn't know the victim. Didn't care. Mainly irritated because she was at the end of her shift and wanted to go home."

"Nice."

"Like I didn't want to go home, too. But a death's a death. You don't just walk off and leave it."

"At hospitals they do."

Mooney made a face.

"You didn't like the nurse," I said.

"Bingo. And she didn't like me."

"And you're so charming, Moon. Tell me, the boyfriend see Tina last night?"

"Nope. So he got good and stewed, far as I can tell. Eyes bloodshot, but you can't tell if it's from crying or booze."

"If Tina was a user, that could be why the hospital let her go," I said.

"I already thought of that," Mooney said.

"There could be money in this someplace. Fiancé had new stereo equipment up the wazoo."

"So?"

I waited for him to mention Tina's new job as a source of the windfall. He didn't.

"The hospital been leaking drugs?" I asked.

"The question crossed my mind," Mooney admitted.

"Anybody answered it yet?"

"I haven't asked yet. I've got appointments with some docs: Chief of Staff. Chief of Medicine. Chief of Pharmacy. Chief trouble-shooter. Probably Chief of PR."

"But you decided to pick on me first? I'm not gonna give you headaches like some medical bigshot?"

"Carlotta, you know that's not—"

"Mooney, it looks to me like you've got an accidental death, and I don't think my client ought to be hassled about an accidental OD. I don't think I ought to be hassled, either." While my mouth was saying *accidental,* I have to admit I was thinking *suicide.* Maybe Tina had quit JHHI. But there was also the possibility that the woman had been dismissed. Maybe she'd done something wrong, screwed up so badly that Rebecca Woodrow had died as a result. What do you do for a comeback if your negligence causes the death of a child?

Maybe return to the scene of the crime and atone for it.

"What do you mean, hassled?" Mooney's voice interrupted my thoughts. "This is hassling?"

"Yeah."

"Hah." He smacked his glass down so hard I thought it would break. "If you want that plate number, owner, you give up your client."

"Unfair," I said.

"So?"

Dammit. Mrs. Woodrow had insisted that a stranger, a doctor, a man in a white coat had been present when her daughter died.

127

Keith Donovan had asserted that Emily was hallucinating the incident. Harold Woodrow had intimated that his wife was a liar. Pablo Peña, JHHI's resident anesthesiologist, had denied shoving anyone out of a hospital room. And now I couldn't ask Tina Sukhia which one, if any, had been telling the truth.

With a sinking sensation in the pit of my stomach, I wondered exactly where Emily Woodrow had been when Tina died. I hadn't yet received the day's mail, but I found myself hoping it wouldn't contain a confession.

"Mooney, let me get back to you."

"Carlotta, the more time goes by, the less chance I've got."

"Don't quote the stats at me. There's no pressure here, Moon. It's not like you found a city councillor with a knife in his back. The press is gonna see a minority nurse dead in some drug scam. Inside page, Metro, under the fold."

"Tomorrow," Mooney said.

"What about the license plate?"

"Tomorrow."

"Moon, please."

"What is this crap? I can wait, but you can't? If this plate has to do with Sukhia, the whole deal's off."

"Mooney, it's Paolina. The plate belongs to a guy who's hustling Paolina."

He gave me a hard look, but then he sighed and yanked his notebook out of his pocket. "This loser's twenty-eight years old," he said.

"That's why I want to stop him fast."

He made a face. "Plate's registered to Paco Lewis Sanchez. One five eight Peterborough, Boston."

"What else?"

"Height: five-ten. Weight: one ninety-five."

"What else?"

"That's all I got."

"You could run him through NCIC," I suggested. "Keep the crime computer ticking."

"It'll cost," Mooney said.

"Repayment in kind," I replied.

"Like first thing tomorrow, everything you know about Tina Sukhia?"

"She's dead," I said. "And the only way I even know that is from you."

"You can trust me on it," he said.

"Trust has to go both ways," I replied.

"Like love?" he asked after a pause. Mooney's been trying to turn my attentions away from Sam for as long as I can remember. He might have succeeded, too, if we'd never worked in the same chain of command.

"Like lust," I said. "I don't know a lot about love."

"Yeah?"

"And what I do know about love," I said, "I don't trust."

18

She'd told me not to phone.

I punched her number as soon as Mooney's footsteps cleared the porch.

I've never yet tossed a client to the cops, but there's always a first time. I figured I'd use Tina's death to throw a scare into Emily Woodrow, speed up the process, get her to level with me. About her promised packet of information. About Cee Co. About why she needed a person with firearms expertise to take charge of her mysterious paperwork. Or else.

As the phone rang, I doodled on my blotter and tried to envision Emily, in her elegant beige suit, plunging a loaded hypodermic into Tina Sukhia's arm. Or, more likely, forcing her to swallow a quantity of pills.

Had Emily ever been a nurse?

If Patsy Ronetti had done her job, I'd already know. Why the hell hadn't she gotten back to me?

"Hello?" The voice was harried, anxious. I'd reached Harold, the husband, which seemed odd in the middle of the day. When I gave my name and asked to speak to his wife, he erupted, but not in the way I'd expected.

"She's not here," he shouted. "She's not with her mother. Her friends don't know where she is!"

"Calm down."

"She didn't come home last night. Her asshole therapist, the jerk, doesn't know where the hell she is."

"She didn't tell you where she was going?"

"Shopping, for Chrisake, something like that. What do I know? How do I know?"

"Have you, uh, called anyone?"

"The police, you mean?"

"Yeah."

"Why on earth would I call the police? Bitch walks out on me. On *me!* What did you tell her about me?"

"Huh?"

"It's not like she's been a comfort lately, you know? A help-mate. If she ever spoke to me in a civil tone anymore . . . It's not like . . . Well, things might be different with us, that's all. Ever hear the one about how there are two sides to every story?"

"I'm not sure what story you're trying to tell me," I said.

His voice grew tight with suspicion. "Is she with you?"

"Yeah," I said sarcastically, "that's why I called to speak to her."

He hung up. I bit my tongue and winced.

Roz came speeding by and homed in on the refrigerator. She wore black from her leggings to her bustier. On the side that wasn't shaved, her white hair was developing greenish streaks. It looked like she was aging in a fashion usually reserved for plants.

I said, "Busy?"

"No more cleaning," she pleaded. "C'mon. My hands stink. Something in Marta's refrigerator went right through the rubber gloves."

"Soak them in turpentine," I suggested.

Instead she displayed them five inches from my nose, full of odd rings and chartreuse nail polish. "Smell." Her toenails were the same chartreuse.

"No, thanks." I described the guy who'd escorted Paolina to her aunt's house. Then I scribbled Paco Sanchez's address on a scrap of paper. "See where this guy lives, what he does, who he sees. Drives a blue Firebird." I wrote down the plate number as well.

"Maybe I can borrow Lemon's van."

"Good idea. See if you can borrow it without borrowing him."

"Two's better." Lemon is her karate instructor and sometime lover. They share a penchant for slogans: hers on T-shirts; his plastered on the bumpers of his van—everything from friendly whales spouting SAVE THE HUMANS to travelers' warnings such as NEW YORK CITY—WHERE THE WEAK ARE KILLED AND EATEN.

"Two's better for what?" I asked.

"Surveillance."

"One's cheaper," I responded. The Woodrow riches weren't going to pay for this investigation.

"If it doesn't cost, you got any objection to him coming along for the ride?" she asked.

"Just don't miss the Sanchez guy 'cause you're busy screwing in the back of the van, okay?"

"Would I do a thing like that?"

"Oh, Roz," I said. "Yes. You have and you would. But why rake up the past?"

19

When I dialed the Foley-Sukhia number, I got the recording again. Tina must have made the tape, and it was disconcerting to hear the cheerful voice of a dead woman over the line. While I listened, I recalled her photograph, white cap perched on glossy hair, smiling unlined face. I left no message.

After a glance at my watch, I quickly changed from torn jeans to black slacks. The grubby sweatshirt hit the laundry basket. I yanked a pea-green cowl-neck over my head, a sweater I've had since my Detroit high-school days, made of some indestructible acrylic fiber that never balls and never rips. I'm sure the clothing industry outlawed it years ago.

I combed my hair with my fingers as I dashed down the stairs.

My house has a stoop. Keith Donovan's house, two doors down, has a porch big enough to call a veranda. I rang the bell and paced, hoping I'd timed it right. Five minutes before the hour to five minutes after the hour, a psychiatrist ought to answer his bell.

He came to the door wearing a gray oxford-cloth shirt and charcoal slacks, his unknotted tie draped around his neck.

"Hey," he said. "Caught me off guard. This patient's always late."

"Spare a minute?" I asked.

"Have you seen Emily? Spoken with her?"

"My questions exactly."

"She's not at your house?"

"She's not at yours?" I returned.

He pulled at one end of his tie and glanced hastily up and down the street. "Why don't you come in?"

His floor plan wasn't much different from mine. Foyer with staircase. Single step down to the living room. Dining room straight through the foyer. There the resemblance ended. If he did his own decorating, he was wasted as a therapist. A job at *House and Garden* beckoned. The foyer had been set up as a waiting room with a hunter-green loveseat and two inviting chairs. The wallpaper picked up the green of the loveseat. The area rug was a plushy Oriental.

He peered into a gilt-framed mirror, executed a flawless Windsor knot. If my foyer looked like his, I could raise my rates.

He'd taken the entire living room for his office, not just a corner of it like I had. It made me wonder about him. Where did he do his entertaining? Where did his friends hang out? Was he the workaholic the room suggested?

His inlaid mahogany desk probably cost more than every stick of furniture in my house. He couldn't have been a practicing, high-earning shrink for long. Cambridge is full of trust-fund babies. I wondered if he was one of them. Maybe he had an exceptionally wealthy practice. Or an extremely rich wife.

If he had a wife, there was no evidence of her existence. No ring on the man's hand. No framed photo on the desk.

I avoided sitting on the nearby couch. Made me feel too much like a patient. I settled for a tall chair with its back to the window. From the expression on Donovan's face, I'd copped his favorite seat.

"I haven't much time," he said.

"Did you and Emily Woodrow ever talk about the nurse-practitioner who was with Rebecca when she died?" I asked, skipping to the meat and potatoes.

"Emily's husband called me, all worked up—"

"I've spoken with him. Any reason he'd expect to find Emily at your house?"

"What do you mean?"

Looking at his guarded face, I could tell he knew exactly what I meant. Lately, you open any newspaper, there's a story about some therapist who's getting sued for seducing a patient.

"I mean what I said," I responded. "Mrs. Woodrow calls you Keith. You call her Emily. I thought you might be close."

"You thought I might be sleeping with her? As part of her treatment?" He sounded amused rather than outraged.

"Not really," I admitted.

"But you needed to ask."

"Unlikelier events have occurred," I said.

"She's not my type," he offered.

"So what about the nurse?" I asked.

"You don't want to ask me what my type is?"

"Not at the moment. The nurse."

"Emily talked about her," he conceded. "Can I call her Emily without you drawing any cheap conclusions?"

"Did Emily talk about her by name?"

His raised eyebrows implied he'd be humoring me by answering such a ridiculous question. I hate that.

"Did Emily use her name?" I insisted.

"If you want to know the name, I'd have to check my notes—"

"Tina ring a bell?"

"Tina. Yes."

Dammit, I thought. "A last name?" I asked.

"Is it important?"

"Start looking at those notes. Did Emily ever seem to blame Tina for Rebecca's death?"

He made no move toward his desk or wherever he kept his files. "In the past three months, Emily has gone so far as to blame Congress for her daughter's death," he said with a twist of his mouth.

"Have any congressmen been found dead today?"

"What's that supposed to mean?"

"The body of a nurse named Tina Sukhia was found at JHHI this morning."

"Sukhia." He recognized the name, all right.

"And now Emily's missing," I said. "And that might be a coincidence."

"It would have to be a coincidence. What else could it be?"

"I can think of a startling number of possibilities."

"Such as?"

"Tina Sukhia came into some money recently. *After* she lost her job." I left out the new job. I didn't intend to discuss Cee Co. with Emily's therapist. If she'd felt comfortable talking to him about it, she wouldn't have invented a ruse to see me alone.

"Maybe she quit *because* she came into money," he said.

"See. You can play the game, too," I said.

"Your turn."

"Emily has money. She could have used it to buy information."

"Such as?" Donovan asked.

"The identity of the man who was in the room when Rebecca died."

"The man Emily *says* was in the room," he retorted.

I got the feeling he was less than happy with the present situation, that he'd much prefer to lean back in his own chair, above the fray, and ponder somebody else's problems. "Another thing you can buy with money is silence," I suggested.

"So? Go on."

Could Cee Co. be some abbreviated form of the Ruhly department-store chain, the source of Emily's wealth? Maybe the Ruhly empire consisted of a group of "Clothing Co-ops" or "Cecilia's Corners." Maybe Tina's new "job" was to blackmail Emily Woodrow.

"Is it possible that Emily could have monkeyed with a piece of machinery, done something that inadvertently caused her daughter's death?" I asked. *And that Tina might have seen her do it,* I thought.

Donovan removed his reading glasses from his pocket, tapped them against his thigh. "Emily feels a basic responsibility for the child's death," he admitted. "Of course, that's not unusual."

"Do you think she could have deliberately killed her own daughter?"

"You have a high opinion of people, don't you?"

"I earned it," I said. "Do you know if the child's life was insured?"

"It would never have occurred to me to ask."

"I suppose the girl could have been wealthy in her own right," I said. "A trust fund. Money from a grandparent that would revert to a parent on the child's death."

"Whenever Emily mentioned money, which wasn't often, she spoke of it as a given, as a matter of fact."

"Was she jealous of her daughter?" I asked.

He paused long enough to swallow, and when he finally spoke, he avoided a direct response. "Women rarely kill," he said softly. "And when they do, they almost always kill abusive husbands or boyfriends."

I was a woman who'd killed twice, once as a cop, once after. My ex was alive and well, far as I knew.

I said, "Emily never discussed what happened in that room that day? Before Rebecca died?"

"I think she's told me every word she exchanged with her daughter, just remembering it, validating it, sharing it. She's talked about the possibility of a medical mistake, never murder."

"Did she ever talk about suicide?"

"About killing herself?"

"Yeah," I snapped. "She's missing. People who go missing sometimes turn up dead. That's what I mean."

"Let me put it this way: Most people who haven't lived sitcom lives, at one time or another think about killing themselves."

"I'm not asking you about most people. Did Emily talk to you about wanting to do it?"

"Have you ever thought about doing it?" The question came out wrong, full of sexual overtones. The silence in the room grew. He polished his glasses, restated himself carefully. "I mean, killing yourself?"

When my mother died. The thought came so quickly I was afraid I'd spoken it out loud.

"Don't analyze me," I said instead, my voice tight with anger. "Or patronize me."

"Okay," he said. "I'm telling you this in confidence. Understood?"

"I'm not a lawyer. It's not a privileged communication. But I'm not a blabbermouth either."

He leaned forward, extending his fingers and steepling his hands. He regarded me for a long moment, as if he were gauging exactly how far I could be trusted. "Okay then. When I first saw Emily, she wasn't sleeping. She said she never slept, or she slept for two hours and then roamed around the rest of the night. I prescribed Dalmane, a very common drug. Minimal side effects. She said it didn't work. I tried another. Serax, I think, was next, more an anti-anxiety medication, with drowsiness as a side effect. Didn't work."

"Is that unusual?"

"Yes. I tried Xanax, a tranquilizer, then something else. She still seemed resistant. And then it hit me. I realized she wasn't taking them."

"Huh?"

"She'd get a two-week supply or a month's supply, and stash it. I figured she was saving up, hoarding a lethal dose of sleep against the day she couldn't take the pain anymore."

"What did you do?"

"I cut her off cold. I spoke to her. She said she threw the pills away."

"Said."

"She seemed to be making progress."

"What kind of progress?"

"Her retaliatory thoughts seemed to become more other-directed than internalized."

"Did she specifically threaten to kill this nurse?"

"Whose side are you on here?"

"Do you have any idea where Emily might be?"

"I've told my answering service to put through her calls night or day. That's really all I can do."

"Psychiatrists not being interventionists," I said dryly.

"What would you suggest?"

"Go through your notes, and try to get in touch with every person she ever mentioned." I could see the protest in his eyes, so I added, "Or go through the notes and give me the list of people."

He nodded grudgingly.

I went on. "With Emily Woodrow unavailable I need a way to get her daughter's medical records. As Mrs. Woodrow's shrink, why don't you apply for the files?"

"I suppose I could do that."

"Too interventionist?" I asked.

"No," he said defiantly. "Why do you need them?"

"I want to know who was in that room at the end."

"I'll try," he said.

"And let me run some names by you, people who've come up in my preliminary check."

"I can give you till the doorbell rings."

"I spoke to Dr. Muir."

"You did?" His voice dropped as if I'd had an audience with the pope.

"Everybody tiptoed in his presence. Treated him like a national treasure. Except for one guy, an anesthesiologist named Pablo Peña. You know him?"

"Never heard of him."

"A resident. Three-quarters asleep."

"That explains it. He was probably too exhausted to salute when he heard Muir's name. You work a hundred and ten hours a week, you get tired."

"Tired enough to get confused? To panic and give the wrong drug?"

"Anesthesiologists don't give chemo."

"Think about it this way. Maybe he's on duty, thirty-fifth hour of a thirty-six-hour stretch, and something goes wrong with Rebecca. Tina Sukhia calls for help—what do they say?—calls a code, and this guy, asleep on his feet, rushes in with a mask, but instead of attaching it to the oxygen outlet, he grabs some cylinder on the emergency cart—"

"Stuff's color-coded. A cylinder on a crash cart would be either oxygen or air—"

"What if he intended to kill her?" I said. "Anesthesiologists have access to killer drugs."

"You're thinking like a cop. Why would he want to kill her?"

"Off the top of my head? Because he gets off on the power, the life-and-death stuff of putting people to sleep and waking them up —or not waking them up. Or maybe Rebecca saw something she wasn't supposed to see. Heard something she wasn't supposed to hear. Maybe the guy's a child abuser, and he'd tried his act on her."

"Carlotta—can I call you that?"

"Yes."

"Have you ever seen a code called?"

"Yeah. I have. Very recently."

"There would have been a minimum of ten people in Becca's room, within seconds. You think Peña would have killed her with all those witnesses?"

"In a mob scene, with everyone focused on a specific task, he might have seized an opportunity."

"If there was anything odd about Becca's death, Muir would have demanded an investigation."

"I'm not so sure about that," I said.

Donovan pressed his lips together and tried to hide his indignation. "You've met the man exactly once."

"Believe me, I was awed. But I got the feeling that he was a man who cared about his reputation. And his reputation is tied up with JHHI's rep, right? Bound together with steel bands."

"Yes," Donovan admitted.

"Who wants to send a kid to a hospital where there might or might not be a killer loose? If I ran that place, I might be tempted to play my cards very close to my chest."

Donovan raised his eyebrows, gave me a look.

"It's happened before," I said, egged on by his skepticism. "Hospitals can be a killer's favorite place. Where else can you wear a mask and not get thrown in jail? Where else can you find such a helpless population? There was a nurse's aide who split his time between Ohio and Kentucky, killed dozens before anyone even considered him as a suspect. Richard Angelo was a nurse who killed four on Long Island."

"And you're ready to add Peña to the list? Just because he's sleepy?"

"I spoke with a guy named Renzel," I said. "Chief of Pharmacy. He didn't seem to think much of Peña."

"That figures."

"Why?"

"I'm talking too much."

"Go right ahead. It's all confidential," I reminded him.

"Renzel's very close to Dr. Muir."

"Is that why Renzel dislikes Peña? Are they rivals for Muir's favor? Is one of them going to take over when Muir retires?"

"Nothing like that. Truly, I don't understand the Muir-Renzel relationship. They're friends. They travel together. Maybe Renzel's a laugh-a-minute conventioneer. I feel like you're asking me to do five-second psychiatry."

"That's because I am."

"I have an impression—I wouldn't call it more than a feeling—that Hank Renzel resents nonwhite physicians. Among men of a certain age-group, it's not unusual."

"Alan Bakke," I said.

"Who?"

"Wasn't that his name? The white guy out in California who sued because he didn't get into med school. Said they dumped him in favor of a less-qualified black."

"For some borderline white applicants, affirmative action was the end of the dream."

"For Renzel?"

Donovan shrugged. "He's a Ph.D. Not an M.D. And his father was a well-known surgeon. Almost as big a name as Muir. Medical careers tend to run in families."

So, I thought, Renzel's comment about Peña—that he might not be as "up-to-date" in his methods as the WASPy-sounding Hazelton—could stem from pure prejudice.

Donovan stared pointedly at his watch. His next patient was tardy.

I decided to try a quick change. "Harold Woodrow. Does Emily know he's having an affair?"

He grinned and refused to bite. "Do you know? Or are you guessing?"

"Let's just say I wondered."

"Here's a question for you. Do you ever feel you do more harm than good, digging around like this?"

"I didn't set this in motion," I said.

"Are you sure about that? Did you see this Tina woman before she died?"

I only wished I had.

"Can I ask you something else?" he said. "If you've run out of questions for me."

"Till the doorbell rings."

"You dating someone?"

It must be something in the air. Now Donovan.

"Yeah," I said flatly. "I'm seeing someone."

"*The* someone?"

"The someone who?"

"The man you're going to marry."

Good sex can blind you to a lot of character flaws, but even with great sex, Sam was not marriage material. Which was fine with me.

"And then would I get to live happily ever after?" I inquired sweetly.

"Where do you think this conversation's headed?" he asked.

"Nowhere."

144

"I was planning to ask you out."

"Because we have so much in common?"

"Because you interest me."

"Clinically? As a subject for further analysis?"

"I haven't met many women who seem as comfortable with violence as you do."

"I'm not proud of it," I said.

"No?"

"Let's sit this one out," I suggested.

"Until Mrs. Woodrow turns up."

"We'll see," I said.

"Just let it simmer?"

"We'll see."

The doorbell rang.

I said, "Did you ever prescribe Halcion for Mrs. Woodrow?"

"In moderation, under the administration and supervision of a doctor, there is nothing wrong with that drug."

"And it makes one hell of a criminal defense," I said.

"I have a patient." He stood and walked quickly across the room, his face rigidly under control. "Good-bye."

20

Tony Foley still didn't answer his phone. When Tina Sukhia's recorded voice cut in, I banged down the receiver.

I dialed the phone again, hung up again. Maybe Tony was home, stubbornly resisting the telephone's lure. Considering the statistics on boyfriends killing girlfriends, the police had probably grilled him past exhaustion. The reporters would be next in line, pursuing him for poignant quotes. Given similar circumstances, I wouldn't answer my phone for a week.

I sat at my desk and twisted a strand of hair, a childhood habit I've never outgrown. Most of my hair is silky, but the occasional kinky filament teases my fingertips. The game is to isolate a lone curly stalk and pluck it out.

I'll probably be bald before I'm thirty-five.

I needed to ask Tony Foley some more questions. And stats aside, I didn't see him as a valid murder suspect. Call me sentimental, but I figured he'd have waited until Tina paid off the VISA bill for the stereo.

I debated phoning the Woodrows. Had Emily reappeared?

I reached into the drawer for the photographs she'd sent me, dealt them face up on the desk: baby, toddler, little girl. All I'd ever seen of Tina Sukhia was a single photograph, a smiling image.

Police photographers would have taken shots of her body, pictures that might hint at the circumstances of her death. But I wouldn't see them, not unless I told Mooney everything, including my client's name.

Roz was momentarily handling the garbage-thief search. I hoped Lilia was looking after Paolina.

I yanked, and six inches of curly copper wire came loose, a lone hair trapped between my thumb and finger. I wrapped it around the photos of Becca Woodrow and thrust them into the drawer.

I took back roads to Buswell Street, avoiding Memorial Drive.

Tony Foley wasn't answering his doorbell any more than he was picking up the phone. I settled into a metal folding chair at a Laundromat half a block away and tuned in to the spin cycle. Read the *Globe*, focusing on the tiny paragraph concerning the discovery of a body at JHHI. Former employee. Identification delayed pending notification of kin. No cause of death implied. What would coverage be like tomorrow?

The Laundromat was slightly too warm and smelled of bleach and Downy fabric softener. I took off my jacket, sat down again. Fidgeting escalated to pacing. If Foley didn't come home soon, I was going to start folding laundry.

He'd been out running; no mistaking the regalia. I stifled the thought that he ought to be wearing a black suit instead of royal blue shorts over gray sweats. Physical activity has always proved a healer for me.

I did a little sprinting myself and was by his side as he turned up the front walk. He glanced at my legs. When his eyes traveled up to my face, he abruptly U-turned and started running again.

"Hey!" I said. He didn't stop.

"Tony," I yelled. "Come on."

No reaction. He ran well, long easy strides down Park Drive. He already had thirty yards on me.

I took off after him.

I don't run long distances for exercise or pleasure. I prefer volleyball, with other people and competition, and swimming, with buoyant water and no shin splints. But I'd waited a long time to talk to Tony Foley and I wasn't about to lose him.

He wasn't racing, just pounding along at a good rhythm, a distance man's run, the kind of pace that he could probably maintain for an hour and that would kill me in half.

He turned a corner at St. Mary's and headed toward the university. Afraid he'd hide in some alley or vestibule, I speeded up another notch. When I caught sight of him again, I'd gained a few yards and he was looking back worriedly. I hoped he'd already done a hard day's workout, a marathon at least. Get tired, you bastard, I thought, my sneakers smacking concrete.

He seemed to be heading toward the river, which made sense since the banks of the Charles are the major running path for those who don't enjoy traffic roulette. Racing across Commonwealth Avenue, I almost got smashed by a red Buick. I heard the screech of brakes, kept my head down, and ran.

I thought he'd take the footbridge to the Esplanade, but he kept going, hung a right, sped over the crest of the B.U. Bridge, cut another right, and headed toward MIT.

The going got easier along the river, turf and muddy ruts replacing the pavement, springier but more uneven. Now I had to look down to keep my footing. When I did glance up, I seemed to be getting closer. But I was starting to breathe hard, and my right side was aching.

I don't know if I'd have caught him if he hadn't stumbled. Stupid ideas were crowding my brain. I saw another runner nearby and thought about yelling at him to tackle Tony, considered a traditional cry of "Stop, thief!" But it would be just my luck to get an avenger on the trail, some bozo who'd shoot first.

I could see myself trying to explain it to Mooney.

He went down near the spot where the geese hang out, across from the Hyatt Hotel ziggurat. I put on a burst of speed. He looked back, lowered his head, and struggled to his knees. I was close enough to see the sweat on his forehead and hear the rasp of his breath.

"What the hell?" I stopped next to him, hands on my aching thighs, panting so hard the words could barely surface.

"Leave me alone." He forced the words out between gasps, and I felt vindictively glad he wasn't daisy fresh after practically maiming me.

"You hurt?" I asked, hoping for a positive response.

I got a stream of expletives.

"Why the hell did you run?"

"I don't have to talk to you."

"You twist the ankle, sprain it, or what?"

He put weight on it, winced. "It's gonna blow up, I don't get ice on it."

"I don't usually carry ice," I said. "Maybe if you wait long enough, the river'll freeze."

He tried to stand, but his foot wouldn't take the weight. He hopped a couple of futile yards before collapsing again.

"You gonna help me here?" he asked angrily.

"Oh, sure," I said sarcastically. "What's in it for me?"

"Yesterday, I didn't figure you for a detective. Today, you're actin' like some fuckin' supercop."

"The fuckin' supercop would like to ask you a couple questions," I shot back.

"I didn't know you were a runner."

"I'm not a runner."

"Your wind's good."

"Thank you very much."

"Think you could help me over to the hotel?"

"Answer the questions?"

"Hell, once I get ice on the ankle and a drink in my hand, I'll tell you my fuckin' life story."

"Deal," I said.

It was plain luck we didn't get run over crossing Memorial Drive.

21

Our sweaty appearance was not greeted by hotel staffers with any great consternation. In fact, we were pretty well ignored. The place was jammed, the seafood restaurant off the lobby filled to bursting, humming with conversation and background music. Velvet theater-lobby ropes and a black-and-white sign declared it off limits to the dining public this evening, taken over by the American College of Gynecologists and Obstetricians.

"Whole shit box fulla doctors," Tony Foley complained. "You see one volunteerin' any aid, you let me know, and I'll go have a heart attack."

I said, "Maybe they can't tell you're pregnant."

"Hell, OBs are regular doctors, too."

A harried maître d' finally noticed us. I asked for a bucket of ice and got the feeling Tony wasn't the first injured runner the head-waiter had encountered.

"Can we get a drink?" My surly companion's request sounded more like a demand.

"Certainly, sir. I'll send a waitress over. Why don't you, uh, take a seat in the lounge?"

I smiled at the maître d' and he ruefully returned the grin. The "lounge" was a couple of chairs plunked near the check-in desk for weary travelers.

Tony limped toward the restaurant proper, glaring. "You want to take a guess how many of these sharks are eatin' on their own dime?"

"You really ought to sit down."

"Every time some Joe takes a friggin' aspirin, it goes into a doc's pocket."

I took an elbow and steered him. He lurched into a yellow armchair, sank into the cushion with a groan.

"Think he'll bring the damn ice today?" he muttered, already bent over untying the laces on his worn left Nike. "Shoulda told him I tripped on the hotel grounds, over some goddamn tree root. Shoulda told him I'm some kinda lawyer. Get him hoppin'."

A waitress approached warily.

"Double scotch," Tony demanded. "And bring it before you go back and serve those fat butts their wine, okay?"

"Beer. Whatever's on tap." I thought I might learn more from Tony if I drank with him. Separate myself from the cops anyway.

The waitress was young and easily flustered. She edged around Tony's chair. "It's real busy," she murmured softly.

Tony glowered. She turned and practically ran.

The maître d' brought not only ice but an ice pack improvised from a folded hotel towel. Foley stopped cursing long enough to mumble a hostile thanks.

The waitress served our drinks in a rush of squeaky shoes and dropped napkins. Foley glared at her and gulped his scotch.

"Ice and a drink," I reminded him. "Life-story time."

"Pretty tame stuff," he said.

"Up till now."

"What's that mean?"

"Now you get to be the number-one suspect."

"Hell."

"Meaning?"

"The cops are full of it." He took a deep breath, then another pull on his drink. "Nobody killed Tina. Nobody ever would."

"Then what happened?"

"She made some kinda mistake is all."

"You saying she used drugs?"

"Not like that."

"She pop pills when you were around?"

"You recordin' this or what?"

"You watch too much TV."

"Hell," he said, "what I figure, Tina—look, I love her. I do, but this is how I see it. I mean, she's a good-time gal. She'll try practically anythin' once. Hell, so will I."

"You think she got the dose wrong?" I asked skeptically. "A nurse?"

"How do I know? How the hell do I know? What I know is I never got to thank her for the stereo. I never bought her a goddamn gift worth more than twenty bucks. We'd go to flea markets, and I'd buy her cheap earrings. That's all I ever bought her. Cheap earrings."

He stopped talking abruptly and applied his mouth to the glass. Sitting so near, he seemed as silent and remote as Tina's photograph.

I took a sip of beer and decided I ought to be more particular about ordering by brand name. "Do you know what Tina was doing at JHHI last night?"

"Try another one. Cops asked me that all day."

"Taking a class, filling in for a sick friend?"

"Look, I been through this."

"You find yourself a dinner companion last night?"

"Ordered in pizza. Hope to hell the delivery boy remembers."

"If he took the stairs, he'll remember." It was warm in the hotel after the race along the river. My sweater was starting to stick to my back. "Think Tina went to JHHI to steal drugs?"

"I don't have to answer—"

"How about if I dump you over by the geese and you can crawl back?"

He summoned a ragged smile. "I want another drink."

I flagged the waitress. If cops could ply suspects with liquor, they'd make more arrests.

"I never guessed you for a private eye," he said as soon as the timid waitress departed. He grimaced as he spoke, either from the pain in his foot or the pain of the admission. The number of people who don't guess my profession is one of my major assets in the field.

"You gave my card to the cops," I said. Why had he run away from me? Because he thought I'd be angry about the stupid business card? Did he think I'd shoot him for telling the cops I was looking for Tina?

Did he think I'd killed Tina?

"Yeah, I sure did," he said. "Why'd you give it to me anyway?"

"I was impatient," I admitted. "I wanted some answers fast. Wanted to know if I was wasting my time checking out some rich woman's fantasy."

"This rich woman hired you to ask Tina questions?"

Not exactly, I thought.

Tony lowered his voice. "If you tell the cops I was hittin' on you, I'll flat-out say you're lyin'."

They must have questioned him long and hard about his fidelity. I said, "The subject won't come up."

"Anybody says I didn't love Tina is crazy. I wouldn't do anythin' to hurt her ever. Hell, I didn't even know where she was last night."

"She stay out all night often?"

"She worked nights, some."

"You had an exclusive thing?"

"Mostly. Look, I'm not saying I been a saint, but Tina, I figure she's the faithful type."

"Sure about that?"

"Sure as anybody is."

"Did you call the police when she didn't come home?"

"I fell asleep. They called me."

A businessman replete with yellow power tie and alligator briefcase gave us a haughty glance, as if to say "Why are these homeless people cluttering up my lobby?"

"Are you taking the day off today?" I asked Tony.

"I'm not workin' right now. Cops loved that. I got fired three friggin' weeks ago. Crummy economy, you know."

"Where did you work?"

"Bicycle shop over on Cambridge Street. Little repair, little sales. Little was about it, that's why they laid me off."

"You looking for a job?"

"You offerin' one? Sorry. I been thinkin' things over, if I oughta go back to school or what." He jerked his head over his shoulder. "I'm not like those fellas. I'm not an ambitious kind of guy, tell the truth. Tina had enough ambition for the both of us." He tried out another smile, but his bottom lip shook. "You know, I had ideas of myself as a daddy, a full-time daddy."

"Tina liked to work?"

"Yeah. She sure did. She was the planner, the one figuring on striking it rich. And no, she wasn't pregnant. It wasn't anything but dreamin', and now it's nothin' at all."

He frowned and took a gulp of his fresh drink. "You ever eat here?"

I glanced at the fern-bar decor. "Nope."

"Looks like a buffet setup. Think they'd miss a few clams?"

"You want 'em, you got 'em," I said.

If the cops could ply suspects with seafood, they'd make more arrests.

I liberated a lavish plateful. A waiter glared at me. I glared back. No one tried to stop me.

"Want one?" Tony asked.

"All for you," I said. "Did you see Tina last night?"

"No," he intoned, like he'd given the same response a hundred times.

"Well, did you talk to her last night?"

He peered at me from under pale lashes, his mouth full of food.

"She telephone you?" I asked.

"Yeah."

"You tell the cops this?"

"Sure, I did."

"If you didn't, you'd better."

"Well, I did."

"Where'd she call from?"

"I dunno."

"Did you tell her about me?"

"I guess. I read her your card."

"Did you ask her about it?"

"Sure."

"And?"

"She said she didn't know what the hell you could want."

I sighed. "How's the ankle?"

"Another drink?"

"Not on my tab. Look, I need some stuff about this Cee Co. place."

"Like what?"

"How did Tina hear about it?"

"I dunno."

"Did she go for an interview?"

"I dunno."

"Did anybody at the hospital tell her about the job?"

He just looked at me blankly.

"Did she want to leave JHHI? Was she unhappy there?"

"She was . . . depressed about somethin'."

"Something that happened at JHHI? Look, last night, you thought I might be from some quality board, a committee that checks on patient care. Right?"

He peered at his empty glass, looked around for the waitress.

"What happened?" I asked softly. "What got Tina upset?"

"Why should I tell you? She's dead. She was a damn fine nurse. They're tryin' to say she was messed up with drugs, one more dark-skinned girl dead from drugs, no big deal, right? But it's not like that."

"Then don't let them write her off," I said.

"Nothin' I can do, is there?"

I shrugged my shoulders. "Maybe not," I said, taking a sip of warm beer, keeping silent, watching him decide.

He started slowly, in a low, flat voice. "A while back, beginning of the year, just before she left JHHI, she came in from work a mess, went right into the bedroom, wouldn't hardly talk to me."

"Yeah?"

"I cooked dinner. She wasn't hungry. I tried talkin', she wasn't listenin'. Wound up watchin' TV reruns most of the night. *The Tonight Show*, but she didn't laugh once. Didn't even hear the jokes."

I kept quiet. He held his empty glass in one hand. The index finger of his other hand traced a circle on the arm of his chair, the same circle over and over.

"She took a shower before bed. I always know it's really bad if she takes a shower at night instead of in the morning. Like she wants to wash somethin' offa her. So when she comes out I ask her flat-out did she lose a kid? Seven years she's a nurse, it still rips her up to lose a kid. And she gets this look on her face and she says, 'You know, I had bad days before, but this is some kinda personal best.' I remember she said that, 'personal best,' 'cause she's a runner, too, like me. And she tells me she lost three. Three in one day, one right after another. All real sick, yeah, but she don't understand it, and she's worried as hell thinkin' maybe, maybe, she did somethin' wrong. Thinkin' about how it'll look and all. Three."

Three.

"Can you pin the date down on that?"

"Huh? How?"

"What did you watch on TV? Anything besides *The Tonight Show*?"

"I don't remember."

"Was it the first week in January?"

"Could be."

Becca Woodrow had died January sixth.

"Did she get fired?"

"No."

"Was there an investigation?"

"I dunno."

"She didn't talk about it?"

"No. And I didn't ask. I didn't want to get her upset again. I was just damn glad when she left that place is all."

"Left for Cee Co."

"She only mentioned the name Cee Co. once. And then she kinda laughed."

"She only mentioned it once?"

"That's what I said."

"You didn't ask her about it?"

"What's to ask? 'You have a nice day, honey?' Yeah, I'd ask her stuff like that. 'Say, what's the real full name of that company you work for?' Naw, that didn't come up."

I swallowed my exasperation along with a mouthful of tepid beer. "How about this? How soon after her bad day at work did she leave JHHI?"

"Maybe a month later."

"Think hard, Tony. Do you ever remember Tina mentioning a woman named Emily Woodrow?"

"No. Sorry. I don't."

"Isn't there anything you can remember about Cee Co.?"

"Honest, no. I didn't pay it hardly any mind, and she didn't seem to work much, to tell you the truth. Put in a few hours is all. Nothing like the hours she worked at JHHI."

"A few hours?"

"Some days she didn't go in at all. Then, the last few weeks she spent a lot of time away. But some of that was at the library."

"What library?"

"I dunno." He seemed momentarily abashed by the scope of his ignorance, but then brightened up and offered, "She was readin' about Pakistan. Know-your-roots stuff, I guess."

"Pakistan? Was she planning a trip?"

"Nope. Just readin' about it is all."

I took a sip of beer and wished I'd had a chance to meet Tina Sukhia.

Not many women are killers, Keith Donovan had said. And he was right. But a nurse in a Texas hospital had killed sixteen children with a lethal drug a few years ago. Made national headlines, that one. She said she'd done it to show administrators how much the hospital needed a pediatric intensive-care unit. The lady was in jail and would stay there till she died.

I wished I'd remembered that little tidbit when I was sparring with the shrink.

I called a Green & White cab for Tony Foley before I left.

22

The light slipped from the sky as I walked back over the bridge into Boston. The air had cooled and a breeze whipped the dark river. A lycra-clad bicyclist swerved to avoid a pedestrian. A dented Volkswagen blared its impatience at the traffic light.

Chase a bereaved man away from his home, buy him drinks, and desert him, friendless, in a bar. I congratulated myself on a job well done. Time was, I'd have stayed with him, munching stale peanuts, nodding and listening. But the plain and simple fact was that I didn't want to hear the precious details of his pain.

I shook my head and plodded on. I've felt empty before, depleted of compassion. I quit being a cop when I felt that way all the time.

Worries slowed me like pebbles in my shoes. Paolina. Marta. Emily Woodrow. Becca and Tina were dead and couldn't profit from my anxiety anymore.

Hell, if I were Tony Foley, would I go home to that solitary apartment, to Tina's peacock feathers and filmy scarves, to the bed they'd shared? I'd moved back to my aunt's house after I'd split with Cal, and he wasn't even dead, although he might as well have died, for all the good he did me, zonked out on cocaine.

I passed a phone—not a booth, just a public phone stuck on a metal stem. The 411 operator took her time before parting with the Woodrows' number. Harold picked up on the first buzz, like he'd been hovering over the instrument, willing it to ring.

No, Emily was not home. No, she had not been home.

"Don't you think you should call the police?" I asked. "She's been missing for more than twenty-four hours—"

"What do you mean, 'missing'? It's her choice. You think that's what she's waiting for? Me to call somebody, let the general public know my wife's turned into a lunatic?"

"Look at it this way. If something's happened to her, if she's in a hospital somewhere, it won't look good if you haven't lifted a finger to find her."

"I've informed my attorney. Desertion is grounds for—"

"This is a no-fault divorce state, Mr. Woodrow, as you know. Look, I hate to bring this up on the phone, but I'm concerned about your wife's welfare—"

"And I'm not, I suppose?"

"Are there pill bottles in your medicine cabinet? Did you notice a lot of prescription bottles?"

He gave an exasperated snort. "What are you getting at?"

"I think you ought to hire me to look for your wife."

"Hire you? Hah. Use the thousand she already paid you, the money you bilked her out of already. Don't come to me for more."

"It's not money I need, it's authorization! I can't tell you what your wife hired me to do, but I can tell you she didn't hire me to find her!"

"I'm hanging up."

"Wait. I'm sorry I raised my voice. I won't do it again. You said her mother hadn't seen her—"

"Her mother's in a nursing home. She can't speak. The attendants haven't seen my wife in days."

"Is there anyone else? A sister or brother?"

"I phoned her half sister in Rhode Island."

"Can you give me that number?"

"You think Emily's there, but she doesn't want to speak to me?"

"It's possible."

"She's not close to her half sister. No love lost there. Greta would have begged me to come fetch her."

"What about her friends from before you got married?"

"Before we married? Well, I wouldn't know about them, would I?"

"This is no good. On the phone like this. I need to see you. It'll take me, what? Half an hour, forty minutes—"

"Not tonight."

"Fifteen minutes of your time. No more."

"Absolutely not. Not tonight."

"Tomorrow, then. Ten o'clock."

"You won't be late?"

"No."

"Nine thirty would be more convenient."

"Nine thirty, then."

"Good-bye." The receiver cracked into the cradle and a rusty dial tone hummed in my ear.

How inconvenient, I thought, to have a missing wife.

Tomorrow. Wait till tomorrow. What the hell would I tell Mooney tomorrow? That my client was missing? That she might or might not have killed Tina Sukhia? That she might have killed herself as well?

I turned blindly and walked uphill toward the bridge. A teenager in a B.U. sweatshirt jogged past, breathing hard. She started to smile at me, stopped with her lips barely stretched, and looked quickly away.

Poor Emily Woodrow. Mother in a nursing home. Husband cold as ice. Daughter dead. I stared at the high iron railing surrounding the bridge. High enough to discourage midnight jumpers? Or did the polluted Charles River beneath, the thought of an unclean death in murky water, do that? For a moment I thought I could see Emily in the gloom, still and small in her neat suit, stockings torn, poised on the brink. Just out of my reach.

My mother used to throw up her hands and cry, *"Eyner vil lebn un ken nit, der tsveyter ken lebn un vil nit."* "One person wants to live and can't, another can live and won't." Her all-purpose comment on the basic injustice and futility of it all.

If Tina had been killed by someone other than Emily, my client could have been murdered as well.

Where in hell were those documents Emily had promised to send? Did Harold know about them? Had she confided in her husband? Would he confide in me?

I walked.

I could have gone back to comfort Tony Foley.

"What is it you do when you're down?" Keith Donovan had asked.

I could have gone home to play guitar and eat frozen pizza.

I called Sam Gianelli.

23

"Hey," I murmured gently, running a light finger over Sam's ear, "wake up."

He smiled and sighed. His eyes stayed shut.

Me, I'm a second-round lover. Unless I have a steady bedmate, a regular night-and-morning man, I find the guy too eager to come, too easily satisfied, too quick to drift off to sleep. I'm slow to rouse and slow to finish. Sam knows that. He forgets.

But when I wake in the middle of the night and reach for him, Sam isn't surprised. That's the coziness of old lovers, who know just where to lick and touch and probe.

"C'mon," I said, a little louder.

Sometimes I miss the craziness of new lovers, who haven't got a clue, but are more than willing to search. My subconscious flashed an image of Keith Donovan knotting his tie. Substituted one in which he unbuckled his belt.

"Mmmmm," Sam said. "That's nice."

"How to put the romance back into your affair," I said.

"You could wear lace," he murmured.

I peeled off my menswear tank-top undershirt. "Black lace?" I asked. "Kinky?"

"Kinky," he agreed solemnly.

I've never been into dress-up sex. Music's my aphrodisiac, and since Sam tolerates my old blues albums, maybe I ought to give itchy lace another chance. I've got a black underwire bra I haven't worn since high school. The push-up kind, bought when I thought every girl needed Miss December breasts. Had I thrown it out?

"Pay attention," Sam said.

165

I did. The sheet and blanket entangled us, but they finally surrendered and tumbled to the floor. We managed to stay on the mattress, me on top, wriggling and slowly, slowly sliding, while Sam, his big hands free and busy, did his own underwiring and encircling.

When the phone rang, I was winded, pleased that it had waited till I'd climaxed.

"Relax," I said to Sam, lifting my hair off my sweaty neck with one hand. "It's probably just a ransom demand for my garbage."

I tilted the receiver off the hook before it could shrill a fifth ring. The woman on the other end of the line cursed me in Spanish. I was tempted to hang up, but I knew the voice too well.

"Marta," I said firmly. *"¡Por favor, repita!"*

That had no effect at all.

"¡Mas despacio!" I demanded.

The flow of sound slowed and started to make sense.

"How long ago? Did she take any money?" I spoke in Spanish. I know better than to try English on Paolina's mother when she's in a state.

"¿Cuanto? Gracias. Now tell me exactly what she said. Word for word. Spanish, English, whatever! If I don't understand, I'll ask." I shut my eyes and ground my teeth to keep from screaming.

Sam leaned over and flicked on the light.

" *'¿Jamás?' ¿Cómo se dice en inglés?* Never? Same as '¿nunca'? Stronger, when you use them both? What else? Okay. Okay. *Cuanto antes."* I hung up while she was still shrieking at me about how it was all my fault and she would sue me, kill me, if anything happened to her daughter.

"Bad?" Sam asked, already sitting up and starting to pull on his pants with the speed of a man who felt guilty about missing the earlier episode with the trash cans.

"Paolina. She ran away." I started punching buttons as soon as I heard a dial tone.

"Cops?"

"Not yet."

"Green and White Cab," Gloria sang on the first ring. She didn't try to interrupt while I sketched the outline. "Poor lamb," she muttered. "Poor darlin'." Then "You hang on two seconds, hear?"

It was more than two seconds, more than two minutes. I spent the time foraging for clothing on the floor, handing an occasional article to Sam, balancing the receiver between my shoulder and chin while donning the rest.

"You called it right, babe." Gloria's voice was so soothing I wondered why I didn't dial her whenever I got an insomnia attack. "Johnny Knight picked her up on Portland Street, dropped her in front of the Delta terminal fifteen minutes ago. Sweet child knew enough to flag a Green and White. No perverts workin' here. 'Course she probably hoped she'd get you."

"I doubt it," I said. "It's not like I'd have driven her to the airport. They don't start flying out of Logan till it's light, do they?"

"I already checked that on another line. No departures till six eighteen. Not from Delta anyway."

"She'll want Delta."

"Should I call airport security?"

"No. I'm on my way."

"Let me know if I can help."

"You already have. Thanks."

Sam was ready when I was.

"How'd you know she'd take a cab?" he asked.

"She took money from Marta's purse, and she's not dumb enough to hitch. Come on."

I slammed the car door, twisted the key in the ignition, and floored the accelerator.

"Want me to drive?" Sam asked quietly.

"No," I snapped. "I should have known."

"Known what? You haven't seen her for months."

"I haven't spoken to her for months. I saw her Sunday, spied on her. Oh, goddamn—" I remembered the envelope the beer-bellied man had passed her, the quick argument that had preceded the exchange, the aura of conspiracy. Money?

"Still—"

"She had a fight with Marta. Usual stuff, but worse. The brothers kept teasing her, she didn't have any privacy. And Marta says, 'You're no better than the rest of us, girl. Don't complain to me.' And it goes on. And gets into the business about her dad, and Paolina says Marta's right, she's not like the rest of them. And then she says, '!Nunca, jamás, volvere a verte!' "

"What's that?"

"She pulls out a bag, already packed, from under her bed. And she says to her mother, 'I'll never, *ever* see you again.' "

"Kids say that."

"And Marta says, 'Wherever you go, they'll send you back.' "

"So?"

"Paolina uses the Spanish word *extradición*. Sounds pretty much the same in English, and you don't use it if your final destination is in the U.S."

"You figure she's going to try to track down her real father? That bum in Colombia?"

There was a long silence in the car and then Sam added, "We'll find her." He tried not to wince as I screeched a corner onto Memorial Drive.

It was sheer negligence on the part of the police that I didn't get a ticket. I flew the route at twenty miles over the speed limit while Sam hung on grimly to the chicken stick and didn't say a word, bless him. I had less than an eighth of a tank in the car. Plenty to make the airport unless the Callahan Tunnel was jammed, an unlikely event in the predawn blackness.

I shot a yellow at Leverett Circle, yanking the wheel hard to the left to bypass a truck already stopped in my lane.

"Why Delta?" Sam asked.

"They do the Miami run," I said. "Miami's halfway to Bogotá."

"She have enough money for that?"

Why would Paco Sanchez give her money? Why would a twenty-eight-year-old hang out with an eleven-year-old? I used to be a cop. I know there are men who steal children—especially

young girls—men who spin them tales of instant movie stardom—or
reunions with long-lost fathers.

"I'm afraid she might. She took sixty bucks from Marta. She's
got her baby-sitting money. And there's this guy who might have
loaned her some." I didn't tell Sam any details about Sanchez; it
made him seem less real.

"And she's that hot to meet her old man?" Sam murmured.

"Wouldn't you be?" I asked. "If you'd never seen him? If you'd
never even known about him till you found out by mistake?"

"I'd be delighted if I found out my father was a mistake." Sam's
voice had an edge to it. It's a sore subject. He's the son of a Boston
mob underboss, the kind of guy who chews a cigar on the evening
news and mumbles "No comment" out of the corner of his mouth.

I fishtailed into the short-term lot at Delta. You want your
wheels stolen, park them at Logan International. The professional
car thief has the brains to boost from the long-term lot, but the
junkies don't care.

I made sure all the doors were locked. My Toyota was going to
have to take its chances.

I didn't want to alert airport security. Once you start your basic
attack dog in motion, it's hard to call him off, and the last thing I
wanted was a bunch of bored gun-happy guards tagging at my heels.

She'd have to buy a ticket at the counter, or, better, talk somebody into buying one for her. She'd want to stay out of sight until
she could blend with a crowd. Maybe find a nice sympathetic family
she could temporarily join. Paolina's a pretty good liar. If she went
up to some lady with a story about how her mom had to drop her at
the door with money and rush Aunt Cecelia to the hospital to have
the new baby, and now the people at the counter won't pay attention to her because she's just a kid . . . well, you'd probably do her
a favor, and take her cash, and put her ticket on your credit card,
too.

If there was a cheap under-twelve fare to Miami, she'd definitely join a family. I tried to think myself in her shoes, but eleven
years old is a lifetime away from thirty-odd. I don't remember

eleven, except that everything—a quiz, a boy, a pimple—was life-and-death important.

The terminal was hushed and fairly empty. Cleaners bused the ashtrays where desperate smokers had stoked up before venturing into the smokeless skies. A skinny young man stared into space as he moved his linoleum polisher in widening arcs. I asked him if he'd seen a little girl hanging around and it took me a while to realize that he was plugged into a Walkman and hadn't heard a word I'd said.

"Nope," he muttered when disengaged. "Ain't seen nothing."

Good witness. Typical.

We tried the restaurant, the snack bar, the bookstore, the two magazine stands, the souvenir shop. There was a special waiting area with cheerful slides and ride-'em airplanes for Disney-World-bound children. Empty. Sam's leather soles smacked the linoleum. My sneakers were silent, except for the occasional hurried squeak. I remembered the elevator and thought she might have taken refuge there. She likes elevators.

The doors slid open on no one.

"Maybe we should wait by the ticket counter," Sam said, grasping my hand.

"You wait, okay?"

"Where will you be?"

"Just make sure she doesn't buy a ticket."

"What am I gonna do? Grab her and carry her out to the car? What if she screams?"

"Do what you have to do, Sam."

"If I get shot by airport security, one of Dad's goons will want to know why. Bear that in mind."

I leaned into a quick kiss, took off in the direction of the rest-room sign.

There are six restrooms in the Delta terminal complex. I pride myself on knowing the location of every ladies' room in Boston—which ones have Tampax machines, which have rats and roaches, which are clean enough to use. The knowledge came in handy as a cop, especially on surveillance, and it comes in handy as a cab driver.

Two flight attendants chatted in number one. A cleaning crew was swabbing the floor in number two. Number three was empty. I opened all the stall doors, ducked into the special baby-changing alcove.

By number four I had to pee. That's what propinquity will do for you.

Number five was it. A hint of Paolina's cologne entwined with the smell of disinfectant. She doesn't wear it often, just on special occasions, and then she always splashes on too much. I waited while a woman patiently helped her daughter sit on the toilet, then washed the girl's hands in the sink and showed her how to start up one of those dumb air blowers that takes so long to use that your flight has left by the time your hands are dry.

The daughter stuck her face in front of the vent and let the hot breeze ruffle her hair. The machine had entertainment value I'd never appreciated.

After the woman and her daughter departed, I stood absolutely still for two minutes. Then I tiptoed to the one closed stall and peered underneath.

She was wearing the red shoes I'd sent for her birthday, flats with big shiny bows. I could never have had a biological sister with such tiny feet. At the sight of them I swallowed hard.

I cleared my throat. The feet tried to scoot out of sight.

I wanted to yell. I wanted to scare her the way she'd scared me. I wanted her to know that there were people in the world who'd take unimaginable advantage of her innocence.

I filled my lungs, but the scalding words wouldn't come because I was so damned relieved to see those little feet. I could hear her breathing, quick and shallow.

"Paolina," I said.

The right foot reappeared, then the left. She started to sob quietly.

"Open the door, baby."

"Go away."

"I can't."

"Let me go. Please."

I didn't make a fuss about opening the door. If I had to, I could crawl under it.

Months ago, Paolina stumbled on a family secret: she doesn't share the same absentee father as her three younger brothers. She's presumably the daughter of a wealthy man, an offshoot of one of Colombia's richest families. Her mother, a servant in the big house, never married Paolina's father, although she says he promised her marriage. The old story. Complicated by the fact that the man ran off, not with another woman, but to the jungle, to lead a revolutionary guerrilla group. Which is where—the popular press declares—he first became involved with drugs. Money for *La Revolución, La Violencia.*

You've seen grainy news photos of Paolina's dad. Carlos Roldan Gonzales. A member of the Medellín cartel.

"Did you tell Paco Sanchez about your father? Did Sanchez promise he'd help you find your dad?"

Silence.

"Paolina—"

"I need to find him. I have to find my dad now."

"Open the door, baby."

"I can't. I can't. I can't get up. I can't leave here."

"Honey, calm down."

More silence, broken by huge gulping sobs. I thought about crawling under the door.

When it came, her voice seemed very small. "I'm sick, Carlotta. There's something really wrong with me, inside me. I think I'm dying."

"What are you talking about, baby?"

"I can't get up. It's happening again. It happened before, but then it stopped, and I thought if I went to church and prayed, and if I helped at home, maybe I wouldn't die."

"What do you mean?"

"It's happening again."

"What's happening?"

"I'm bleeding. I'm bleeding. Down there."

Eleven years old. Oh, my God. Eleven years old, with a mother who hadn't told her what to expect.

"Oh, honey," I said, "please open the door."

I'd gotten my period at eleven, too. A Wednesday, I remember, dance class in gym. How I'd hated, *hated* dance class. Flat-footed foxtrots with boys half my size. And then a sudden dampness spreading between my legs, and pointing fingers, and smothered giggles.

I'd been ashamed to ask the gym teacher for permission to go to the bathroom. I'd fled, convinced that death by embarrassment was truly possible. And then the horrific stain. The fear.

There was no hiding anything from my mom. The slightest shading in my afternoon greeting would tell her whether I'd passed the test or failed, met a new friend, lost an old one.

She'd been brusque and congratulatory. Squeezed me in a tight embrace, and taken me out for a grown-up lunch at the corner deli.

"If I stand," Paolina said, her voice quavering, "I'll get blood on my clothes. I have blood on my pants. I can't go out. Everything's spoiled. Everything's ruined. I'll never see my father."

"Sweetheart, just lean forward and open the door. There's nothing wrong with you, nothing at all." I made my voice as calm, as soothing, as gentle as I could, trying to force my words through the gray steel door, will her hand to flip the lock.

"I'm bleeding," she wailed.

"I know you're scared," I said. "But you're okay. I'm coming in. Don't be afraid." I sat on the floor, eased myself down on my elbows, stuck my head, my chin, under the door, and inched my way backward under the stall.

She was sitting on the toilet, her stained panties and tan pants rolled into a ball and hidden behind it.

I knelt by her side in the cramped space, put my arms around her shoulders. "Listen to me. Listen, honey. There's nothing wrong with you, Paolina. Every healthy woman bleeds like that. Till she gets too old. It just means she's healthy, she's ready. Her body's getting ready. When you bleed, it's because your body's saying that everything's in working order. Your body's ready to have a child."

She looked up at me, momentarily startled out of her tears. "A baby? I don't want any baby."

"Of course not. Not now. Your body's ahead of the rest of you, that's all. But someday, if you want to, honey, when you want to, you can have a kid. It's a choice you can make because your body's telling you it's in gear, it's working just fine."

She looked up at me with red swollen eyes, the panic and the pain still at the surface.

"I'm so sorry it scared you," I said, hugging her closer. "I'm so sorry I wasn't there to tell you."

"I'm not dying?" she said. "I don't have cancer or leprosy?"

Leprosy. Jesus.

"You're not dying. You're just older. You're a girl turning into a woman. You menstruate, that's what it's called. You bleed."

"But what do you do? How do you—?"

"Pads. You use pads." There was a Tampax machine outside the stall, but I remembered from somewhere in my past that tampons weren't recommended at first, for virgins.

Paco Sanchez. No. I wouldn't think about it. I wouldn't ask. Instead I started wadding up a stream of toilet paper, folding it over and over into a makeshift pad.

"We'll stop at a drugstore," I said. "This will do till then."

"But—are you going to make me go home?"

"Honey, you're only eleven."

"My dad's getting old. He could die. He must be fifty, my mom says."

With a life expectancy that diminished with each photo in the international press.

Paolina said, "I can't wait much longer. I need to meet him is all. To see what he looks like. If he looks like me. Can't you understand?"

I was tempted to get on a plane with her. Forget about Emily Woodrow and Tina Sukhia. Go to South America. Find the delinquent father. Get it the hell over with.

I didn't relish the thought of being arrested for kidnapping in Miami. Bad class of people in the jails down there, I hear.

"Oh, honey," I said softly. "I'm so sorry."

"You won't let me go?"

"Can't."

Tears filled her eyes and welled over. I held her until the sobs turned to sniffles. We used up more toilet paper blowing her nose and wiping her eyes.

"Well, if I'm not going to die," she announced solemnly, "maybe I could wait just a little longer. I'm really, really tired."

"Come home with me?"

"But I'm so messy." Her voice started to shake again. "I'm such a mess."

"I can fix that," I said, patting her shoulder, squeezing her hard.

We found other clothes in the battered gray carryon that she'd shoved to the side of the stall—underpants, dark slacks. She seemed to have packed half clothes, half stuffed animals, all in a jumble. I rinsed her tan slacks and bloody underwear in icy water and stuck them in a plastic bag she'd used to hold a pair of sneakers.

"You look great," I said, after she'd patted her swollen eyes with a soaking paper towel. She was taking big deep breaths, trying to accept that she wouldn't die in the airport ladies' room after all.

My little sister.

"Ready?" I asked.

"Ready."

Holding hands, we went out of the bathroom.

24

I could hear far-off shouting as soon as I opened the door, coming from the direction of the ticket counter. I thought I recognized Sam's voice.

I tugged at Paolina's arm.

"I can't run," she moaned. "I can't. My stomach hurts."

A six-foot-long black vinyl bench stretched along one wall of the corridor.

"Sit right here and don't move," I said. "I'll be back for you in five minutes. Don't move, Paolina. Promise me."

"Come soon."

I was already twenty yards down the hall, running toward the commotion.

I saw Roz first. Flanked by two much-taller men, ringed by curious onlookers, she stood out because everyone else seemed to be staring at her, either mesmerized by the green-white hair and partially shaved skull or taken with her black leather shorts and metal-studded T-shirt.

The heavyset man was the same one I'd seen walking with Paolina.

"Leave her alone." That was Sam. His voice was low, but its menace carried.

The two of them, Sam and Roz, were herding Sanchez in my direction. If they kept him backing up, he'd bump smack into me.

I swiveled and searched for uniforms—airport security or Boston police. I saw neither, just some gold-braided flight attendants. One was speaking urgently and softly into a red phone.

Security would be on its way.

I couldn't wait for Roz and Sam to push Sanchez closer. I sped toward him. "Forget about going anywhere with Paolina," I said firmly. My voice turned him around. If I'd had a gun, I would have aimed it, kept him immobile until the cops arrived. Maybe done something worse.

That's one of the reasons I don't usually carry.

"Do you own a gun?" Emily Woodrow had asked.

"Can you use it?"

"Have you used it?"

"Would you do it again?"

Use it for what, Emily? Couldn't you have told me that before you disappeared?

The defiant grin on Sanchez's face altered when he saw me. Two to one, he'd seemed almost comfortable with. Three made him sweat. "What the fuck you talking about? Get the hell out of my way."

He lowered his head and tried to charge past me, but Paolina was down that corridor and I wasn't planning to let him get a single step closer to her. I faked to the left, let him pass me on the right, did a fast reverse, and dived for his ankles. Damn, damn, damn. It stings so much less when I wear my volleyball kneepads and fling myself across a wooden gym floor. I cursed while I brought him down, and hoped it hurt him more than it did me.

He was quick, up in an instant, sprinting the other way, toward an automatic exit door, past a suddenly frozen Roz and a Sam who'd gallantly stopped to help me.

"Get him," I yelled, standing and rubbing one aching knee before scurrying back to Paolina. I could have joined in the chase, but I figured she'd be worried, all alone.

Besides, I didn't think they'd catch him. Too many places to run, too many places to hide. Roz is a good karate student; a sprinter, she's not. Sam's big, but slow, and once outside the terminal building, Sanchez's dark pants and shirt would ease him into the shadows.

So I wasn't surprised when the two of them came back, Sam

empty-handed; Roz shaking her oddly coiffed head and clutching a flat manila envelope.

Both greeted Paolina, who was practically asleep, her relief converted to exhaustion, her head lolling against my shoulder.

"You can pick that creep up again, can't you Roz?" I asked quietly.

"Sure, but he's no creep," she said.

Never trust Roz's judgment, that's one thing I've learned.

"Surprise!" she went on. "The creep's a PI, same as you."

"You're kidding," I said after a pause.

"Hey, like, I tailed him all day. The maggot works for Griffith. You know, old Carl Griffith, that slime in the Pru Center?"

I admit that Carl Griffith, an ex-cop with a colorful reputation, has never struck me as a stand-up prince on the few occasions we've met, but—"I don't understand this," I muttered.

Sam said, "Hey, how are you, Paolina? Long time. You sure have grown."

She kept on staring at the floor, but a faint, pleased smile spread over her face.

"What's in the envelope?" I asked Roz.

"Jerk dropped it."

"On purpose?"

"I don't think so. It was early on. See, I didn't know he knew I was tailing him. I thought I did a hell of a job, by the way, him being a pro, and not knowing I'd tracked him all over town. Lemon's van—"

"That jerk is nothing more than a semipro at best. I tailed him to the Pru and he never—for Chrisake," I said, "look at this."

Inside the envelope was a passport. A single navy-blue U.S. passport, for one Maria Elena Vargas, age 13. The photo was of Paolina.

There it was. Proof that Paco Sanchez had planned to help Paolina leave the country. Had he also intended to accompany her? And why?

"Honey," I said, nudging her awake. "You know anything about this?"

"No," she said.

"You had to pose for the picture."

"I remember when Paco took it. See, that's the wall over by the school, next to the playground."

"Here," I said, pointing to Maria Elena's signature, scrawled across the photograph. "Did you sign that?"

"No. Honest. What's wrong?"

"Good. Nothing. Listen." I motioned Sam to sit next to Paolina while I pulled Roz aside. "Roz, go back to Sanchez's home address. Pick him up and stick to him. Use Lemon. I'll even pay him. Follow this guy everywhere."

"But he's seen me."

"Wear glasses," I said. "Get a wig. Change into something conservative. I want to know who he sees, what he does. If he goes near a train station, a bus depot, an airport, stop him."

"Oh, yeah," she said sarcastically. "How?"

"Use your charm," I suggested. "If that fails, try a karate kick."

25

Paolina dozed in the car and so was spared the additional embarrassment of a stop at a Store 24 where the register was operated by a teenage boy who blushed at the sight of a box of maxi pads.

I placed them on the bedside table in the guest room. She didn't wake, just moaned softly when Sam carried her up the stairs. I decided to let her sleep in her clothes.

After ten minutes of telephone sparring, I managed to convince Marta that Paolina would hardly come to grief in a single night spent under my roof.

"I'm surprised Paolina didn't know," Sam said, when I explained. "Street-smart kid like her."

"Street-smart, right. Means she's heard the jokes, not the facts. She gets her period and panics, so she goes to church. Period ends; prayer works. When it starts up again, she figures she's gonna die any minute. Goddamn Marta."

"Marta's mom probably never enlightened her either," Sam offered.

"You defending her?"

"Not if it pisses you off."

I smiled grudgingly. "It doesn't." I put my arms around him and nestled my face into his neck. "Thanks for coming along."

"Will it piss you off further if I go now? I've got a major meeting tomorrow, and I could use a couple hours of sleep."

I'd have liked him to stay, but after a few hard hugs and a little body massage—just enough to get me started—he went home.

Morning came quickly, a raw gray morning more like February than April. Paolina breathed quietly, the blankets wildly scattered, as if she'd attacked them in the night. An untidy sleeper, she sprawled across three quarters of the big bed, arms outflung, as if she needed to occupy all available space.

I hesitated, hating to wake her. But I couldn't stick around. I had a nine-thirty, don't-be-late appointment with Harold Woodrow. Maybe I'd leave a note on the kitchen table, along with breakfast. She looked so happy asleep, so unconcerned and childlike.

Downstairs, the mail carrier had littered the foyer with Stop & Shop coupons and ads. No blue envelopes. Nothing from Emily Woodrow. The message counter on the answering machine stood at zero. Roz hadn't called in.

Just as well I had a date with Woodrow. I'd have to stay out most of the day to keep a step ahead of Mooney. Once he discovered the relationship between Emily and Tina . . . well, maybe I could put the threat to good use. Cooperate, I'd order Harold Woodrow, or I talk to the police.

After Woodrow, I'd try to track down Savannah, Dr. Muir's gorgeous second-string receptionist. Approached the right way, she might tell me a lot about the day three patients died.

If I were a more domestic soul, I could have left a nice platter of homemade waffles for Paolina, on one of those warming trays, along with a glass of freshly squeezed juice. As it was, with Roz responsible for stocking my shelves, there was nothing to eat.

I opened the freezer in hopes of a frozen bagel, stared at glacier formations, and wondered if Roz would ever defrost it short of an engraved invitation. I found sixteen cans of peaches at the back of a cupboard; she must have hit a sale. Also a suspiciously large number of cans of jellied cranberry logs. Maybe she was planning to use them for hair dye. Or finger paint.

I wound up eating peanut butter straight from the jar, a trick I've picked up from watching Roz too often. About all she eats is peanut butter; she uses her finger for a scoop, as part of her continuing effort to avoid washing dishes or silverware. I'm proud to say I used a spoon. A can opener is the only kitchen utensil Roz ever needs.

The phone shrilled, and I figured it must be her, reporting from surveillance. I'd have her come in and take Paolina out to breakfast at the IHOP. Lemon ought to be able to cover Paco Sanchez for a couple of hours.

The phone blared twice before I caught it.

"Hello," I said.

Nothing.

"Hello?" I thought I could hear faint breathing on the other end.

"Roz?" I said, breaking the first commandment of answering the phone to possible dial freaks: Never give them a name to use. I heard more breathy noises and a distant grunt, then banged the receiver down.

Since I already had my hand on the phone, I called Donovan. If Emily had been in touch with him, I wouldn't have to tackle Woodrow.

The psychiatrist picked up after I'd started my standard answering machine spiel. I hate that. What am I supposed to do, feel grateful that, after careful screening, somebody's decided to accept my call?

"Heard from Emily Woodrow?" I asked.

"Who is this?" He sounded angry.

"Carlotta. Your friendly investigator down the street, remember?"

"Sorry about the machine. I keep getting hang-up calls. That's why I—"

"I got one, too. Just a minute ago."

"They're out there," he said. "The weirdo patrol. And no, I haven't heard from Emily, and I'm pretty worried about it."

I'd have to threaten Harold after all. "You get Rebecca Woodrow's medical records yet?"

"No. And hello, good morning, how are you?"

"Busy."

"Me, too. That's why I haven't picked them up."

"Good."

His voice took on an edge. "Now you don't need them? I went through a lot—"

"I do need them. And more. I need the records of two other patients who died the same day as Rebecca."

"How am I supposed to—"

"You're the doctor. Use your imagination. Snow the clerks at the medical records office. Wave your M.D. in front of them."

"Who are these other people?"

"I don't have names."

"You don't have names?"

"Stop repeating me. Three patients died under Tina Sukhia's care that day."

He took his time responding, and when he did, he spoke in measured flat tones. "At a smaller hospital, like JHHI, that would be unusual."

"Find me three deaths on the same day—I assume from complications of acute lymphoblastic leukemia, certificates signed by the same doctor—"

"Dr. Muir?"

"Probably."

"I don't see where you're headed."

"Can you do it?"

A pause again. "Probably. I can fudge it. Research subjects. Family reactions. Follow-up therapy. I don't know."

"Good."

For the shadow of a second, before hanging up, I thought about asking him what I should say to Paolina when she woke. There's a temptation to listen to experts. I resisted it. Hell, he didn't even know her.

I glanced at my watch; I'd have to leave in twenty minutes. Better wake Paolina, ferry her back to her mom. Maybe I'd have time to ask her a few questions about Paco Sanchez, how he'd approached her, who'd brought up the possibility of travel—

It didn't make sense.

He worked for a detective. And it had to have something to do with me, because of the garbage.

Now, I was a cop for six years, and I've put a few pimps away for pretty long spells. There are felons and ex-felons and ex-husbands who might think they'd be better off if I'd never entered their lives.

One of them might hire a not-too-savory investigator to get the goods on me. But hurt me by stealing Paolina?

The doorbell rang. I hurried, envisioning a UPS man holding a fat, detailed file sent by Emily Woodrow.

There were cops on the doorstep.

26

"You didn't have to send the storm troopers!" I said in a voice so dangerously soft it was almost a whisper. I controlled the volume carefully; if I let myself get a single decibel louder, I'd scream.

Mooney glanced innocently up from his desk. "Hey," he said, shoving back his chair and standing abruptly, "what is this? Paolina? Honey, I'm sorry. What the hell, guys? A kid?"

The younger of the two cops smirked. "You said pick her up. She wouldn't budge without the kid."

Mooney closed his eyes and sighed deeply. "Right. I'll talk to you later. Go back to work." As soon as the door slammed, Mooney shrugged and turned to me. "Traffic patrol," he said. "I'll stick 'em both back in traffic."

"Heavy traffic," I suggested, tight-lipped and angry.

"Carlotta, look, it's for your own good. There are guys from Winchester looking for you with a warrant."

Winchester was Emily Woodrow's backyard. A muscle on the right side of my neck tightened like a fist.

"Mooney, is anybody dead?"

"Carlotta, believe me, I had no idea Paolina would be with you. Those guys. I can't believe them."

"*Is anybody dead?*" I repeated.

"No. No, honest. Paolina, come on over here and give me a hug, okay?"

"She hasn't even had breakfast, Mooney."

Paolina marched over and threw her arms around Mooney's neck. "I missed you," she said. "Those guys, they wouldn't even run the siren or flash the lights. Are they for-real cops?"

"Hey, that's my girl!"

"Mooney, I hate to interrupt, but what's going on here?"

"A minute," he said. "Paolina, Jo Triola was asking me about you the other day. When's Paolina coming by? And you know, she's got a whole boxful of doughnuts in her room. Smelled 'em when I came in."

"Mooney, just tell me quick, and let me take her out to breakfast. Okay?"

"Are you two mad?" Paolina asked anxiously.

"No, honey. But I need to talk to Carlotta alone. For a little while."

"My mom didn't call you, did she?"

"It's not about you, Paolina. Honest. Come on, let's find Jo and the doughnuts."

I waited. I fidgeted. Winchester cops with a warrant? Dammit, I ought to be in Winchester right now, chatting with Harold Woodrow. Maybe I ought to make a run for it. Hah.

Mooney's not in Donovan's league as an interior decorator. Not even a poster on the wall to take my mind off the institutional paint and the smell of police station. I glanced at his compulsively neat desk top. He'd left a single file folder dead center, labeled *Tina Sukhia*. Sealed.

I was fingering it when Mooney opened the door. He pretended not to notice. "Here," he said, holding out a napkin-wrapped bundle. "Paolina sends you a glazed doughnut, with love."

"Mooney, you can't keep ordering your hounds to pick me up. I don't work for you anymore."

"I know that. And I also know who your client is. So maybe we can have a meaningful conversation."

"I don't see where the two points follow," I said. "You think you know who my client is. So what?"

"Where were you last night?"

"You recording this?"

"Come on. I know you weren't home."

The doughnut was sticky. "Is there coffee to go with this?" I asked.

"I can get some. Hang on."

I waited.

"You break the seal on the file yet?" Mooney asked when he came back, two plastic foam cups steaming in his hands.

"You can't break it yourself?"

"I called you last night. Late. No answer."

"I was out partying," I said. "Need the gory details?"

"This is not about your social life, Carlotta. Harold Woodrow, a Winchester big shot whose name rings bells with some well-connected people, says you were busy breaking into his house."

I chose one of the coffee cups. Didn't matter which. Mooney takes cream and sugar, same as me.

So. Harold wouldn't have been too surprised when I didn't turn up at nine thirty. Harold might have arranged the whole thing so I wouldn't turn up at nine thirty. But why?

I toyed with my cup. "This Woodrow, he happen to see me?"

"He wasn't home."

I licked my sugary fingers, thought fast. "Where was he?" Out with the girl friend, I'd bet.

"Nobody thinks he trashed his own place, Carlotta."

"The cops actually went out and looked?"

"Yeah."

"So why don't they think he did it himself? Because he's a big shot?"

"Damage."

"He's probably insured." I caught a chunk of my lower lip between my teeth, worried it. Who'd break into Harold Woodrow's house? Kids out for kicks? Professional burglars? Someone who wanted whatever material Emily was supposed to send me?

"Let's talk about you instead of him," Mooney said.

I sipped coffee that was too hot to taste.

"He named you," Mooney went on when I said nothing. "Gave the cops your address and phone number. One of the guys knew me. Otherwise you'd be making the acquaintance of the Winchester lockup."

"Did I take anything, or was I just out burglarizing the homes of the well-connected?" I asked. "Does that mean mob-connected, by the way?"

"Government-connected. Important-people-connected. He's a lawyer."

"Yeah, and we all know no lawyers are mob-connected."

"Woodrow told the locals his wife hired you to keep tabs on him."

It made me angry; it really did. Here I'm prepared to spend time in jail to shield Emily Woodrow, and her husband goes and loudmouths his jackass theories to the cops.

I managed a smile.

"Did Emily Woodrow hire you?" Mooney asked.

I was sure he'd heard about the thousand bucks, maybe even seen the cancelled check. "What if she did?"

"Then you make the connection between the Woodrows and Tina Sukhia, right?"

I kept silent.

He leaned back in his chair, big feet on the desk, hands clasped behind his head. "I talk to this Woodrow on the phone, drop the name 'Sukhia,' and he hesitates, says Sukhia might have been a nurse at JHHI. Well, I know damn well she was. So I figure maybe his wife wasn't paying him much attention while their kid was in the hospital, and maybe he got together with Sukhia, who was no bad-looker. The wife guesses something's wrong, hires you, and you tell her about it."

"Good figuring," I said. "Why did I break into the house? I forget."

"Can't you just talk to me? Aren't we on the same side here?"

"What side is that?"

"Somebody killed Tina Sukhia."

"Or maybe she killed herself," I maintained, although I was less and less inclined toward that theory.

"I don't buy it."

"Intuition?" I asked.

He stuck his tongue out, gave a halfhearted raspberry. "I have to take an educated guess," he said. "Nobody's gossiping in my direction."

"What do you expect? You look like a cop," I said. "I wish you'd brought me another doughnut."

"I want to know where your client is."

"So do I."

"Come on."

"You never believe me when I tell the truth."

"Sure I do. Try it."

"Let's trade." Mooney and I have an ongoing, years-long game of *Let's Make a Deal* in progress.

"What?"

"You wouldn't have left that folder on your desk if you didn't want to tease me."

"Maybe I've got zip."

"Maybe I don't know where my client is."

We stared at each other.

"Even exchange?" I said.

"I'm not giving gifts."

I smiled at him. "Keep your precious file sealed. Just answer a few questions. Appease my curiosity. Tina stopped working at JHHI. Why?"

"Resigned."

"Not fired?"

He considered it. "She left pretty quickly. Could have turned in her resignation under pressure, I suppose. But I've read the letter on file. Nothing unusual."

"She have a new job?" I made it casual, like I'd just thought of it as a possibility.

"Told the boyfriend she did." There was something in his voice, hesitancy beyond his usual circumspection.

"Lying to him? Maybe stepping out?"

"She was earning money, getting paid a lot. And get this: no pay stubs. No checks. Cash."

Damn. I wanted an address for the elusive Cee Co. Did they even exist?

"Maybe she was more than stepping out, maybe she was hooking," I said, just to keep talking.

He scribbled a note on a scratch pad. "I'll have Triola run escort services. But a nurse hooking? I figure cash payments, plus location of death, makes it swiping drugs from the hospital."

"If that's why she was fired, for stealing, they'd tell you, wouldn't they? Once she was dead."

"Hospital pharmacies aren't corner drugstores, Carlotta. Somebody knows the right procedures, the right computer codes, they could probably steal a hell of a lot before they got caught, if they ever got caught."

"Sukhia was a nurse, not a pharmacist. Would she know?"

"Computers are computers. If one person can rig them one way, another person can rig them another way."

"You got somebody checking?"

"My turn. Is the Woodrow guy telling the truth?"

"About me breaking into his house? Forget it. Was anything stolen?"

"He doesn't think so. Is he telling the truth about why you were hired?"

I exhaled, waited.

Mooney smiled. "The romantic link to Sukhia, it's crap, right?"

"Intuition, Mooney? Instinct?"

"Better than that. Here, take a look." He grabbed a flimsy sheet of paper out of his top desk drawer, flapped it in front of my face. "You're gonna love it."

"What is it?"

"Read it. Take your time."

It was a photocopy of a typewritten note.

The salutation was heavily inked out, so heavily I didn't think

even the police lab could make heads or tails of it. The meat of the
message was simple:

SHE WILL LIVE WHEN YOU ALL DIE!
THERE IS NO PRICE FOR LIFE BUT DEATH.
TORTURERS. KILLERS. MURDERERS.

"You met the Woodrow woman," Mooney said evenly. "Did she
write that?"

"How would I know?"

"She seem okay? She seem odd?"

"Her daughter died."

"According to the husband, she sees a shrink."

"That doesn't make her a psycho."

"Read it again. I'm glad I'm not a doc at the hospital where her
kid died. Or a nurse, like Tina Sukhia."

I shrugged. "Where'd you get the note?"

"One of Muir's partners. Man named Piersall."

I hadn't seen Piersall. Could he have been the man in the
white coat who pushed Emily Woodrow out of her daughter's room?

"He the only one who's received a letter?"

"Only one who's told us about it." He lowered his voice. "I
need to find that woman, Carlotta. I don't like how the note says,
'you all,' like she's planning more than one death here."

I didn't like it either.

"I don't know where she is, Mooney."

"Convince me."

"Ask her stupid husband how many times I've called, trying to
reach her. Ask the jerk if she's written me any more checks. He
keeps tabs on her checkbook."

"What did you tell her about Tina Sukhia?"

"Nothing."

"What did she tell you about Tina Sukhia?"

"Nothing."

"I ought to let Winchester lock you up."

"You'd have to look after Paolina."

"This Woodrow woman gets in touch, you call me."

"Right."

"I didn't book you. I didn't read you your rights. I didn't embarrass you in front of Paolina—"

"I'll call you, Mooney. The minute I hear. And you?"

"Me?"

"Are you looking for Emily Woodrow? Hard? Is there an APB? I'm worried about her. Honest-to-God worried."

"If you were so worried, you should have named her yesterday."

Somebody banged loudly on the door, opened it before the echo died. "Oh, hi. Didn't know anyone was in with you. Maybe I'll—"

"Wait," Mooney said. "You get the lab report?"

"That's why I'm here."

"Those spots on her dress, they get a reading on those? Blood?"

"Rust," the man said. He was slight and thin. His moustache drooped. "Common rust."

"Rust," Mooney repeated. "Thanks. I'll catch the rest in a minute."

The man shrugged, closed the door.

"Tina Sukhia?" I asked.

"Yeah."

"Rust on her dress?"

"A few spots. In front, near the hem. That suggest anything to you?"

"What color dress?"

"Tan, beige, sorta light brown."

I thought it over. Maybe nothing more than a lousy dry cleaner. "No," I said.

"Too much to ask," he muttered.

"You have time to run that guy for me? Sanchez?"

"The Firebird guy? He's clean," Mooney said.

"Just hasn't been caught yet," I corrected him. "Mooney—"

"What?"

"Is there really a warrant out on me in Winchester? Are they going to pursue this? I need to call my lawyer, or what?"

"You got an alibi?"

"Yeah."

"Good one?"

"Yeah."

"The Gianelli guy?" Mooney stuck his chin out. He doesn't approve of Sam.

"Gianelli," I admitted.

"Well, I might be able to kill it."

"Why don't you do that?"

"As a favor," he said.

"Does that mean I'll owe you?"

"A very big one. Keep it in mind."

27

Paolina, full of doughnuts and good cheer, chatted with the desk sergeant while I dropped change into a pay phone and placed a call to Woodrow's house.

He'd involved his wife in a murder investigation. And he'd been worried about *me* being indiscreet.

Was he just stupid and angry, or worse?

Had someone actually broken into his home? Why?

I'd intended to search the house. Armed with the now-useless threat of police involvement, I'd planned to check whether Emily had left any vital information under her mattress. Had someone beaten me to it?

"Come on," I ordered the ringing phone.

Woodrow didn't answer. And if he had, he'd probably have hung up at the sound of my voice. I cradled the phone in disgust. I'd have to drive out there, maybe break in after all. If you're going to do the time, you might as well do the crime, I thought.

I got the number of Harold's law firm from Information. A snotty-voiced clerk who informed me that Mr. Woodrow didn't wish to be disturbed, reluctantly took a message.

I couldn't involve Paolina in a Winchester trip. I'd promised Marta I'd have her back in the morning, and it was almost noon.

I glanced at my little sister, grinning and joking with the sergeant, so far removed from the waif of last night. A quick-change artist.

Maybe if Emily Woodrow had been younger when her daughter died, she could have made the adjustment. Younger, she could've had another child.

I stared at Paolina. If something had happened to her, if she'd caught her plane last night, vanished entirely—

"Come on," I said to her, my voice rough. "Your mom's worried about you."

I rang Marta's buzzer as a formality. Paolina's got a key. She used it and we ascended the steps in silence. I could hear the TV from the landing, even louder than usual.

Marta staggered to the door as we entered, in a torn nightgown, her long hair uncombed. Murmuring in Spanish, she lunged to hug Paolina, missed, and landed on the floor, a tangled heap of arms and legs, making a keening noise somewhere between laughter and tears. Her unfocused eyes stared at an unseen horizon.

"Mama, Mama, what's wrong? What's wrong with her?"

I thought she was drunk, so I didn't answer. I knelt near her head, bent forward, and tried to sniff her breath. Sour, but no trace of alcohol.

"Marta!" Her eyelids fluttered. I found her pulse, which seemed strong, arhythmical.

"*Creo que esto enfermo,*" she mumbled.

"Is it your stomach?"

"*No. Sí.* I get *pastas. Estómago.* They say maybe is *úlcera.*"

"What pills?"

She waved an arm in the direction of the kitchen, then clutched her stomach. "*Por favor, llame al médico.*"

"Paolina, see if you can find a new pill bottle. It'll have the doctor's name on it. I'll get her into bed."

"She's not gonna—"

"She'll be okay," I said as reassuringly as I could.

Marta's sudden full-blown laughter was more disconcerting than weeping. Scary. She looked like a harpy, like a Victorian caricature of a madwoman, all snaky hair and crimson fingernails and white nightgown.

"See what's on the kitchen counter," I urged Paolina. "Maybe she took too much of whatever it was."

Marta babbled and giggled while I half carried her into the

other room and tucked her into bed. Her forehead was icy. She stared at me as if she didn't know me, called me Lilia. Abruptly she threw all the bedcovers on the floor.

"*Muy calor.* I'm hot," she said. "Freezing hot."

"Here." Paolina rushed in, speaking fast. "It's a doctor I never heard of."

"Call four-one-one and get his phone number," I said.

"Is she—?"

"She'll be fine. Call." I humped the sheets and blanket back on the bed, made soothing noises, and hoped the phone company had delivered on its promise.

"I called," Paolina said, five long minutes later, on the verge of hysteria. "He's on hospital rounds. He'll call back."

"Let me see the bottle."

I read it and something clicked.

Marta seemed calmer. "Sit with your mom for a minute," I said. "I'm gonna make a call."

Paolina, her cheeks pale, was far too quiet and obedient.

I grabbed the pill bottle from her unresisting hand.

Information gave me Donovan's number quickly. Maybe they heard the urgency in my voice. He did.

"What's wrong?"

"Xanax. You gave it to Emily Woodrow."

"So?"

"What is it?"

"It's a tranquilizer. A benzodiazepine."

"A friend of mine went to a new doctor who said she had an ulcer. She's got rheumatoid arthritis, too, and she takes a lot of drugs that hurt her stomach. He gave her Xanax and now she's talking crazy and she doesn't know who I am."

"Wait a minute. She said Xanax, not Zantac?"

"I'm holding the pill bottle in my hand."

"Which?"

I spelled it.

"Shit. She got the wrong one. Maybe the doc wrote illegibly. Maybe the pharmacist screwed up."

"She's hot and cold and confused as hell."

"Look, Xanax is like a big aspirin. It's mild. It's almost impossible to OD on Xanax."

"She said her stomach hurt pretty bad."

"Count the number of tablets."

"There're a lot of them."

"Count them!"

Eleven were missing.

"Get her to an ER," Donovan said.

28

I don't recommend visiting both a police station and a hospital in the same day.

Mass. General made the cop house look both efficient and humane. Of course, if I'd entered the police station under arrest, I'd probably have had a different take on the situation. In the emergency room at MGH, Marta came off as a prisoner.

Nothing against the individuals—the nurses couldn't have been nicer, even the ones stifling exhausted yawns. A young Hispanic woman with placid brown eyes took Paolina under her wing while I answered questions and filled out forms and waited, waited, waited. The doctor, once we saw one, clucked sympathetically. I found it amazing, considering the surrounding sights and sounds, that he could still summon sympathy.

Overnight hospitalization was recommended. Observation. An unusual reaction, white-coated strangers declared. Definitely atypical. No acute danger.

Words I didn't understand floated past my head. Alprazolam and Ranitidine. IV infusion and polypharmacy. Codes and colors were called over loudspeakers. Beepers bleeped, and machines that looked like they'd be at home in spaceships flashed their lights and sang electronic songs.

I dropped change into a pay phone. Lilia swallowed her indignation and agreed to fetch and temporarily care for Marta's boys. The sour-voiced receptionist at IWP insisted that Harold Woodrow was still unavailable. In a meeting. Again.

"An in-house meeting?" I inquired.

"If you don't wish to leave a message, you might try again in an hour," she said, slamming the phone down before I got a chance to reply.

It was past four o'clock. I wondered if she would deign to pick up the phone after official quitting time. I checked the street address of Irwin, Woodrow, and Place, Attorneys-at-Law, in the Boston directory. Then I hustled back to Paolina.

The Hispanic nurse nodded vigorously when I said it was time to leave. Her mother would be in the best of hands, she assured Paolina, and when her own shift ended, she'd make sure that responsibility for Marta's care passed to a Spanish-speaking night nurse.

"*Gracias,*" Paolina said.

"You're terrific," I added. "Thanks."

Paolina denied any hunger, but I stopped at a nearby Burger King anyway, ordered a bagful of assorted takeout.

"Where are we going?" she finally asked, settling back in the passenger seat and glancing out her window for the first time in ten minutes.

"Nowhere," I said disgustedly. We were crawling up Huntington Avenue behind a loaded Green Line train, at rush hour, an experience to be avoided. Traffic was snarled as Northeastern students tagged across the street like a flock of abandoned sheep.

"You okay, Paolina?" I asked.

"Yeah," she replied, her voice unsteady.

"Your mom will be fine."

"Yeah."

"You feel okay? Cramps?"

"No."

"Look," I said, "I've got a problem. I don't want to drop you at Lilia's. I don't want you to be by yourself—"

"Why can't I stay with you?" she asked quickly.

"Exactly. I want you to stay with me. But I have work to do, and it's not the kind of thing where I'd normally take you along."

"Is it dangerous?" She perked right up; I knew she would.

"Boring, more likely. Here." I groped in my purse, handed

over my case notebook. "This should be on page three or four. Read me the make and license plate number for any car registered to Harold W. Woodrow. Do you need the overhead light?"

"Not yet. He a crook?"

"Not that I know of, baby."

"I wish you wouldn't call me baby."

"I won't. I'm sorry."

"Two cars," she said, wrinkling her forehead over the scribbled notes from my conversation with Patsy Ronetti. "A BMW seven-three-five-I and a Saab nine-thousand. Rich guy?"

"Lawyer."

"We going to his house?"

"His office. The slow way."

"Why?"

"To see if he's there."

"Is he a bad guy? Is he doing something bad?"

"I have to keep secrets in my business, Paolina."

"Oh," she said, disappointed.

"But, if you want to, you can help me out."

"And stay with you?"

"Sure. As long as you do exactly what I say."

"Deal," she said.

Most Boston law firms, I wouldn't have had a chance. They're huddled around Federal Street, jammed close together with no parking, except for the major underground lots. But IWP has offices in a converted brownstone on Newbury Street—very tony, very quiet, with private parking off the back alleyway.

Once I abandoned Huntington, the crush eased. I semicircled the Pru and eased onto Boylston, turned left at Berkeley, passed Newbury, turned left again.

I drove behind the IWP offices, not too slowly. The alley was a one-way affair, wide enough to admit a garbage truck. The mouth of the tiny parking lot was visible, but not the cars.

"Okay," I said to Paolina. "You know the plates?"

She rattled off two sets of six numbers and letters.

"This lawyer might recognize me," I said. "So I'm gonna send you instead. I want you to walk back as far as the lot, stop, and look around like you're lost."

"Okay," she said.

"Be casual about it. Don't come racing back if you spot his car. Just decide you're going the wrong way and look at your watch, like you're late."

"I'll be cool," she assured me. And then she was out of the car and walking.

The Back Bay is Boston's safest neighborhood, far less crime-ridden than Paolina's project. Still, I felt funny, sending her like that. Even if it would take her mind off her mother.

I don't think I breathed until she climbed back into the front seat.

"The BMW's there," she said excitedly. "What do we do now?"

"Eat dinner," I said.

"In the car?"

"Don't worry about the upholstery. Ketchup could only be an improvement."

I parceled out wrapped bundles—sandwiches, shakes, and fries —and we ate heartily, having devoured nothing but doughnuts all day. I kept an eye on my rearview mirror and I even rigged up the side mirror so Paolina could assist. And, after a little prodding, Paolina started to tell me more about Paco Sanchez and how she'd met him in the neighborhood, and liked the way he looked at her and talked softly to her and treated her like a grown-up woman.

"Did Paco suggest the plane trip?" I asked.

"No," she said firmly, looking me straight in the eye, which could have meant she was lying. Could have meant she was telling the truth.

"He loaned you money."

"Yeah."

"Why?"

She set her jaw. "Because he likes me."

Sure, I thought.

"Was he planning to go with you? To Florida? To Colombia?"

"He always wanted to visit Colombia," she said defensively.

"You gonna finish your hamburger?"

"You want it?" she asked.

"I'd rather see you eat it."

"I'll get fat," she said.

Fat's good at eleven years old, I thought. Keeps the boys away.

The sky darkened steadily as we ate. By seven o'clock it had turned to navy velvet. If Woodrow worked past eight thirty, I decided, I'd let him go for the night.

"Hey," Paolina said. "Isn't that the car? Yeah. Look. Come on."

"Is he alone?"

"Just him. Hurry up. Aren't you gonna follow him?"

Alone, I thought. Dammit. Then he'd most likely head back to Winchester. If he *was* having an affair, I thought it likely that the object of his affection was an office mate. When long-married men stray, they rarely venture far from accustomed paths.

"Relax," I said, pulling out into moderate traffic. "I'm gonna tail him. A loose tail. Far back. Not like on TV. Just get a clear image of his taillights in your mind, and tell me if you see them turn. You'll be my extra eyes."

"He took a left."

"I'm on him."

"This is neat," Paolina said. "Like a video game."

After two more turns it was obvious that he wasn't heading home. For a moment, I thought he might be driving to JHHI, but he kept on going into the area known as Mission Hill.

"Lock your door, Paolina," I said firmly.

"Where is he? I lost him."

"He took a left. He's doing a lot of zigzags."

"Do you think he knows about us?"

"At night, all he can see is headlights. And headlights look the same," I said, taking my eyes off the target vehicle for an instant to glance at my companion.

She was leaning forward, her eyes sparkling, her lips parted.

Watching her, I experienced a moment of sheer panic: What if she became a cop?

"He took a right," she said. "He stopped!"

I wouldn't have left my Toyota on the street where he parked his BMW, streetlamp or no streetlamp. Maybe he had a fancy alarm system. Maybe he wanted his car stolen.

I drove by as he got out of his car. He bounded up the stairs of a nearby apartment building. He wasn't carrying a briefcase.

I stared at the five-story building. No lights blossomed. Either he'd entered a back apartment, or he was visiting someone whose lamps were already turned on—possibly someone who expected him.

"What now?" Paolina breathed.

I pulled into a slot three quarters of the way down the block, in a no-parking zone. Across the street, a wire fence drooped around an abandoned playing field.

"We wait," I said. "He could be dropping off something on his way home. Paperwork."

I didn't think so. IWP's clientele might own some of the surrounding tenements, but I doubted they'd live here, in a poor, ethnically diverse, racially tense enclave.

We waited almost an hour. He didn't come out. Paolina yawned with increasing frequency. "I'm going to need to go to the bathroom soon," she announced.

"Keep your door locked," I ordered her. "I'll be right back."

I walked purposefully down the block, ducked quickly into the apartment's vestibule, wrote down all the names as they appeared on a row of rusty metal mailboxes. One—Savannah Cates—caught my eye. The rest were men's names. Or initials. Or Mr. and Mrs. So-and-so.

Savannah. I flashed on exotic eyes, tilted eyebrows, an engaging smile. Mooney hadn't been so far off base after all. Harold Woodrow *had* met a woman at the hospital. Not Tina Sukhia, but Savannah Cates, Muir's young receptionist . . .

SNAPSHOT

I drove my little sister home to her suitcase full of crumpled clothes, and held her hand till she fell asleep in the guest room.

I had my shirt halfway over my head, getting ready for my own bedtime, when the phone rang.

Mooney must have found Emily. I grabbed it.

Roz.

"You get my messages?" she hissed.

"Haven't had a minute."

"Dammit, I don't know how much longer I can keep him here."

"Calm down. Where are you?"

"South Station. At the oyster bar."

"Where's old Paco headed?"

"One-way, New York."

"Keep him there."

"Carlotta—"

"I have every confidence in you, Roz."

"Just get here."

"Half an hour," I said. "Bye."

29

I lied. It took me almost an hour, what with changing clothes, waking Paolina, dialing Gloria, making sure Paolina felt okay about staying home alone, assuring her that Gloria was a phone call away.

Oh, and I had to run back upstairs to get the nicely altered passport Paco had been civil enough to drop.

As I drove, I found myself peering down empty cross streets, checking the surroundings the way I used to when I was a cop on patrol. Searching the black-and-white shadows for Emily Woodrow. Wishing I knew her haunts, knew exactly where to focus. Hoping I'd find her before Mooney. Or she'd find me.

Had she killed Tina?

Had Tina killed Rebecca?

Was that what it was all about—an eye for an eye?

Or had a third party killed both Tina and Emily? Tina, for what she knew about Rebecca's death; Emily, because she'd learned the secret from Tina.

I blared an old Taj Mahal tape full volume. The music filled my head, answered no questions.

South Station has been recently renovated. An interior designer crisscrossed the floor and walls with beige-and-raspberry tiles, put in a French bakery, and sold vendor permits to hawkers with cute green carts filled with ties, fudge, and sun hats, as well as toys to bring home to the kiddies. Huge fans did their best to circulate the cigarette smoke and train fumes. You can get your shoes shined, buy a bouquet of fresh flowers and a chocolate croissant. The hurrying footsteps, whooshing doors, groaning diesel engines, and clanging bells are all that remind you that you're not in a shopping mall.

The oyster bar is tucked in a street-level corner.

I recognized a couple of veteran prostitutes right off, old friends I'd rousted years ago, no doubt rehabilitated through the wonders of our prison system and social service agencies. One was giving a brazenly outfitted hooker the unfriendly glare reserved for new talent on already-taken turf.

It took me a minute to realize that the woman of the hour, the one drawing hostile eyes, was Roz.

I guess she figured that with her clothes sense and general flair, there was no point in shooting for subtlety. But green hair, I thought, except on St. Patrick's Day, is going a little far.

Her wig made the stuff they sew on the heads of Barbie dolls look real. Nor had she taken my advice about conservative clothing —not that I'm naïve enough to think Roz possesses a knee-length shirtwaist dress. Her low-cut green taffeta number looked like a fifties prom dress gone astray.

One thing you have to say for her: She didn't look like the shaved-headed, black-clad karate warrior of the airport. No way would Sanchez link the two. Roz wore spike heels to change her height. Glasses completed the ensemble. Harlequins, with rhinestones in the corners.

She didn't look like anyone I knew. Or wanted to know.

"Don't worry, Yolanda," I murmured to the tiny platinum-haired pro. "You are totally out of her league."

"Hey. You back with the cops?"

"Relax."

"No, sugar. You check that babe. She's young and hot and she ain't let go that dude all night. Man couldn't even take a pee if he wanted one. And look at the bod on her. She's messin' up business is what."

"Good," I said. "She works for me."

"You pimpin' now? Hell."

"Yolanda! I'm private heat, and she is, too. Go peddle it some-place else."

"You gonna bring cops on me?"

"You're hopeless," I said. "Go home."

"Spot me twenty?"

"Ten," I said. "Home."

"Later, babe."

I caught Roz's eye and she sagged with relief. I could see her point. Even after Paolina had sung his praises, I couldn't ID the sterling qualities in Paco Sanchez.

Either he hadn't changed clothes since the weekend or he had many identical T-shirts and bagged-out jeans. His five-o'clock shadow had turned into scruffy three-day growth. His eyes looked bloodshot under the fluorescents.

"Hey," I said, approaching Sanchez and borrowing Yolanda's all-purpose greeting.

His face changed when he saw me. He recognized me, no doubt about it.

"Don't go anyplace till we've talked," I said.

"And why the hell not?" he blustered.

"Cause this green-haired lady, the one you been boring to death with your sorry life story, will be glad to kick you where it hurts anytime I say. Right, Roz?"

"How about now?" she said. "What took you—"

"Hang on a minute." I removed the doctored passport from my purse, held it well out of Sanchez's reach. He grabbed for it anyway. "Something you want?" I asked, tucking it out of sight.

"Hey," he said. "Maybe we can deal."

"Exactly what I had in mind," I said. "Roz, why don't you take a walk?"

"Can I stay in sight? Just in case? I'd like to kick him."

"The restroom, Roz. Lose the hair."

"That's a wig?" Paco said. He sounded disappointed.

"Let's deal," I said.

30

Roz disappeared.

"See, I want to understand something," I said to Sanchez, sipping my assistant's leftover Pepsi and thinking that for the day, I was probably well over the maximum daily caffeine intake for a small country.

"I'll bet." His moustache barely moved when he talked. It made me wonder what deformity he was hiding under its bushy growth. "Your friend have to leave?"

"I'll give you her phone number later," I promised, tongue in cheek. "Why'd you boost my garbage?"

He lit a cigarette and I inhaled fumes. "Guy I work for said to do it."

We shared a small round table, the stand-up kind meant for rushed commuters. The bar was empty except for two serious drunks in a corner, a scattering of working pros. "Carl Griffith," I said. "The investigator. He musta been ripped when you took the cans too. You know, stealing the cans makes it sort of obvious."

Paco blew a puff of smoke my way. "He doesn't tell me how to handle it. He kinda leaves stuff like that up to his ops."

I don't mind inhaling smoke. I used to do a pack a day myself, before my dad died. "You started working for him recently?" I inquired.

Sanchez opened his mouth, paused with his tongue sticking halfway out. "Nah," he said.

"Come on," I said. "This your first case?"

"Third," he said, stung.

A miracle he'd lasted this long. "And what about Paolina?"

"Griffith told me to check her out."

"He tell you to get her on a plane?"

"That was her idea," he said. "Honest. I wanted to help the kid out. That wasn't business, that was personal."

Personal, bullshit. Now *I* wanted to kick him. "Who's the client?" I asked.

"Huh?"

"Who's Griffith working for?" I repeated impatiently.

"Lotsa people."

"On the Paolina Fuentes thing."

"He'd kill me."

"He won't know."

"You don't understand."

"I don't want to understand, Paco. I want to know why you gave Paolina money."

"It was a personal loan. Nothing to do with Griffith."

"It probably comes under corrupting a minor. You know what kind of prison time child molesters get?"

"I never touched her. I liked the kid is all. Felt sorry for her."

"Who's Griffith's client?"

"He won't tell me. He won't tell you, either. Man, it's all he talks about, how nobody can push him around."

Sounded like a nice guy. The kind of guy who'd employ a creep like Sanchez. There was an ashtray on the table. Sanchez dropped his ciggie butt on the nicely tiled floor, ground it out with his heel.

"He keeps you in the dark?" I said.

"Hell, yeah, and if I get in any trouble, I'm on my own, too."

"You're in trouble."

"Well, I don't know anything." He gave an elaborate shrug.

"Let's go," I said.

"Go where?"

"Two choices, Paco. And one is the Feds. Passport forgery is Federal, right? As in Leavenworth."

He swallowed, his Adam's apple jiggling up and down. "Uh, I thought you wanted to deal."

"What time does Griffith open his office?"

"Hey, not till late. Not till after noon, at least."

"I don't want to have a lot of conversation about this, Paco. I'm kinda on a tight schedule. The way I see it, if you love Griffith like a brother, and you're gonna get all bent out of shape when I suggest visiting his office after hours, we might as well talk to that uniform over there. I'm sure he can get through to a Justice Department suit who'd love to see how you doctor a passport."

He swallowed again. "Say we do visit Griffith's place. What do I gotta do?"

"Sign in. Sign out. Work the security system. No reason the boss should know about our visit. Then you go back to work for him, you split for New York, whatever you want."

He considered the situation.

"And then you'll give me the passport?"

"I never said that, Paco."

"Come on."

"It's either the Feds or a quick peek at Griffith's files."

Before we left the train station, I found Roz sheltering behind a column and told her to get home to Paolina. Sanchez couldn't pry his eyes off the shaved section of her scalp.

When you work the middle-of-the-night shift, you don't have to worry about parking. I got a perfect slot on Boylston Street, and Sanchez and I strolled into the Prudential Center like buddies, almost arm in arm. I kept the funny passport in my handbag, its strap double-looped over my arm. I didn't trust my new buddy.

Like a lot of office-tower tenants, Griffith had unshakable faith in the building guards, uniformed do-nothings who could be counted on to make sure visitors signed in and out. His office locks wouldn't have baffled a toddler. Even worse, he'd lavished a key on Paco.

How does a guy who employs squirrelly ops like Sanchez rate a plush office in the Pru? It baffles me; it really does. The rents there are astronomical, and Griffith Investigations wasn't squeezed into any broom closet either. My socialist mom would have ranted on about inequality for weeks. Me, I just noted the thick pile carpet, the fancy Roman shades, the leather chairs, and got down to business.

Griffith was an organized bastard, maybe that was the key to his success. He kept his current cases at the front of a tall metal filing cabinet. Six of them. I should be so lucky. I studied the file tabs, spotted no familiar names.

I started with the first file, an assets search for a potentially messy divorce, read it through, looking for my name or Paolina's. Next case, another divorce, I did the same. Third case, also marital.

The fifth file was it. There was my name, heavily underlined. My address. My phone. My Social Security number. The file was headed *Vandenburg*. Some kind of code? No. Thurman W. Vandenburg. Of Miami Beach, Florida.

I glanced at my watch. It reminded me that I needed sleep. "Hey," I said to Sanchez, who was folded into one of the leather chairs, chewing the ends of his moustache. "Xerox machine in here?"

"Yeah."

"What's the warm-up time on it?"

"It's one of those little jobbies. Pretty fast."

"Turn it on and copy this. Don't 'forget' any pages either."

I didn't know a Thurman W. Vandenburg from Miami or anyplace else.

Sanchez did a good job handling the copy machine. Maybe paperwork was his forte.

"Can we get out of here?" he asked when he'd flipped off the machine and tidied up.

"My pleasure," I said.

"I dunno," he muttered, shaking his head.

"You considering calling your boss and fessin' up?" I asked.

"Nah," he said.

"Because you ought to think before you do it, long and hard. If you spill it, I'll tell him you sold me the file. And I'm a good liar. He'll believe me."

We walked out of the building after signing out with the guards. We'd used names other than our own upon entering.

"Now for one last thing, Paco," I said as we reached the sidewalk.

He said, "I'm finished doing business with you, lady."

"My garbage cans, Paco. Where are they?"

"Huh?"

"You using them?"

"I dumped 'em."

"Damn, that is too bad."

"Tough," he said.

"I expected more sympathy, Paco. I was fond of those cans. You know, you can help make up for my loss. True Value Hardware Stores. The gray wheeled cans. Two of them. By tomorrow night."

"You're kidding."

"Tomorrow night is garbage night, Paco. Would I kid about that?"

"You're crazy."

"Yeah." I sighed. "I guess I am. But if I don't get my garbage cans, the Feds get the passport, with your name, and probably your prints on it. They'll ask questions. They won't be as polite as I am."

"Shit," he said.

"Just put them by the side of the house," I said. "No need to ring the bell."

I got in my car and sped away while he was still searching for words.

I don't normally listen to the news. Usually my tape deck goes full blast, but I'd played all my tapes twenty-seven times, so I hit the radio button instead. Not a news station, a blues-and-oldies station. But even they have news breaks and I caught one. I heard talk of the thirty-seventh recent health-care proposal and slaughter in Bosnia. It sounded the same as last week's horrors, so I leaned forward to punch it off.

"A spokesperson for the pharmaceutical firm Cephagen Company has announced that a man shot dead today at the Marine

Wharf Hotel in downtown Boston has been identified as company president and CEO David Menander."

She pronounced Cephagen with a long *E* sound. Cee Co.

More, I commanded silently. More. Come on.

Three teenagers wounded in a drive-by shooting in Boston's Grove Hall area had been taken to Boston City Hospital for treatment. Police suspected gang involvement.

No! More about Cephagen with a long *E*.

The woman's voice slid into the weather forecast, fair and sunny, while rain spattered my windshield.

I drove faster, checking my rearview mirror for cop cars, and hitting fifty in the thirty-mile zones. A Store 24 had one tattered *Globe* left. I hurled my thirty-five cents across the counter top to the bored and indifferent clerk.

It was one of those inside-page late-breaking Metro stories. Splashy because the Marine Wharf is no fleabag, and soft-pedaled because tourists are easily discouraged from spending two hundred a night to endanger life and limb. Hotel PR would have been all over this one. Bad luck, the victim being a notable. That would hinder further efforts to soften the impact. My eyes skimmed the print. Possible robbery of a male Caucasian. Wallet removed. Wristwatch ignored.

I climbed back into the car. Cephagen Company. Cee Co. Cee Co. Pharmaceuticals. They had to be related. Had to be. I drove quickly through the rain. Oncoming headlights dazzled my eyes. My tires squealed on the slick pavement.

At home, all was quiet. Paolina slept.

31

I was tired enough to fall asleep in the car, but I still had one phone call to make—to Mass. General, where according to Patient Information, Marta Fuentes was in satisfactory condition and resting comfortably. "Resting comfortably" had such a nice ring to it that I hurriedly splashed water on my face, brushed my teeth, stripped, and yanked on my in-lieu-of-nightgown tank top. Then I slowed to enter Paolina's bedroom in barefoot silence, listening to her hushed, regular breathing and smoothing the rumpled sheets.

When I do fall asleep, I slumber soundly and rarely remember my dreams. I recalled this one only because the phone woke me before it ended.

"Hello?" The shrill of a phone in the middle of the night summons the elemental power of childhood terror, as well as the adult knowledge that no one calls with good news past midnight.

"Hello," I repeated loudly. The line was open. I heard something at the other end, a crashing sound, then silence.

"Who is it?" I demanded. "Is someone there?"

I muttered a curse and slammed down the receiver.

I could hear the clock tick. Ten past four in the morning. I was drenched in sweat and my pulse drummed in my ears. I gulped deep calming breaths. My throat felt scratchy. Not from an oncoming cold, from my interrupted dream.

I'd been spinning, whirling along with my bed, which floated above the floor, abruptly released from gravity. The sheet and quilt became restraints, imprisoning my arms and legs. The mask had begun its descent, covering my mouth, my nose, choking me, stealing my breath. . . .

Why had I assumed oxygen, air, *anything*, in the mask? Why not the simple absence of air? Nose and mouth covered, airways blocked . . . would Rebecca have lashed out, squirmed, and kicked? Would Tina Sukhia have recognized her distress for what it was? Suffocation.

What it might have been, I amended. I could hardly ask Tina now, and I doubted "suffocation" would appear on Becca's medical chart. I shut my eyes and tried to force myself back into the dream, to view the resolute face above the mask.

When I woke again, my alarm clock was on the floor where I must have hurled it. Sunlight flooded the curtains.

The house was still. Paolina slept, catching up for two late nights in a row. I tiptoed downstairs, brunched at my desk on crackers smeared with peanut butter.

The phone book gave only one number for JHHI. I didn't want Admissions. I didn't want Muir. I didn't particularly want Personnel. I closed my eyes and came up with the name of the floor on which I'd spent so much time waiting: Eastman Two. I dialed and repeated the words to the operator.

I was almost certain the woman who picked up was Barbara, the dragon-lady receptionist. "May I speak to Miss Cates?" I said clearly.

"Who?"

"Savannah Cates."

"Oh, Savannah. Right. She's no longer with us."

Damn. "Is she ill?" I asked.

"Who is this?"

"Her sister. I've been trying to reach her at home—"

"Can you hold, please?" Barbara said, zapping me into limbo.

She was back in a minute, sounding harried. "Look, Savannah was temping with us. Try her agency, okay?"

The line went dead. There was an S. Cates in the book. I let the phone ring twenty times before I gave it up.

Harold Woodrow and Savannah Cates. An odd couple, but if

Emily had hired me to prove infidelity, I'd have gone a long way toward earning my fee.

I gathered my uncombed hair into a messy topknot and yanked it, leaning way back in my chair and trying to figure a connection between Harold and Savannah that amounted to anything more sinister than sex. Could they have caused Emily's disappearance? Could they be implicated in Rebecca's death?

I didn't see it. Savannah wasn't the white male who'd entered Rebecca's room on her final day. And I couldn't buy Woodrow as the murderer of his own child. Arrogant, self-centered, yes. A killer, no. It was psychologically wrong.

Psychologically . . . I released my hair and hustled upstairs.

Dressed in jeans and my last clean shirt, I pushed Keith Donovan's bell, toe-tapping impatiently until he wrenched the door open with an exasperated grunt. His legs were hairy beneath a blue robe, his feet bare.

He said, "I thought it was the mailman, special delivery."

I said, "I didn't think you'd be sleeping."

"Thursdays," he said. "No patients. You heard from Emily?"

"No. You?"

"No." With that resolved, he hesitated. "Uh, how's your friend?" he asked. "The one with the pills."

"She'll be okay. Pharmacists do that often?"

"Not if they want to stay licensed. But, yeah. There are always a few cases a year, and everybody's got a horror story about some drug sounds like some other drug, and how they were just about to pop a killer dose into somebody's vein when the internal alarm bells went off. I remember—"

"Yeah?"

"See. I'm doing it."

"You get the medical records?"

"I did."

"Can I see them?"

"Right now?"

"Right now," I said. "And I'm gonna need help on the technical

221

stuff. Also now. But I don't mind seeing a doctor in his bathrobe; my doctor's seen me in less."

He shrugged and smiled. "Come in, then. You want coffee?"

"Sure."

"Make some in the kitchen while I pour cold water on my face, okay?"

The kitchen, unlike the foyer and living room, hadn't been renovated or redecorated. I liked its uneven floorboards, battered oak cupboards, and faint smell of cinnamon. Green plants hid some of the cracks in the yellow plaster. One of those automatic-drip coffee makers, bristling with buttons and dials, looked out of place on a countertop. I was hunting for instant and a spoon when he came back, looping a belt through khaki pants.

"You got dressed," I observed. His shirt was alternating bands of tan and blue, with a placket closing. I preferred it to his oxford shirt and tie.

"Professional ethics," he responded with a grin, removing a can of coffee grounds from the freezer. He counted spoons into a filter cone, inserted it into the recesses of the clinically white machine, and pressed buttons. The gizmo gave a contented beep.

"While we're waiting for the coffee, you want to tell me your horror story?" I asked.

"The drug story? It isn't mine. A friend of mine. Anesthesiologist."

"Like Pablo Peña."

"Not him. Somebody else."

"What happened?"

"He had a patient hooked up to a continuous epidural pump. On Fentanyl. For pain. It's a narcotic, side effects are nausea and itching. Had an old lady on the pump, she's complaining about itching. Nurse calls my friend, and he says give her some Narcan. Works out the dose. All set."

"But."

"Gets paged back right away. Lady can't breathe. So my buddy goes to check it out and he finds one frightened old woman. She's more than willing to itch, just don't give her any more of that stuff. So my friend checks, and the nurse didn't give any Narcan, she gave Norcuron."

"Close," I said.

"Norcuron is used to paralyze patients during surgery. Pharmacist had no business even delivering it to a nursing floor. Sent up ten vials of the stuff, enough to kill everybody who itched and then some. See, Narcan's a liquid and Norcuron had just switched over to liquid, and there was a mix-up. There's always a new form of a drug coming out. Always something new."

"Nice story," I said. "Remind me to stay out of hospitals."

"Advice I try to follow myself," he said.

"Where are the records?" I asked.

He walked toward a small desk. "I left them down here. You know it was hard enough getting access. Copies were a bitch."

"I'm sure you did a great job."

He offered me a stack that must have been close to a foot high. "I pulled five files."

"Five?" I said sharply. "I asked for three."

"Five fit your specs."

"You're telling me *five* kids died in a small hospital on the same day and nobody rang the alarm?" I asked.

"I'm not telling you anything," he said. "I'm just handing you some extremely private files."

"This looks like fifty files, not five."

"Disease generates a lot of paper."

Each file consisted of an unburst sheaf of computer printout, with MEDICAL RECORDS, JHHI, 259 LONGWOOD AVENUE, BOSTON, MA 02117, DO NOT REMOVE, at the top of the first page.

I read the names of the dead in alphabetical order:

Avalone, Renee F.
Eaton-Fitzgerald, William P.
Milbury, Heather C.

Schulman, Justin A.
Woodrow, Rebecca E.

"Common factors," I murmured, sitting unbidden at the kitchen table. "I need common factors."

"That's how I yanked these," Donovan protested.

"All acute lymphoblastic leukemia patients, and they all died at JHHI on the same day. I know. But I need more."

After each patient's name, age was noted, then date of birth. Renee Avalone had lived the longest. She'd been eleven, almost twelve—the same age as Paolina—when she died.

I'd started with a question: Why had Rebecca Woodrow died? It was no longer that simple. Not "Why this child?" but "Why these children?" Not "What could Rebecca have heard or seen or done?" but "What could these children have heard or seen or done?"

Please, I thought. Please, let me find it in the files. Let me not have to interview Heather's mom, William's parents, Renee's loved ones.

People think the hardest part of being a cop is shooting it out with bad guys on some dark street corner. The toughest thing I ever did when I was on the force was tell a dazed woman kneeling by the side of a busy road that her four-year-old had been hit by a car.

"But he's okay," she'd insisted, even though she must have seen what I'd seen, known the truth. "He's going to be okay." She wouldn't let go of my arm. I remember she wouldn't let go of my arm.

"You all right?" Donovan asked.

I tapped a finger on the laminated table top, found it reassuringly sticky. "Yeah," I said quickly. "I'll need a list of all medical personnel in common. And treatments in common, and drugs in common. It was on my mind with my friend and the Xanax–Zantac thing, even before you told about your Narcan–Norcuron mix-up. I want to know if they all got the same drug or the same combination of drugs on the day they died."

His phone rang. "Damn," he said, making no move toward the wall-mounted instrument. "Ignore it."

"Why?"

"It's another hang-up. I've been getting them all morning."

"I got another one last night. Answer it, okay?"

He picked up the receiver.

"Hello?" He shook his head and made a face, repeated his greeting, then said, "Nothing."

"Can you hear breathing?" I asked.

"Not now. Dial tone."

"Could it be Emily?"

"Emily? I hadn't thought of it. I don't know . . ." Almost to himself, he murmured, "What do hang-up calls mean?"

"You're the shrink," I said.

"Rhetorical question," he responded dryly. "Sometimes I can't help myself."

"If I'm after a runaway," I said, "I'll put a trace on the home phone. The kid'll always call. Won't talk, but she'll call. Just to hear Mom's voice."

"Reassurance," he said.

"What else?"

"Hate calls, love calls. Annoyance calls. Anything you can imagine, people do."

"Anything that would fit with what you know about Emily?"

"I don't know enough about Emily."

"Look, I saw her for fifteen minutes," I said. "You've been her therapist more than three months. You have to know more than I do."

"Three months. Twelve weeks: a scratch on the surface with someone as reserved as Emily."

"You found her reserved? Cold?"

"Afraid. Maybe shy is a better term," he said, sitting across from me at the table. "I don't mean that she was afraid of anything specific. More frightened of life, which isn't unusual in someone who's experienced a devastating loss. She felt out of control. Lost in space. If Rebecca could get leukemia and die, she saw no reason why Harold wouldn't crack up the car on the way home from work. She expected to be struck by lightning."

"She had been."

"Exactly. It was like trying to convince someone who's been mauled by a shark that there are really very few sharks in the water."

Each file was divided into sections with subheadings: *Diagnoses and Notes, Hospitalizations, Therapies, Test Results, Internal Consultations.*

"You know," Donovan said, frowning, "I don't think Emily's fear started with Rebecca's death. I think she was timid before that."

"Why?"

Frowning, he laced his fingers together and rested them on the table. "I'm speculating now, but if she hadn't married Harold, she'd probably have stayed out of sight, hidden behind that camera of hers."

"Her camera?" I said.

"Emily Ruhly, she was. E. J. Ruhly. Ever hear of her? She took pictures—you probably saw some of them. Studies of migrant workers, Native Americans. I guess you'd have called her a photojournalist. She didn't keep up with it after she married. Harold objected to the hours and the travel, and then when she had Rebecca, she gave it up entirely."

The snapshots. So clear, so sharp, so illuminating. And yet, there was nothing in her photos of Rebecca that I'd have labeled *technique*, nothing that cried out *professional*. No tricks. Just the child, caught at the perfect moment.

"Very shy people sometimes become addicted to cameras," Donovan went on. "Or sketchbooks. It's a way to shift the eyes of the world away from themselves. To stay in the background. Oh, I know it smacks of dime psych, but the obvious is sometimes true."

My gut reaction was: Patsy Ronetti never told me, damn her! She'd never come through with the promised employment check on

Emily. My second reaction was to examine my first: If Patsy *had* told me, would I have given more credence to Emily's story? Was unfocused speculation from a mother less believable in my eyes than unfocused speculation from an ex-professional photojournalist?

"Coffee," Donovan said.

"Thanks. I need it. I mean, I'll need some before tackling these. Rebecca's file alone is what? Two-and-a-half-inches thick. It's . . . daunting."

"She was sick for months. She put in a lot of hours at JHHI."

So had Emily Woodrow. E. J. Ruhly.

"All you really need to focus on is the end," Donovan said. "Right? The final day."

"Maybe."

"They all died from complications of ALL," he said.

"On Becca's death certificate, it lists ALL and then something else. Sepsis. What's that?"

"Septic shock. Bacteria in the bloodstream."

"What would cause it?"

"Sepsis? Contamination of some sort."

"Would it kill somebody quickly?"

"That would depend on all sorts of things."

"Is sepsis unusual?"

"I don't study death certificates. I'd certainly expect the hospital to check it out. Hospitals have review boards, morbidity and mortality reviews, all sorts of governing bodies."

He drank coffee and I read. It was slow, tortuous going, like reading a foreign language, jammed with multisyllabic words I had to break down into parts before they yielded information.

"Hepatic," I said. "That's liver, right?"

"Pertaining to functions of the liver. Maybe I should cook some eggs." He didn't sound enthusiastic at the prospect.

"Don't bother on my account."

"Coffee cake?"

"Sounds great."

He pulled a Sara Lee ring out of the freezer, started messing with the microwave oven while I waded through sentences laden with *extravasation* and *myelosuppression.*

"Alopecia," I said.

"Hair loss," he countered.

"Couldn't they just say that?" Several times I came close to quitting in a fit of frustration, but strong coffee and the aroma of defrosting coffee cake glued me to my chair, and I soldiered on. Occasionally I asked a question, and Donovan gravely responded.

If I gave up on the files, I'd have to face the bereaved families, rip away stitches on wounds that had scarcely crusted over.

"This," I said into silence. "What is this?" I must have spoken loudly. Donovan gave me a look.

"What? Cephamycin?" he said. "I think it's a chemotherapy drug."

"Who makes it?"

"You mean who manufactures it?"

"*Where does it come from?*" I said, very slowly.

"I don't know. Here. Look it up in the PDR."

He handed over a hardbound *Physician's Desk Reference* the size of the Yellow Pages, but heavier, with tinier print. I located the drug but got bogged down on "cytotoxic anthracycline antibiotic."

"What's a naphthacenequinone?" I asked, murdering the pronunciation.

He made a wry face. "Go to the beginning of the entry for the name of the lab."

Cephagen. The Cephagen Company. An Orlando address.

"Keith," I said, very quietly. "The president of this company was killed in a Boston hotel yesterday."

"Killed?" he repeated.

"How do you administer Cephamycin?"

"Give me the book."

"With pleasure."

"Here," he said after a long two minutes. "Intravenous. 'Slowly administered into the tubing of a freely running intravenous infusion of Sodium Chloride injection USP or five percent Dextrose injection USP.' "

"Huh?"

"In an IV drip," he said.

"How's Cephamycin packaged?"

"Let me check." He ran his fingers over the three-columned page, dense with print. "Two ways. As a liquid, you can get it in ten-, twenty-, or fifty-milligram vials. And it comes in a powder, too. You reconstitute that."

"If contamination—sepsis—was in an IV drip, how long would it take someone to die?" I asked.

"If the contamination were in an administered fluid—which would be extremely unlikely—the patient would get shaking chills, spike a high fever, blood pressure would drop. The patient could die within hours, sooner."

"Can I make a phone call?" I asked. "Long distance?"

"Help yourself."

My fingers hit information for area code 407, and I requested the number of the Cephagen Company.

"Cephagen. How may I direct your call?" The receptionist was female. She sounded both harried and hostile.

"Sales, please."

"We are not accepting any calls from the press." She practically spat out the last word.

"No. no, nothing like that," I said. "This is Diana Hudson. We've talked before. I'm calling from the JHHI pharmacy. Boston."

"Oh." She sounded only slightly mollified.

"Things must be really hectic there," I went on, oozing sympathy. "I hate to bother you with this. I'd call another time, but you know how it is, everybody wants things done yesterday."

"I think Mr. Knowlton is in."

"That would be great. Thanks."

He came on the line with no further secretarial interference. A gentleman pretty far down in the food chain, I guessed.

"Knowlton," he said. "How may I help you?"

I gave the Diana Hudson name again, the JHHI affiliation, the apology.

"What do you need?" he said, apparently taking me at my word.

Encouraged, I went on. "It's not an order, Mr. Knowlton. We're, uh, updating our list of approved chemotherapy drugs, with emphasis on ALL treatment. And I'm the lucky one who's supposed to make sure all the spelling's correct before we go to the printer—"

"Hah. Then the printer'll louse it up."

Good. He was buying it.

"I know, but you've got to try, don't you?" I said. "My boss is a real stickler for spelling. So could you please spell out the brand names of any drugs Cephagen would want placed on that list?"

"We just have the one."

"Go ahead."

"It's Cephamycin. I know it as well as my own name, but let me check to make sure. C–E–P–H–A–M–Y–C–I–N. One Y and one I."

"Thanks," I said.

"You're welcome. Good luck."

"Oh, one more thing. A friend of mine used to work for you. She really had great things to say about the company, and how nice it is in Orlando. The weather up here is just vile, you know?"

"Don't tell me. I used to live in New Hampshire."

"Really? Where?"

"Hollis."

"No kidding. I used to date a guy from Nashua."

"I don't miss the winter."

"I'll bet," I said. "Anyhow, my friend had to move away from Orlando, and I was thinking, you know, if her job's open, I'd really like a change of climate."

"What division was she in?"

"Gee, I can't remember."

"Well, hey, Diana—you say your name was Diana?"

"Diana Hudson. What's yours?"

"Peter. But I wouldn't know about job openings. Let me transfer you to Personnel."

"Mr. Knowlton, please. Peter. Wait a second. You transfer me to Personnel, we both know what'll happen, right? They'll just say they're not hiring, or tell me to send a résumé."

"Look, Diana," he said, softening. "I'll try to transfer you to Janet Lee. She's a friend of mine and she might be able to help."

I hung up on him. Then I quickly placed the call again, going through the same harried receptionist. "Personnel," I said this time.

"To whom may I direct your call?" She was really trying to weed out the uninformed.

"Janet Lee, please." Names are power. Any good skip tracer knows that.

When I got through to Lee, I immediately mentioned Peter Knowlton, and repeated my tale. She wasn't from New England. We had less rapport.

"We're not hiring," she said flatly. Careful, I warned myself. Don't push too hard.

"Well, this wouldn't be like new hiring, this would be just replacing somebody who left."

She relented. "What was your friend's name? At least I can check the department, to see if they've already filled the requisition."

"Tina Sukhia."

A pause, then, "That name's not familiar."

"Well, I'm sure she said Cee Co. Pharmaceutical research."

"That's what we do. Sukhia?"

It was my turn to spell. "S-U-K-H-I-A."

"Sorry," she said after a long interval. I could hear the quick clicks as she punched away at her computer terminal. "No one with that name has ever worked here."

I hung up.

"You're a good liar," Donovan said.

"And I'm comfortable with violence. An attractive combination."

"I think so," he said.

"But you haven't acted on it."

"You're the one who said to cool it. Until Emily's found. I took you at your word."

"Good. I like to be taken at my word."

"You don't look happy," he said.

"Shrinks are certainly perceptive."

"And we love to be called 'shrinks.'"

"Tina Sukhia is not the connection," I muttered.

"Still think there is one?"

"Yeah." But only Emily Woodrow knows it, I said to myself.

I left him, taking the files and an extra napkin-wrapped slice of Sara Lee with me. Now, I thought, would be a terrific time for a fat special-delivery envelope from Emily Woodrow to arrive at my front door.

Nothing came.

I studied the files, circling all references to Cephamycin. I hammered my fingers on my desk top and yanked at strands of wayward hair.

What did I know?

Five children had died at JHHI on the same day. *Five.*

Three, including Becca Woodrow, had been Tina Sukhia's patients.

Tina Sukhia administered chemotherapy drugs.

Cephamycin was a chemotherapy drug. All five patients had received Cephamycin the day they'd died.

Tina Sukhia was dead.

The CEO of Cephagen was dead.

My fingers moved to my temples and inscribed deep circles. Oh, for Chrisake, Emily, Emily, Emily.

I wished I'd made a copy of the anonymous note Mooney had shown me. "*She will live when you all die!*" Something like that.

Had Emily written the text? Who would die next?

I swallowed. Me. Mooney would kill me.

I took the photocopies of the file I'd lifted from Griffith Investigations out of my handbag. I'd been too tired to read it the night before. I couldn't take time to deal with it now. I stuffed it into a desk drawer. Locked it.

I changed from jeans to dark blue slacks. My white shirt would do, thank goodness. And I had a hat I'd once borrowed from a meter maid and forgotten to return.

I woke Roz. Placated by coffee cake, she agreed to take Paolina out to breakfast, then to the hospital to visit Marta. I admonished her to behave nicely and not frighten the nurses with obscene language or vulgar T-shirts.

"I'll be a good girl," she mumbled sleepily and sarcastically, her mouth full of crumbs.

"Then, if Marta's up to handling Paolina, I have a research job for you. Find out anything you can about a company called Cephagen. Not on any of the exchanges, so they're probably closely held. Offices in Orlando."

"Can I take a field trip?"

"No. And stay awake."

Downstairs, I hurriedly unlocked the desk drawer where I store dangerous or incriminating items, including my unloaded .38. I reached behind it to grab a set of slender picklocks—handcrafted by a former and future resident of the state prison at Walpole— thrust them into my handbag, and raced out to the car.

3 2

I had to crack my Arrow Street Guide to locate the Woodrow house, a huge mock-Georgian brick set on a couple of gently rolling acres bordering a golf course. Distant marker flags flapped in the breeze.

As a native Detroiter, I'm happiest surrounded by concrete, but I could see the charm of the area. Anyone who looked like Paolina's buddy, Paco, would be arrested on sight here. I, on the other hand, in my uniformlike dark slacks, with my meter maid's hat squashing my curls, would closely resemble the person who reads the gas meter, or delivers the mail.

B&Es, such as the one I now contemplated, are easier to pull off on busy city streets, where no one notices another car parked on a teeming block, a new face in the crowd. Your suburban crook banks on absence and indifference: closed curtains, housewives hypnotized by soap operas, dads and kids away.

I strolled up the walk and pressed the doorbell, feeling like a suspicious person.

Harold Woodrow yanked the door open and put an end to my criminal fantasies. He was dressed for the office, but his navy suit was wrinkled, his expensive tie askew, his thinning hair unkempt. The lines under his eyes had turned to gray pouches. *Pathetic* and *arrogant* don't generally go together, but he managed to look both down-in-the-mouth and insufferable at the same time.

I whipped off the hat and stuffed it under my arm. Maybe it was the shape of his nose that made him seem forever arrogant. I could sympathize with that: I've had my nose broken three times and it may say things about me that nature never intended.

I read recognition in Woodrow's eyes, anger.

"Savannah Cates," I shouted, leaning my weight against the rapidly closing door.

I almost fell into his arms when he suddenly reversed motion.

A flicker of uncertainty crossed his face. He made a stab at denial. "Savannah who? What did you say?" He applied pressure to the door again.

I held my ground. "Don't try it," I advised. "Any jury would convict. Guilty as charged."

"What do you want? More money?"

"Let's discuss it inside," I said.

He released a pent-up breath and held the door ajar. "This way," he said tersely, leading me down a long hallway lined with framed hunting prints, into a room shelved with law books and furnished in deep red leather. I sat, without permission, on a buttoned-down loveseat.

"Have you heard from your wife?" I asked.

He remained standing. "No."

"Did you really have a burglary?"

"Someone broke in through the kitchen window."

"No burglar alarm?"

"Emily always sets it. I forgot."

"Let's look at this logically," I said. "If your wife had hired me to break in—to conduct a little asset search, let's say, just in case she were interested in divorcing you—would I need to crawl through the kitchen window? Don't you think she'd lend me a key?"

He contemplated the theory, his lips stretched into a tight line.

"Is anything missing?" I asked.

"I don't think so," he admitted.

"Where did this supposed burglar search?"

"There *was* a burglar, dammit. And he searched this office, for one."

"How do you know?"

"I keep my things extremely neat. Does this look neat?"

It looked average to me, papers strewn on the desk in multiple piles. Stacks of books on the floor.

"What was the burglar looking for?" I asked.

"I have no idea."

"Papers? An address book?"

"I have no idea," he repeated stubbornly.

"Do you keep files from your firm here? Legal documents?"

"My office has a safe."

"Savannah might be interested in your financial situation."

"She doesn't care about money," he said. I didn't see how his lips could draw themselves into a thinner line, but they succeeded.

"Yeah," I agreed. "Absolutely. She seemed like the spiritual type to me. But you probably don't entertain her here, what with a wife and curious neighbors and all. And she might just happen to have a friend in the burglar business."

"You're as bad as that oaf at the hospital," he said. "I consider that a racist remark."

"Which oaf is that?"

"Savannah's a beautiful woman, elegant, passionate—"

"And you'd be proud to introduce her as your bride at the next office Christmas party. I know. And the fact that she works for a temp agency and lives in a tenement, while your present bride has millions, that's never crossed your mind. So let's leave it be, and you answer my question, okay?"

He seemed to consider his options for a moment before angrily responding, "I resent your assumptions."

"Fine with me. Who was this oaf at JHHI?"

He sat on the companion loveseat, deftly yanking the knees of his trousers to preserve their careful crease. "A friend of Dr. Muir's saw us holding hands at a coffee shop near the hospital. An indiscreet bit of foolery. I'd met the man before. Socially and professionally. Renzel, Hank Renzel."

"Professionally?" I leapt on the word. "Does that mean you represent him? Do you legally represent anyone at JHHI? Jerome Muir, for instance?"

"I won't answer that. I won't answer a single one of those questions."

"Did Muir introduce you to Savannah?"

"No."

He'd answer questions, all right. As long as they didn't involve his legal practice.

I said, "Let's get back to Renzel. What oafish thing did he do?"

"Stared at me. Stared at Savannah. He knew us both. He—he shunned us. Like we carried the plague."

"Maybe he has a thing about infidelity."

"He has a thing about race," Woodrow blurted. "Before she started temping, Savannah had a steady job at the pharmacy. Until he forced her to resign."

"Really?" I made my tone skeptical.

My disbelief seemed to loosen his tongue. "He faked an incident, said she miscounted pills on purpose. It happens to every person of color who gets assigned to pharmacy," he finished awkwardly.

It never ceases to amaze me, this man-woman thing, this astonishing chemistry. "Person of color." Even Savannah's choice of words sounded wrong tripping off Harold Woodrow's staid establishment tongue. Oh, I could see what might be in it for him: a fling, a tonic for male menopause, escape from his wife's preoccupation with their daughter's illness and death, a way to forget his own pain at Becca's loss.

For Savannah, what?

"Let me ask you something," Woodrow said abruptly. "Do you think Emily will come back? What's happened to her?"

"I might be able to answer your questions after I go through her things."

"Impossible."

"Do you want a divorce?" I asked. "If she *is* alive, I'll find her. How do you think she'll react when I tell her you're having an affair with the receptionist at the hospital where your daughter died?"

"Get out of my house," he said, but there was no menace behind the words. He sounded exhausted, drained.

"As soon as you let me look through Emily's things."

"Let me understand this. If I allow you to invade Emily's privacy, you'll keep quiet about my, uh, personal business."

"Your wife never hired me to spy on you," I said.

"Why, then? Why did she hire you?"

"I won't answer that," I said, perversely echoing his earlier refusal.

"What could pawing through her belongings tell you? How would that help?"

I got to my feet.

He rose as well, took a deep breath, and stared around his study, seeming to view the disorder as a shambles, the rest of his life as the same. "The room at the top of the stairs to your left," he said.

"I won't be needing your company," I replied.

3 3

Top of the stairs to the left.

It was a large overdecorated room—finished, perfect, and yielding few signs of human habitation. The queen-size four-poster, shrouded in yellow-and-rust-flecked paisley, matched the chaise lounge and the curtains. The scallop-edged pillows contrasted. The framed watercolors looked as if they might have been selected for an upscale hotel room. Even the knickknacks seemed impersonal, like books chosen by the yard for their attractive spines.

I rested my meter maid's hat on the top of the bureau and started opening drawers.

Emily folded her sachet-scented bras and panties. Organized her closet rigorously by color. Harold maintained a separate closet and dressing room, also unimpeachably neat.

I wondered what Keith Donovan would make of the room. Compulsive personality disorder?

A full-time maid with too much time on her hands, I concluded.

The only papers in the tiny desk, which the decorator had doubtlessly called an "escritoire," were contained in a single drawer and amounted to one box of blameless blue stationery. Two gold pens huddled in a leather case.

Three skin magazines were crumpled at the back of a bedside drawer on what I assumed to be Harold's side of the bed. Very tame stuff.

I worked my way through Emily's scarves and stockings. Her jewelry box, a large leather case, gave me hope, but the only thing I discovered in a promising envelope was a handful of pearls awaiting restringing.

Nothing taped to the bottoms of the drawers. Nothing lurked under the mattress. I ran probing fingers over the back of each picture frame, hoping to find an attached manila envelope.

Where were these documents I was supposed to receive? Did Emily travel with them? I recalled her ultraslim handbag. Did she keep them in her car?

Mooney would be looking for her car.

The master bedroom's medicine chest was packed with over-the-counter cure-alls, vitamins, and bath oils. A muscle in my neck unknotted when I found the prescriptions Donovan had mentioned —Serax, Xanax, Dalmane—all intact, unsampled. I discovered a vial labeled Halcion.

Since the sleeping pill had received such unfavorable press, I counted the Halcion tablets carefully, slowly. None was missing.

I returned to the bedroom, sank into the desk's padded chair, and stared around me.

Was this where Emily had sat while slipping photos of her dead child into blue envelopes? Here, in front of a deep-red paperweight and a chunky crystal vase?

If Emily had wanted to keep secrets from Harold, she'd hardly have hidden them in a room he shared. I snatched my hat off the bureau, plunked it on my head so I wouldn't forget it. I listened for a moment at the head of the stairs, heard no footsteps, and hurried down the hall.

Of seven doors lining the second floor hallway, three were shut. I twisted the handles with care. They opened noiselessly, one to reveal a spacious linen closet, the next, a bathroom.

Rebecca's room had suffered under the same interior decorator as her mother's, resulting in an overblown "little-girl's" room, all pastels and florals. But the housekeeper had been kept away, and a bit of the child who'd lived there remained with the dust.

She'd collected stuffed animals. A large lion crouched in a corner next to a propped-up giraffe and a kangaroo with a baby in its pouch. Smaller animals crowded the bed. Hippos had been a favorite.

A large wooden chair seemed out of place in a corner. I lifted it and found that the marks it left on the carpet were shallower, newer, than the marks left by a nearby rocker, the only other chair in the room. Had someone brought it in recently? Did Emily sit for hours in her late daughter's room?

Did she keep her secrets here?

I started with the bureau, opening each drawer, working methodically, bottom to top, left to right. My fingers sorted through piles of white undershirts, cotton panties, colored turtlenecks. Rebecca's socks were neatly rolled, some banded with lace.

I surveyed a shelf of dolls: worn Raggedy Anns and much-used baby dolls, stiff porcelain collectors' items, foreign figurines in exotic outfits, a row of Barbie dolls with wasp waists and clouds of hair.

Her closet was a miniature of her mother's, color coded, excessively neat. Her shoes were paired: patent leathers, sneakers, tiny pink-and-white saddle shoes.

I sat in the big chair, bit my tongue, and tugged at my hair. The chair was positioned oddly; it faced neither window nor bed. What had Emily looked at when she sat here? Why here?

Was the view unimportant, only the fact that she was in her daughter's bedroom, pretending Rebecca might rush upstairs, home from school, ready to change into play clothes? Did she keep her eyes closed to strengthen the fantasy? To better smell any lingering scent? At seven, Paolina had smelled of cherry Life Savers. Rebecca's room smelled of mint.

I stared at the ceiling and read nothing on its white surface. I glanced down.

Faint tracks led from the foot of the chair toward the closet, as if something had been dragged over the high-pile carpet. I traced the drag marks to a rectangular laundry hamper, hesitated. If the woman communed with her daughter's soiled clothes, I wasn't sure I wanted to know about it.

The hamper was heaped with photographs: scrapbooks, loose snapshots, paper envelopes from Fotomat and One Hour Photo. FREE DOUBLE PRINTS! screamed a coupon. JOIN OUR PHOTO CLUB! I hauled the hamper back to the chair, using the old track marks as a guide.

While Harold went to his office, Emily sat in a straight-backed chair and reviewed her daughter's life. I lifted five fat volumes from the left-hand side of the hamper. A pink and lacy baby book had a brass plate inscribed REBECCA, HER FIRST YEAR. Four subsequent albums in peacock-feather design—one per year—were as methodically organized as the color-coded clothing.

Most parents keep a baby book—even my erratic mother attempted one—but the majority decrease their obsessive photo taking after the second or third year. Emily had never tired of her subject matter. Was she validating her choice of motherhood over career by selecting her daughter as sole model over and over again? By choosing a cheap automatic camera, the kind so many mothers seem to use? By taking her too-well-composed photos to the one-hour developer?

A racehorse hauling hay? A promising poet penning limericks? A labor of love?

I'd leave stuff like that to Dr. Donovan.

I skimmed each book. Rebecca in a swimming pool, supported by a Mickey Mouse inner tube. Rebecca on her first sled, a red Flexible Flyer. Rebecca wearing a bright yellow dress, her white tights bagging at the knees and ankles, holding a toy camera made of bright red plastic, aiming it awkwardly, beaming.

All shots carefully preserved under plastic. I lifted each collection by the binding and shook it. No loose items fluttered to the floor. I stacked the books on the bed, started in on the packets and loose photos. More of the same.

She'd sent me photographs. She'd concealed photographs in a laundry hamper. Before her marriage, photographs had been her life.

I started to organize the envelopes by date, from Becca's final

birthday to her last days. I hefted each packet. None seemed notice-
ably lighter or heavier than the others.

She'd sent me photographs, dammit.

I started leafing through the most recent envelopes, dated just
before Becca's death, working my way backward through her life.

Nothing out of the ordinary. Nothing.

"What—what the hell are you—" I heard Harold Woodrow's
outraged splutter from the doorway. "Who said you could pry
through Becca's—through *her* things? How dare you?"

"Your wife must have had a darkroom," I observed calmly.

"No. Only a bathroom in the basement. And she hardly ever
used it. It smelled the place up. I didn't like it."

"After Becca died—"

"Don't use her nickname. You have no right."

"After your daughter died, did your wife use her darkroom?"

"She might have. Once, twice."

"Recently?"

"Get out of here. Get out. Put everything back exactly the way
it was, and get out!"

His mouth twitched with fury as he spoke. I stuffed photos into
envelopes, dumped them into the hamper, restored it to the closet.

"Before I leave," I said, facing off with Woodrow near the doorway, "I'm going to search the darkroom."

"There's nothing there."

"Not even a shot of Savannah Cates? Bet she's photogenic."

He pressed his lips together, parted them enough to say, "This
is nothing but blackmail. If I don't cooperate, you'll talk."

"At least you've got that straight," I said. "Could you show me
the basement stairs?"

3 4

If you want to know the age of a house, check the basement. Two hours ago, I'd thought the Woodrow place was practically brand-new. Now I recognized it as a modernization job, a good one. The basement, with its seamed cement floor and exposed beams, its old oil tank in one corner—just in case the modern gas furnace became obsolete—added fifty years.

Down a single step, in a corner that might once have housed a root cellar, a chemical smell oozed from under a partially open door.

If the door had been locked or closed, I might have hesitated, even with the picklocks screaming in my pocket. I don't know much about photography; my workaday needs in that area are met by Roz.

If I discovered undeveloped film inside, I'd need to call her, get her to come over.

Woodrow was sure to enjoy that. I shrugged. Who knew? Maybe a conservative lawyer type like Harold would get a charge out of Roz.

I eased down the step, shoved open the door, and ducked under the low transom.

E. J. Ruhly's career was represented by three newspaper clips, mounted in cheap black frames. As grainy news photos go, they were impressive, but the meager display was hardly in the same league as Dr. Muir's power wall.

I hoped the originals were superbly framed and proudly displayed on the Woodrows' living room walls. I doubted it.

Preconversion, the bathroom had been Spartan, with simple white fixtures, bare-bulb lighting. A sanded plywood workbench had been constructed to fit around the tiny sink, a larger metal sink installed nearby. A second bare bulb, this one red, stuck out of a wall-mounted socket.

Compared to Harold's leather-and-walnut office, Emily's darkroom looked like Cinderella's quarters. Inferior, indeed. Had it angered Emily, this dismissal of her work, this relegation to the cellar, this diminishment of her former career?

Maybe not, but it angered me. I studied the three grainy prints, the cheap frames. I always worry that if Vincent van Gogh had been Virginia van Gogh, she'd have been consigned to paint in the outhouse. Keep all the smelly things together, my dear.

I surveyed the room. It should have been easy going, such a small place. But the various pieces of machinery, of which I could only dubiously identify an enlarger, the shallow trays, the storage bins and files, were foreign to me, hardly everyday stuff like bureaus and desks.

I knew enough not to mess with lightproof envelopes.

There were three of them stacked on the toilet-seat cover. I examined them gingerly. Unsealed.

I flicked off the white bulb, located a second switch, and the room was bathed in a red glow. Now I couldn't inadvertently destroy what I was searching for.

The unsealed envelopes were empty.

Wooden shelves held large tinted-glass bottles. Fixative, developer, unlabeled liquids with sharp and pungent odors. Manila folders contained magazine clips of ancient, abandoned, stone dwellings.

Spider webs filled the corners.

I found the pictures strung like laundry on a line, over my head, across one end of the tiny room. Six shots, six photos that were definitely not of Rebecca.

Were these what Harold's break-in artist had sought?

My hands fumbled with the edges of the first photo. It was small, dark, grainy. The interior of a building. Metal pipes and buckets. Machinery.

I held up the next one. More pipes. Vats and coolers. Hoses. A cement floor with a drain. JHHI? Damn. Weren't there any identifying details in the dim shots? I studied each one. Drains and pipes and vats. No context. No meaning. No words.

I attacked the files. *Artists* consisted of a series of portraits, eight-by-ten blowups of unknown intriguing faces. *Bears* had been shot in zoos. Metal cages loomed and threatened, more terrifying than tooth or claw. No *Hospitals*. No helpful clues. No packets marked: Open in case of my disappearance or death. No explanation of the six photos. By the time I reached *Wampanoog* my fingers were stiff from opening and closing envelopes, my eyes tired of focusing, refocusing.

I flipped the light to full spectrum, blinking rapidly. I took one of the empty lightproof envelopes, tucked the six photos inside, and shoved the thin packet down the waistband of my slacks, snug against the small of my back.

Harold Woodrow saw me out. He didn't seem disposed to chat. As I got into my car, I knocked the long-forgotten meter maid's hat off my head and onto the grass. I retrieved it and stuffed it unceremoniously into the dash compartment.

Maybe Harold Woodrow thought I moonlighted as a meter maid. That could account for his hostility.

35

Before entering my house, I checked the side drive, the yard, even under the back porch where I usually store the garbage cans. No replacements. Was I going to have to send an illegally altered passport to the Feds, live through their intensive questioning, fill out forms for the rest of my life over eighty bucks' worth of trash containers?

I'd been so sure Paco Sanchez would jump at the deal.

One more bright idea gone awry. Now Roz and I would have to stuff the week's garbage into Hefty bags for the dogs to plunder. The neighbors would complain.

I dumped my purse on the hall table with a heavy thud. There were no messages on my answering machine. No packets from Emily Woodrow. Finding Emily was the key, dammit. Were there any bases Mooney wouldn't have covered? He'd check the local hospitals. Airports and bus stations. Credit card charges. The morgue.

If she'd killed Tina, and then killed herself . . . if she'd driven to one of the local beaches, disrobed, and kept on swimming out to sea—stroking, paddling, pushing her endurance until she was too exhausted to turn back, how long could her body stay submerged, undiscovered?

I'm a strong swimmer. When my mom died and I found myself wrenched away from everything I'd known, suddenly propelled from Detroit to Boston, the ocean had almost sucked me down. Dour November mornings, my seventeenth autumn, I'd ride the subway to East Boston, walk slowly to the sandy shore, all the time thinking that I could keep on walking, walking . . . walk till I had to swim, swim in cold, endless green till I'd never have to do anything again.

If Emily *had* killed herself after disposing of Tina Sukhia, then what about the death of the Cephagen CEO? Chalk it up to random urban crime?

Had Emily been murdered like the others?

In the kitchen, I popped the top on a Pepsi. Someone had killed the president of a pharmaceutical lab, a drug company that made a chemotherapy drug, this week of all weeks, in this town of all towns. Cephagen might not have employed Tina Sukhia, but there had to be a connection.

The *Globe* was hiding under the hall table this time; nothing is ever where it's supposed to be in this house. After the first bracing sip, the cola turned unappetizing, so I made myself a cup of instant soup from boiling water and a packet of powder and sat down to learn what I could about Cephagen's late David Menander.

Ringing tributes from colleagues, outraged cries for more police protection, those I could live without. Facts. Where were facts? The who, what, where, when, why journalists used to jam into the first paragraph, and now rarely bother to include at all if juicier details are available. I learned the per-night cost of his plush hotel room before I discovered that Menander had not come here as a tourist.

Body discovered after he'd failed to attend a scheduled meeting at the Jonas Hand/James Helping Institute. If that didn't raise a red flag for Mooney, I'd eat my picklocks.

Who would Menander have dealt with at JHHI? Not peons. CEOs were accustomed to dealing with CEOs. Muir, certainly. Renzel, as Chief of Pharmacy? A humble resident anesthesiologist like Peña?

The police were questioning several unnamed individuals. No one had heard the two shots, which indicated a silencer. A front-desk receptionist thought she remembered that flowers had been delivered to Mr. Menander's room.

As good a way as any to get his room number.

Menander, thirty-nine, had been considered something of a whiz kid, although his company never seemed to take off after the early promise it had shown with the development and marketing of its premier drug, the costly but effective Cephamycin. Menander had been criticized for taking a soft approach to marketing, for keeping the company private, for not raising massive capital and diving headlong into the biotech future. His decision, some years ago, to repackage Cephamycin, using a fancy holographic logo, had been seen as sheer extravagance by several members of the board of directors who'd almost voted him out of office. Others had regarded it as a logical counterattack to the drug-tampering craze that had temporarily driven Tylenol off the shelves. This was from the business section, not the news update.

I finished the oversalted soup, rinsed the cup, shook it dry, and stuck it back in the cupboard. Then, returning to my desk, I spread out my borrowed treasures. Six dimly lit photographs. I rubbed my eyes, shook my head, went back to the kitchen, and burrowed in the fridge till I found the already-opened Pepsi. I ought to buy caffeine pills.

I went over the first photo with a magnifying lens, trying to identify the machinery. The lighting was so bad, the shadows so deep, I couldn't be sure what I was seeing.

Same with the second. Same with the third, although I could sense some order, some setup that made me think of an assembly line. A large metal vat had no visible markings in the fourth shot. The fifth and sixth were even darker and murkier.

Had Emily blundered in taking these shots, or deliberately misprinted them?

Disgusted, I turned them facedown on the blotter, and immediately noticed a legible symbol, a faintly penciled notation in the bottom left-hand corner of the fourth photo.

Tiny numerals: 6, 3, 2. A letter: L. A word: WOOD.

I stared at it until my head hurt, but no illumination came, so I unlocked the upper desk drawer and removed the file I'd forced Paolina's friend, Sanchez, to xerox. Working two or three cases at once isn't bad. When you hit a brick wall on one case, concentrating on the other can free enough brain cells to generate a breakthrough on the first.

Sometimes you just double your frustration level, shoot it straight into the danger zone.

The more I read about Mr. Thurman W. Vandenburg, the bastard who'd hired my garbage thief, the less I knew. An attorney, that most secretive of beasts, he was working for a client named Jaime Valdez Corroyo. Valdez Corroyo was interested in the whereabouts of one Marta Fuentes Giraldo, whom he believed to be his long-lost cousin. A question of inheritance was involved, but while he wished Mrs. Fuentes located, he did not wish to contact her directly. First, he needed assurance that she was not addicted to excessive gambling and drinking, as were so many other members of the Fuentes family. Codicils in the will could preclude her from inheriting if she were a gambler. Therefore it would be best not to raise her hopes until her character and her sources of income were evaluated by a reputable local firm.

Huh?

A list of Marta's "associates" was appended, with an asterisk preceding my name. The client was particularly interested in learning as much about me as possible, including my relationship with Marta's only daughter.

The phone rang. I let it go for three rings, trying to find the magic combination. Maybe the phantom caller would only hang up at the sound of my voice. I lifted the receiver, said nothing.

I heard faint muffled noises, grunts or groans.

"Hello?" I said softly. "Is that you, Emily?"

A slow, seemingly deliberate click.

Damn.

I closed the Vandenburg file, turned back to the photos.

Emily had developed them, therefore they were valuable. They meant something. They were part of the story she needed to tell. I would concentrate on the photos, the location shown in the photos.

632 L wood.

SNAPSHOT

Six thirty-two Longwood Avenue?

Why not check it out? Paolina was safe, either with Roz or with Marta. If Sanchez chose to replace my trash cans, he wouldn't need me to greet him with a brass band.

I already had my picklocks in my pocket.

I sat back in my chair and closed my eyes. Less than a week ago, I'd met Emily Woodrow for the first and only time. . . . So many things remained unseen. Emily's daughter, Rebecca: I'd only viewed her snapshots. Tina: a single photograph. The CEO of Cephagen: a blurred likeness in a newspaper. For a moment the invisible dead seemed more real to me than Emily Woodrow. Through their photographs they had substance, a single frozen form. Emily had moved, walked, talked. Sobbed and whispered. If she entered my doorway, wearing other clothes, would I recognize her?

The intense blue eyes. The terse sudden speech.

"Do you own a gun?"

"Can you use it?"

"Have you used it?"

"Would you do it again?"

While I waited for darkness, I cleaned, oiled, and loaded my .38 police special.

36

Six thirty-two was the place I'd pegged as a former factory, an eye-sore lowering JHHI's property value. I drove around the block, circling it twice, checking the area.

You can learn a lot from looking. Cops who walk a regular beat know who keeps the lights on, who turns them out, who draws the curtains, the angle at which Mrs. Patterson sets her shutters before going to sleep every night at 9:37 P.M. sharp. Especially in small towns, or small neighborhood enclaves, such habits keep the police informed. If I'd known the cops working the medical area, I'd have bought them a few beers and steered the conversation around to 632.

If I'd known them. If I hadn't had the sense that time was running out for Emily.

If again. That ugly stammering word.

Since I saw no beat cop—nor was I likely to see one since most of Boston's patrolmen are locked into speeding vehicles—I decided to pretend that the cop on the beat was me.

I was still wearing my Winchester break-in outfit, so the imper-sonation was fairly convincing. The meter-maid hat had suffered slightly in the dash compartment, but a few pats straightened it enough for night wear. I added a black jacket, one of many articles of clothing I keep in my car, to blend in with the dark and hide my gun.

I strolled the perimeter of the block. Six thirty-two was larger than I'd expected, edging up against the narrow alleyway that ran behind JHHI. While it didn't share any walls with Helping Hand, one forty-foot section almost touched. I wondered if there was inside access from one to the other. An underground tunnel. If so, it might make the property a good acquisition for the hospital.

The front windows were plugged with plywood, crisscrossed with one-by-eight pine planks. Weathered boards. Rusty nails. Dust and cobwebs, dead leaves, and dirt. The front door didn't need plywood; a shuttered metal grille, padlocked and rusty, did the job.

Maybe the Boston Housing Authority had plans to destroy the structure, rebuild from scratch. I wondered when 632 had last been occupied. It was no architectural treasure, nothing worth renovating. Far as I knew, it wasn't an historic site. A few high windows had been smashed and left broken. A bird's nest bridged a gap in a gutter.

Did it already belong to JHHI? Was it awaiting a construction crew? Lying fallow till some golden goose passed on and bequeathed a substantial legacy?

Two winos gave me the eye as they passed. I nodded and one dropped his head in a tipsy greeting.

Instead of walking around the block this time, I found a way to squeeze between JHHI and 632, thinking I might gain access to an unobstructed interior view, a place from which Emily might have taken her snapshots. Why bother to nail plywood across a window that faced a brick wall? Most likely, I'd find no such opeining, but it couldn't be taken for granted. Builders erected their walls not knowing that five years later city planners would turn their picture windows into sunless, brick-view squares.

No window. I snagged my jacket on a nail and had to backtrack to keep the rip from becoming a triangular tear. A sharp smell permeated the narrow space.

I had to hold my breath to make it into the alleyway. The odor almost made me gag. In back, it was better. The windows were boarded and barred. The door mesh-grilled.

Somebody once warned me against learning to fire a gun. If

you know how, he said, you'll do it. Same thing with picking a lock. If you know how, if you take pride in it, you tend to do it. If your day's been frustrating and you don't know where your client is or who's going to sign your next paycheck—well, I admit my picklocks were weighing heavily in both my pocket and my mind.

I glanced right and left. A drizzle had thinned out the foot traffic, and while I could hear the occasional pedestrian, see car headlights shoot by the mouth of the alley, the temptation was high, and the risk seemed low.

The adjoining buildings were so close, so towering, it seemed almost as if I were in an air shaft, concealed by the sheer height of the surrounding walls. I reached in my shoulder bag and grabbed my flashlight, shining it on the back door lock.

It glistened. I knelt in front of the door, my tongue between my teeth, my pulse racing in my ears. The padlock reinforcing the Yale lock was almost new. Underneath it, a tiny plaque had been affixed to the doorjamb with two brass screws. Nothing fancy, the kind of item you could buy in any hardware store. Plastic-covered to keep out the rain, with a slot at the side big enough to insert a business card. DELIVERIES FOR CEE CO., it read in small precise letters.

I stood, ran the light over the edge of the door, felt the hinges. I rubbed my thumb and forefingers together, held them under my nose. Oil. The hinges had been recently oiled. I expanded the circle of light. Fresh tire tracks, deep wide tracks, scored the mud in the alleyway.

I'm not your meet-me-in-the-abandoned-warehouse-at-midnight kind of gal. I'm too tall to play a convincing damsel in distress. I've seen too many horror movies.

Still, I might have gone in. But the edge of the flashlight beam caught the crease of my pants as I got ready to kneel again.

Rust.

Spots of rust.

Like the ones on Tina Sukhia's dress.

Had it been Tina, not Emily, kneeling, camera at the ready?

Tina who'd taken the ill-defined shots? Given the precious film to Emily Woodrow?

I scurried out of the alley, listening for the faintest footfall. I checked the backseat before I got into my car.

No abandoned warehouses, thank you very much.

37

I drove straight home. I didn't even slip my jacket off before dialing Mooney. I tapped my fingers on my desk. Answer, dammit, answer.

Someone picked up.

Mooney was out. Could they reach him? Maybe. Yeah, if it was really urgent, they'd try.

"Have him call Carlotta."

"Yeah."

"Mister, this is not some boyfriend-girlfriend thing. This is business."

"Hey, I said I'd have him call."

"Fast," I said.

Draping my jacket over the back of my chair, I bent over and stared at the six grainy photographs. Rubbed dust off the magnifying glass. Turned on the desk light and edged the photos closer. My .38 dug into the base of my spine. I thought about returning it to the drawer, stuck it into my handbag instead.

I caught the phone before it completed one full ring.

"Mooney—"

"Hey? Hi? You there?"

The voice was slurred, familiar. I couldn't place it.

"Who is this?"

"This is Tony. 'Member? Tony Foley?"

Christ. I hoped he wasn't still at the Hyatt bar.

"Hi. How are you?"

"Rotten," he said with a quick, bitter laugh.

Struck by sudden suspicion, I said, "You haven't been pestering anybody with hang-up calls lately, have you, Tony?"

He stayed quiet so long, I thought I might have hit a nerve. "Tony? You there?"

"Look," he said, "I don't know what you're talking about hang-up calls. Maybe I got something for you. I dunno. Maybe I ought to throw it away, forget I saw it. I dunno what Tina would want me to do. I can't figure it."

"Are you okay?"

"You wanna have a drink with me?"

I glanced at my watch. Past midnight. "Now?"

"Hell, it's nothin'. I'll forget about it. Just make trouble is all—"

"Where are you?" I asked.

"My place. Tina's place."

"I can't leave here," I said.

"Oh, well . . . I'll just toss it—"

"Wait. Is it something you can carry?"

"Sure, but can't you come over here? I'm not feeling real good." Not sounding good, either. Sounding drunk.

"I need to stay by the phone," I said.

"Oh."

"Bring it to me."

"I dunno. I can't really—"

"You won't have to drive," I said quickly. "A cab will pick you up in fifteen minutes. A Green and White. He'll honk."

"A cab? I dunno."

"You won't have to pay," I promised. "Not even a tip. All taken care of."

"Hey, okay! Green and White?"

"Remember, bring it with you."

"I'm puttin' it in my pocket right now."

I dialed Gloria.

Maybe Mooney tried to reach me while the phone was busy.

38

The cabbie honked before discharging his cargo. The neighbors must have loved that, but when I saw Tony's condition I understood. The way he weaved across the sidewalk, Tony was as likely to wander into the bushes for a snooze as he was to ring my doorbell. The warning blast on the horn was pure courtesy.

"Hey," he said, trying not to stumble down the single step to the living room. "Nice."

"I'll make coffee," I said, backing off from a handshake that threatened to turn to a sodden embrace.

"Beer. Ya know, I could use a beer."

"Are you going to be sick?"

"I'm never sick."

"Yeah, well, don't sit on the couch, okay? I had it cleaned once."

Real coffee may taste better, but instant is a blessing. Tony Foley regarded it and me reproachfully. I centered the cracked blue mug carefully on an end table, where he'd be less likely to knock it to the floor.

I said, "Is this important or what?" Maybe the jerk was lonely.

"You're no cop, right?" He made no move toward the steaming coffee.

"I'm no cop."

"Maybe I don't want cops knowin' this, okay?"

"Tony, you phone me for advice at midnight, you gotta let me make the judgment calls."

He leaned back in my aunt's rocking chair and scowled. His eyes were half closed, puffy.

263

"It would help if I knew what you were talking about," I said.

"Once you're dead, it's over? Right?"

"I'm not in the mood for mind games, Tony."

He got a crafty look in his eye. "Gimme another beer. I'll trade for a beer."

Another beer, he'd probably pass out, I thought. One beer coming up.

He took a long swallow, tilting the Rolling Rock bottle toward the ceiling. A silly grin creased his face and he slumped in the chair.

"Tony, dammit—"

He didn't straighten up, but he opened his eyes. "I done nothin' but drink since I found it."

"Nothing but drink since you found *what*?"

"It doesn't make Tina look too good, you know what I mean? I don't want her mama hearin' this on the news."

"Hand it over, Tony."

The silly grin spread wider. "You wanna fight for it, lady?"

"Hell, no."

"C'mon, let's fight. Jus' wrestle a little, okay?"

"Jesus, Tony. You call me. I pay your cab fare. I bring you a cold beer. Don't you think you owe me?"

He considered it for a while, then stood on shaky legs, and dug his hand deep into the pocket of his stained khakis. "Sorry," he mumbled suddenly, slapping a hand over his mouth, dropping a crumpled envelope to the floor. "Which way's your—"

"Upstairs. First door on the right. Hurry."

I watched him lurch for the staircase. Either he'd make it or he wouldn't. I'd have to have the runner taken off the steps soon anyway. T.C.'s sprayed it once too often.

When I didn't hear any alarming noises, I strolled over and bent to pick up the envelope.

Addressed to the World Health Organization, Berne, Switzerland, it bore no street address, just two lines of block print. I examined the flap. It had never been sealed. Or stamped.

Handwritten in blue ball-point on onionskin sheets, the enclosed letter could have been a first draft, or it might have been written in a hurry. How else to account for the corrections and alterations?

"Dear Mr. _____:" it began. That was crossed out and "To whom it may concern:" had been substituted.

"Where'd you find this, Tony?" I yelled upstairs.

No answer.

I read:

Why haven't I heard from you? I don't know whether to call the FDA or the police. Everyone who comes to my door, every time the doorbell rings, I'm afraid they've come to arrest me. Then I'm relieved, because if I'm arrested it will be over. And even if I took the medicine from the wrong place, I know I'm not really to blame. Dear God, if I could have one moment of my life to live over again, that would be the one.

Maybe because I took the money, you think I was part of it from the beginning. Maybe you don't trust me and that's why I haven't heard anything. But I swear, I never would have taken a penny if I'd known. To keep quiet about a mistake, that's one thing. And I was scared for myself, too, scared he'd find a way to make it seem all my fault.

One of the mothers I mentioned in my first letter is very persistent, and I think I owe her an explanation.

That entire sentence had been crossed out with a single thin blue line.

I haven't figured it all out yet, but I'm enclosing part of a Cephamycin package, the kind that contains 25 mL (50) mg single-dose vials. Can you check to see if the seal has been tampered with in any way? You must have laboratories where you can do that.

I saw another container that's ready to be shipped overseas, to Karachi, like the rest. Before I send this, I'll get the exact address so you can stop it and make sure it's what it's supposed to be.

My parents grew up in Karachi, and I'm glad that I can help people there. But in another way, it bothers me. I ask myself, if I weren't Pakistani, would I keep silent like the rest? There's so much money.

Please send someone quickly. I can't believe the people at JHHI know what's going on, but if they do, I need to find out. I need to know.

There was no signature.

I read it twice, then shifted my attention to Tony Foley, who was inching downstairs, clinging to the banister as if he were attempting a rope descent from a snow-capped peak. His head nodded to one side. His jaw was slack. I marched over, grabbed him by the arm, and deposited him in the nearest chair.

"Where's the package?" I demanded.

"Wha—"

"She enclosed part of a box. Where is it?"

"Huh?"

I waved the letter in his face. "Where'd you get this?"

"Wait. Wait. Slow down, okay? She forgot to return one of the library books. Books on Pakistan I told you about. I thought maybe I'd read it, see what was so excitin', why she had to spend so much time readin' and all. Damn book, I picked the thing up and threw it against the wall. And then I saw that letter on the floor."

"It just fell out?"

"Honest. Fell out."

"You haven't been holding back on me? Thinking you might keep Tina's money supply coming?"

"Hell, no."

"You still have the book?"

"At home."

"Did anything else fall out of it, Tony?"

He squirmed and swallowed, made a face as if he'd tasted

something sour and bitter. I hoped he hadn't left a mess in my bathroom. "Just a little slip of shiny paper."

Shiny paper. Shiny paper . . .

I dived across the living room, yanking open the top drawer of my desk so fast it nearly crashed to the floor. Where had I put it, the envelope with Rebecca's death certificate, the envelope Emily had handed me in secret?

I scrabbled through bills and letters. Shoved neat piles into disordered heaps.

There. I upended it and shook it onto the blotter. The shiny, Mylar-like stuff floated slowly to the floor.

"Tony? Wake up, dammit!"

"Hey, hey, there it is. There it is. What're you so upset for? I didn't lose it or nothin'. There's the stuff."

"This?"

"Yeah. Pretty, huh? You hold it right, you can see colors in it. Hologram. Neat, huh?"

I lifted it to the light. Blue, red, and green *C*'s—a design I'd earlier misread as crescents—swam to the surface, wavered, and disappeared as I shifted the angle. Part of a Cephamycin package. Maybe the seal of a Cephamycin package.

The phone rang. Mooney, finally! I grabbed it.

"Hello?"

Nothing. Faint murmuring.

"Hello?" Was that a bell in the background?

I said, "Emily, please, where are you?"

Silence. I heard a distant beeping, a bell ringing again, but not like a telephone or a doorbell.

"Mrs. Hodges, dear, what do you think you're doing?" The voice was faint and far away, a voice I didn't know, a brisk voice, cheerful, but impersonal.

There was a clatter on the other end and a far away voice said, "Code Sixty, Code Sixty."

Then the phone clicked and went dead.

I held it to my ear for a long time.

39

I rang five times in quick succession, pressing my thumb against the bell until my knuckle hurt. I pounded the brass knocker, then hit the bell again. I was ready to kick in the door when I heard footsteps and the jangle of the chain lock.

The porch light snapped on.

"Goddamn," Keith Donovan said, hauling open the door. "This time I was *sure* you were Emily Woodrow."

He wore the same blue bathrobe. Blinking back sleep, his eyes looked unguarded and very young.

I stepped inside. "Code Sixty," I said. "I heard a Code Thirty called while I was at JHHI. Does Sixty mean it's some other hospital?"

"They call Sixty at JHHI," he said, looking bewildered. "Thirty's a child. Pediatric cardiac arrest."

"They double it," I guessed. "Sixty's an adult."

"Right. Can I—"

I said, "I need your help. Now."

He rubbed his hands over his eyes, then squinted at me as if he thought I might disappear. When I didn't, he followed me into the living room. I fumbled with the switch of a floor lamp, lifted the receiver on his desk phone.

"Call JHHI," I said. "Find out anything you can about a patient named Hodges. Mrs. Hodges."

"What the hell time is it?"

The floor lamp cast shadows against the deep green draperies, illuminated barely half the room. "Past two. It doesn't matter."

"Hodges?"

"That's all I know."

"You can't do this from your own house? In the morning?"

"I'm not a doctor," I said. "All I can do is call patient information and find out Mrs. Hodges's condition. Period. That's it."

"Have you tried that?"

I tugged at my hair. "Dammit, I should have." My fingers hit 411. I counted the rings. Five. Six. Pick up!

Donovan said, "JHHI's number is five five five seven three eight oh."

"Thanks."

I didn't know her first name, so I decided to let a quaver creep into my voice. I referred to the operator as "dear." I dithered and repeated myself. Yes, the operator said after a maddening pause, a Thelma Hodges was listed. Was that my friend? Yes? Well, she was in "guarded" condition.

"Over to you," I said to Donovan, reestablishing a dial tone, then brandishing the receiver.

"What? What's over to me?"

"Get me a room, a location. A diagnosis. A prognosis."

"If she's 'guarded,' they don't know the outcome."

"Get any information you can. Please," I said.

"Is this about your friend? The one who took the wrong pills?"

"This is about Emily Woodrow. Make the calls."

He stared at me as if I might want to make an immediate appointment for therapy, but then he leaned over the desk and started fanning through his Rolodex. I paced while he debated between two cards, dialed, and joked easily with someone on the other end of the line. Seemingly as an afterthought, he asked for Thelma Hodges's room number.

He did it well. The man was almost as good a liar as I am.

"Fifth floor west," he told me as he hung up. "It's a cancer ward. Adult patients. Why exactly am I doing this?"

"Do you know anybody who works on the fifth floor? Anybody who works nights?"

SNAPSHOT

"I might know a couple of nurses."

"By name? By sight?"

"Both. Calm down, okay?"

I faced him. "Call a nurse. A specific nurse, by name. Ask her about Mrs. Hodges."

"What should I ask?"

I spied a notepad on his desk and started scribbling. "How long has she been there? Who admitted her? What's wrong with her?" I hesitated. "Is she confined to her room? Does she have access to a phone?"

"Anything else," he asked sarcastically.

"Lots. But let's start with these."

This time, with his permission, I listened in on the kitchen extension, holding my breath. Mrs. Hodges's care presented certain problems, he learned from a motherly sounding woman named Ava. Wasn't it a shame? So young and in such ill health. First the early onset of Alzheimer's Disease, so disorienting for the poor thing, and now the cancer as well. Hard to explain to her what they were doing, and that it was all for her own good. Like treating a child, really. But harder. Was Dr. Donovan doing some work on early-onset Alzheimer's?

Yes, well, Thelma Hodges wasn't confined, but they did their best to keep an eye on her. She tended to stumble around the hospital and disturb the other patients. And they were always finding phones off the hook. He probably should have placed her in a more secure facility, under greater restraint, but it must have been so hard for him, knowing that excellent care could be obtained for her right at JHHI.

He? Why, Dr. Muir, of course.

I wished I'd written more questions, different questions.

Donovan struck off on his own, started ad-libbing.

Dr. Muir? Oh, he never came to visit, but you really couldn't blame him. They'd been very close, Ava understood. Uncle and niece, yes, but really more like father and daughter. Poor Thelma's

271

parents were separated, her mother dead. No one came to see the patient, no one at all. But then, Dr. Muir was such a busy man. And it would be so painful for him to see his niece the way she was now.

Yes, he'd engaged a private duty nurse. Would Dr. Donovan like to speak with her? Not now? Well, Mrs. Hodges was coping very nicely. Everything had been arranged with her comfort in mind.

And, might Ava ask, what exactly was Dr. Donovan's concern?

Enough, I urged Donovan silently. Don't push it. I tapped the phone stem up and down to make clicking noises, but he kept chatting away. I hung up and went after him, drawing a line across my throat with a finger to indicate that a quick farewell was in order.

"Hey, I thought you wanted to know all about her," he said defensively, rubbing sleep from his eyes. "Look, I suppose I owe you one. I barged in on you with a client, and now you get to barge in on me, but at least I phoned first—"

"She's Emily Woodrow," I said.

His finger stayed frozen at the corner of one eye. His lids blinked. He had dark lashes for a man with such pale hair. "What are you talking about?"

"Thelma Hodges is Emily Woodrow. Your Dr. Muir is holding her prisoner.

"Oh, come on," he said.

"She's probably drugged out of her mind."

His hair was cut so short it barely moved when he shook his head. "I can't believe that."

"Don't believe it," I said. "Come *see* it."

"Try me in the morning. After you get a good night's sleep."

I crossed the rug, so that only the width of the desk separated us. "This nurse you just talked to, Donovan—she doesn't exactly sound like the soul of discretion."

"Ava? She'll talk your ear off. You heard."

"Think she's gonna keep quiet about your call? Think she's not curious about why a psychiatrist's interested in Dr. Muir's sick niece? She's probably checking to see if Muir's on duty right now."

"It was Dr. Muir who recommended me, who brought me into this," Donovan protested. "To help Emily."

"And why didn't you tell me that before?"

Donovan lowered his eyes as if he were studying the grain of the desk. "He asked me to keep it confidential. He has other therapists he generally recommends. He didn't want them to feel that he was planning any major changes . . . didn't want them to feel threatened."

"So he doesn't normally refer patients your way?"

"She's actually the first. I'd hoped—"

"He chose you because you're inexperienced, Donovan. Or else to help him keep an eye on her. Was that part of the deal? Did you report to him?"

The therapist hesitated. "He asked about her occasionally."

"Did you tell him Emily had hired me?"

"No," he said. "You were essentially Emily's own idea. And I wasn't sure he'd approve."

"He's got her," I said. "He's holding her against her will."

"Why on earth would he? You wake me up in the middle of the night to tell me a—some kind of Gothic horror story! What? Do you think the man's suddenly gone mad? Do you imagine he keeps some kind of captive harem in the middle of a respectable hospital?"

I paced, pressing the heels of my hands against my temples. I could feel my pulse pounding. "Okay, try this," I said. "Come back to my house. There's a guy passed out in my living room."

"That's not my problem," he said angrily.

I softened my voice. "The man's name is Tony Foley. He lived with Tina Sukhia; they were engaged. He's drunk. Wake him and he'll tell you. And I can show you."

"Show me what?"

"Pictures of a bottling plant used to manufacture phony chemotherapy drugs."

He shook his head again, lifted a hand to the back of his neck. I wanted to grab his arm, force him to move. I made myself speak slowly, deliberately instead. "Someone's manufacturing phony Cephamycin right next door to JHHI. It killed Rebecca Woodrow and four other children. God knows how many other kids have been killed."

"Others?"

"Tina Sukhia used the wrong Cephamycin. She grabbed a package meant for faraway places, faraway deaths. Deaths where the mortality statistics are so grim that a few more deaths wouldn't be noticed."

Both of Donovan's hands were active now, kneading the muscles in his neck.

With effort, I kept my voice low. "Come with me. Talk to Tony. You're the one who told me you couldn't understand the relationship between Dr. Muir and Dr. Renzel. Well, here's a connection: they travel together, Chief of Staff and Chief of Pharmacy, to international conventions. They peddle phony drugs together, to backwater nations."

"You're absolutely wrong."

"Tina Sukhia didn't believe it. She's dead. Your hero's feet are not just made of clay, they're made of shit, and I can prove it."

He didn't bother with slippers or an overcoat. If any of the neighbors peered out from behind their closed blinds, they must have raised their eyebrows at the sight of us hustling across the damp grass.

In my living room, Tony Foley snored loudly. A red light flashed on my answering machine.

"Even if we could wake him—" Donovan began distastefully.

I waved the *Globe* in his direction. "Here. Four years ago, the Cephagen Company voluntarily repackaged Cephamycin, at great expense, to come up with a tamper-proof package, a package sealed with a trademark hologram. Why?"

"Why? Because of Chicago and the Tylenol scare."

"Cephamycin's not stocked on regular pharmacy shelves."

"So?"

"They must have *had* a counterfeiting problem. Or anticipated one. Do you know how much a dose of Cephamycin costs?"

"No."

"The *Globe* calls it extremely expensive."

"Research costs run high," he said.

"Hundreds of thousands?" I asked. "Millions?"

"Hundreds of millions," Donovan said, "to get a new drug on the market. Years of research."

"Could Cephamycin go for as much as a thousand dollars a dose?" I asked.

"I suppose it could. Maybe more."

Tina had mentioned fifty-dose cartons. Fifty thousand dollars a pop, I thought. Enough for expansion, a new wing, a whole new sterile floor. "Look at this," I said.

Donovan held the shiny paper gingerly between his index finger and thumb. I watched his expression shift while he read Tina Sukhia's appeal to the World Health Organization; he scanned it once, twice.

He lifted the silvery paper to the light, eyeing the three-dimensional *C*'s. "Was this enclosed with the letter?" he asked gravely. "Is this the genuine seal from a Cephamycin package?"

"I don't know for sure," I said. "Emily Woodrow gave it to me, the morning you brought her over. When she said she'd lost her glove."

"She didn't trust me."

"You had ties to JHHI," I said. "When I showed the hologram to Tony Foley, he swore it was the same as the one Tina'd enclosed in her letter."

"He's drunk. He might say anything."

"You want proof, help me load him into my car. The matching hologram should be at his place. You can see for yourself."

Donovan sank into the chair near my desk, fingered the sash of his robe. "Once we've got that kind of evidence," he said slowly, "we'd need to go to the authorities."

"Yes," I agreed. "Absolutely. The minute Emily Woodrow's out of that hospital."

The red light on my message machine flashed accusingly. I punched the button, listened long enough to hear Mooney's voice. Hit "reset."

I wouldn't call him back. I'd been a cop too long. I knew too much about bureaucratic delays and foul-ups. The police are a necessary force, not a perfect one. They're big and sloppy and secrets have a way of spreading like wildfire through the ranks.

You don't do brain surgery with a chain saw. It wasn't one of my grandmother's Yiddish maxims, but she would have agreed with the sentiment.

40

Cancers grow with no regard for the clock. Incisions heal and scar, babies wail indignant cries, and the elderly rattle their last breaths in their own due time. Hospitals know no night or day.

I fronted into a metered space scarcely a block from the hospital entrance. It was close to six A.M.

"I'm not sure we should do this," Keith Donovan said.

I ignored him. It wasn't the first time he'd voiced his doubts.

"Go home," I urged. "Walk. Take a cab."

"You won't know how to take care of her."

"I'm surrounded by hospitals. You did your part. I appreciate it. Now go home."

"I can't."

"Wait in the car, then. Can you drive?"

"Of course I can drive."

"Give me five minutes, then move to a loading zone or a fire hydrant, something right in front of the ER. Keep the engine running."

"I'm not afraid to go in."

"Then quit stalling."

Still harnessed by his safety belt, he stared at me searchingly.

Tina's white hospital smock was short and a trifle tight, but topping my own white pants, it looked okay. I hadn't bothered trying on any of her slacks when Donovan and I had deposited her drunken fiancé at the Buswell Street apartment. Donovan had helped me maneuver Foley's bulk into the tiny elevator, which had made lurching progess to the fourth floor. I doubted I could have handled Tony without him.

I'd certainly never have located the tiny but convincingly identical holographic seal without his help.

Donovan wore hospital greens, a relic of med school.

In addition to the smock, I'd taken a few props from Tina
Sukhia's closet: a stethoscope, a clipboard, a flashlight more powerful than the one I normally keep in my handbag. A name tag hung
from the pocket of the smock, but its photo ID was so small no one
could distinguish Tina's dark smiling face from my own pale grim
one. Not at a distance.

I'd yanked my hair back and up, wound it into a tight knot, and
secured it with the dead woman's bobby pins, still scattered on a
tray in the bathroom. I'd asked if I should bring the cap, but that
was only for ceremony, Donovan said. For graduation photos.

A shaft of early sunlight pierced the windshield of my Toyota
and scattered into dust motes.

"Please," Donovan said. "Leave the gun in the car."

"No," I replied firmly.

He released his seat belt, opened the door, and I breathed
again.

We entered through the swinging doors of the ER, two doctors
—or a doctor and a nurse, depending on the viewer's assumptions—
in earnest conversation, heads bent over a clipboard, reviewing vital
charts. Donovan had suggested the ER approach. The general
lobby, he'd declared, was the stronghold of security guards.

We walked through the electric-eye doors of the first available
elevator with a purposeful stride. No one stopped us; I didn't expect
to be stopped. A tiny elderly Indian woman joined us, smiling and
nodding as if she'd smiled and nodded to us a hundred times before.
It was probably a nervous tic, but it gave me confidence, made me
feel like we'd get away with the charade.

"Fifth floor," Donovan murmured, although my hand was already on the button.

"I know," I said. "If this is too interventionist for you, you can
peel off on two."

"You'd get lost," he said.

We slipped past the second floor, the third. The Indian woman got off on four.

"I hope there's a wheelchair up there," I muttered.

"There's always a wheelchair. You bring one along, they'll wonder about you. Procedure."

"That's why you're here," I reminded him. "Just find the wheelchair, get the patient into it, and waltz," I continued.

"I still think we ought to wait. There's more confusion during visiting hours—"

"Look, we've been through this. I want it done now, before the shift changes. If news of your phone call gets to Muir, Emily might disappear along with the next wave of personnel. New name, new location, or worse. Tell you the truth, Donovan, the main thing I can't figure is why she's still alive."

"From the Alzheimer's and cancer diagnosis—the drugs indicated for that diagnosis—her memory may have been destroyed or altered in such a way that she could never be a credible witness," he said.

I said, "Maybe you should have stayed in the car."

The elevator slid to a stop. The doors opened.

"To the right," Donovan said crisply. "Past two corridors, hang left. We'll circle behind the nurses' station. If they see us coming out of the room with her, they might assume we went through proper channels. Out is easier than in."

We stopped at a utility closet, found and opened a lightweight chromium wheelchair.

"Good so far," I told Donovan.

Room 508 displayed the name HODGES to the left of the door. A private room. Nothing but the best for Dr. Muir's niece.

The quiet hum of the place jangled my nerves. I pushed down on the lever and noiselessly swung the door of 508 inward. Donovan scooted the wheelchair inside. I joined him and flipped the light switch.

On the narrow bed, a woman slept, her mouth open, a faint snore emerging. A sour smell issued from the twisted sheets.

Her resemblance to the photos of the little dead girl was all that connected the sleeper to my memory of Emily Woodrow. Her matted blond hair showed dark roots. Her hands were ringless, the nail polish stripped. The area around her eyes seemed swollen and dark, her cheeks rough and large-pored. All her surface elegance was gone.

I glanced at Donovan to make sure. He nodded.

I shook her, murmuring "Shhhh." She shifted, grunted in protest, but her eyes didn't open. Donovan lifted the chart at the end of the bed, studied it with pursed lips.

"What's she on?" I asked.

"I can hardly decipher a single word," he said.

The door opened. "Excuse me. Is there a problem?"

The private duty nurse hadn't wandered far. Maybe to the nurses' station to chat. Probably just to the bathroom; she had a nervous, rabbity look about her. She seemed to expect to be scolded for leaving her charge.

"Nothing you need concern yourself with, Nurse," Donovan snapped rudely. "Mrs. Hodges is taking a ride down to, uh, Radiology. Help me disconnect her from this monitor."

The nurse blinked pale lashes. "How long will she be gone?"

"Twenty minutes, half an hour. I'll have an orderly wheel her back up."

"Radiology?" She pressed her lips together firmly to keep them from shaking. "No one mentioned anything about Radiology."

Donovan said, "What's your name, Nurse?"

"Helen Robins. Sir."

"Helen. Make sure the IV line's secure."

She came, cowed by his arrogance. I briefly considered knocking her on the head, gagging her, dumping her in the bed. She seemed so harmless that I wavered, and then she was back near the door.

"May I go now?" she asked.

"Certainly," Donovan said.

The door hissed shut and we swung into action.

Moving an unconscious person is tricky. I'd hefted my share of drunks when I was a cop. Protesters who recommend passive resistance know what they're talking about.

"You should have ordered the nurse to jack her into the chair," I said. "They know how it's done."

"She made me nervous," Donovan responded. "I thought her nose was going to twitch."

"Forget the robe," I told him. "Let's just get her in the chair. She won't freeze to death."

"Protocol," he insisted. "We'll be stopped."

"Not if we don't get going," I snapped. "Take her legs, and for Chrisake, make sure the brakes are set on that thing."

"Make sure the IV unit's ready to roll," he said.

We were starting to shift her when the door opened. Our rabbity nurse had been joined by another, obviously her superior.

The more forbidding of the two said, "I've paged Dr. Muir. There is nothing in the written orders for this patient concerning Radiology."

I smiled at her winningly. "He must have hated getting such an early wake-up call."

"Hardly," she said. "He's right here at the hospital."

Great.

"When was the last time the patient was medicated?" Donovan asked.

"I gave her the regular meds when I came on at eleven," the little rabbit responded.

"What's your name?" The nursing supervisor stood toe to toe with Donovan.

"Woodrow," I said while he hesitated. "When Dr. Muir shows up, tell him Mrs. Woodrow's gone home."

"Home?"

"Home. And the name is Woodrow. Get it right."

"I thought you said Radiology." The older nurse turned on the younger accusingly.

"He did. He did," she said, wringing her hands, almost clasping them in prayer.

"Call security," the supervisor said.

"Um, can I see your badge?" our rabbity nurse asked Donovan, obviously more afraid of offending a doctor than a nurse. "Please?"

"I'll call them myself." The older nurse's footsteps thundered down the corridor. I quickly traded my clipboard for the chart Donovan had replaced at the foot of Emily's bed.

"Wake up," I said to her loudly, to no avail. We propped her with pillows, got a good hold and moved her to the wheelchair. She slumped forward and started to fall out. The young nurse gazed at us openmouthed.

I swore and jammed my body up against Emily's. They ought to make the things with shoulderbelts.

"Nurse!" Donovan ordered. "Give us a hand here."

She couldn't seem to help obeying. Must be the tone, I thought. The impersonalized "Nurse!"

Emily grunted and snored.

He entered the room quietly, a graying shadow of his portrait, his speckled bow tie askew, his mane of white hair tousled. Perhaps he had been sleeping. One corner of his mouth drooped.

He forced a ghastly smile and tried to seize control of the situation by sheer force of personality; he must have been able to do that easily in his prime.

"Oh, it's you, Keith," he said. "You've got the whole floor in a muddle. Ruth must have misunderstood. Radiology, my eye. Please explain yourself. What's this foolishness about taking a patient home?"

"Explain yourself," I returned sharply.

He eyed my mismatched uniform with distaste. "Who are you? Do you work here?"

"Does this patient suffer from Alzheimer's Disease?" I demanded. "Does she have cancer? Leukemia?"

He peered closely at the woman in the wheelchair. Raised a hand to his forehead, dropped it, and wiped it across his mouth.

"How dare you?" he said to Donovan, lowering his voice in fury. "This is outrageous. Where is her chart?"

"We know who she is," I said. "Dr. Donovan, can you identify this woman as your patient, Emily Woodrow?"

Donovan said, "I can and I do."

"You interfering bastard," Muir rumbled.

At the same time, Donovan said, "Dr. Muir, are you okay?"

"Mrs. Woodrow's leaving," I announced. "Now."

"Security," Muir said softly. He didn't call out to them; they were there. Two guards had silently materialized, one grizzled and stooped with age, one quite young.

"Take me as far as a phone," I told them. "You can even dial it for me: nine one one."

The guards seemed puzzled. I gave the wheelchair a push. It went nowhere. I released the brake. Donovan stood frozen.

Muir was blocking the way. His skin looked waxy in the overhead fluorescents. He said softly, "Give me her chart. You can't take a chart out of the hospital—"

I said, "Out of the way."

He rested a hand at his throat, breathed in and out audibly. "You may mean well," he said. "Please, just leave. I don't want trouble. Dr. Donovan, I'll speak with you later. I don't blame you for any of this."

"We're not going without Emily," I said.

Muir's face looked grayer by the minute.

"Out of the way," I repeated. "Or tell your guards to shoot. They're armed, aren't they?"

The younger one bobbed his head quickly, patted his holster as if he needed reassurance.

"Great," I said. "And then, after they shoot us, Doctor, you can try to save our lives. *Doctor,*" I repeated scathingly. "Look what you've done to her."

If he'd brought the full authority of his presence to bear, the guards would have stopped us. Maybe not shot us, but stopped us. Muir stared at Emily, wiped his hand across his mouth again. He made his way to the edge of the rumpled hospital bed and sank onto it slowly, like an old man.

I wheeled Emily out the door.

The guards looked to Muir for instruction. The younger one said eagerly, "Should we stop them?"

"It doesn't matter," I heard Muir whisper.

I took off, walking with increasing speed. Down the corridor, past the nurses' station. I could feel eyes boring into my back. Donovan walked stony-faced at my side, a steadying hand on Emily's shoulder. The elevator took about two hours to make the ascent from the first floor.

No one stopped us as we pushed the wheelchair out of the ER. The automatic doors whooshed behind us and I took a deep breath.

"Where?" I said.

"The Brigham ER's closest," said Donovan. "I don't know how to get her down from these kinds of dosages without risking an MI and God knows what else."

"See," I said. "You know the lingo."

"You were good in there," he said.

"Thank you."

"You didn't shoot anybody," he said.

The Brigham's emergency room was jammed. While I was still reeling from the number of awkwardly bandaged arms and legs, the welter of wheelchairs and crutches, the incoherent cries of pain, Donovan collared a nurse, identified himself, and informed her that his patient had complained of chest pain just before collapsing.

In less than five minutes, Emily had moved to the head of the queue. In ten, she was in possession of a bed and full monitoring equipment.

41

I called Mooney from a pay phone. He answered immediately, and the more I talked, the angrier he sounded. He made the trip from Berkeley Street to Brigham and Women's in record time. He brought along two uniformed men.

"Look, I phoned," I said, as soon as I saw the tilt of his eyebrows. "We missed each other about a million times, but I did phone."

"I'm the only one in the department? Nobody else?"

"Mooney," I said, "this may surprise you, but I don't have great faith in the department. Especially when there might be political strings attached."

"Political?"

"There's money and power in hospitals. Politics can't be far behind."

Mooney's eyebrows lowered, and I took advantage of the lull to introduce him to Keith Donovan.

"She really sick?" Mooney said skeptically, as soon as I mentioned the word *psychiatrist*.

"Not only is Emily Woodrow really sick, Mooney," I said, "she didn't kill anybody, so we wouldn't have to pretend she was sick if she wasn't. I *want* you to talk to her."

"You couldn't have waited until I was available before you went stealing her out of Helping Hand?"

"Stay in your office."

"Soon as people quit knifing each other, I'll be delighted." Back from a ruckus in the South End, he was less than cheerful. "I'm not the only cop in town."

"The only one I trust, Mooney. You want to put me in jail for that?"

"Has her husband been notified?"

I said, "I didn't call him."

"Nice," Mooney said. "I guess you leave us a few scraps."

"C'mon, Moon."

He made a face. "The way I understand it," he said, "you've got some pictures, you've got two bits of shiny stuff, and you've got an unmailed letter."

"Right. And we've got Emily Woodrow."

"Who might not remember anything," Donovan added.

"That's it?" Mooney asked.

"Yeah," I said defensively. "That ought to be enough."

Mooney said, "Give me details. The pictures are of some kind of machinery—"

"It's a bottling plant," I said, "an assembly-line kind of thing."

"Wait—and you think it's at six thirty-two Longwood Avenue?"

"Soon as you get a warrant, we'll know," I said.

"I need probable cause for a warrant."

"Find out who owns the place. I'll give you ten to one it's JHHI. Check the ground near the rear door. It's covered with rust —again ten to one it matches the stains on Tina Sukhia's dress. There's some kind of chemical smell. Brand-new locks on the back door. A tiny sign that says 'Deliveries for Cee Co.' Cee Co.'s got to be a knock-off of Cephagen Company—the cut-rate division."

I remembered what Tony Foley had told me. That Tina Sukhia had laughed when she'd told him her money came from Cee Co. Muir must have had fun selecting the name.

"Jerome Muir is a respected and powerful man," Mooney said. "Even with all that—"

"Jesus, Mooney," I exploded, "don't you know a judge who owes you a favor?"

"I know a lot of people who owe me a favor," he said pointedly.

"Donovan," I said. "Tell him."

"Tell him what?" Donovan and Mooney had disliked each other

SNAPSHOT

on sight. Mooney hates psychiatrists. As for Donovan, I guess he was only fascinated with women who felt comfortable with violence, not men.

"What you told me," I urged. "About how much it costs to manufacture and market a drug like Cephamycin."

"It costs plenty," Donovan said shortly.

It seemed like I was in this on my own.

"I'm worried about Dr. Muir," Donovan continued. "He must be ill. You can see that, just looking at him. Did you notice the left side of his mouth?"

I kept a close watch on the door to Emily's room. It stayed ominously shut.

Donovan said, "We have to be missing something. It doesn't make psychological sense."

"Psychological sense," Mooney echoed. "What's that called? An oxy-something? Oxymoron? Psychology doesn't make sense most of the time, Doctor."

"Donovan," I said. "You *saw* Muir. You saw his face when he realized we recognized Emily."

"I saw him," Donovan agreed, "but I can't comprehend it. It's like—like learning my father was a thief, or a casual adulterer—someone who betrayed my trust over and over again, in terrible ways. I know it can happen. I've heard it from patients. But I know the man."

"Yeah," Mooney said, "but what do you know about his lousy childhood?"

"*I know the man,*" Donovan repeated.

"You called him a genius," I said quietly. "He could have fooled you."

"But this sort of thing, this basic lack of caring . . ."

"Mooney," I demanded as Donovan's voice trailed off into anxious silence. "Did you find out why the president of the Cephagen Company was up here? Who he was meeting with?"

"You could have paid back a lot of favors by making that connection for me, Carlotta."

287

"We can argue that later, Moon. Did you find out?"

"The meeting was supposed to be with Muir, but Muir says he had no idea of the agenda. Never spoke to Menander directly. Hang on, okay?"

He spent two minutes conferring with his uniforms, gesturing and talking full speed. In another two minutes, he'd have a team scouring city records, searching for paper concerning JHHI, 632 Longwood Avenue, Cephagen, and Cee Company.

Maybe they'd run into Roz.

"You need to get in touch with somebody at the World Health Organization," I reminded him when he turned his attention back to me. "About Tina's letter."

"Oh, yeah," Mooney said, raising an eyebrow. "Switzerland."

"Berne."

"Narrows it down."

A doctor hurried out of Emily's room. Mooney clapped a hand on his shoulder, blocked his way.

"How is she?"

"Hard to say at this point. She's unconscious."

"When can I see her?" Mooney demanded.

"She's not going anywhere," the doctor said. "What's so urgent?"

"Tell me when I can speak to her."

"You can see her when she wakes up. Now, ask me when she'll wake up, and I'll say I don't know, okay? It could be five minutes; it could be five hours. She's not a hunk of machinery, officer."

I got between them. "Is she going to wake up?" I asked quietly.

His voice softened. "Are you family, miss?"

"No," I said.

He stiffened up again. "If's she's not responding in twelve hours, we'll try a stimulant. She's not in a coma. That's our major concern, making sure she doesn't slip into one. It would be better if she woke up on her own." With that, the doctor broke away and strode down the hall.

"Shit. I'll have to assign somebody. I can't wait around," Mooney said.

"I'll stay," Donovan said.

"Me, too," I volunteered.

Mooney reconsidered. "I can give it a little while," he said grudgingly. "Until the warrant comes through, anyway."

Half an hour later, with Emily still asleep, a uniformed officer bustled in, a young guy I'd never seen before. He stopped at the nurses' station and held a whispered confab. A white-haired woman pointed him in our direction.

"Lieutenant Mooney?"

"Yeah."

"We got a stiff. Nearby. Called it in, and Officer Triola said to get you on it right away."

"Where?"

"Helping Hand. My partner and I caught the squeal. Doctor name of Muir. Important guy, I guess."

Suicide, I thought, slamming my hand down angrily on a nearby seat back. Dammit to hell.

42

Donovan stayed at the Brigham. I trailed Mooney out to the cruiser and either he didn't notice or else he'd forgotten that I no longer worked for him.

The young cop sped the two hundred yards, siren blaring, lights flashing, and dropped us in front of the ER doors. Two nurses greeted us with a stretcher, but Mooney waved them off. Guided by the cop's directions, we boarded an elevator.

Someone had posted a hospital security guard on the fifth floor. He opened his mouth to question us. Mooney flashed his badge in response.

"Room five forty-six," the security guard said excitedly. "Head of the whole damn hospital croaks. And not a thing they can do about it." He sounded perversely satisfied, as if death's triumph over a doctor was something to cheer about.

Two uniformed cops controlled the scene.

"Randall," one announced with a military snap, apparently recognizing Mooney.

"Talk."

The man consulted a spiral-bound notebook gripped tightly in his left hand, began haltingly, then spoke with increasing confidence. "According to the nurse who found him, Doreen Gleeson—that's two E's in Gleeson—this Dr. Muir was found in a supply room. Got a man there, but a whole medical team's already tramped through it. She, uh, Gleeson, yelled for help and another nurse sounded the alarm. Carried him in here and tried to resuscitate. Thought he'd had a heart attack or something. Used those paddle things, a defibrillator, right? A bust. Couldn't get his heart started.

Gleeson, the nurse, goes back into the supply room and spots a syringe lying on the floor. I've got it safe in an evidence bag, but I had to practically threaten three doctors to make her give it to me. They wanted to send it to the hospital lab, have it analyzed here, can you believe it?"

"I'm surprised they bothered to call us," Mooney said.

"Doreen Gleeson did that. After she saw the syringe."

"Observant."

"And she knew that other nurse who died here."

Mooney said, "A syringe on the floor doesn't make it homicide. What's against the doc using the needle on himself and then dropping it? Or it could have fallen out of his arm or wherever when the medical team grabbed him."

"Yeah, I suppose," the cop said, his nonchalance not quite hiding an underlying excitement, "but I've got a witness—not to the moment of death or anything—but a witness who says he saw somebody leaving the supply room, kind of sneaking out, and he says he can describe her."

"Her?"

"Yeah. A woman."

"Crime-scene unit ought to be here by now," Mooney said, checking his wristwatch.

"Yeah, well, they're on the way."

"Witness?"

"Guy named Renzel. A doctor. But I don't know what kind."

"He's involved, Moon." That's all I had time to murmur before the man himself was in earshot. His tan had yellowed and paled, and behind his glasses he looked older, sunken, almost as old as Muir had looked the last time I saw him.

"God, I don't know if I can talk about this," Hank Renzel said. "He was my best friend."

Mooney gave me a long look. "Let's find a place to sit down," he said.

He didn't tell me to stay away, so I followed. I figured he

wanted me as a witness, in case Renzel decided to do any confessing about the phony drug setup. Juries prefer nonpolice witnesses.

We found an empty lounge across from the double steel doors of an operating theater, the kind of place where anxious relatives await word.

Renzel looked like he'd already heard the worst. He sank into a blue couch and Mooney sat next to him. I took a chair facing them both. Renzel gave me a single glance, didn't recognize me without my blond wig.

"I can't believe it," he mumbled. "Muir. Like that. It was bad enough with the nurse . . ."

"Tina Sukhia."

Renzel nodded at Mooney. He seemed surprised that he'd spoken loud enough for anyone else to hear. "Yes. Her. And now him. Who else, I wonder? Who else?"

He was silent so long I wondered if he'd fallen asleep behind his heavy frames and staring eyes. I took Interrogation 101 from Mooney. I know how reluctant he is to prompt a witness, but even he was finally forced to talk.

"Can you tell me what you saw, Dr. Renzel?" Mooney asked.

"I told the other officer."

"Tell me. Sometimes, when you go over it, you remember something."

"I'd never have seen anything out of the ordinary if I hadn't felt like taking a stroll. I pass that supply room on the way to the cafeteria. I wanted a brownie. They make good brownies. Sometimes the pharmacy workers bring them in for me. They know I like them . . ."

This time Mooney and I outwaited him.

"I saw a woman come out of the room."

"How sure are you that she came out of the supply room and not out of one of the adjoining rooms?"

"Well, I'm absolutely sure of it because I thought to myself, why is she coming out of the supply room, what was she doing in there? You know, you read things where doctors have all these, well,

sordid meetings, trysts? In magazines. Made-up things. I've never
seen behavior like that at an actual hospital. Not here, anyway, and
so I just took notice."

Renzel paused. "Do you want me to describe her?" he asked.
"Yes."

"She seemed to be a patient."

"A patient," Mooney repeated.

"Or else she was wearing a patient's johnny and robe," Renzel
said, sounding as if he'd just that minute considered the possibility
of such a deception.

Had Muir and Renzel decided to keep Emily alive in case they
needed a patsy for Tina's killing? Someone to blame for the death of
the Cephagen Company's president?

Had Renzel alone decided to make use of her again? Why kill
Muir? Why now?

I bit my lip. Why didn't the Chief of Pharmacy know that
Emily was no longer trapped in her JHHI cell? Why hadn't Muir
confided in his partner?

"I'd say she was forty," Renzel continued, giving each word
due weight and consideration. "Maybe older than that. Very fair
skin. Blond hair, medium length. Not anyone you'd consider the
criminal type."

"What do you mean?" Mooney asked gently. "By 'the criminal
type'?"

"Well," Renzel said in a low confiding tone. "Around here, in
this neighborhood, it's the minorities who generally cause trouble."

"Ah," Mooney said. "Do you remember when I spoke to you
before, right after Tina Sukhia died? You thought she might have
been stealing drugs from the pharmacy. Was that, in part, because
she was dark-skinned?"

"The woman I saw today was definitely Caucasian," Renzel
said quickly, defensively.

Was he going to try to sell Mooney some tale about Emily
Woodrow admitting herself to the hospital under a false name?
Feigning cancer, so she could get a good shot at Muir? How was he

planning to explain "Thelma Hodges's" medical chart, with Muir's handwriting all over it?

My throat felt dry. I wished I'd paid closer attention to that chart. Undecipherable, that's what Donovan had said. Undecipherable.

Mooney glanced at me and I gazed steadily back at him. He didn't nod or smile. Maybe he moved a fraction of a second slower. Maybe his jaw worked.

Renzel slapped both hands to his head, then leaned abruptly forward. His hand smacked against Mooney's thigh.

"Oh, my God," he said. "If I'd checked right then, gone to see what was going on, I might have saved him. I'll never forgive myself. Never. Muir was a fine man. A decent man. He treated me like a son."

He was good, this Renzel guy, very good.

"What time was it?" I asked quietly, speaking to him for the first time, "when you saw this woman?"

"Not even fifteen minutes before Jerome—before his body was found in the supply room. She could still be posing as a patient. She could be anywhere by now. I know your man posted guards, but there would be no reason for her to stay once she'd done what she did—"

Hadn't he had time to check "Mrs. Hodges's" whereabouts? Doreen Gleeson, the observant nurse, must have discovered the body too soon.

"You know that a syringe was found in the supply room?" Mooney asked.

"I didn't. You mean . . ." He paused and licked his lips. "It's almost like the other one. I know this: Jerome got a threatening letter, an anonymous letter. I told Jerome he ought to take the letter to the police, but ignoring it would be more like him. He wouldn't want to make trouble for the poor woman."

"The poor woman," I repeated. "Then Dr. Muir knew who'd sent the letter?"

"He suspected the mother of a former patient," Renzel said.

"Did he tell you her name?" Mooney asked.

How far would Renzel go? I wondered.

"I might recognize it," he said, waiting for Mooney to name Emily Woodrow.

Instead Mooney said, "Dr. Renzel, I think we should continue this conversation downtown."

Mooney didn't say a word about calling an attorney. He didn't do anything stupid like trying to cuff Renzel or read him his rights. It must have been in Mooney's eyes, the knowledge that he'd caught a killer.

"Don't move, don't speak, don't do anything," Renzel commanded. He was staring at me as if Mooney's compliance was a foregone conclusion.

It was. Mooney sagged on the couch, his eyes unfocused, his mouth open. He was trying to speak, but he couldn't.

"What—"

"Shut up." Renzel's hand came out of his pocket and I got a glimpse of the tiny syringe tight between his index and middle fingers. Mooney hadn't seen it at all. Had he felt the jab?

"Stand up."

I did.

"Stand next to me."

My feet moved.

"Walk to the elevator." He grabbed my right arm above the elbow in a firm left-handed grip. The syringe, in his right hand, shrouded by the folds of his lab coat, was close to my side.

If it were a gun, I'd know. Know whether it was cocked, whether the safety was off, know what my chances were, what organs the bullet would pierce. I'd know whether it was a .22, which would give me a faint chance, or a .9mm cannon, which wouldn't.

But a syringe . . . what had its poison done to Mooney? Was it the same stuff that had killed Tina Sukhia? Jerome Muir?

"That cop *knew*. You knew," Renzel said, his hand biting into my arm. "What did I do wrong?"

"Emily Woodrow's not a prisoner anymore. Didn't Muir get a chance to mention that before you killed him?"

"Where is she?" was all he said.

"Police custody."

"Push the button," he said. "Down."

Most drugs, you have to hit the vein. Intramuscular's not as good. I learned that from junkies. Had he hit a vein with Mooney? How much time did Mooney have?

I stared at a silent loudspeaker, willing it to life. Code Something. Call the code for reviving a police lieutenant pumped full of a substance that might or might not prove lethal.

I didn't intend to get into any elevator with a maniac holding a loaded needle. Once inside, it would be too easy. A quick slap on the butt, a shot in the vein if he got fancy. Carlyle on the floor, and him out the door, and on the way to the airport.

My handbag hung over my left shoulder, occasionally bumping my hip. My handbag with my gun inside, the gun I'd taken because of Emily's insistent questions.

"Can you use it?"

"Would you do it again?"

Not when I can't reach it, dammit. Could I manage to swing the handbag, knock the syringe away?

I had a quick vision of Mooney, head lolling against the arm of the couch. How long before anyone strolled over to the lounge by the operating theater? How long before someone went looking for the officer in charge?

How long before they searched the elevators?

"Dammit. Why doesn't this thing come?" Sweat was beading on Renzel's forehead. Obviously, this wasn't his style, this immediate, physical crime. He preferred long-distance hits, where you never got to see your victim.

"I thought Muir was the boss," I said. "But I guess it was your show all the way."

"Shut up. We're going to try a staircase."

That was fine with me.

Maybe security had turned off the juice to the elevators. That would mean someone had found Mooney, someone knew what was going on. They'd be looking for us.

The silent speaker suddenly boomed. Code Red.

Dammit, I thought they used numbers here.

"What's that?" I asked.

"They probably found your cop friend."

"Did you kill him?"

"I'm not a killer," he said.

"What do *you* call it?"

"Profit and loss. Business, that's what I call it."

How much could the man see without those heavy glasses? How could I knock them off?

"It's hard to believe Muir never knew what was going on," I said.

Renzel flushed, and I realized it was with pleasure. Pleasure at having duped Muir, the man who'd "treated him like a son."

"Muir's a fool." The Chief of Pharmacy's voice seemed harsh, grating. How could I have ever thought it appealing? "He's been losing it for years, but they all cover up for him. They know what his name's worth."

Dr. Jerome Muir. An M.D. doctor, a medical doctor, like Renzel's father, the well-known surgeon. Was that the root of Renzel's delight? That he'd put one over on the substitute old man?

If I survived, I'd ask Donovan.

"Dr. Muir never knew you were holding Emily Woodrow prisoner? Even though you used his name," I said, my voice full of pretended admiration.

"I sign his name better than he does," Renzel said.

"But how did you manage the drugs, the medical chart? You're not an M.D."

"I'm as good a doctor as anyone here," he said. "Better than most."

Renzel's glasses had sidepieces that curved firmly around his ears. It would take more than a quick sideswipe to dislodge them.

"Now stop jabbering and walk faster," he ordered.

"Where's the staircase?"

"Keep going. There's one around the next corner. Not many people use it."

We were walking down a broad, empty corridor. If someone had found Mooney, the place ought to be a hive of police activity. I imagined Renzel's profile in cross hairs, a target for unseen sharpshooters. Suddenly I envisioned them everywhere, siting just a little off, high and to the right, at my head.

"Backward," I muttered, my mouth dry as dust, speaking to keep my mind off the shooters.

"What?"

"I got it backward," I said. "Once I started to believe Emily's statement, to accept what she'd seen—a man shoving a mask over her daughter's face—I called it all wrong. I assumed the man—I assumed you were trying to kill Rebecca, not save her."

Renzel said nothing, kept walking.

"Why did you bother?"

"I don't expect you to understand."

"I'd like to understand."

He swallowed. "It . . . the children here . . . Rebecca's death was different."

"You ran into the chemotherapy room. You pushed Emily Woodrow out the door. You risked your entire operation."

"Look, the other stuff I do . . . No one cares. Everyone does it. I ship bogus high-tech drugs to sink-hole countries with no sewage treatment. Sick people—people who'd have died anyway, from bad water or third-rate physicians—die a little sooner. Keep it off the U.S. market and nobody cares. The profits are unimaginable. Millions. I would have gotten everything I wanted."

"What?"

He stared at me blankly.

"What?" I repeated. "What was it you wanted?"

"Everything." His eyes blinked rapidly behind his thick glasses. "Money," he said carefully, as if he were explaining a difficult concept to a child. "Here we are. Now shut up and open the door."

The stairwell was cool. Silent. Gray walls. Gray steps.

"You're nuts," I said.

He held more tightly to my arm. I didn't think he'd do anything while we were actually on the stairs. The landings, where he'd have better footing—I'd have to watch for the landings.

"I would hate to have to kill you," he said softly, his face so close I could feel his breath on my neck.

"Like you killed Tina," I said.

"If she hadn't taken the carton off my desk—if she'd followed standard procedure, none of this would have happened. But she was in a hurry and she grabbed the first carton she saw."

"Why was it on your desk? Why not keep the mess over at six thirty-two? Why risk contaminating your own hospital?"

"I needed to check the bar codes, make sure the packaging was current. It was her error. Not mine."

"Why didn't you kill Emily Woodrow?"

"I could have. I found them prowling the hospital together: proof that Tina'd never keep quiet no matter how much I paid her. But it would have been too many deaths too fast. Even old Muir might have woken up and asked questions. And I had plans for Emily. You might call her a little pharmaceutical research project of mine. The police will probably find her quite willing to confess to Tina's death. Any death. Even her daughter's."

I studied the concrete-block walls, listened for approaching sirens, ascending or descending footfalls. Nothing.

"The black nurse," Renzel said confidingly, "Tina. Killing her . . . I have no regrets about it. No feelings. Except possibly . . ."

"Yes?"

"That I'd have preferred to kill a black doctor. Yes. A minority M.D. Someone my own age."

"Someone whose acceptance to medical school meant you didn't get in?"

"Exactly," he said coolly. "Perceptive of you. But I do regret the children *here*. I regret Emily Woodrow's child."

I stared down at Renzel's feet, left, right, left, right. He wore brown loafers, well polished, expensive. Leather soles, I thought. No traction. I watched my own feet in conjunction with his. I couldn't do anything obvious, but I tried to match my stride to his, to measure the distance my foot would have to kick in order to trip him up.

"The doors are probably guarded," I warned, just before we reached the landing. "You'll need me. You'll need me, as your ticket out."

I could feel his hesitation.

"You might not be so lucky with your next hostage," I said hastily. "Cops are very careful when a woman's taken hostage."

"We'll go out the ER," he said.

How many steps could I fall and still get up? How quickly would he have to stab with the syringe? Could I count on his impulse to throw out his arms and save himself? Would his damn glasses fall off?

I watched and counted, felt his rhythm. When he was between steps with his right foot I lurched as far away from him as I could, hurled myself down the stairs.

He shouted, toppled as well.

Seven steps was all I wanted to fall. And I was ready for it. And it hurt like hell.

When I dive on the volleyball court, my knees and elbows are padded, and the floor is level, forgiving wood. Dammit, dammit, dammit. The staircase was cold concrete and hard right angles. It's the knees and elbows that get it every time. Knees and elbows because I was rolled in a ball to protect my head.

He wasn't holding on to me. Even as I was falling, I knew that. And somebody was yelling. Me.

I grasped my handbag to my chest and hugged it. I could feel the outline of the gun.

Would the tiny syringe break? Would he squeeze it inadvertently? Disarm it? Would he break his goddamn hand?

We landed in a tangle of limbs and I found I could move. I threw myself on top of him and I kept yelling and thrusting my hand in my handbag until I could bring out my weapon and hold it at the base of his skull.

I couldn't see the syringe.

"Just lie there," I told him.

He squirmed and I dug the barrel into his neck. "Don't move!" I yelled, my mouth an inch from his ear.

He lay still.

"I can pay you," he said.

"Like you paid Tina Sukhia?"

"Listen," he said softly, like he was imparting a great secret. "There's nothing you can't fix with money."

"Yeah," I said. My knees ached. I could feel wetness under one of them and hoped the cut wasn't deep. I felt bruised and shaken. Time for some cop to open the door.

"Nothing money can't fix," I said. "Be sure and tell that to Emily Woodrow."

43

It took two days for the fallout to hit. I don't mean the newspaper headlines; those were fast and immediate, and mostly inaccurate as hospital PR kicked into overdrive, handing out misleading press releases by the bushel. But the reaction to my role in Renzel's arrest came more slowly.

Part of the delay was due to Mooney's hospitalization. Some of it was weekend inertia. Another element was jet lag, but I didn't know anything about that until after my Monday morning summons to Mooney's office.

Mooney had taken a 1-cc intramuscular jolt of a drug called Ketamine. Hospitals don't keep Ketamine under lock and key; you can find it on any anesthesia cart. It's what they call a dissociative anesthetic. Keith Donovan told me about it.

He stayed at the Brigham, camping outside Emily Woodrow's door, leaving only to see his regular patients. I don't know if he acted out of guilt; I don't much care. I just liked the way he remained after others went home, noting the changing shifts of nurses and police guards, reading psychiatric journals, chatting.

We talked about anesthesia, third-world medicine, general topics, skating-on-the-surface stuff. He brushed my hair back from my face once, when the arguing got a bit heated.

He offered to see me to my Toyota when I left. In the descending elevator he asked if I wanted to talk about it.

"What?" I said.

"Did you feel tempted to use the gun? When you had him down on the floor, when you had him cornered?"

I considered possible replies. I thought about dating, even sleeping with a very attractive guy who'd analyze my every move.

I got in the car and drove away, watching Donovan grow small in my rearview mirror.

The next day, while I was at JHHI waiting to visit Mooney, a bouquet of wilting jonquils in my hand, Pablo Peña, the sleepy anesthesiologist, told me more about Ketamine. They use it on kids. Horses, too, he believed. Unless given supplemental drugs to offset its effect, patients wake from Ketamine-induced sleep soaked in sweat, screaming of gruesome nightmares. A biker he'd once sedated had specifically requested Ketamine, asking for that "angel dust stuff." He'd come down shrieking, "They're ripping my flesh off! Man, I'm charred by fireballs!"

Over the weekend I wondered about Mooney's dreams.

Monday morning, at headquarters, I thought I might actually be offered a congratulatory handshake, a collegial pat on the back. Mooney hadn't died. Emily Woodrow hadn't died. The poison plant at 632 Longwood had been shut down. A receptionist at David Menander's hotel had picked Renzel out of a lineup as the "flower delivery man."

"Mooney? In a meeting," I was told when I arrived. I waited long enough to drink one cup of coffee. Long enough to hunt for doughnuts, tracking their cinnamon smell to an empty box in the trash.

Through a slit in the shade on Mooney's door, I could see that he was entertaining two suits. They didn't look like plainclothes cops. They looked like politicians or businessmen. Possibly lawyers. Maybe I ought to take a hike, call, and reschedule.

"Hey, thank goodness," JoAnn Triola said when she caught sight of me.

I glanced behind me. We went to the police academy together and we get along okay, but Jo doesn't usually offer up prayers of thanksgiving on making visual contact.

"What?" I said cautiously.

"You'd better go right in."

"Why?"

"Mooney's been asking for you every five minutes," she said.

"Maybe I'll leave," I said.

She took two long strides across the floor and rapped on his glass before I could stop her. He glanced up, startled, saw me and pushed back his chair.

The door opened.

"Carlotta, get in here."

"I hope you're feeling better," I said sweetly.

One of the men in the office popped out of his chair like a jack-in-the-box. He was wearing a pin-striped navy suit. A crisp white handkerchief peeped from his breast pocket. On his lap, he cradled a small round hat with a flipped-up brim. The other man rose more slowly. He wore wire-rimmed glasses, a brown suit.

If I'd known it was going to be formal, I'd have worn a suit, too.

"Sit down," Mooney ordered firmly, nodding me into a chair. "This is Mr. Kuh—"

"Kurundi, madame." The man who'd popped had a clipped, almost British accent, dark skin.

Mooney said, "Mr. Kurundi is a representative of the World Health Organization, and this is Mr. Wiley from the FDA."

"Food and Drug Administration," I said warily. "Hi. Carlotta Carlyle. Let me guess. You got a letter from a woman named Tina Sukhia."

Wiley said, "We should have been contacted immediately."

I shrugged, gestured at Mooney, said, "He was in the hospital. I was busy sitting on a killer."

Mr. Kurundi spoke in a high voice with a melodic lilt. "You read a letter which was intended for the World Health Organization."

"It hadn't been sent," I said. "I didn't exactly tamper with the mail."

His tone became more severe. "Nevertheless, once you read such a letter, we should have been informed with utmost speed."

"In Switzerland? What's going on here?" I asked.

"Exactly this," Wiley, the Food and Drug man said. "If the proper authorities had been activated at the proper time, we would now know the names of Renzel's suppliers, wholesalers, middle men, exporters. The whole bag."

"And Emily Woodrow would be dead," I pointed out. "Unless she was getting ready to stand trial for multiple murder. Sounds to me like your beef's with this Kurundi guy. Ask him what the hell he's been doing with the letter Tina Sukhia sent him months ago."

"Excuse me, madame," Kurundi said, fiddling with his hat, "but you did not read that letter. It was, shall I say, both a vague and confusing communication. Also, the World Health Organization is a large tree with many branches. Prompt action was indeed taken once Miss Sukhia's letter reached its correct destination. However, we began our investigation from the other end, you might say. We were grateful to Miss Sukhia for pointing us toward Cephamycin. We discovered it was, as she implied, arriving into several third-world countries in a contaminated form—"

"I'm sure she appreciates your gratitude," I said. Mooney fired me a warning glance.

"In conjunction with the Food and Drug Administration of your country, we were working with the Cephagen Company's president—"

"Menander? The guy who got shot?"

"Yes," Wiley admitted.

"I'm sure he appreciates your work as well," I said.

Mooney said, "Menander had noticed that his orders from JHHI had picked up considerably."

"So Renzel would have access to more packaging materials," I said. "While Muir and JHHI paid the bill."

"Renzel could counterfeit the drug at minimal cost," Mooney added, "but he couldn't counterfeit the holograms. When the World Health Organization started questioning Menander about unusual ordering practices—"

Kurundi interrupted. "Which we did because the packaging was so perfect, everything absolutely correct. We assumed the coun-

terfeit drug must have been coming directly from the Orlando manufacturing plant."

"Menander must have realized that JHHI's orders had more
than doubled," Mooney continued. "But he couldn't believe Helping Hand would have any truck with counterfeiters. He came up
here, figuring Muir must have a good explanation."

"And Renzel got to him first," I said. "Renzel had a hell of a
nerve. And Muir—I can't believe he didn't figure it out. Five deaths
in one day."

Mooney said, "He didn't want to figure it out, Carlotta. He
knew he had a problem; we've got that in his own writing, notes and
letters left in his desk. He was trying to hold off a scandal until a
bequest came through. He was expecting a twenty-million-dollar
legacy—"

"Why didn't he hide the medical records?" I asked Mooney.
"He did."
"No," I said. "Donovan got them."
"He hid them in plain sight," Mooney said. "Shunted them into
general records instead of bringing them up for review. He planned
to recall them, after the bequest—"

Mr. Kurundi interrupted again. "Madame, you perhaps do not
take this seriously enough. Counterfeiting of drugs is a major problem worldwide. In Africa, in Nigeria, more than a quarter of the
medicines on the market are not what they seem to be. Millions and
billions of dollars are involved. In Burma, men, women, and children believe they are taking good medicine to counter the effects of
malaria, and they die from it. Hundreds of them die."

Wiley broke in. "And now, what do we have? A minor operation closed, a tiny dent in an enormous machine. We could have
placed operatives inside this plant. We could have traced shipments
and made arrests up and down the chain of command."

"You've got Renzel," I said.
"He's not talking."
"Make a deal with him. Isn't that what you guys do? Offer him
a cushy cell in a country club jail."

307

"Maybe I should have said that he's talking," Wiley admitted slowly, "but he doesn't make a lot of sense."

"A team of psychiatrists could have a field day on that guy," Mooney offered.

"He tried to save the kids," I said, "the children at JHHI. He seemed genuinely grieved by their deaths."

Wiley said, "Self-interest. You don't shit in your own back-yard."

Kurundi looked so shocked at the FDA man's language that Wiley colored and apologized. To me.

"Renzel's reaction seemed like more than self-interest to me," I said. "He had some kind of moral code. Them and us. Black and white. The code got so twisted, it probably snapped."

"Him along with it," Mooney muttered.

Kurundi ran his fingers around his hat brim. "It seems," he said bitterly, "that the Sukhia woman was correct. I read your newspapers: An airplane crashes; no Americans are aboard, so all is well. You dump cigarettes on foreign markets. You dump waste products, some of them toxic, on any country so poor and debt-ridden they cannot refuse. You move slowly, cautiously, in this case, even though the suspect lab itself is located here—"

"Now wait a darn minute," the Food and Drug man said. "Most of the labs aren't here. This stuff mainly goes on in Turkey and Greece—"

Maybe I could get the two of them going and slink out the door. I stood, and they immediately ceased arguing.

"Mooney," I said, "why am I here?"

"These gentlemen are gonna try to suspend your PI license, Carlotta. Yank your ticket. They're gonna do their best."

"I don't believe this."

"Believe it."

"I had to move in a hurry, Mooney. You know that. Emily Woodrow would be dead if I hadn't—"

"Madame, you say it yourself," Kurundi observed. "You saved one life. We could have saved thousands of lives."

I counted to ten, counted to ten again. "Excuse me," I said. "What exactly would you have found out, in this perfect situation, if I hadn't acted so hastily?"

"We've told you."

"Repeat it, please."

"Renzel's suppliers."

"He used water. Arrest the water company. He probably used red food dye. Arrest whoever the hell makes food coloring for birthday cake frosting."

"Suppliers of machinery," Kurundi went on, "pharmaceutical bottling machinery. And especially, we would like to net the wholesaler, probably someone this man Renzel met at one of his international conferences. The wholesaler would then sell to a brokerage house. It's a vast network, a chain. You break it at one place, it starts up again. It's a huge industry, this counterfeiting, as bad, even more dangerous, than illegal drugs."

Illegal drugs. I could almost hear the puzzle pieces click in my mind. *Illegal drugs.*

"Carlotta?" Mooney said. "You okay?"

"I'm not the one got shot full of dope, Mooney."

"You looked funny for a minute."

"Mr. Kurundi," I said. "Mr. Wiley. If you were to get a lead to the next link in this chain, the wholesaler, would you consider ignoring the matter of my license? You probably have more important things to do than pick on me."

"What do you know, Carlotta?" Mooney said too quietly.

"Absolutely nothing, Mooney. Pleased to make your acquaintances, gentlemen."

"Carlotta—" Mooney said.

"Arrest me, or I'm gone," I said on my way out the door. Under my breath, I added, "I hope you have technicolor nightmares, Moon." He didn't hear me, or if he did, he ignored it.

44

"Professional pride, Patsy," I said insistently, "don't you have any?"

"Carlotta, look, I'm sorry I didn't get back to you with the woman's job history—"

"It's water under the bridge. But I want a little satisfaction here."

"Sounds like you want a freebie."

"This is right up your alley and I'm gonna sit on your phone till I get it, Patsy. Miami lawyer named Vandenburg. Thurman W. Vandenburg. I want to know if he's a defense attorney, and I want to know if he defends drug runners—"

"He's earning a living in Miami? Of course he does."

"In particular, a guy named Jaime Valdez Corroyo. I want to know if Valdez Corroyo's ever been arrested, if Vandenburg ever got him off. I want to know if Valdez Corroyo was tried alone or with anybody else."

"When can I—"

"Start punching names right now, Patsy. Time-and-a-half rates."

"Double?"

"No way."

I could hear her fingernails tapping the keys. I spelled Vandenburg and Valdez Corroyo, and within eight minutes she hit gold.

"Bingo," I said. "Send me the bill."

"Will do."

"While it's on your screen, read me Vandenburg's phone number, okay?"

The lawyer's secretary took my "absolutely urgent" at face

value. Thurman W. Vandenburg returned my call within six minutes.

"Get in touch with C.R.G.," I said, after giving my name and phone number. "Or I could call him Carlos. Have him call me. I'll be sitting by this phone for the next four hours—and if I don't hear from him, tell him I doubt he'll ever see his daughter."

That was bullshit, but I wanted a call fast.

"I don't understand you, miss."

"You don't have to understand. What you *do* have is a number to call on the 'Jaime Valdez Corroyo' business. Not Valdez Corroyo's real number. No point in phoning the state pen, huh? Do yourself a favor and call Carlos."

Vandenburg said nothing.

"Time is passing," I warned.

"I may have, uh, some little difficulty reaching this man you speak of," the lawyer said.

"That's life," I said.

I fidgeted around for a while, trying to organize my files. Gave that up, brought my National steel guitar downstairs, and started picking out old fiddle tunes, playing faster and faster until the fingerwork required total concentration. Usually music can fill my mind, empty it of everything but melody and harmony, bass line and chords.

I jumped when the phone rang half an hour later. Vandenburg again.

"The man we spoke of earlier cannot call you on your own line."

"Can he call me on somebody else's line?"

"I am not trying to amuse you. Is there a pay phone near your house?"

"Yes."

"Somewhere quiet?"

That would rule out any phone in Harvard Square. There was a booth in the back of a drugstore on Huron Avenue. "Yes."

"Go there now, call collect, and give me the number."

"Okay."

"I warn you. I'll check to see that it really is a pay phone."

"Hey, I'm not trying to set the guy up."

"Our friend is a cautious man."

"No kidding."

"He has business enemies."

"I'm not surprised."

We did the whole song and dance. I was relieved he didn't make me change pay phones until he found one he liked. At the drugstore, I bought a copy of the *Globe*, read a lengthy article about restructuring at the top at JHHI, and waited. Twenty, thirty, forty-five minutes went by. I studied the Op/Ed page, the funnies, Ann Landers, "Ask Beth." She advised a self-described "mature" ten-year-old to avoid attending sex parties with her best friend's father.

The phone rang. I grabbed the receiver, heard a hollow sound, a faint hum, a click.

"Señora?"

"Señorita, and I'd rather speak English."

"I can do that."

"Who am I speaking to?"

"The man you wish to speak to. We will avoid names, I think."

"Are you her father? Paol—my sister's father?"

"Let us say this: A woman you know well made a trip to my country last year, to beg an old man for money. She was accompanied by her daughter. Soon afterward the old man, my father, died. My father and I, we were not reconciled at the time of his death, you understand, but the housekeeper, an old and faithful friend, spoke to me of this visit."

"And you hired somebody to kidnap her, just in case she turned out to be your daughter? To check her out?"

"What is this?"

"What do you call it?"

"We speak at odds, señorita. I no longer understand you."

There was an echo after every phrase. Pauses made the conversation awkward. The man's voice was deep and smooth, heavily accented. It had both warmth and power. A caressing voice.

"The girl was encouraged to take a plane ride," I said.

He sounded puzzled. "Not on my orders," he said.

The trip could have been Paolina's idea. But Paco Sanchez had loaned her money, encouraged her, obtained a false passport for her, planned to accompany her.

"If you're telling the truth, you may have a problem, señor," I said. "In the future."

"I may have many problems in the future," he said evenly.

"In all innocence, your—my sister may have confided a secret to a man who would take advantage of it," I said slowly. Paco Sanchez had asked Paolina leading questions about herself. Most likely he'd learned of the connection to Roldan Gonzales. Figured a rich father would be willing to pay for his daughter's safety. Figured the chance to get in good with a big-time drug dealer would be worth the price of plane fare.

I went on. "If you should come in contact with a man named Paco Sanchez, a man who says he knows your daughter, and could arrange to bring your daughter to you—"

"It would not be advisable for her to visit," Roldan said. "I will speak to my attorney about this matter."

"Will you deal with Sanchez?"

"As it is necessary," he said in a tone that almost made me shiver. "Is that all?"

"No," I said quickly. "May I ask, why the need to find out about her? After all these years?"

There was a long pause and I wondered if the connection had been broken. The deep voice, when it spoke again, seemed uncertain. "I don't know. How do you say it? A whim of mine, perhaps. Maybe old age approaches. A child—she is part of me. My friend, the old housekeeper, said she looks very much like me."

"Then you must be a handsome man," I said. "Your daughter—my sister—this girl—is lovely."

He chuckled. It amazed me, this monster I'd read about, this killer. He chuckled.

"I know about you, señorita," he said.

"Yeah? What?"

"Many things I like. Some I dislike."

"Such as?"

"You are a divorced woman, and you sleep with a man whose father is not in a good line of work."

"Yeah. That's good, coming from you!"

"You don't know me," he said somberly.

"Oh, yeah, but you know me, right? You think you found out anything about me by hiring a thug too dumb to steal my trash without getting caught? Mister, if it's true that you know somebody by the caliber of people they hire, I'm wasting my time here, you're too dumb to help me."

I heard a sharp intake of breath, a long hollow pause, and then the chuckle again. This time it grew into a laugh.

"What is it you want, señorita?" he said. "Much as I might enjoy trading these insults, I cannot stay on the line."

"The connection isn't very good."

"I can hear you."

"Do you want her? With you?"

"No. She would be no good to me here. She would be someone my enemies could use against me. It would be dangerous for her. All I want is to know about her. To help her, if I can. I have money to send, for her education. Enough for anything she wants."

"You should talk to her mother."

"If I send money, it will be for the child alone."

"You could send it to me," I said into a long echoing pause.

"I hear the beginning of a bargain."

"You're a businessman."

"I can smell a deal," he said.

"Listen. I need to know something about your business. Or rather, a related business, and I can't find it out any other way. A small counterfeit drug company called Cee Co."

"Counterfeiters of regular medicines? That's a nasty business."

Nasty. Coming from someone like Carlos Roldan Gonzales. Nasty.

"Our two worlds don't often intersect," he said.

"My world doesn't intersect at all."

"Understand this, señorita. What I sell, people want to buy. I make no pretense about what I sell. I am not a thief or a murderer."

"I make no accusations," I said flatly. "I made a request. I asked a favor."

The silence stretched. I swallowed, remembered to breathe.

"I might be able to find out something," he said reluctantly. "But these are dirty people."

"I need a wholesaler of a fake chemotherapy drug called Cephamycin—a name, a place to start."

"Do you know in what country this person operates?"

"The drug enters Karachi. In Pakistan. That's all I know."

"Is this important to the girl, to Paolina?" It was the first time I'd heard him speak her name. He hesitated before he said it.

"If I get an answer I'll stay employed, so I'll be able to look after her a little."

He said, "I must go now."

"How will you—"

"The man from Miami will contact you."

"If I get no information, there'll be no money conduit to Paolina. Not through me."

"Will it trouble you? The origins of this money?"

"I'll have to think about it," I said. "It would bother me to tell Paolina she can't go to college."

"You have been saving money for her. This I know about you."

"Yes."

"But not enough."

"I'm working on it. She might not need your money."

"I would like to give it to her. It surprises me that I would."

"Why?"

"I'm a man of causes. I thought I would always only give my money to causes."

"Maybe you should keep on doing that."

"Why?"

"I like Paolina the way she is. I don't know how you bring up an heiress."

"Not as I was brought up, señorita." Across thousands of miles I heard a deep sigh. "That is all I can tell you."

The line went dead.

Señor Carlos Roldan Gonzales had hung up first.

4 5

"Ma nish-ta-nah ha-lai-lah ha-zeh mi-kol ha-lay-los?"
"Why is this night different from all other nights?"

At their best, my seders bear little resemblance even to my mother's radical gatherings, little resemblance to most seders at all. Haphazard is the word I'd use to describe them, and true to form, this year I was celebrating belatedly, having missed the traditional first-night and second-night observances. A small group assembled at my house on the eighth and final night, to eat, sing, and drink. I rarely miss the holiday altogether.

We each have our appointed tasks. Gloria makes potato kugel, a kind of enormous rectangular pancake, because she has a knack for greasy and fattening dishes. When she brings along one or more of her huge brothers, she makes multiple kugels. Roz buys enormous jars of gefilte fish at the supermarket, and white horseradish sharp enough to make your eyes water. She also brings men. Lemon's a regular.

This year, to my surprise and chagrin, Roz had invited the therapist-almost-next-door, Keith Donovan, evidently her latest conquest. Donovan's eyes met mine more than once during the evening, and I'm pleased to report that, on each occasion, he was the one who glanced away.

Ah, well, I thought philosophically, she's more his age. And he could continue his study of women comfortable with violence, even branch off into the behavior of women who wear strange T-shirts and shave their heads. Roz's shirt of the evening was hot pink and read: WILL WORK FOR SEX.

I make the chicken soup. From scratch. Its slow simmering

319

constitutes my major religious observance of the year. I have no recipe. No matter what quantity I make, there always seems to be enough. No matzoh balls ever remain in the pot. Sometimes I can almost feel my grandmother's hand guiding me as I add water, salt, and dill, debate the merit of a parsnip over a sweet potato.

I never met my grandmother, my mother's mother, the dispenser of Yiddish sayings.

Fish, kugel, soup, that's it. The entire menu. Chopped liver is traditional, but no one at my seders has a taste for liver except the cat, and T.C. shares his liver 'n' onions with no one.

At my mother's seders, fish, soup, matzoh balls, and kugel were all appetizers. The entrées—dried-out soup chicken, overcooked beef—were so anticlimactic no one ever ate them. So I forget about them. If anybody complains of hunger, we go to Herrell's for ice cream.

I skipped seders for years after my aunt Bea died, started them up hesitantly, almost secretively. I'm often the only Jew present.

Sam Gianelli brings good Italian wine. Mooney came once. His mother, who hates me, told him attending a seder was an occasion of sin.

Paolina attends. So do Marta and the boys. It's a time for families to be together.

I hadn't told Paolina anything about the phone call. I hadn't mentioned it to Marta either. Carlos Roldan Gonzales had come through with a single name and an address. I was off the hook with the WHO and the FDA, and Mooney now regarded me as a probable member of the underworld.

I'd have to deal with Roldan Gonzales's largesse, his guilt money, in some way. Some way that would satisfy the tax man. That would satisfy me.

Charities, maybe—with Paolina the major beneficiary.

Marta's smallest boy squirmed and wiggled when it came time for the youngest participant to ask the four questions, the set piece around which the Passover ritual revolves. Eventually Paolina read them, speaking hesitantly in her clear sweet voice.

" 'Why is this night different from all other nights?' " she began.

My *Haggadah,* the official rendition of the Passover story, gets pared down every year until it's more a distillation than a discussion. "Because on this night we celebrate the going forth of the Hebrew people. Because we were slaves and now we are free."

We take turns reading, in English, not Hebrew. Marta refuses to take part, embarrassed by her illiteracy. Sam reads in a rich deep baritone that reminds me oddly of Roldan Gonzales's voice.

Two days earlier, I'd gone to visit Emily Woodrow. In the waiting room, I'd met up with her husband, who'd beckoned me closer with a stiff and imperious gesture.

"I'm just leaving. Back to the office. I've been here for hours," he said. "She hardly talks."

I said nothing. I didn't know what he wanted to hear.

"I'm grateful to you," he muttered. "The police have mentioned your role."

Kind of them, I thought.

He went on. "What I'd—excuse me. My wife, have you told her about me?"

"I don't think she needs any additional burdens right now, Mr. Woodrow."

"I intend to stick by her through this, you know," he said.

How does he see himself? I wondered. What does he glimpse when he looks in the shaving mirror each morning? A hero forswearing his true love for an invalid spouse? A martyr?

"Well," he said lamely, glancing at his gold Rolex, "I have to go now."

"Are you planning legal action?" The words came out of my mouth. I hadn't planned to ask.

"Yes," he said. "I am. You may be called to testify."

"If your *wife* asks me to, I will."

I watched him as he waited impatiently for the elevator, wondering uncharitably if he'd come back to Emily for the imagined profits of the lawsuit.

I knocked on her door. No one answered. I entered slowly, in case she was asleep. The television in her private room was on, but she stared out the window at the parking lot below. Her hair was neatly parted and combed. The dark roots showed.

It seemed impossible that we'd met once, just once while she was conscious. I'd seen her through her husband's eyes, her therapist's eyes. I'd seen her through her photographs.

Her face looked puffy and swollen, her eyes bewildered. On the television screen Fred Astaire danced with Ginger Rogers, spinning her in widening circles.

She was fine, Emily murmured. Just fine. Was there ice water? Oh, yes, there was. How nice. Ice water.

A nurse described her as disoriented. The doctors weren't sure what she remembered, what she would remember.

She remembered that her daughter was dead.

At the seder table, I thumbed through my *Haggadah*. It's more than a story of slavery and freedom. It's a tale of God's wrath. There are dreadful events. Plagues.

I remember the plagues from my childhood seders as nothing more than a game. Stick your finger into your wine cup and splash a drop of sticky redness on the edge of your plate, one drop for each plague. Chant the unfamiliar, meaningless words:

Daam. Tz'far-day-a. Keeneem. O-rov. Dever. Sh'cheen. Ba-rad. Ar-beh. Cho-shech. Ma-kat B'cho-rot.

Don't suck the wine off your fingertip, Carlotta, my mother would say.

Why, Mama?

It's bad luck to taste a plague.

Ma-kat B'cho-rot. I know what it means now. The killing of the firstborn.

I know that killing is not the Passover message. I know we spill the wine to show that we cannot rejoice in full measure when our enemies have been so harshly treated.

But a single drop of wine for the killing of the firstborn? I turn the page quickly. My mouth will not shape the words: *Ma-kat B'cho-rot.*

I remember Emily, what she said to me, glancing up suddenly. I'm not sure she recognized me or knew who I was.

"It's just—I don't know. I think I'm dying." Her voice was still rough, her tone flat, unexpressive.

"That's not what I heard. The doctors say you're going home soon," I said.

She murmured on. I had to bend low to hear her words. "No. It's not—it's that I don't know how to keep going. I kept on all this time, because I thought I'd find out what happened and then I'd—I don't know—that it would change things. That if I found out how she died, I'd see things differently. That if someone had to pay for her death, if someone else had to die even, it would make it easier."

"But it isn't?"

"It doesn't make anything different. It doesn't make anything easier. They gave me drugs—Renzel, I think I remember, he gave them to me—and there are things I forget. He made me forget. I'd hallucinate. I thought she was alive. He should have wiped my memory clean. I remember the wrong things. I forget the wrong things. He should have killed me and let that other woman live. She was young, you know. Tina. A beautiful woman. Young. She could have had children."

"You can still have a life, Mrs. Woodrow."

"It's like you read about people who've lost limbs, an arm or a leg, and they still feel pain in them."

"Phantom pain," I said.

Fred Astaire and Ginger Rogers pirouetted and bowed.

"Yes," she said. "I have a phantom daughter."

On this night that is different from all other nights, I wish I could tell the story of the coming out from Egypt to Emily Woodrow, tell it the only way I can understand it.

"It's April, Mrs. Woodrow . . . Emily," I would say. "I don't know if you're a religious woman. I'm not. But I was raised a Jew, and April is when Jews celebrate the Passover. It was always a hard holiday for me as a kid, and it hasn't gotten easier. Do you know the story?

"I'm going to explain this badly," I'd say. "I'm no rabbi. But this is the part that always gets to me. God punishes the Egyptians for enslaving the Israelites, and not obeying the word of God. There are ten punishments, ten plagues: blood, frogs, gnats, flies, cattle disease, boils, hail, locusts, darkness—and the last plague is the slaying of the firstborn."

"God does that?" she might ask.

"The God of my fathers," I'd admit. "But first this God tells all the Hebrews to put a mark on their front doors—lamb's blood—so the Angel of Death will pass over their houses. Passover."

I see her in my mind's eye, turning her face to the wall.

"I think about it," I would say, "especially in April. And I think sometimes that if God had told the mothers, it might have turned out differently. They might have acted the way you did. Because you did it, Emily. You defeated the Angel of Death. You marked the doors with the blood of the lamb. Strangers' doors, the doors of Egyptians and Nigerians and Pakistanis. You made the Angel of Death pass over their houses. You saved their children, the children of strangers."

"It doesn't help," she would say faintly.

"Maybe someday it will."

"Carlotta," Paolina said. "You're not listening."

"Sorry."

"Can I have wine? Please? A little?"

"If your mother says okay, you can taste the wine. Taste."

Marta, her arthritis under temporary medical control, smiled broadly and poured a thimbleful of Barolo into a stemmed glass. I stared at my little sister, a girl in search of a father, and saw Emily Woodrow, a mother in search of a daughter.

"Carlotta?" Sam said. "More wine?"

"Yeah," I answered, my voice sounding too loud in my ears. "Is it the fourth cup yet?"

"Way past the fourth."

"Good."

When I heard the rumbling outside, I thought it was distant thunder. It grew louder, gave a curious squeak. At the first crash, I was on my feet.

What with all the shouts and questions, the delay while I found my keys, I got outside just in time to see a car's taillights disappear around the corner.

I'd run straight down to the sidewalk, over the grass. I almost tripped over them heading up the walk.

"What?" Sam called to me from the stoop.

It took me a while to answer. I was laughing.

"What is it?"

"The trash cans, Sam," I said. "They came home."

Start Reading

The 100 Best Business Books of All Time

The
100 Best Business

Books of All Time

What They Say, Why They Matter, and How They Can Help You

JACK COVERT AND TODD SATTERSTEN

PORTFOLIO

PORTFOLIO
Published by the Penguin Group
Penguin Group (USA) Inc., 375 Hudson Street, New York, New York 10014, U.S.A.
Penguin Group (Canada), 90 Eglinton Avenue East, Suite 700, Toronto, Ontario,
Canada M4P 2Y3 (a division of Pearson Penguin Canada Inc.)
Penguin Books Ltd, 80 Strand, London WC2R 0RL, England
Penguin Ireland, 25 St. Stephen's Green, Dublin 2, Ireland (a division of Penguin Books Ltd)
Penguin Books Australia Ltd, 250 Camberwell Road, Camberwell, Victoria 3124, Australia
(a division of Pearson Australia Group Pty Ltd)
Penguin Books India Pvt Ltd, 11 Community Centre, Panchsheel Park,
New Delhi – 110 017, India
Penguin Group (NZ), 67 Apollo Drive, Rosedale, North Shore 0632, New Zealand
(a division of Pearson New Zealand Ltd)
Penguin Books (South Africa) (Pty) Ltd, 24 Sturdee Avenue,
Rosebank, Johannesburg 2196, South Africa

Penguin Books Ltd, Registered Offices: 80 Strand, London WC2R 0RL, England

First published in 2009 by Portfolio, a member of Penguin Group (USA) Inc.

10 9 8 7 6 5 4 3 2 1

Copyright © Jack Covert and Todd Sattersten, 2009
All rights reserved

Pages 337–339 constitute an extension of this copyright page.

LIBRARY OF CONGRESS CATALOGING IN PUBLICATION DATA
Covert, Jack.
    The 100 best business books of all time : what they say, why they matter, and how they can
help you / by Jack Covert and Todd Sattersten.
        p.   cm.
    Includes bibliographical references and index.
    ISBN 978-1-59184-240-8
1. Business—Bibliography. 2. Management—Bibliography. 3. Businesspersons—Books and
reading—United States. 4. Executives—Books and reading—United States. 5. Best books—
United States. I. Sattersten, Todd. II. Title. III. Title: One hundred best business books of
all time : what they say, why they matter, and how they can help you.
    Z7164.C81C85 2009
    [HF1008]
    016.65—dc22   2008036664

Printed in the United States of America
Designed by Joy Panos Stauber

I dedicate this book to A. David Schwartz, who saw something in me that I didn't, and who is either really proud or is rolling over in his grave. Either way, thanks!

Jack Covert

To Eric and Sue Sattersten—For your love and support from the very beginning.

Todd Sattersten

The 100 Best Business Books of All Time

11,000. That was the number of business books published in the United States in 2007. Placed one on top of another, the stack would stand as tall as a nine-story building. And the 880 million words in that nine-story pile would take six and a half years to read. Locked somewhere in this tower of paper is the solution to your current business problem.

In fact, a book publisher recently shared research with us that showed the number one reason people buy business books is to find solutions to problems. Sitting at the educational crossroads of "I know nothing about this" and "Let's hire a consultant," good business books contain a high-value proposition for twenty dollars and two hours of your attention.

But it is more than that. Business books can change you, if you let them. *The Lexus and the Olive Tree* will lead you to a paradigm shift from local to global. *Now, Discover Your Strengths* quizzes you, then encourages an exploration of your talents, not your weaknesses. And *Moneyball* shows that any industry is ripe for reinvention.

It is difficult to find those gems, though. The endless stream of new books requires a filter to help discern the good and the better from the absolute best. The solution to *that* problem is this book, *The 100 Best Business Books of All Time*.

Recommending the best in business books is in our company's DNA. In the early days of 800-CEO-READ, Jack manually compiled a new acquisitions list every week to keep customers informed of the latest releases. This weekly list evolved into a set of monthly reviews called "Jack Covert Selects." When Todd joined the company in 2004, the recommendations were further expanded to include a daily weblog, a semiweekly podcast, and the monthly publication of essays on ChangeThis (change this.com). The latest additions are the annual 800-CEO-READ Business Book Awards and the publication *In the Books*, both of which highlight the best of the year in business books.

After sifting through "the new and the now" of business books for a quarter-century, we decided it was time to bring together the books that are most deserving of your attention.

OF ALL TIME?

Our choices for the one hundred best business books of all time will certainly find detractors. So early on we want to make clear our criteria for selecting these books. First, the most important criterion was the quality of the idea. Recognizing that judgment of quality is subjective, we found the only route to choosing the best was to ask of each book the same set of questions: Is the author making a good argument? Is there something new to what he or she is presenting? Does the idea align or contradict with what we intrinsically know about business? Can we use this idea to make our business better? After asking these questions of thousands of books, we found ample candidates. However, a good idea was not the only consideration in selecting the *100 Best*.

The second factor in choosing these books was the applicability of the idea for someone working in business today. We dismissed books that described dated theories that have since been replaced or those containing anecdotes for success about companies that no longer exist. For example, Frederick Taylor's turn-of-the-century view that laborers were merely replaceable cogs in some organizational machine has been largely replaced by a more humanistic view that individuals bring the diversity of their strengths to the work they do. The selections in our book represent a more contemporary (and thus, more applicable) point of view and in this way diverge from other "best of" lists.

Finally, the books needed to be accessible. A good idea is indecipherable when conveyed using cryptic language, and worthwhile messages get lost when surrounded by pointless filler. For all the love we have for Adam Smith, we didn't select *The Wealth of Nations* and its nine hundred-plus pages because of the sheer magnitude of the undertaking. We suggest Geoffrey Moore's *Crossing the Chasm* as a more accessible substitute for Everett Rogers's *Diffusion of Innovations*. In this sense, we champion the reader's need for clear access to whatever idea the author is selling.

HOW TO USE THE BOOK

This book contains twelve sections, organized by category. We start with the most important subject of all: you. Then, leadership, strategy, and sales and marketing follow. We include a short section on rules and scorekeeping, after which you'll find sections devoted to management, biographies, and entrepreneurship. We close with narratives and books on innovation and creativity and big ideas.

We leave you with a section called Takeaways. Constructed differently from the others, this part gives you a quick look into the world of business. All of these books serve as proof that business books can provide value for even the busiest person.

In the reviews themselves, we aimed to stay true to the promise of our subtitle, "What They Say, Why They Matter, and How They Can Help You." This was an ambitious task in the 500 to 1,000 words we allotted for each book, but the effort resulted in reviews that are an amalgamation of a summary of the book, our own stories, the context for the ideas presented by the authors, and our take on how the book might best be used. Since we divided the task of reviewing the books, we've identified the reviewer (Jack or Todd) at the beginning of each entry.

We were as careful with the design of this book as we were with the selection of the books included. We drew on a wide variety of inspirations to create the layout that makes it something different. The browse-friendly style of magazines inspired our use of highlighted quotes, large headings, and rich illustrations. We mimicked the Choose Your Own Adventure children's book series by giving readers the opportunity to choose their own path through the listings. And finally, scattered throughout *The 100 Best* are sidebars that stand independent from the reviews, taking the reader beyond business books, suggesting movies, novels, and even children's books that offer equally relevant insights.

We truly hope you enjoy the book and use it to find solutions to your business problems. We'd love to hear whether you agree or disagree with our choices, and of any successes that resulted from reading one of the recommended books. Jack is available at jack@800ceoread.com, and Todd is at todd@800ceoread.com. You can also find more material online at 100bestbiz.com.

YOU Yes, you! How about spending some time on you for once?

You have things to do.

You have some habits to break and some new ones to form.

You have a life you want to live.

You need to start by reading this chapter.

Flow

MIHALY CSIKSZENTMIHALYI

Reviewed by Jack

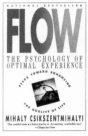

T he pursuit of happiness has been contemplated by many thinkers over the ages, from Aristotle to Thomas Jefferson to Viktor Frankl, and the conversation continues today. No matter how much society has evolved in physical comforts or cultural achievements, happiness remains elusive. We talk about it, we write books about it, and yet we barely recognize it.

But we have all experienced it. Happiness comes in those moments of effortless concentration when minutes, even hours, seem to pass without so much as a glance at the clock. It's the point guard unconsciously dropping three-pointers in the big game. It's the writer sitting at her keyboard while the story writes itself. In those moments, we have experienced what Mihaly Csikszentmihalyi calls *flow*, when we are totally focused and completely un-self-conscious. This achievement of flow captures that longed-for state of happiness.

These moments appear to us as fleeting and unpredictable, though Csikszentmihalyi's research shows otherwise. Certain pursuits and activities lend themselves to reaching a state of flow. Csikszentmihalyi describes the common characteristics of these activities as including "a sense that one's skills are adequate to cope with the challenges at hand, in a goal-directed, rule-bound action system that provides clear clues as to how well one is performing." Games, in the broadest sense of the word, contain those elements. Rules provide boundaries. Practice builds skills. And scoring systems offer immediate feedback on your performance.

If jobs were constructed like games, Csikszentmihalyi posits, flow would be reached more often at work. He offers surgeons as an example of workers who reliably achieve flow. A surgeon's goal is clear: fix what is broken. The feedback is immediate and continual: check heartbeat monitor. The intense challenge is recurring, though no surgery is the same. The operating room itself is designed to block out distractions. And because the risk is so great, a surgeon is in a state of concentration "so intense that there is no attention left over to think about anything irrelevant, or to worry about problems. Self-consciousness disappears, and the sense of time becomes distorted." All of these features create an emotional rush for a surgeon. The only time a surgeon loses that level of engagement is when he or she gets into a position of rote repetition and the game becomes predictable.

Flow is "the state in which people are so involved in an activity that nothing else seems to matter; the experience itself is so enjoyable that people will do it even at great cost, for the sheer sake of doing it."

The premise of this book is based on an experience we have all had: those precious moments when time flies and we find we have accomplished a great deal. I have included *Flow* here at the beginning of this section as a starting point, a broad discussion about our mental approach to accomplishing tasks. But the significance of these optimal experiences extends beyond productivity and lies in their ability to provide us with periods of happiness. I *know* the feeling of flow, the kind of high it gives, and as with all good things, I want to learn how to tap into that feeling more often. There seems to be no more worthwhile endeavor. **JC**

Flow: The Psychology of Optimal Experience, Harper Perennial, Paperback 1991, ISBN 9780060920432

WHERE TO NEXT? ↠ Page 279 for **the art of possibility** ↠ Page 50 for **the art of leadership** ↠ Page 295 for **the art of self-awareness** | EVEN MORE: *Man's Search for Meaning* by Viktor E. Frankl; *The Pursuit of Happiness* by David G. Myers; *Group Genius* by Keith Sawyer

Getting Things Done

DAVID ALLEN
Reviewed by Todd

Most efforts to get organized fail. Even given one's diligent use of a FranklinCovey planner or PDA, tasks change hourly based on priorities of the corporate moment. Calendars capture but a fraction of our total responsibilities, and simple to-do lists prove, as author David Allen puts it, "inadequate to deal with the volume and variable nature of the average professional's workload."

In *Getting Things Done*, Allen suggests productivity comes from a quiet state of mental being. Distractions easily disrupt conscious thought. Poorly defined to-do's force the brain into repeating loops of infinite alternatives. *Getting Things Done* shifts the focus from the commonly defined problems of time, information, and priorities, to action with a capital A. By defining and managing actions, ambiguous tasks are turned into clear next steps. And once those actions are captured using a reliable system, the mental noise clears, allowing space for more substantive thought.

"The big problem is that your mind keeps reminding you of things when you can't *do* anything about them."

Allen introduces a "workflow method" made up of five distinct stages. Everything that commands attention—unread e-mails, a pile of magazines, the never-ending list of household projects—is collected and processed, and decisions are made about subsequent actions. The results are organized into lists, calendars, or projects. The overall flow is reviewed weekly, allowing a wide-angle view of the progress. The final step is doing: writing the e-mail, returning the call, buying the groceries. As Allen

THE FIVE STAGES OF
MANAGING WORKFLOW

We . . .

1. *collect* things that command our attention
2. *process* what they mean and what to do about them
3. *organize* the results
4. *review* as options for what we choose to . . .
5. *do*

says, despite most people's declaration that there is just not enough time in the day, time is not the issue; clarifying the actions needed is where people fall down.

The modularity of Allen's system makes it attractive to all people looking to be more productive. While the highest possible Getting Things Done mind-set is achieved with devotion to all five interlocking steps, adopting a single discipline or stand-alone technique can bring measurable benefit. For example, Allen suggests using a tickler folder to hold items that can be dealt with at a later date. I recently took his advice and started an electronic tickler folder (as opposed to the physical folder system he recommends), and I'm happy to report that the simple benefit of a reliable system for follow-up calls and forthcoming business books clears a perceivable portion of my personal RAM.

To say *Getting Things Done* has a following would be an understatement. Programmers and technology enthusiasts were early adopters, attracted to its simple but methodical approach to eliminating mental clutter. These same individuals tested and experimented with the most effective use of software, often writing their own code to create a solution that best fit their unique needs. Several dozen stand-alone applications have been brought to market, as well as supplements for industry standards like Microsoft Outlook. New *Getting Things Done* converts can do a simple Google search to discover forums, blog posts, and vendors of all sizes to help with their organizational metamorphoses.

High-level athletes train for years to perfect the smallest aspects of their performance. Allen is suggesting the same in *Getting Things Done*. Mental loose ends and overflowing in-boxes sap our ability to perform. By implementing processes and focusing on action, businesspeople share with athletes the same benefits of a clear mind and forward momentum. TS

Getting Things Done: The Art of Stress-Free Productivity, Penguin Books, Paperback 2001, ISBN 9780142000281

WHERE TO NEXT? ➤ Page 18 for **personal effectiveness** ➤ Page 313 for **early effectiveness** ➤ Page 91 for **organizational effectiveness** | EVEN MORE: *Ready for Anything* by David Allen; *Mind Hacks* by Tom Stafford and Matt Webb; *Lifehacker* by Gina Trapani

Jack Covert Selects

Karen Sherlock, Milwaukee Journal Sentinel, 1995

"Jack Covert Selects" book reviews morphed out of a memo I produced each week in the late 1980s called the "New Acquisitions List." Every Saturday I typed up the new book titles (yup, on a typewriter) from that week along with twenty-five to fifty words directly from the books' flyleaf copy. I would then mail the list to my customers, mainly corporate librarians and the rare dedicated business-book reader. This piece filled an information void until Amazon arrived in 1995 and made reviews on specific genres, like business books, more readily available. My customers also changed during that time; corporate purchasing began to go the way of the woolly mammoth due to easy access to new information through the Internet.

For the new millennium, David Schwartz, my mentor and owner of the Harry W. Schwartz Bookshops, from which 800-CEO-READ originated, suggested that we grow the "New Acquisitions List" into a monthly review of recommended books—reviews that would consist of *my* words, not those of the publishers. The reviews would continue the conversation with our customers about good books while differentiating our suggested titles from the information available online. "Jack Covert Selects" was our first step toward branding our company as the arbiter of good business books. My reviews have become a cornerstone of the wide range of information products we offer to all avid business book readers.

Through the years, we have reviewed over 350 books. Eighteen titles featured in this book were originally featured in "Jack Covert Selects."
Written by Jack Covert

The Effective Executive

PETER F. DRUCKER
Reviewed by Todd

Peter Drucker's theories and arguments always start at the most basic level, assuming little or no previous knowledge of a topic on the part of the reader. The premise of *The Effective Executive* is no different. Drucker starts by asking: if the ultimate measurement of manual labor is efficiency, what is the corollary measurement for knowledge workers? Drucker argues that rather than *doing things right*, knowledge workers must strive for effectiveness by *doing the right things*. This powerful insight into how individuals need to work led to this book's inclusion in *The 100 Best*.

"Nothing else, perhaps, distinguishes effective executives as much as their tender loving care of time," Drucker begins. In his classic style of driving to the core of an issue, Drucker quotes studies that show how humans have a poor perception of time and are worse at remembering how they spend their time. Because the typical executive is at the mercy of those he serves, the issue of time becomes more acute. Drucker suggests keeping a log, and if more than one-half of an executive's time is being dictated by others, it is time to wrestle back control. Three common time sponges that need to be considered include: doing things that don't need to be done, doing things that could be better done by others, and doing things that require others to do unnecessary things.

Effective executives use the strengths of individuals in an organization. Drucker talks about the importance of strengths in this book, almost thirty-five years before Gallup's popular theory was discussed in *Now, Discover Your Strengths*. In leveraging extraordinary strengths, however, you must also put up with weaknesses. Drucker has no qualms about hiring the prima donnas and geniuses, saying any managerial discomfort is simply a part of the deal. Contribution is the only measurement of success that matters.

To that point, Drucker spends a whole chapter on contribution, asserting that this type of measurement provides focus for the effective execu-tive. At the organizational level, an eye on contribution shifts attention from downward and inward to upward and outward, toward clients, cus-tomers, and constituents. "To ask, 'What can I contribute?' is to look at the unused potential in the job," Drucker writes. He believes that com-munication, teamwork, self-improvement, and development of others all become natural extensions of contribution.

Contribution itself comes only with concentration. Drucker felt this was the one true secret to effectiveness, and his statement, "Effective ex-ecutives do first things first and they do one thing at a time," foreshadows the rise of David Allen's *Getting Things Done* philosophy. With a focus on singular activity, executives ask important questions about abandoning often benign initiatives and programs, especially ones that have never met expectations. Leaving the past is central to progress. The very nature of an executive's job is to make decisions about committing resources to the possibilities of tomorrow.

"Effectiveness is, after all, not a 'subject,' but a self-discipline."

Decision making is Drucker's final practice of effectiveness. Effective executives solve problems once. They look at problems as generic to be-gin with, and try to solve them with rules that will be simple and easy to follow for everyone, not just those involved in the current issue. Decision makers also understand that doing nothing is an acceptable option as well. Effective executives know that a decision is not complete until it is put into action. Simple solutions that everyone in the organiza-tion can understand improve the likelihood of their adoption. We hear echoes of Bossidy and Charan's *Execution* here as Drucker emphasizes the idea that a decision is merely intent if it is not a part of someone's responsibilities.

Time. Strengths. Contribution. Concentration. Decision making. Each of these subjects has been covered in myriad works since Drucker first addressed them in *The Effective Executive*, but his book stands alone as an indispensable handbook for the leader, covering the topics at just the right level of detail and from just the right perspective to enable action.

The book can serve as both a starting point for the novice and a firm reminder for the experienced that our labor is not about doing things, but rather doing the right things. ᴛs

The Effective Executive: The Definitive Guide to Getting the Right Things Done, HarperCollins, Paperback 2006, ISBN 9780060833459

WHERE TO NEXT? ▸ Page 177 for **building strengths** ◂ Page 9 for **narrowing your focus** ▸ Page 91 for **turning decisions into actions** | EVEN MORE: *Managing for Results* by Peter F. Drucker; "What Makes an Effective Executive" by Peter F. Drucker, *Harvard Business Review* in June 2004 (also included as the introduction to the 2006 edition of *The Effective Executive*)

How to Be a Star at Work

ROBERT E. KELLEY
Reviewed by Jack

To excel in business you need to rise above your peers and be noticed for all the right reasons. *How to Be a Star at Work* is the book that will show you how to accomplish that feat without selling your soul to the god of hubris.

The core concepts of this book revolve around research compiled from Bell Labs during the mid-1980s and after the breakup of "Ma Bell." For twenty-four months, Robert E. Kelley and his team worked as consultants to management at Bell Labs to discover what separates a star performer from all the rest. First, they surveyed senior and middle managers, asking what they thought was the difference between star performers and average performers. The managerial responses were what you would expect: stars would be smarter, better problem solvers, more driven, more outgoing, and greater risk takers. The company then gave multiple tests to a number of stars and average performers. The results were surprising. The researchers found no measurable difference. For Bell, this was a good news/bad news situation. It was bad news in that there wasn't one trait management could look for to provide a shortcut to finding stars. The good news was the realization that all employees can be shown the elements needed to become stars and then escorted down that path by aware managers.

Kelley presents nine strategies one can learn to reach "star-hood." One of the nine points he delineates is "Organizational Savvy":

> What average performers think it is: The talent for brownnosing and schmoozing in the workplace to help me get noticed by the right people. What star producers know it to be: A work strategy that enables me to navigate the competing interests in an organization, to promote cooperation, address conflicts, and get things done.

To help readers gain organizational savvy, Kelley offers a six-step approach that is wholly doable: find a mentor; understand the "real" organizational chart, not the one in the annual report; master relationship building; learn to manage conflict; create a niche; develop credibility.

Another of Kelley's strategies is "Initiative," which he describes as: "Blazing Trails in the Organization's White Spaces." Kelley gives examples of people who have taken initiative with some amazing results. He tells about a state bureaucrat who was afraid of losing her job during a potential downsizing within her department. In an effort to establish her value to the organization, she took all the Medicare and federal funding manuals home to study and found an accounting "wrinkle" between the way the state and the Feds calculated hospital costs and income. As a result, the state was getting much less from the federal government than was deserved. In the end, the state got a check for $4.89 million and our bureaucrat kept her job. Kelley believes that stars show initiative when they: "Seek out responsibility above and beyond the expected job description," "Undertake extra efforts for the benefit of coworkers or the larger group," "Stick tenaciously to an idea or project and follow it through to successful implementation," and "Willingly assume some personal risk in taking on new responsibilities." In the author's research, 60 to 80 percent of average performers in the workforce don't have inherent initiative and are resistant to the extra effort because they view it as doing somebody else's work.

"Stars are made, not born."

Interestingly, Kelley's research helped some groups succeed even more, the details of which he added in a chapter in the revised paperback edition. For instance, he discovered that women and minorities sometimes had difficulty with three of the strategies—initiative, networking, and teamwork—due to a history of discrimination in the workplace. While Kelley found that, generally, when all employees incorporated the star strategy into their day-to-day routine the company's productivity rate increased an average of 100 percent, he also discovered that when women and minorities incorporated this strategy, productivity rates rose to over 400 percent.

Kelly clearly comes down on the nurture side of the nature-versus-nurture debate, concluding that performance can be nurtured even in large organizations. That speaks well enough for the effectiveness of the strategies in this book. *How to Be a Star at Work* is a practical book needed by both employees and employers to move to the next level. **JC**

How to Be a Star at Work: 9 Breakthrough Strategies You Need to Succeed, Three Rivers Press, Paperback 1999, ISBN 9780812931693

WHERE TO NEXT? » Page 317 for **what the boss expects** » Page 121 for **how to network better** » Page 198 for **how people are programmed** | EVEN MORE: *Sink or Swim* by Milo Sindell and Thuy Sindell; *You're in Charge, Now What?* by Thomas J. Neff and James M. Citrin; *Know-How* by Ram Charan

The 7 Habits of Highly Effective People

STEPHEN R. COVEY
Reviewed by Todd

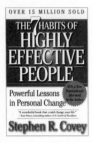

The 7 Habits of Highly Effective People is the outcome of Stephen Covey's doctoral research into personal development literature. He studied two hundred years' worth of self-help, popular psychology, and self-improvement writings, and identified two distinct philosophies of self-improvement. The first is what we identify with principles found in the works of early-American visionaries like Benjamin Franklin: principles such as integrity, industry, humility, and simplicity. Covey calls this the "Character Ethic," and it was the dominant philosophy in American success literature until the early twentieth century. But Covey found the literature changed significantly after World War I, with a shift in emphasis from quality of character to improvement of personality, behavior, and attitude: the Personality Ethic. He takes aim at books, though not by name, like *How to Win Friends and Influence People*, *Think and Grow Rich*, and *The Power of Positive Thinking*, saying at best these books focus on secondary traits and at worst teach deception using a quick-fix mentality.

Covey divides the first six habits equally between habits of private victory and habits of public victory. The first private habit, "Be Proactive," describes the freedom of choice one has between stimulus and response, between loss of a job and loss of self-worth. The initiative to learn a new skill is a simple incarnation of "Let's look at the alternatives" versus "There's nothing I can do."

> **"Management is efficiency in climbing the ladder of success; leadership determines whether the ladder is leaning against the right wall."**

Then, his second habit, "Begin with the End in Mind," encourages the use of imagination to envision a set of creative choices about the future, the same energies employed in leadership. Covey advocates the development of personal mission statements to codify the varying roles and responsibilities of home, work, and community. "Put First Things First" takes that newly defined identity derived from the mission statements and matches up tasks and priorities to ensure alignment. When Covey asked readers which habit was the most difficult to adopt, this management process ranked number one, and he wrote another book, *First Things First*, to further explore the challenges.

THE SEVEN HABITS

1. Be Proactive
2. Begin with the End in Mind
3. Put First Things First
4. Think Win/Win
5. Seek First to Understand . . . Then to Be Understood
6. Synergize
7. Sharpen the Saw

"Self-mastery and self-discipline are the foundation of good relationships with others," Covey writes, and then moves forward with his three public habits: "Think Win/Win," "Seek First to Understand . . . Then to Be Understood," and "Synergize." All are based on relationships. "Think Win/Win" is interpersonal leadership that creates mutual benefits for all parties. The classic negotiation book *Getting to Yes* uses the same philosophy, calling for individuals to use an abundance mentality in their interactions and look past the confining paradigm of the zero-sum game.

Being a good listener is a skill that is helpful in any relationship and sits at the core of "Seek First to Understand . . . Then to Be Understood." When someone is speaking to us, our natural response is to listen autobiographically: agreeing or disagreeing, asking questions from our point of view, giving advice based on our own experiences, trying to figure out what is making someone feel the way they do based on how we would react. Covey spends much of the chapter on an extended example of a conversation between a disillusioned son and well-intentioned father. Covey replays the conversation a number of times showing how ineffective listening with our biases can be. When listening, the author writes, *"rephrase the content and reflect the feeling."* Then he shows how the conversation completely changes. The second half of the discussion of this habit is about presenting ideas, and Covey returns to Aristotle's rhetorical philosophy of *ethos* (character), *pathos* (emotion), and *logos* (logic).

"Synergize" encapsulates the entire Seven Habits process. When people join together, the whole is greater than the sum of the parts, and greater insights and previously unseen results are achieved. Covey suggests synergy is the third alternative to "my way or the wrong way." All relationships grow when trust and cooperation grow.

The seventh habit, "Sharpen the Saw," returns to the individual but "will renew the first six and will make you truly independent and capable of effective interdependence." Covey believes we all have four dimensions that need continual renewal: the physical, the mental, the spiritual, and the social/emotional. He suggests spending an hour working on the first three every day. Find time for a cardiovascular workout. Read the classics. Keep a journal. Meditate or pray. It is only through recharging that we have the energies to succeed in the other aspects of our lives. **TS**

The 7 Habits of Highly Effective People: Powerful Lessons in Personal Change, Free Press, Paperback 2004, ISBN 9780743269513

WHERE TO NEXT? ▸ Page 21 for **the philosophy Covey takes to task** ▸ Page 295 for **more on empathic listening** ▸ Page 36 for **keeping the end in mind** | EVEN MORE: *Man's Search for Meaning* by Viktor E. Frankl; *First Things First* by Stephen R. Covey; *Eat That Frog!* by Brian Tracy

How to Win Friends and Influence People

DALE CARNEGIE

Reviewed by Todd

"Hello, 800-CEO-READ. This is Meg. How can I help you?"

"This is Jane Doe from Any Company. My order hasn't arrived and I needed it today."

This is the call every service company hates to get. The customer didn't get what they needed and now there is a relationship to fix. It is the same as being late for dinner when your spouse cooks your favorite dish: an expectation was not met and someone's feelings are now hurt. Whether you are a customer service representative, a division president, or a loving spouse, a set of skills is needed to mend the emotional break and maximize the potential in every relationship.

How to Win Friends & Influence People is often touted as *the* text for the hard-core personal development crowd. The title itself implies backslapping, sweaty handshakes, and always a friendly word for a new networking acquaintance. As a result, many readers react instinctively with skepticism to Carnegie's message. Even Carnegie admits that after relating a story of complimenting a post office clerk on his fine head of hair, the listener asked him, "What did you want to get out of him?" Yet Carnegie refutes such a cynical interpretation and quotes psychologist Alfred Adler to convey the lens through which the book must be read: "It is the individual who is not interested in his fellow men who has the greatest difficulties in life and provides the greatest injury to others. It is from among such individuals that all human failures spring."

When complimenting the man at the post office, Carnegie was obeying what he believes to be the most important law of human contact: always make the other person feel important. "Please," "Thank you," and "Would you mind . . . ?" are simple extensions of the precept. "Make the other person feel important . . ." is the common wisdom, but how Carnegie ends the statement frames the whole book: ". . . and do it sincerely."

Carnegie divides the book into four main sections. In the first section, he explains the three main tenets of relating to people. Next, he takes six short chapters to describe how to make people like you. In the third section, he shows how to win people to your way of thinking with twelve principles. And in the final section, Carnegie takes on the topic of leadership, with headings like "Talk about Your Own Mistakes First" and "Give a Dog a Good Name."

"Always make the other person feel important."

Regardless of whether you are dealing with a missed shipment or a missed dinner date, Carnegie provides several tools to smooth the stormy waters. Start by using the person's name and state how sorry you are for the misstep. Admit the mistake and let the crossed individual air his or her grievances. And—the final token of sincerity—say, "I don't blame you one iota for feeling as you do. If I were you I would undoubtedly feel just as you do."

Over seventy years and fifteen million copies later, people are still reading *How to Win Friends and Influence People* because there are simple truths found throughout Carnegie's book. Over time his principles have been criticized with claims that the anecdotes are too dated for the new century, but, truly, the book delivers the ever-needed reminder that all we have are the relationships with those around us, and there is always a better way to manage those relationships. **TS**

How to Win Friends and Influence People, Pocket Books, Paperback Special Anniversary Edition 1998, ISBN 9780671027032

WHERE TO NEXT? ◀ Page 18 for **Covey's rebuke of Carnegie** ▶ Page 193 to read about one of **Carnegie's examples** ▶ Page 200 to **see our list of classics** | EVEN MORE: *Think and Grow Rich* by Napoleon Hill and Arthur Pell; *The Power of Positive Thinking* by Norman Vincent Peale

GLOBALIZATION OF MANNERS

In 1990, Roger Axtell wrote *Do's and Taboos Around the World,* the best-selling guide to international behavior, inspired by the experiences of more than 500 international travelers. Today, the need to understand the diverse cultures of the countries with which we do business has increased due to globalization.

Did you know? Singapore prides itself on being the most corruption-free country in Asia. Consequently, it has strict laws against bribery, so Government employees may not accept any gifts at all. (From *Kiss, Bow, or Shake Hands: Asia,* by Terri Morrison and Wayne A. Conaway)

Did you know? In the Middle East, a deal is not done even after the terms have been agreed upon. Negotiation continues until the signing of the contract. (From *Multicultural Manners: Essential Rules of Etiquette for the 21st Century,* by Norine Dresser)

Did you know? In traditional negotiations, Chileans consider feelings more important than facts. The truth is considered to be subjective and personal. (From *Kiss, Bow, or Shake Hands: Latin America,* by Terri Morrison and Wayne A. Conaway)

HERE ARE SOME TITLES TO CHECK OUT:

Do's and Taboos Around The World

Multicultural Manners— Essential Rules of Etiquette for the 21st Century

An American's Guide to Doing Business in China

Kiss, Bow, or Shake Hands: How to Do Business in Sixty Countries

Cultural Intelligence: A Guide to Working with People from Other Cultures

Written by Aaron Schleicher

Swim with the Sharks Without Being Eaten Alive

HARVEY B. MACKAY
Reviewed by Jack

Harvey Mackay has always been a "can-do" guy. After college, Mackay took an entry-level job at a local envelope company and worked up into sales. Three years later, he bought a different small envelope company and turned it into a $100 million business. He now is a best-selling business book author who has sold over four million copies in thirty-five languages of this debut book. But his reach stretches past the sphere of his own personal accomplishments. He helped organize a campaign to keep the Minnesota Twins baseball team in Minneapolis, raised the money needed to build the Metrodome there, and has also raised money for cancer research for the University of Minnesota. There is much about Harvey Mackay to be inspired by, including this classic motivational book about how to handle yourself in business situations, surviving and thriving amid the "sharks" who are out to eat your lunch.

The original edition of this book was published in 1988, but the 2005 paperback has an "author's note" in which Mackay talks about the changes that have taken place between these publications. In the updated version, he has added material on how to apply technology to save time and reach out to others more efficiently. The new material is proof positive that, like Mackay claims, "sharks change," and staying up to date with all the assets that are available is key to your continued success. But the real meat in this book is the everlasting original content.

Swim with the Sharks is divided into four sections: sales, management, negotiations, and a final section called "Quickies." With almost 90 chapters in this 250-page book, you will find succinct lessons that are easy to absorb. For example, Lesson 9 in the sales section, "Create Your Own Private Club," was eye opening to me because I recognized that I have been on the receiving end of this lesson when visiting publishers in New York City. Mackay explains how you don't need to have a fancy club membership to impress a client. He offers step-by-step instructions on how to call the best restaurant in town and know what to ask for so that when you walk in, you are greeted personally, and when the meal is complete, you just walk out, because everything is prepaid. End result? You've given your client the impression that you are a big shot and deserving of his business. Lesson 19, "Show Me a Guy Who Thinks He's a Self-Made Man and I'll Show You the Easiest Sell in the World," is a concise chapter containing only this insight: "All you have to do is make him think it's his idea." Simple yet effective, with just the right amount of real-world boldness to know that Mackay means business.

Other examples of Mackay's wisdom are counterintuitive. From the Management section comes Lesson 64, "The Acid Test for Hiring": "Ask yourself, How would you feel having this same person working for your competition instead of for you?" From the same section is Lesson 44, "Your Best People May Spend Their Most Productive Time Staring at the Walls": "If you discover one of your executives looking at the wall . . . instead of filling out a report, go over and congratulate him or her. . . . They're thinking. It's the hardest, most valuable task any person performs." These are certainly obvious concepts—hiring good people and supporting a creative environment—but Mackay comes at these insights with an alternate perspective that enables us to internalize the lessons because they are so unexpected.

"I used to say that networking is the most underrated management skill. Now I believe it may be the most important management skill, bar none."

In his final section, called "Quickies," he includes an amusing story titled, "How to Get to Know a Celebrity." When Mackay was set to meet Castro, he did a little research and found that Castro enjoyed bowling. Upon meeting the man, Mackay asked him how he kept in such good shape. Castro, who supposedly didn't understand English, replied before the translator translated, "Bowling." Mackay told Castro that he was a three-time bowling champion in college and . . . suddenly Castro and Mackay were communicating in English. Mackay believes that to connect with celebrities, you need to avoid the "fan syndrome" and instead talk to them about their interests.

There are books that break new ground and then there are books that show you a new way to think about the basics. Harvey Mackay has written a classic version of the second type of book, with the added imperative that your survival is on the line. The information offered here is truly timeless, presented with humor, and will be around to save many business lives for years to come. JC

Swim with the Sharks without Being Eaten Alive: Outsell, Outmanage, Outmotivate, and Outnegotiate Your Competition, Collins Business, Paperback 2005, ISBN 9780060742812

WHERE TO NEXT? » Page 314 for **more irreverence** » Page 316 for **more quick quotes** » Page 130 for **another animal** | EVEN MORE: *Fish!* by Stephen C. Lundin, Harry Paul, and John Christensen; *Eating the Big Fish* by Adam Morgan; *It's Not the Big That Eat the Small . . . It's the Fast That Eat the Slow* by Jason Jennings and Laurence Haughton; *What They Don't Teach You at Harvard Business School* by Mark H. McCormick

The Power of Intuition

GARY KLEIN
Reviewed by Todd

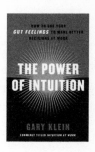

S tories of a fake Greek statue at the Getty Museum and John
Gottman's "Love Lab" at the University of Washington
turned Malcolm Gladwell's sophomore effort, *Blink*, into a best
seller and brought the topic of intuition to the forefront of
cocktail conversation in 2005. Tucked into one of Gladwell's
key stories, however, was a man named Gary Klein. The Ohio-
based PhD has been studying decision making for three decades
and is well known in the field for his work with professionals in
high-intensity occupations.

Klein found that firefighters, U.S. Marine lance corporals, and neona-
tal nurses don't make a conscious effort to consider all the options before
taking action; instead, they quickly gather information and act. As more
information becomes available, these specialists reassess and change
course if needed. When asked how they came to such quick decisions,
Klein's subjects used vague, mystical references like '"The Force" and
"ESP" to describe their abilities. Klein, unsatisfied, probed deeper.

As you read *The Power of Intuition*, the deconstruction of split-second
decision making feels disorienting. How often do you think about how you
think? We all can reflect to when we were faced with such life-changing
decisions as moving to the big city or deciding whether to take a new job,
but the vague hunches we receive from our cavemanlike brains are difficult to articulate, often harder to act on. Studies show that professionals
in fields ranging from naval command to offshore oil platform management use intuition 90 percent of the time in their decision making. By
choosing individuals whose own lives, and others', depend on the accu-
racy of their intuition, Klein found subjects who were attuned to this unconscious mental process. He delineates the process to develop a teachable
framework.

Klein's decision model is illustrated in a loop that starts with the
situation as a whole. First, we look for cues: a firefighter searches for the
heat source or an account rep looks for common threads in prior sales

proposals. Those cues lead to the recognition of patterns, whether dangerously unknown or comfortably familiar. And then our brains start running "action scripts," in which we simulate an effort and evaluate each potential action singularly until we find a satisfactory answer. With a decision made, we act and start the process over again.

Recognizing the process gives you the chance to improve your intuition, and Klein suggests a variety of ways. Throughout the book, he provides a wide array of decision games. These are simple stories which drop the reader into murky hypothetical situations. In one case, the president of your company asks you to lead a new product development effort with workers idled by weak revenue. Klein then presents twenty-six pieces of information that appear as the project progresses, ranging from coworker gossip to company-wide e-mails, and asks you to note your reaction to each and its impact on your project. This exercise squarely focuses on developing the early skills of the model: filtering cues and seeing developing patterns.

"I define intuition as *the way we translate our experience into action.*"

Intuition is not some magical power or extraordinary mental attribute that some have and others don't. Improved intuition comes from recognition of this unconscious routine and the accumulation of real-world experience. While the stakes are clearly higher in the lives of Klein's research subjects, the world of business shares the need for quick and accurate decision making. And *The Power of Intuition* shows you how to trust your gut and improve your own sixth sense. TS

The Power of Intuition: How to Use Your Gut Feelings to Make Better Decisions at Work, Currency/Doubleday, Paperback 2004, ISBN 9780385502894

WHERE TO NEXT? ›› Page 99 for **what else influences our decisions** ›› Page 304 for **how crowds make decisions** ›› Page 29 for **making decisions about your life** | EVEN MORE: *Blink* by Malcolm Gladwell; *Sources of Power* by Gary Klein; *Decision Traps* by J. Edward Russo and Paul J.H. Schoemaker

What Should I Do with My Life?

PO BRONSON

Reviewed by Jack

P o Bronson was at a turning point in his life. His job as a TV screenwriter had dissolved when the series he wrote for was canceled. He was unemployed with his first child on the way. Not succumbing to the worry over getting his next pay-check, Bronson instead asked himself the universal question, "What should I do with my life?" His introspection made him curious about how other people were able to envision a new kind of future or identity for themselves when standing at that same career crossroads. So, he decided to investigate, determining to "travel the country tracking down the people whose stories spoke to me." The stories he collected here in *What Should I Do with My Life?* are about regular people, some with families, some with little education, some with money—all everyday folks from whom we can learn a great deal.

What Should I Do with My Life? was published in 2002, during what Bronson describes as "a time when we were losing our respect for corpo-rate leaders, we no longer believed new technology would make our lives better, and the attack on our freedom made life precious and weighty. People were reassessing what mattered to them and what they believed in." What he presents here are stories about the ghosts and stumbling blocks that prevent us all from pursuing what Bronson names "our true calling."

The organization of this material is unconventional. Eight sections are aligned with just what ghost the person is struggling with or the obstacle they have succeeded in clearing. There is something rich and satisfying about this interpersonal way of grouping stories. For example, in explain-ing why he featured people who have demonstrated patience and persis-tence, Bronson writes: "I include them not to admonish the young and urgent, but to respect the Big Picture. Most of us take the slow road, no shortcuts." Bronson relates to his subjects so intimately that it is impos-sible to not become engaged in their stories yourself.

Bronson interviewed individuals from every social strata. His willing subjects bared their souls and took confession with the writer. Bronson makes no attempt to distance himself, serving as subject and scribe. While that is sometimes a sign of an author's ego, here it feels natural and integral to the subject matter. Bronson has lived a fascinating life, suffered through much the same uncertainty; his own stories add connective tissue to the chapters.

"The most common question I'd get asked was, 'So is your book about life, or about careers?' And I'd laugh, and warn them not to get trapped by semantics, and answer, 'It's about people who've dared to be honest with themselves.' "

In the opening section, Bronson shares a story about a seventeen-year-old Phoenix boy who receives a letter from the Dalai Lama, who instructs the teenager to go to India and fulfill his destiny as the reincarnation of an ancient Tibetan warrior. The boy agrees and begins a twelve-year journey to becoming a monk. In another case, a PR executive in England passes on a plum promotion that would double her salary, and instead pursues a degree as a landscape designer. Both of these stories have in common an unexpected decision, a choice to take the road less traveled. Guided by an internal compass, the actions of these two people exemplify what Bronson calls "rightness." Many times we make decisions to change the course of our lives by following a hunch stemming only from passion, a direction not based in real-world experience but one that satisfies some unfulfilled need.

Po Bronson hopes this book will give us the courage to step out of our comfortable nests armed with the inspirational stories of regular folks who have taken the leap before us. For himself, he learned a valuable lesson that he shares with us: "I used to think life presented a five-page menu of choices. Now I think the choice is in whether to be honest, to ourselves and others, and the rest is more of an uncovering, a peeling away of layers, discovering talents we assumed we didn't have." JC

What Should I Do with My Life? The True Story of People Who Answered the Ultimate Question, Ballantine Books, Paperback 2005, ISBN 9780345485922

WHERE TO NEXT? ▸ For inspiration, read one of the biographies reviewed in this book. Start on page 191. ▸ | EVEN MORE: *I Could Do Anything If I Only Knew What It Was* by Barbara Sher with Barbara Smith; *I Don't Know What I Want, But I Know It's Not This* by Julie Jansen; *Free Agent Nation* by Daniel H. Pink; *What Color Is Your Parachute?* by Richard Nelson Bolles

Oh, the Places You'll Go!

DR. SEUSS/THEODORE GEISEL
Reviewed by Todd

A number of years ago we got a substantial order for *Oh, the Places You'll Go!* from one of our corporate customers. When we received subsequent orders, we became curious. What would an international manufacturer need with such a supply of Dr. Seuss books? A call to the company's HR department revealed to us that they were using the book in their new-employee orientation.

While your employer may never have presented you with a copy, perhaps you received the book as a graduation present or at a baby shower. And perhaps you are wondering what on earth *Oh, the Places You'll Go!* is doing on a list of must-read business books. If you haven't cracked open your copy for a while, take this opportunity to pull it from the bottom shelf of your bookcase, where it is probably wedged between an old geometry textbook and a dog-eared atlas. Here's why.

Oh, the Places You'll Go! was published in 1990 and was Theodore Geisel's (aka Dr. Seuss) last book. The book spent its first two years on the *New York Times* best-seller list, and Geisel remarked, "This proves it. I no longer write books for children. I write books for people."

It is this book's broad appeal and keen effectiveness that demands its mention here. Jack and I often say that we have seen the same book regurgitated dozens of times, just between different covers. To watch how many times a subject has been covered or a cliché has been reanimated can be disheartening. What keeps you coming back to some, however, is the magic that's created when an idea and the way it is packaged conveys new (and true) meaning.

Oh, the Places You'll Go! is self-help at its finest—self-help in the same way that Thoreau and Emerson championed self-improvement on the individual level. The book couldn't begin on a more positive note:

Congratulations!
Today is your day.
You're off to Great Places!
You're off and away!

At just under six hundred words, the book covers the gamut of human experience. Our unnamed young man is told that choice is within his power and that all he has to do is decide. But deciding requires judgment and is not without consequence. Seuss points him to the less-traveled path because "there things can happen and frequently do."

It is the reality of the negatives that makes the book so believable and motivating. Confusion, loneliness, and procrastination all make appearances. Each is a challenge, but Seuss never doubts that our little man will get through his difficulties. Geisel said the only thing all of his books had in common was hope, and *Oh, the Places You'll Go!* will provide you with a healthy dose to face each new experience or disappointment that lies on your path.

"And will you succeed? Yes! You will, indeed! (98 and ¾ percent guaranteed.)"

Many nights I find myself reading this book to my children. I am not sure if its frequent appearance at bedtime is for them or for me. I do know that this book taps into the ideal that we can all be better people and help make the world a better place for us and for our children. Every book should deliver on such a promise. **TS**

Oh, the Places You'll Go!, Random House, Hardcover 1990, ISBN 9780679805274

WHERE TO NEXT? » See the next page for **more business books for all ages.**

Business Books
for Kids
of All Ages

Sometimes to think outside the box you have to draw outside the lines. Draw inspiration, that is, from unlikely sources. "All grown-ups were children first," wrote Antoine de Saint-Exupéry. Whether it's time to reevaluate, rejuvenate, or simply escape the demands of our busy lives, we recommend returning to the stories and lessons that were most impressive to us as children. The truths you'll find there are timeless. Here are a few stories in which we find inspiration again and again.

Le petit prince, or *The Little Prince,* is Antoine de Saint-Exupéry's classic novella about a small, extraterrestrial boy who changes a grown man's life by reminding him of simple truths too often forgotten with age: Children learn by asking questions. Flowers bloom when they are nurtured. Work is futile when it lacks purpose. You must experience the world to appreciate it. There is still time to make friends. And, perhaps most profoundly, *"On ne voit bien qu'avec le cœur, l'essentiel est invisible pour les yeux"*—"It is only with the heart that one sees rightly; what is essential is invisible to the eyes." *The Little Prince* will put you in a renewed frame of mind; you might even look up at the stars tonight.

Based on a short story by Leo Tolstoy, Jon J. Muth's *The Three Questions* follows a small boy, Nikolai, as he searches for answers to three questions: "When is the best time to do things?" "Who is the most important one?" and "What is the right thing to do?" As Nikolai visits his animal friends and helps a few in need, he learns—with a little help from an old turtle named Leo—that he already possesses the answers. Muth's concise prose and serene watercolors make *The Three Questions* a contemplative read for children and adults alike.

Kevin Carroll's *Rules of the Red Rubber Ball* is a creative little book with a big message for people of all ages: no matter what you do, pursue that which makes you most happy . . . and pursue it with abandon. For the young Carroll growing up on the streets of Philadelphia, the playground was his refuge and passion. *Rules of the Red Rubber Ball* is both his remarkable story of chasing that red rubber ball for the rest of his life, and also a powerful charge to dream big, take chances, and make time for play in everything you do.

In *Walk On! A Guide for Babies of All Ages,* Marla Frazee uses Baby's experience of learning to walk as a metaphor for knowing how to get out of a rut, take chances, overcome obstacles, and determine who and what to trust. It's the earliest "try, try again" experience we have as humans. With its universal observation, "See how different everything looks from here?" *Walk On!* reminds us that sometimes you have to stand on your own two feet to find a new perspective on the world.

Written by Rebecca Schlei

Chasing Daylight

EUGENE O'KELLY
Reviewed by Jack

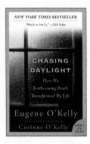

An advance review copy of this book had been sitting on my office table for three weeks, untouched—one of many review copies I receive from publishers. I was clearing off the table for a new delivery of books when I finally read the back cover:

> On May 24, 2005, Eugene O'Kelly stepped into his doctor's office with a full calendar and a lifetime of plans on his mind. Six days later he would resign as CEO of KPMG. His lifetime of plans dwindled to 100 days, leaving him just enough time to say goodbye.

I closed my office door, forwarded my telephone calls, and read this amazing little book, *Chasing Daylight*, in one afternoon. I am not ashamed to admit that tears flowed.

The book details the three and a half months between the diagnosis of O'Kelly's terminal brain cancer and his death. His haunting yet extraordinarily hopeful voice narrates the book and reminds us to embrace the fragile, fleeting moments of our lives—the time we have with our family, our friends, and even ourselves. O'Kelly is totally honest about his fears. But what really moved me was his simple yet profound writing style. For example, consider this brief passage:

> The business of dying is hard. The wrapping up. The paperwork, the legal work. The stuff that's boring and maddening about life when life is going well. Of course, the other stuff that's happening when dying—the physical stuff and the huge emotional stuff—can be unspeakably awful. But if paperwork is enough to break your spirit—and it is—then how can you have anything left?

The impact of those few sentences continues to move me no matter how many times I read them. He could be writing about anything: selling a house or making plans for a trip. But it becomes clear that he is talking about courage, about leaving this earth the right way.

Just imagine you are the CEO of a major accounting firm, where you started your career as an assistant accountant in 1973. You are only fifty-three years old and still have so much of your life in front of you. Or at the very least, a tempting retirement plan. But then you learn that you have inoperable brain cancer. It is the end of life as you planned it. *Chasing Daylight* speaks to us simply because we are human. Perhaps this book moved me because I am of the same generation as O'Kelly. Or perhaps it is because I had lost a good friend, a mentor, the year before to lung cancer, and was still shaken by the loss. But for anyone reading *Chasing Daylight*, it is a singular insight into the mind of a man who knows he is going to die—simply a part of the human condition met early and thus, greatly feared.

"I was blessed. I was told I had three months to live."

I was concerned that the author would tell a story of spiritual enlightenment, or, as with many end-of-life memoirs, spend the book listing his regrets—maudlin passages about his young daughter and loving family. Not that there isn't room for some of that, but those are songs we've heard sung. And that wasn't in O'Kelly's nature. When he discovers the seriousness of his disease, he does what he was trained to do as an accountant—he makes lists: "1. leave my job, and 2. choose a medical protocol that allowed me to . . . 3. make the time remaining the best of my life, and as good as it could possibly be for those most affected by my situation." Next, he creates a to-do list for his final days: "*Get legal and financial affairs in order, *'Unwind' relationships, *Simplify, *Live in the moment, *Create (but also be open to) great moments, 'perfect moments,' *Begin transition to next state, *Plan funeral." A bean counter to the end.

The title of the book comes from O'Kelly's routine of playing golf with his wife after getting home from work—playing golf throughout that summer, chasing daylight. His love of his family is deep, and the end of the book is truly staggering. His wife writes the last chapter, telling the story of how he died. She also corrects his reporting of his final days since his brain cancer was spreading and *his* reality was not reality.

Chasing Daylight is an eloquent confirmation that our lives and the people in them are temporary joys, but the time we spend enjoying them is never lost. And if we conquer our fears—even the fear of facing the end of our lives and leaving those we love—we can conquer anything. This was my favorite book of 2006 and will remain one of my favorites for all time. I urge you to read *Chasing Daylight*: this book will change your life. JC

Chasing Daylight: How My Forthcoming Death Transformed My Life, McGraw-Hill, Paperback 2008, ISBN 9780071499934

WHERE TO NEXT? » Put this book down and spend some time with the people you care about. | EVEN MORE: *Not Fade Away* by Laurence Shames and Peter Barton; *The Year of Magical Thinking* by Joan Didion; *The Last Lecture* by Randy Pausch and Jeffrey Zaslow

LEADERSHIP

LEADERSHIP is this seemingly unidentifiable quality we all wish for in politicians, chief executive officers, and—whether we admit it or not—parents. This section proves there is nothing elusive about what it takes to lead people. All of these authors take different routes to the same destination: everyone wants a leader to define what the future will be and take them there.

On Becoming a Leader

WARREN BENNIS

Reviewed by Todd

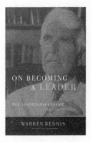

Warren Bennis postulates that leadership cannot be taught: "[M]ore leaders have been made by accident, circumstance, sheer grit, or will than have been made by all the leadership courses put together. Leadership courses can only teach skills. . . . Developing character and vision is the way leaders invent themselves." Interviews with almost thirty leaders from all walks of life, and Bennis's own experience as leader, academic, and consultant (advising even U.S. presidents), give *On Becoming a Leader* incredible depth. The evergreen interest in this title reflects its unique prescriptions for leadership. The book also addresses beautifully the timeless search for meaning in one's own life and how that can affect your success as a leader.

Successful leaders are those who can access and then express their true selves, Bennis says—a nod to his belief in humanistic psychology. Developed by Abraham Maslow, this branch of psychology concerns specifically what it means to be human; its main goal for the individual is self-actualization. What might sound like some mystical Eastern path to enlightenment is instead a philosophy central to Maslow's hierarchy of needs. You may have come across this philosophy more recently in Gallup's strengths-based tools. Let me put it another way: to be successful you must figure out what you are good at and do it.

"No leader sets out to be a leader," Bennis says. "People set out to live their lives, expressing themselves fully. When that expression is of value, they become leaders." Bennis asks us to consider, then, our lives and how family, friends, and school have shaped our beliefs, stressing that those relationships and experiences don't define us but rather provide the material to discover or reflect upon a true and unique self. Though the logical left brain often competes with the emotional right, instinct serves a leader well only if he or she can listen to a balanced inner voice. To do so, we must examine our motives and strive for healthy expressions of value while abandoning selfish pursuits.

There is no direct path to personal enlightenment, and the structure of *On Becoming a Leader* seems to mimic the anfractuous course we must all take. The chapters, with provocative titles such as "Knowing Yourself" and "Operating on Instinct," provide a loose framework. Bennis then draws from a wide range of sources and interviews that lend the book a conversational tone. On page after page, wisdom from multiple sources challenges readers to consider leadership from diverse perspectives. For example, the late film director Sydney Pollack observes that "Driving a car, flying an airplane—you can reduce those things to a series of maneuvers that are always executed in the same way. But with something like leadership, just as with art, you reinvent the wheel every single time you apply the principle." This extra content provides another point of contrast with the more commonplace and neatly packaged how-to type of leadership guides.

"[M]ore leaders have been made by accident, circumstance, sheer grit, or will than have been made by all the leadership courses put together."

In *On Becoming a Leader*, Bennis treats leadership with a certain gravitas that is perspective changing. He references a scientist from the University of Michigan who asserts that after nuclear war and worldwide epidemic, the greatest risk to society is the quality of leadership in our institutions. Then Bennis follows with a challenge to his readers: "Our quality of life depends on the quality of our leaders. And since no one else seems to be volunteering, it's up to you. If you've ever had dreams of leadership, now is the time, this is the place, and you're it. We need you." TS

On Becoming a Leader: The Leadership Classic, Basic Books, Paperback updated and expanded 2003, ISBN 9780738208176

WHERE TO NEXT? ▸ Page 285 on **how to lead during uncertain times** ▸ Page 50 for **another leadership book with the same vibe** ◂ Page 29 for **help figuring out what you should do** | EVEN MORE: *Judgment* by Noel M. Tichy and Warren Bennis; *Organizing Genius* by Warren Bennis and Patricia Ward Biederman; *The Maslow Business Reader* by Abraham H. Maslow and Deborah C. Stephens

The Leadership Moment

MICHAEL USEEM
Reviewed by Jack

On August 5, 1949, Wagner Dodge and his team of fifteen firefighters were called to parachute into Montana's Mann Gulch to fight a grass and forest fire. In the language of "smoke jumpers," it was a ten o'clock fire, one that they would fight through the night and have under control by the next morning. As they fought the flames, the wind unexpectedly spread the fire, and their escape to the river at the base of the gulch was blocked. Dodge and his team abandoned their attempts to fight the fire and simply tried to escape, but found themselves cornered by the advancing blaze. In the chaos, Dodge stopped, lit a match, and threw it into the prairie grass. With this counterintuitive move, he hoped to create a fire within the fire to protect him and his men. But by this point, he had lost the confidence of his crew. They ignored his emphatic motioning for them to join him, and instead sought their own route to safety. For thirteen of Dodge's men, this proved to be a fatal choice. In his book, *The Leadership Moment*, Wharton School professor Michael Useem uses this story, along with a series of others, to illustrate the singular moments that leaders face.

Useem uses masterful storytelling, focusing on real people who experienced a leadership moment to teach nine leadership principles. He defines this moment as a time when our credibility and reputation is on the line, when the fate or fortune of others depends on what we do. Leadership at such moments is best when "the vision is strategic, the voice persuasive, the results tangible." Useem draws from a wide range of occupations and incidents, showing what real leaders do, or don't do, when the chips are down. This sweeping perspective results in an inspiring work that broadens the definition of what it means to be a leader.

Useem starts each chapter with captivating episodes, but then dissects the actions taken and, in some cases, the mistakes made in order to emphasize the underlying lesson. During the Mann Gulch fire, Dodge's first mistake came earlier that day when he instructed his crew to advance without him toward the fire while he returned to get supplies from the drop site. Upon his return, the fire was much further developed and their only option was to flee. At that time, Dodge commits another error, telling his crew to drop all their tools. Useem says the use of this command was the equivilent of Dodge "ordering his soldiers to shed their uniforms." Both decisions were the right reactions to the set of circumstances Dodge faced, but Useem believes there is an additional, less apparent, reason his crew lost faith in him. Dodge's style of communication was quiet and instructive, and over time he had not established a rapport with the men. When he presented an uncommon solution in an unexpected environment, his crew had no reference point from which to trust him.

"Leadership is at its best when the vision is strategic, the voice persuasive, the results tangible."

Other leadership moments happen when a decision is made to serve a greater good. Useem tells the hopeful story of Roy Vagelos, Merck & Co., and his mission to combat a pervasive disease called river blindness. In 1988, over 20 million people worldwide, most of them poor, had the disease; one-third went blind. The disease is caused by a waterborne parasitic worm. Merck chemists had discovered that a drug for heartworm in animals could also kill the parasite. As the head of research, Vagelos was presented with these findings and left in a quandary: a new product with no profit potential, since the recipients had no money to pay for the treatment. Also, the transfer of drugs from animal use to human use frequently failed, and given the nature of the disease, those inflicted would need annual doses for up to fourteen years to completely eradicate the parasite. Despite those significant drawbacks, Vagelos green-lighted the project and the trials showed immediate success. When the time came to make the decision to commercialize the product, Vagelos, by then CEO of Merck, decided again to support the project, but this time he was supporting a project that flew in the face of his fiscal responsibility to shareholders. Vagelos took the heat and supported the initiative despite the outcries, showing that doing the right thing is leadership at its best.

Although much of the material included in *The Leadership Moment* relates incidents from outside traditional business, Useem's wealth of knowledge from his position at Wharton allows him to draw parallels to the challenges contemporary business leaders face throughout their careers. The story format provides the reader vivid access to the high level of intensity withstood by leaders in all situations, and inspiration for how to make the most out of every leadership moment. JC

The Leadership Moment: Nine True Stories of Triumph and Disaster and Their Lessons for Us All, Three Rivers Press, Paperback 1998, ISBN 9780812932300

WHERE TO NEXT? » Page 66 for **another leader in history** » Page 85 for **a great leadership moment** » Page 252 for **a poor leadership moment** | EVEN MORE: *The Killer Angels* by Michael Shaara; *Leading at the Edge* by Dennis N.T. Perkins; *It's Your Ship* by Michael Abrashoff

Leadership

in Movies

A movie can be pure entertainment, or it can influence what you do in your everyday life. While few of us will ever need to learn how to defuse a booby trap while leading shipwrecked survivors on a quest for lost treasure, many of us face challenges of leadership at the office. For inspiration and even some ideas about leadership, here is a guide to films that depict leadership at its finest.

12 Angry Men [1957]

Starring Jack Klugman, Jack Warden, Henry Fonda, and Ed Begley. Directed by Sidney Lumet. Nominated for three Oscars and four Golden Globes. | On almost every critic's "must see" list, *12 Angry Men* exemplifies the leadership, drive, and negotiation skills needed by many managers and CEOs. It revolves around a court case and the twelve-man jury that debates the fate of an accused man. All but one of the jurors believes the accused is guilty, and what follows is a tense and dramatic debate that reveals in depth the character of each of the twelve men. Within the story, important tools of persuasion and dealing with confrontation are available for the attentive viewer.

Apollo 13 [1995]

Starring Tom Hanks, Bill Paxton, Kevin Bacon, and Gary Sinise. Directed by Ron Howard. Nominated for nine Oscars (won two) and nominated for four Golden Globes. | In 1970, three astronauts set out to put a man on the moon. Though not one of them stepped on the moon, the mission was deemed a "successful failure." An explosion during liftoff left them with a deteriorating spacecraft and the astronauts' survival in jeopardy. On Earth, Flight Director Eugene Kranz pushed the NASA crew beyond its creative limits to find a solution that would bring the astronauts home alive. In space, Commander James Lovell kept his team focused on the task, working together, and, given the circumstances, optimistic. The extraordinary leadership displayed by these two men is, like the mission, legendary.

A Midwinter's Tale [1995]

Starring Michael Maloney, Joan Collins, Jennifer Saunders, and Julia Sawalha. Directed by Kenneth Branagh. Winner of the Golden Osella and nominated for the Golden Lion. | *A Midwinter's Tale* is the old "Hey, let's put on a show!" motif that appears often in literature. Here, it is a community group that aims to put on a production of Hamlet in order to save a church. Whether a stage show or a new idea in the boardroom, one person always owns it, directs the plan of action, and works hard to implement it. Certainly not all of these shows run smoothly. But in real life, the skills needed to get everyone pulling on the same oar are critical for success. Some conflict inevitably arises, and employees (in this case, the actors in the play) aren't motivated or don't grasp the bigger picture. It takes a great leader to clarify the main objective, keep each member motivated and on task, and maintain a level of intensity that will ultimately culminate in something quite meaningful.

Additional Leadership Movies:
Aliens [1986]
Dead Poet's Society [1989]
Elizabeth [1998]

Written by Roy Normington with Sally Haldorson and Kate Mytty

The Leadership Challenge

JAMES M. KOUZES AND BARRY Z. POSNER

Reviewed by Todd

To begin their research for *The Leadership Challenge*, Jim Kouzes and Barry Posner asked people of all backgrounds this open-ended question: " 'What values, personality traits, or characteristics do you look for and admire in a leader?' " Twenty characteristics captured the wide range of responses, and four of them came up consistently: *honest, forward-looking, inspiring*, and *competent*. The findings correspond to what communication experts call "source credibility." Successful newscasters, salespeople, and politicians all exhibit these qualities, but it is particularly the ability to be forward-looking that lifts someone from being credible to being a leader.

The authors continued their research, studying individual leaders to determine how they work when they are performing at their best. After gathering several hundred case studies (now several thousand) on personal-best leadership moments and searching for common themes in those experiences, Kouzes and Posner developed five governing practices: Model the Way, Inspire a Shared Vision, Challenge the Process, Enable Others to Act, and Encourage the Heart. When they found parallels between their initial research into what followers valued in a leader and the common themes underlying leadership's best, the authors knew they were on to something. They further tested the validity of their research by correlating those leadership behaviors with external measurements such as increased financial performance and team satisfaction.

To see how Kouzes and Posner's copious research was then applied, consider the leadership characteristic *forward-looking* aligned with the authors' second leadership principle, "Inspire a Shared Vision." Leaders imagine what is possible; as one interviewee said, " 'I'm my organization's futures department.' " Yet senior managers say they spend only 3 percent of their time looking forward. Those who operate on the front lines, the authors claim, should be spending five times that, and even more time with each step they take closer to the executive suite. The authors suggest reading publications to spur inspiration; *The Futurist* and *Popular Science* come to mind.

Another trick the authors recommend, labeled the "Janus Effect," is to widen your time horizon. Start with the past, thinking about where you and your company have been . . . and then think about the future. Professor Omar El Sawy is referenced here, having found that starting with history allows prognosticators to see twice as far into the future. Then, to truly bring vision to life, the vision must be "shared," enlisting others in the process.

Due in part to the appeal of the authors' extensive research and to their practical approach, *The Leadership Challenge* has sold over 1.5 million copies since 1987 and was recently published in its fourth edition. But the book is not the end of the road for readers interested in applying the authors' lessons. A unique variety of supplements gives *The Leadership Challenge* added depth. For example, three million people have taken the thirty-question Leadership Practices Inventory and helped evaluate the hundreds of thousands of leaders they work with. The Leadership Challenge Workshop provides a kit which gives corporate trainers and independent facilitators the tools to share the principles with groups of all sizes. Workbooks, videos, and worldwide seminars further emphasize that leadership is a skill set that anyone can learn.

"Leadership is not a gene and it's not an inheritance. Leadership is an identifiable set of skills and abilities that are available to all of us."

The book and its additional resources provide a framework for seeing how leadership fits together with all aspects of business. Jim Kouzes refers to *The Leadership Challenge* as a Christmas tree: businesspeople have all sorts of thoughts and ideas about how they and their companies should

operate, much like shiny ornaments and strings of bright lights just waiting for a tree on which to be hung. TS

The Leadership Challenge, Jossey-Bass, Hardcover fourth edition 2007, ISBN 9780787984915

WHERE TO NEXT? « Page 9 for **a strategy on getting organized** » Page 308
for **a strategy on making ideas "sticky"** » Page 74 for **a strategy on strategy** | EVEN
MORE: *The Offsite* by Robert H. Thompson; *The Leadership Challenge Workbook* by James
M. Kouzes and Barry Z. Posner; *Christian Reflection on* The Leadership Challenge by
John C. Maxwell, James M. Kouzes, and Barry Z. Posner

Leadership Is an Art

MAX DE PREE
Reviewed by Jack

Art has always been an integral part of the success of Herman Miller, Inc. From the beginning, the Michigan-based manufacturer of modern furniture collaborated with some of the century's greatest designers, such as George Nelson and Charles and Ray Eames, to create icons of industrial design. These collaborations deeply influenced the values of the company. Today, Herman Miller continues to align its goals of innovative design with innovative leadership practices. In *Leadership Is an Art*, Max De Pree, former CEO of Herman Miller, describes this art of leadership as "liberating people to do what is required of them, in the most effective and humane way possible." De Pree conveys this message through stories and ideas rather than practices and rules.

In the early days, Herman Miller's factory used a central driveshaft to run the machines. The millwright supervised this system and was a key person within the factory. One day the millwright died. De Pree's father, founder of the company, visited the widow to give his condolences. While he was there she read him some poetry. The elder De Pree asked who wrote the poems and she told him that her husband, the millwright, had. Now, sixty years after that revelation, Max De Pree wonders: "Was he a poet who did millwright's work, or was he a millwright who wrote poetry?"

The younger De Pree seems saddened by the lost opportunity. The secret poet could have been the public copywriter. "When we think about leaders and the variety of gifts people bring to corporations and institutions, we see that the art of leadership lies in polishing and liberating and enabling those gifts." Doing this eliminates the separation between the life we lead at home and that which we lead at the office.

Even with such a people-first perspective, a leader must be able to put theory into practice. One practice De Pree advocates is "roving leadership." He writes that in many organizations there are two kinds of leaders—the traditionally hierarchical and the roving. The rovers are the people who step up and take charge or ownership of a situation, regardless of their position or assignment. He tells the moving story of a person who passes out at church and is helped when the roving leaders swiftly take charge of the crisis. I spent some time reflecting on my own and my employees' ability to be roving leaders, and it was refreshing to see that I had created a corporate culture that attracted and retained just such people. Particularly in a small company like mine, where employees' duties tend to ebb and flow depending on what is essential to the company at any given time, roving leaders are crucial to making every project a success.

"Understanding and accepting diversity enables us to see that each of us is needed."

De Pree fills his book with compelling and heartfelt passages about what it truly means to guide a company and its employees: "The first responsibility of a leader is to define reality. The last is to say thank you. In between the two, the leader must become a servant and a debtor. That sums up the progress of an artful leader." It is never too late to pick up *Leadership Is an Art* and find yourself, or the leader you wish to become, within its pages. JC

Leadership Is an Art, Currency/Doubleday, Paperback 2004, ISBN 9780385512466

WHERE TO NEXT? ‣ Page 173 for **proof that listening helps** ‣ Page 230 for **business by trial and error** ‣ Page 88 for **the other companies with soul** | EVEN MORE: *Servant Leadership* by Robert K. Greenleaf; *Synchronicity* by Joseph Jaworski; *Stewardship* by Peter Block

The Radical Leap

STEVE FARBER
Reviewed by Jack

Fables and parables take complicated ideas and, as part of well-written stories, deliver easily comprehendible lessons. The use of storytelling enables the reader to internalize the message the author is communicating. And when the right combination of characters, plot, message, and conclusion collide, magic can happen. Steve Farber has accomplished this synergistic coming-together marvelously with his enjoyable 160-page parable, *The Radical Leap*.

The Radical Leap offers more than a few plot twists. In a story that takes place during a single week, Steve Farber plays himself, and, as with most business parables, he is searching for an answer. A management consultant, Steve is called by a friend who is in an untenable situation at a company she really loves. Janice is the SVP of marketing who has become the de facto second in command when the charismatic president suddenly disappears and is replaced by a real bean counter, Bob Jeffers. This new guy has no people skills. Janice is so upset about the change in her company that she is thinking of quitting and turns to Steve for help with that decision. She also asks Steve to try and find the president who had left. She was very close to him and wants his counsel.

Luckily for Steve, earlier that week he had gone out for a cup of coffee and found himself in a conversation with a person who looked like a beach bum. Edg, one of the most colorful characters in business fiction, becomes Steve's guide. Edg explains to Steve that leadership is "'always substantive and rarely fashionable. It is intensely personal and intrinsically scary, and it requires us to live the ideas we espouse—in irrefutable ways—every day of our lives, up to and beyond the point of fear.'" To deal with this fear, Edg advocates "extreme leadership." Edg's advice helps Steve determine how to help Janice.

Extreme leadership is living in pursuit of the OS!M, a catchy acronym for an "Oh Sh*t! Moment." Edg defines OS!M as the "'natural, built-in human indicator that you are doing—or about to do—something truly significant, and you are—rightfully so—scared out of your gourd.'" Edg also teaches Steve about LEAP, which stands for: cultivate Love, generate Energy, inspire Audacity, and provide Proof.

For many business practitioners, the individual aspects of LEAP can be a bit hard to swallow on first read. Love and energy are not considered "real" business practices by most businesspeople and may seem a little touchy-feely. But when you think about work that you were really passionate about and how you just loved getting up and doing that job . . . this is the love and energy Edg talks to Steve about. It is an intense passion that can actually end up "changing the world." Big-picture thoughts can and will inspire audacity, and, in the end, you will end up providing the proof, or results.

" 'Do what you love in the service of people who love what you do.' "

I am not going to give away how this story ends. But trust me, this is a special book. It shows that extreme leadership is the best and most successful way of leading. *The Radical Leap* is also special because it stands on its own as a work of fiction. The characters are fun, easy to get to know, and the plot has many twists and turns. As a result, you will be invested in the characters' attempts to solve problems, and, in turn, be inspired to take a LEAP and radicalize your own leadership. JC

The Radical Leap: A Personal Lesson in Extreme Leadership, Dearborn (Kaplan), Hardcover 2004, ISBN 9780793185689

WHERE TO NEXT? « Page 47 to **meet Farber's friends** » Page 167 to **read a great novel on management** | EVEN MORE: *The Radical Edge* by Steve Farber; *Leadership and Self-Deception* by the Arbinger Institute; *The Fred Factor* by Mark Sanborn

Control Your Destiny or Someone Else Will

NOEL M. TICHY AND STRATFORD SHERMAN

Reviewed by Todd

In 1994, I accepted a position with General Electric in their Manufacturing Management Program, one of several training programs used to groom college graduates. It was sometime in that first year that I received my first copy of *Control Your Destiny or Someone Else Will*. The book had been published the year prior and was being warmly received within the company. Noel Tichy was instrumental in redeveloping the leadership training programs at GE, and the book, written with Strat Sherman, opened the doors to show the evolution of the conglomerate under CEO Jack Welch.

Control Your Destiny came out before the accolades, before Jack Welch was named "Manager of the Century" by *Fortune* magazine, before the company's market capitalization reached $450 billion. Professors and pundits now can easily look back and call Welch's twenty-year turnaround remarkable, but Tichy and Sherman were the first to recognize and write about it. Though GE fell short of the financial metrics needed for recognition in Jim Collins's seminal work *Good to Great*, read *Control Your Destiny or Someone Else Will* to see how Jack Welch took an organization from good to great.

The situation Jack Welch inherited when he became CEO in 1981 was one of the toughest for any leader: life at GE was good, but he believed it could be better. Not exactly a situation that encourages a change-oriented agenda, and the new leader had 420,000 employees to convince that a new course was needed. To spur change, in 1982 Welch made his now-famous declaration that every GE business would be number one or number two in their markets and vowed to " 'fix, close, or sell' " any business that did not meet those standards." The incumbent managerial class yawned; "same story, different leader" was their reaction.

Over the next ten years, Welch made good on his declaration. He sold 125 businesses in the first four years alone, including many consumer-based brands central to the company's long-standing identity. In that first decade, 300,000 people left GE through the sale of laggard divisions or company-encouraged means. "I think one of the jobs of a business-person is to get away from the slugfests and into niches where you can prevail," Welch said, and by 1993, every part of GE held one of the top two rungs in each of their markets. Welch referred to this time as "getting the hardware right," building the business engine that has allowed GE to succeed as a conglomerate.

Welch knew there was a limit to gaining through reduction, and in the second half of his tenure, the focus shifted to "the software." Welch pumped money into the revitalization of Crotonville, the company's New York–based facility that would train 10,000 employees yearly and "indoctrinate managers in the new principles." He quickly realized those direct efforts would only reach a fraction of the workforce and that something more than the typical videotaped messages and company newsletters were needed. The new values needed to be experienced at GE's manufacturing plants and office buildings around the world.

"Peter Drucker . . . greatly influenced [Jack] Welch by writing, 'If you weren't already in the business, would you enter it today?' "

This insight served as the seed for Work-Out, town hall–style meetings where thirty to one hundred employees, over the course of a few days, would discuss "their common problems." Bosses were not allowed to attend until the final hours when they were forced to make on-the-spot, yes-or-no decisions on the groups' compiled action items. In a five-year period, more than 200,000 GE employees, or 85 percent of the company's workforce, experienced a Work-Out session. This cultural breakthrough empowered employees to take the steps required to eliminate unnecessary work, and built trust across pay grades and business functions, an effort Harvard Business School professor Len Schlesinger called "one of the biggest planned efforts to alter people's behavior since Mao's Cultural Revolution."

The current version of *Control Your Destiny* is quite daunting at 694 pages, but do not let the heft scare you away. The first half is a narrative about Welch and the company he started with, while the second half details the challenges and associated initiatives Welch took on, ranging

Questions from a Jack Welch Business
Review:

• What does your global competitive
  environment look like?

• In the last three years, what have
  your competitors done to you?

• In the same period, what have you
  done to them?

• How might they attack you in the
  future?

• What are your plans to leapfrog
  them?

Source: "It's All in the Sauce," *Fortune*, April 4,
2005

from globalization to speed. In 2001, as Welch was leaving his post, a revised edition included over 160 new pages of his letters from twenty years of annual reports. A second revision was published in 2005 that again revised material and added a new opening note from Sherman and an afterword from Tichy. The last bit of heft comes in the form of a seventy-page "Handbook for Revolutionaries," written by Tichy, that delivers a challenge to leaders to assess their organizations against the radical change GE went through.

I count myself lucky to have been employed by GE, and I will personally vouch for the impact, the absolute culture change, engendered by Jack Welch's actions at General Electric. I never met Welch, but the knowledge and experience that I gained in my six years at the company will likely never be matched. While GE may build aircraft engines and issue credit cards, its true core product is creating world-class managers. All of GE's CEOs have come from within the organization, and Boeing, Chrysler, and Intuit are just a few of the companies now run by former GE executives. Tichy and Sherman's portrait of Jack Welch gives leaders everywhere a strong example of leadership at its best. TS

Control Your Destiny or Someone Else Will, Collins Business Essentials Edition, Paperback 2005, ISBN 9780060753832

WHERE TO NEXT? ↦ Page 180 for **another take on changing knowing to doing** ↦ Page 85 for **another great corporate turnaround** ↦ Page 74 to **see which companies Jim Collins did recognize** | EVEN MORE: *The Cycle of Leadership* by Noel M. Tichy; *Winning* by Jack and Suzy Welch; *If Harry Potter Ran General Electric* by Tom Morris

Leading Change

JOHN P. KOTTER

Reviewed by Jack

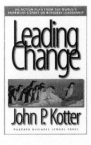

After 9/11, our business hit a speed bump, as did many others. The shake-up altered the typically positive atmosphere of our book company; at the same time, there wasn't much we could do to fight the slowdown in the market. I brought in a consultant to introduce a change initiative that would get us all working together again. The change initiative failed to catch on, however, despite being embraced by the employees in its initial push. John Kotter's *Leading Change* reveals why. A change initiative is like redirecting a river. Build a wall of rocks on the riverbed and still the water will rush around and over—and eventually through—it, determined to continue on its natural path. Thus, to change the course of a river requires constant maintenance. The payoff from this book is that Kotter shows us how to change the course of a company permanently.

Kotter named the book *Leading Change* because he believes that for change initiatives to succeed, a company needs leaders, not managers. In fact, he asserts that successful change requires 70 to 90 percent leadership and 10 to 30 percent management. Many organizations don't have enough leadership bandwidth for this to work. Contemporary organizations have institutionalized management at the expense of leadership, which only adds to the change woes. Reflecting on my company's dilemma, I can now easily see that while I knew change was imperative—and indeed, I was the one who called for it—I regarded it as a managerial mandate and didn't realize that I needed to lead the change, to be the first to put change into action.

The book is built around "The Eight-Stage Change Process." The first process is "Establishing a Sense of Urgency." Sounds simple enough, but as Kotter states: "In an organization of 100 employees, at least two dozen must go far beyond the normal call of duty to produce significant change. In a firm of 100,000 employees, the same might be required of 15,000 or more." Because my company uses open-book management, I felt that showing our employees the numbers was enough to inspire such urgency, but the numbers, nebulous "factoids" for most employees, were not enough to jolt us out of our complacency.

Kotter's discourse on complacency reveals how the "but" in a conversation about change dooms any change initiative. His chart of ways to raise the urgency level is loaded with practical examples on how to motivate people. With suggestions that include setting targets so high that success can't be reached by conducting business as usual, and sending more data about customer satisfaction and financial performance to more employees—especially information that demonstrates weakness vis-à-vis the competition—Kotter shows how to help people understand the seriousness of the problem management faces. I am quite aware now that I missed an opportunity to make the company's challenges real for my employees.

"Enterprises everywhere will be presented with even more terrible hazards and wonderful opportunities, driven by the globalization of the economy along with related technology and social trends."

"Creating the Guiding Coalition" is another process Kotter advocates, asserting that the solo CEO is destined to fail in promoting change because the initiative needs a well-rounded team for success. Kotter suggests characteristics needed for the guiding coalition: position power, expertise, credibility, and leadership, with trust and sincerity as the glue to keep the team together. He emphasizes that "[y]ou need both management and leadership skills on the guiding coalition, and they must work in tandem, teamwork style. The former keeps the whole process under control, while the latter drives the change." In our case, I was struggling to maintain the change against the stronger current of complacency and had not created a solid team to continue the push toward making the change habitual.

As I have learned, change is easy to start, difficult to grow, and really hard to sustain over the long haul. Whether you are trying to energize a company, save a failed strategy, or reorganize teams, you'll find value in what Kotter has done in *Leading Change*, presenting ways to redirect the river by providing us with sandbags and step-by-step instructions on where to place them for maximum, lasting effect. JC

Leading Change, Harvard Business School Press, Hardcover 1996, ISBN 9780875847474

WHERE TO NEXT? ↦ Page 94 for **how the future is all about change** ↦ Page 82 for **a zealot's version of change** ↦ Page 186 to **choose your approach to change** | EVEN MORE: *Our Iceberg Is Melting* by John P. Kotter; *Managing at the Speed of Change* by Daryl R. Conner; *Managing Transitions* by William Bridges

The Economist

The Only Magazine You Need to Read

There isn't always time to read a book, so if you can find time to read only one business publication a week, make it *The Economist.*

The Economist has been at the nexus of business, politics, and community since British hatmaker James Wilson founded it in 1843. The mission of the weekly paper was to promote free trade and oppose the protectionist trade policies of the British Parliament.

The now-worldwide publication continues to advocate for free trade. And because of the strong devotion to that mission, *The Economist* staff is not confined to reporting only on the business community, but covers all aspects of contemporary life—political movements and trends, government policy, international debates, science, and culture—that may affect that community. These aspects include how its members go to work, do business, and interact with others.

This approach serves the business community well, for business is intricately tied to these forces—the political and social landscapes surrounding it.

Whereas magazines like *Forbes* and *Fortune* focus more narrowly on following American politics and financial markets, and tend to be influenced by Wall Street, *The Economist* examines and reports on the larger context in which those markets exist. Staff members are anonymous when they write for *The Economist,* which lends the periodical an objective credibility and turns the spotlight on the issue at hand rather than on an individual writer's perspective.

Every issue of *The Economist* offers in-depth coverage of the week's events with sections devoted specifically to the United States, the Americas, Asia, the Middle East and Africa, Europe, and its native country, Great Britain. Its content includes analysis and insight on the overall business and political climate, sections devoted to books and the arts, and quarterly reports on science and technology.

Written by Todd Sattersten
with Dylan Schleicher

Questions of Character

JOSEPH L. BADARACCO JR.

Reviewed by Todd

Stories play a central role in business books. Whether it is the tale of how Richard Branson created his Virgin companies or the investigation of Ken Lay and Jeff Skilling's shell games at Enron, stories convey powerful lessons. However, when the episodes of a business leader's career are recounted via a journalist's profile, a formal case study, or a reflective autobiography, we the readers often wonder if the events are "true" or distorted by time or even intentional misdirection. Former Hewlett-Packard CEO Carly Fiorina and board member Tom Perkins clearly have different perspectives on the events surrounding Ms. Fiorina's departure from the company, and such differing perspectives can lead to alternate but completely plausible conclusions, making the lessons to be learned unclear.

Instead of wrestling with the inevitable complexities of real-life business studies, professor of business ethics at Harvard Business School Joseph Badaracco felt fiction could be used as a learning tool. Fictional stories have the unique advantage of not being tied to reality. This provides, ironically, a more reliable view into the thoughts, motivations, and actions of the characters, either directly or via a narrator. Badaracco searched extensively for classic works of fiction that specifically address the challenges and nuances of leadership, and he developed a course at the Harvard Business School around this idea. *Questions of Character* is the hardcover version of that curriculum.

Each chapter addresses one of eight questions about leadership through a concise summary of a fictional work, followed by a careful reflection of the protagonist's struggles. The first four stories focus on situations one might face early in a career, while the final four illuminate the challenges a leader with growing responsibilities faces.

To consider the question "How Flexible Is My Moral Code?" Badaracco recounts the lessons learned in Chinua Achebe's *Things Fall Apart*. Okonkwo, the story's African tribal leader, works hard as a young man, eventually earning wealth (along with the associated respect) and becoming the tribe's leader. His village and its way of life are challenged physically and morally by the arrival of white colonists, but Okonkwo is unable to react to the siege, confined by his ritualistic, inflexible moral code. Badaracco contrasts this with a moral code that is like an "old, weathered tree"—one that has deep, value-based roots and tall branches that sway or even bend to the surrounding environment.

The stories that Badaracco uses effectively move us past the rote rules most business books offer and more realistically reflect life's variability. Willy Loman from Arthur Miller's *Death of a Salesman* embodies the very real consequences dreams can have on their holders in Badaracco's chapter: "Do You Have a Good Dream?" The captain in Joseph Conrad's *The Secret Sharer* shows how difficult it is to truly know the answer to the question "Am I Ready to *Take* Responsibility?"

"[S]erious fiction gives us a unique, inside view of leadership."

In each example, Badaracco challenges readers to slip into the shoes of the protagonist and ask him- or herself, "What would I do?" In this unique approach to the business book, Badaracco engages the reader's imagination and forces each of us to ask questions of our own character. TS

Questions of Character: Illuminating the Heart of Leadership Through Literature, Harvard Business School Press, Hardcover 2006, ISBN 9781591399681

WHERE TO NEXT? ❱❱ Page 63 for **how to use stories as a leader** ❱❱ Page 252 for **serious questions of character** ❱❱ Page 256 for **more subtle questions of character** | EVEN MORE: *Things Fall Apart* by Chinua Achebe; *The Love of the Last Tycoon* by F. Scott Fitzgerald; *I Come as a Thief* by Louis Auchincloss; *A Man for All Seasons* by Robert Bolt; *Antigone* by Sophocles

The Story Factor

ANNETTE SIMMONS

Reviewed by Jack

Storytelling has long been a valued method of communication for many people and in many cultures. The effectiveness of this art is difficult to quantify and even more difficult to apply to business. And yet, Annette Simmons, president of Group Process Consulting, contends that storytelling is the best way for leaders to persuade and motivate their people. But for many leaders, storytelling does not come naturally and is hard to learn because of its amorphous nature. Simmons explains: "Breaking storytelling down into pieces, parts, and priorities destroys it. There are some truths that we just know, we can't prove it but we know them to be true. Storytelling moves us into the place where we trust what we know, even if it can't be measured, packaged, or validated empirically."

Most businesspeople, Simmons contends, have had their ability to storytell trained out of them; facts, research, and PowerPoint skills are favored over the art of storytelling. Yet Simmons warns that because people have easy access to too much information, they don't want or need—and perhaps may distrust—facts. Facts can be manipulative and limiting. People want to believe in what a leader has to say, to have faith. "It is faith that moves mountains, not facts," she says. And only stories, Simmons believes, can tap into this desire. In *The Story Factor*, Simmons presents a convincing argument for the unique power of the story to inspire and influence, and offers advice on improving your storytelling skills to garner the best response from your audience.

To help us rediscover our innate talent for storytelling, Simmons presents six different types of stories that have the power to influence others: Who I Am; Why I Am Here; the Vision; Teaching; Values-in-Action; and I Know What You Are Thinking. She gives examples of each type along with instructions on how to create your own story. For example, in the beginning of any story, you must tell people who you are and why you are speaking to them. Personal stories work best to explain your motivation and allow you to explain your position before your audience can draw assumptions.

When you have a significant point to make to an audience—whether you are a new leader coming onboard an organization or an activist detailing the effects of poverty—"you need to see it, feel it, smell it, hear it . . . to 'go there' in your mind. The difference in your delivery will be dramatic. Most people hold back. They hang on so tightly to 'here' they don't go 'there' where their story is." But Simmons believes that most leaders are afraid to open themselves up to such an approach for two main reasons: "The first reason is that they are afraid they will look stupid, corny, manipulative, or 'unprofessional.'" Our image of the professional is of someone who is straightforward, gets to the facts, and refrains from being too emotional. But, Simmons warns, when that happens our delivery becomes cold and ultimately fails to influence listeners.

"Values are meaningless without stories to bring them to life and engage us on a personal level."

The second reason people hold back is that "we are a bunch of control freaks. Losing yourself in the telling of your story means you are not as 'in control' as when you are reading bullet points off slides or reading from notes." Take Tom Peters, for example, who's often lauded as a brilliant presenter and storyteller. Anybody who has seen a great presenter like Peters knows that staying to the facts and refraining from using emotion aren't Tom's traits. When he is done with an all-day seminar, he has given us everything he has to give, and he has really "gone there" with the attendees.

It is one thing to be like Peters and present your stories to an audience that is paying for the opportunity to listen, but trying to influence the unwilling takes some special handling, and Simmons offers a chapter on that subject. She suggests that storytelling offers a real advantage in high-risk circumstances. In this case, you can't lose. You may not win, but you can't lose. When you are in the middle of serious negotiations and dealing only with facts or rational thinking, you are actually drawing a line in the sand. This gives your opponent the opportunity to say no, to disagree, to prove you wrong. When you use stories, you can sometimes move around that obstacle, and even if you can't move around it, you can revisit the subject because there is no clear "no."

In delving into the do's and don'ts of storytelling, Simmons emphasizes that we need to use this influential tool for good. An accomplished storyteller herself, Simmons explains:

> Storytelling is like any other art. It can be done well. It can be done badly. And sometimes the ones who do it really well get the big head and fly too close to the sun. Power is power. When you tell a powerful story of influence you will feel this rush of power. You will look out at a sea of faces or even into the eyes of one enraptured face and know that you are *inside* the head of the person listening to you. You have gained access to a secret place where their imagination paints new realities and draws new conclusions based on the stories played there. Although you might not control the whole show, you are one of the stars.

This passage speaks to how intimate a relationship between storyteller and audience member can become, how there must be trust in that intimacy. A storyteller should never betray that trust.

Simmons uses various stories and parables as examples throughout the book, along with practical advice on becoming a better communicator. As a leader, knowing how to influence a situation or group of people is a valuable—no, essential—asset, and *The Story Factor* is the book to help you hone your skills. JC

The Story Factor: Inspiration, Influence, and Persuasion Through the Art of Storytelling, Basic Books, Paperback 2006, ISBN 9780465078073

WHERE TO NEXT? ➤ Page 183 for **a story about teams** ◄ Page 52 for **a story about leadership** ➤ Page 167 for **a story about constraints** | EVEN MORE: *The Hero with a Thousand Faces* by Joseph Campbell; *The Leader's Guide to Storytelling* by Stephen Denning; *What's Your Story?* by Craig Wortmann

Never Give In!

SPEECHES BY WINSTON CHURCHILL,
SELECTED BY HIS GRANDSON, WINSTON S. CHURCHILL
Reviewed by Jack

Here's the scene: Your organization is being attacked by the same competition that has beaten you badly in the past. Your organization is on its own, much like an island, without many options for escape or for immediate help. The board has tried to negotiate with this competitor and reached an agreement that was quickly broken. The board decides to dump the CEO and bring back an old guy out of retirement to try and rally the people. This guy is known for unconventional management methods, but is a great communicator; in fact, he is arguably the greatest communicator of the twentieth century.

If you haven't guessed by now, this hypothetical organization is actually the United Kingdom in 1940 and the reinstated CEO is Winston Churchill.

Churchill was presented the ultimate turnaround situation . . . only his company happened to be the United Kingdom, not the United Motors Company. Consider June 1940: The Germans kicked the British army off the European continent. It was one of the worst defeats in modern warfare and ended just off the coast of England at Dunkirk. The United States was not prepared to help Britain defend herself, so she was on her own. Enter a sixty-six-year-old man who proved to be history's greatest turnaround artist.

The similarities between Churchill's position and that of a modern-day CEO are compelling. Communication and motivation are crucial to any change, the hallmarks of good leadership. To turn around the country, Winston Churchill called upon his innate talents as one of the great orators of modern times. *Never Give In!* is a collection of Churchill's speeches selected by his grandson. The speeches in this volume range in time from his first speech, delivered in 1897 at the age of twenty-two to the Primrose League, called "The Dried-Up Drainpipe of Radicalism," to a 1963 address at the age of eighty-eight at the White House after receiving his honorary United States citizenship. These selections are only representative of his work, as a complete collection of his speeches would run eight volumes.

Each selection begins with a short preface to put the featured speech into historical context. For example, the preface to Churchill's speech after the evacuation of Dunkirk explains: "National rejoicing verged on euphoria, which Churchill was anxious to dampen down." This setting of the scene prepares the reader for what follows in the speech. In this case, Churchill, after many minutes of desperately needed upbeat and positive statements about the evacuation, added, "We must be very careful not to assign to this deliverance the attributes of a victory. *Wars are not won by evacuations.* But there was a victory inside this deliverance, which should be noted. It was gained by the Air Force" (emphasis added). Churchill was careful not to depress his audience, and yet he remained committed to portraying a realistic picture. Many times a leader's first reaction is to counter the opinion of the masses with a large dose of reality, but, in truth, the ability to choose a milder tone or first acknowledge the emotions of the majority can help spread the message more convincingly than a heavy hand.

"I would say to the House, as I said to those who have joined this Government: 'I have nothing to offer but blood, toil, tears and sweat.'"

In his final speech to the House of Commons in 1955, Churchill advised the English people, "The day may dawn when fair play, love of one's fellow-men, respect for justice and freedom, will enable tormented generations to march forth serene and triumphant from the hideous epoch in which we have to dwell. Meanwhile, never flinch, never weary, never despair." Clearly, Churchill's oratory and writing talents were manna considering the historic circumstances in which he found himself. And while few if any of us may be brought out of retirement to save a country at war, each day we have the opportunity to lead.

Never Give In! is a book that should be on your bookshelf, ready to serve as a motivator the next time you must present your best self. **JC**

Never Give In! The Best of Winston Churchill's Speeches, Hyperion, Paperback 2003, ISBN 9780786888702

WHERE TO NEXT? ▸ Page 108 for **more on selling the invisible** ▸ Page 99 for **the psychology of persuasion** ▸ Page 308 for **why we still read Churchill today** | EVEN MORE: *The Second World War* by Winston S. Churchill; *The Lost Art of the Great Speech* by Richard Dowis; *Churchill on Leadership* by Steven F. Hayward; *The Wit and Wisdom of Winston Churchill* by James C. Humes

STRATEGY is the sum of all a company does to compete in the marketplace. Decisions range from whether or not to offer free shipping to determining if Omaha is the best place for the new plant. Are you going to thrust or feint? There are an infinite number of ways to put the pieces together, and these books show that some combinations are better than others.

In Search of Excellence

THOMAS J. PETERS AND ROBERT H. WATERMAN JR.

Reviewed by Todd

I n *Search of Excellence* marked a turning point in the evolution of business books, and so it makes the appropriate starting point for our recommended books on strategy. Prior to its 1982 release, historians and academics controlled the discussion about the organization of business, and to no one's surprise, their reportings were often dry and outdated. With this book, Tom Peters and Robert Waterman popularized the exploration of organizational success and created a contemporary conversation that was accessible to a wider audience. The importance of this title in the narrative arc of business thought, as well as the findings themselves, cannot be overstated.

Peters and Waterman first write a capsule history of organizational theory on their way to making a broader case for how organizations must be designed. The arc starts at the turn of the century with political economist Max Weber and mechanical engineer Frederick Taylor. Most are familiar with Taylor for his popularization of time studies and the 1911 publication of *The Principles of Scientific Management*, but it was Weber who suggested bureaucracy as the optimal form for human organization. Then, in *Strategy and Structure* (1962), Alfred Chandler presented the idea that businesses should organize themselves in response to the strictures of the marketplace.

In writing *In Search of Excellence*, Peters and Waterman arrived at a conclusion about the success of an organization that couldn't be more different from those early theories on business organization: *people are irrational and the structures that organize them must account for that.* This argument was 180 degrees counter to the historical modeling of business organizations after the military approach, in which managers fixated on the control of their homogenous teams while following the established five-year strategic plan. Instead, Peters and Waterman advocate humanistic values, including meaning, a small amount of control, and positive reinforcement as a postmilitaristic model. The conclusion is that the soft stuff matters. Culture matters. People matter.

Through this lens, Peters and Waterman spent five years researching such stalwart companies as Boeing, HP, and 3M, which engaged their employees as vital contributors to the success of the company and not simply as rank and file. The second half of *In Search of Excellence* reveals eight principles of organizational behavior gleaned from conversations with these companies:

1. A Bias for Action
2. Stay Close to the Customer
3. Autonomy and Entrepreneurship
4. Productivity through People
5. Hands-On, Value Driven
6. Stick to the Knitting
7. Simple Form, Lean Staff
8. Simultaneous Loose-Tight Properties

Over the twenty-five years since this book was released, others have taken on the challenge of finding the magical model for business success, and as a result, these ideas may look familiar. However, they deserve to be looked at, without preconceptions, as trailblazing concepts providing a prescription for business excellence, and for how surprisingly seldom they are adopted.

> **"In observing the excellent companies, and specifically the way they interact with customers, what we found most striking was the consistent presence of *obsession*. This characteristically occurred as a seemingly unjustifiable overcommitment to some form of quality, reliability, or service."**

In contrast to earlier management texts, *In Search of Excellence* provides a reading experience to be enjoyed, not slogged through. Peters and Waterman write from the viewpoint of passionate observers, and the result is the near-equivalent to sitting in a conference room and listening to these executives recount their tales. The enthusiasm is contagious. (Try listening to the audio sometime with Peters narrating if you really want contagious enthusiasm.) This quality imparts a certain realism to the book that will inspire immediate new behaviors. The book has acquired a historical level of interest, like reading from the journal of an industrial archaeologist. It reported on Wal-Mart fifteen years before its emergence into retail dominance; it talks about the HP Way as a cultural positive; and, before Google, 3M was held up as the company that encouraged employees to spend a portion of their time pursing their passions.

In Search of Excellence advances a timeless vision of business organization: employees—with all of their irrational quirks and natural craziness—are embraced for those very same characteristics. Peters and Waterman posit a truism that has only become more established with time—that the human variable is the fuel that runs the organization. ᴛs

In Search of Excellence: Lessons from America's Best-Run Companies, Collins Business Essentials Edition, Hardcover 2006, ISBN 9780060548780

WHERE TO NEXT? ❱ Page 74 for **a structured view of strategy** ❰ Page 66 for **an example of great leadership** ❱ Page 52 for **taking a leadership leap** | EVEN MORE: *Re-Imagine!* by Tom Peters; *Give Your Speech, Change the World* by Nick Morgan; *Mavericks at Work* by William C. Taylor and Polly G. LaBarre

Good to Great

JIM COLLINS
Reviewed by Todd

N
o one in the last fifteen years has had a greater impact on the discussion of organizational success than Jim Collins. *Good to Great* has sold over two million copies since its 2001 publication, and when you ask chief executives about the books that made a significant impact on their decision making, this book is referenced more often than any other. With *Good to Great*, Collins introduced a new lexicon into management meetings, using memorable metaphors like "the hedgehog concept" and "the flywheel." Most important, he changed the conversation.

Collins's previous book, *Built to Last*, detailed the habits of century-old institutions that had long since established their reputations. Collins wrote *Good to Great* in response to business leaders who wanted to know if they could alter the course of their average companies and achieve the greatness won by the titans characterized in *Built to Last*. He spent five years searching for the answer . . . and the answer was yes.

Collins and his team looked for companies that showed a period of average (or below-average) market returns followed by a run of sustained success. These good-to-great companies were required to return 300 percent over and above the S&P 500 and to have sustained those results over a fifteen-year period. Only eleven Fortune 500 companies passed Collins's strict criteria.

The good-to-great companies were notable for another reason: they were not notable. The list lacked blue chip stalwarts (and media darlings) like General Electric and Coca-Cola. Missing were firms from fast-growth, high-tech sectors, like Intel. Instead, readers will find a steel-maker, three retailers, a couple of financial services providers, three well-known consumer package goods companies, a health-care product company, and another that sold postal meters. This was exactly the message that leaders wanted to believe: if Pitney-Bowes and Fannie Mae can do it, so can we.

Comparing good-to-great companies with a set of peers, Collins discovered a series of practices that were put in action even before the companies transitioned to greatness. During this time, companies identified and promoted leaders who were ambitious—not about their careers, but rather about the overall success of the company. These modest leaders then spent unusual amounts of time selecting the right team before deciding where to take the company, and may have allowed for limited growth until the right talent could be found. Then, these leaders created an environment that allowed employees to voice opinions and take on responsibility.

When companies finally made the transition, they built upon those preparation practices and brought a focus to their efforts. To bring concreteness to this idea, Collins references the ancient Greek fable "The Hedgehog and the Fox," using essayist Isaiah Berlin's analysis, "The fox knows many things, but the hedgehog knows one big thing." The Hedgehog Concept sits at the center of three intersecting circles:

1. What you can be best in the world at
2. What drives your economic engine
3. What you are deeply passionate about

To illustrate the "Hedgehog Concept" at work in business, Collins points to Walgreens. Pharmacists founded and still run the drugstore chain today, which lends authenticity and passion to its mission. The company altered its measurement for economic success by shifting its focus from profit per store to profit per customer visit, because management had the insight that winning loyal customers was about more than being a chain store and having a brand name. Being the most convenient drugstore was the company's differentiator and what it could be best at in the world. This focus now informs all aspects of Walgreens' strategy, from determining the street intersections for store locations to choosing products that best serve their customers.

"Good is the enemy of great."

All good-to-great companies have just such a deliberate nature. Collins describes a disciplined culture that provides constraints while still letting individuals decide the best course of action. Also, he finds that in these companies, technology is assistive, not a driver. Collins compares these efforts to pushing on a gigantic flywheel; the initial efforts are difficult, but the companies slowly build momentum and the ever-increasing rotations propel them forward. This slow and steady mind-set stands in stark contrast to the Tom Peters technicolor "dream big or go home" view of the world.

The book's rational approach to success finds a welcome home on the bookshelves of accountants, lawyers, MBAs, small-business owners, and entrepreneurs. With never-ending pressure from customers and shareholders, every manager is on a quest to find a path to success, but *Good to Great* offers more than that. Collins writes an inspirational tale that gives readers permission to believe they and their companies can achieve what the limited few can do. TS

Good to Great: Why Some Companies Make the Leap . . . and Others Don't, HarperCollins, Hardcover 2001, ISBN 9780066620992

WHERE TO NEXT? « Page 71 for **a supporter of good** » Page 144 for **more strategic methodology** » Page 219 for **how to get started** | EVEN MORE: *Good to Great and the Social Sectors* by Jim Collins; *Built to Last* by Jim Collins and Jerry I. Porras; *Blue Ocean Strategy* by W. Chan Kim and Renée Mauborgne

One of the difficulties in choosing which books to include in this compilation was evaluating the accessibility of the book itself versus the value of the idea contained within. There are many superb ideas that don't translate well into the book form, and there are thousands of books whose ideas never should have been published at that length.

Two books in particular deserve mention for the quality of their ideas, but are ones we cannot recommend in their popular book form. In both cases, the book is dense. The diligent reader is welcome to pursue the original works, but let us suggest more practical routes to accessing their valuable ideas.

The Best Route to an Idea

① Michael Porter's *Five Forces of Strategy*

Porter's defining work on competitive strategy is arguably the most important development of business theory in the last three decades. Business students can recite, from memory, the five forces (now repeat with me: suppliers, customers, competitors, substitutes, and new entrants). Porter's book, *Competitive Strategy,* provides an exhaustive 592-page academic view of the material, inappropriate for the majority of readers.

→ Start instead with Porter's *"The Five Competitive Forces That Shape Strategy,"* the 2008 revised version of the original article he wrote for *Harvard Business Review* in 1979. It encompasses all the basics of competitive strategy in nineteen pages.

② Peter Senge's *Learning Organizations*

Upon cracking open Senge's best-selling *The Fifth Discipline,* the casual reader is seduced by the fluidity of the opening chapter, only to find himself bogged down in the author's impenetrable writing style. Senge's primary insight that organizations compete by learning faster than their counterparts builds on the works of Chris Argyris and bears consideration in the discussion of pinnacle business thought.

→ The way to painlessly access the material is with *The Fifth Discipline Fieldbook* and *The Dance of Change*. Written by Senge and a team of writers, both paperback titles are filled with essays, sidebars, and exercises that make *The Fifth Discipline* concepts a pleasure to absorb.

Written by Todd Sattersten

The Innovator's Dilemma

CLAYTON M. CHRISTENSEN
Reviewed by Todd

Many in book publishing have a romanticized view of the industry's origin, beginning with Johannes Gutenberg and the movable-type printing press he invented in 1453. While that treasured form has changed little in the past five and a half centuries, the way the book is sold and distributed has changed dramatically in the last thirty years. Independent bookstores first struggled against the mall chains of Waldenbooks and B. Dalton, then the big-box retailers such as Barnes & Noble and Borders, and now the online superstore, Amazon. And these retail redistributions pale in comparison to the tectonic shifts that lie ahead in the form of print-on-demand and electronic distribution of books. In *The Innovator's Dilemma*, Clayton Christensen shows how management practices that typically serve executives well fail in the face of just such disruptive innovations.

Christensen begins by drawing a distinction between two types of innovation. In the first, everything from new products to customer service is designed to meet customers' demands. In the normal course of business, customers pay the bills, and writing those checks gives them significant influence over an organization's decision making. New ideas and opportunities, evaluated on the ability to serve existing customers and earn the necessary margins to support the company, are called *sustaining innovations* and are always successful ventures for existing (and dominant) firms.

But sometimes, innovation creates a new technology or reveals a new way to organize a firm's resources. This *disruptive innovation* does not offer the performance needed in the existing market, and entrant companies are forced to find a new set of customers who value innovation on a different set of metrics than those of the traditional market. Existing companies disregard the disruptive innovation because of its lower margins, and the newcomers find a small beachhead outside the existing market, using that market space to develop further. As the performance of disruptive innovations outpaces the sustaining innovations, entrants move into established markets and their lower cost structure forces incumbents further up-market, forfeiting existing profitable markets.

Clayton Christensen provides an array of case studies in *The Innovator's Dilemma*, including how the steel industry is still at the mercy of the disruptive innovation of minimills. Using scrap steel over iron ore, minimills require one-tenth the scale and can produce steel at 15 percent lower cost than traditional integrated steel mills. When minimills first emerged in the 1960s, they were able to produce only low-quality steel whose only market was construction rebar. The integrated mills were happy to cede this low-end, price-sensitive market. What the incumbents missed was the minimills' desire to move further into their markets. With a completely different cost structure and technology that was improving faster than existing methods, minimills began producing structural steel and sheet steel. Minimills now account for 50 percent of the steel made in the United States, and here is the amazing part: at no point did an existing steel company using integrated mills construct a minimill to take advantage of the disruptive innovation.

"To succeed consistently, good managers need to be skilled not just in choosing, training, and motivating the right people for the right job, but in choosing, building, and preparing the right *organization* for the job as well."

To suggest that the integrated steel mills simply hid their heads in the sand would be too easy. Christensen says most markets that serve as the launch point for disruptive innovation are too small for large organizations to concentrate on. These emerging markets lack clear evidence that they will turn out profitable. When disruptive technologies are being developed, the applications for them are unpredictable, and worse, companies are misled when they attempt to use the same tools from their mature markets. In nearly every case of disruptive innovation, a new set of companies rises to dominate the industry.

For disruptive innovation to flourish, says Christensen, companies need to create the right organizational structure. Companies often start by promoting successful managers to lead new efforts, but without addressing the processes and values of the new group, the leadership will start to make decisions the same way it always has. Disruptive innovation requires an autonomous organization with the appropriate cost structure to address the emerging markets. In the 1970s, the motor controls industry was disrupted by programmable logic controllers (PLCs), and the only company to successfully traverse the disruption was Rockwell Automation (then Allen-Bradley). The Milwaukee-based company did so by investing in two smaller companies shortly after commercial introduction of PLCs and combining them into a separate division, which it pitted against its existing electromechanical division. Rockwell showed that it is possible to establish dominance during a period of disruptive innovation while maintaining market leadership in the traditional product.

While the innovator's dilemma stems from uncontrollable external pressures, dealing with it is an internal dilemma. Managers lack the information and experience needed to make confident investments in disruptive technology. The tried and true resource allocation process favors current customers and their needs, starving incubatory projects of needed love and attention. And to survive the innovation pipeline, the disruptive technology needs the marketing leader to find new clients who appreciate its current capabilities. As performance improves, the customers who showed no interest in the initial idea are exactly the ones who will be clamoring for it. TS

The Innovator's Dilemma: The Revolutionary Book That Will Change the Way You Do Business, Collins Business Essentials edition, Paperback 2006, ISBN 9780060521998

WHERE TO NEXT? » Page 244 for **the disruptive story of steel** » Page 321 for **the story of global disruption** » Page 183 for **a story of team dysfunction** | EVEN MORE: *The Innovator's Solution* by Clayton M. Christensen and Michael E. Raynor; *Competitive Strategy* by Michael E. Porter; *Innovation and Entrepreneurship* by Peter F. Drucker

Learn From Experience

Case studies are an effective way to show theory in practice. These three Harvard Business School case studies further one's thinking about a business issue, and each is from an author with a book that provides the perfect next step for the reader looking for more depth. Find complete case studies at www.harvardbusiness.com.

Learn how to **establish a unique competitive strategy.**

↓

CASE:

Matching Dell
by Jan W. Rivkin and Michael E. Porter.
Michael Dell has used competitive analysis to become a leader in the PC industry by offering his products where consumers want them most. Shifting between direct and retail trends, Dell found and followed a strategy that is now the industry standard. By focusing on products and services and building an infrastructure to support his strategy, Dell has become the longest-tenured CEO in the PC industry.

BOOK:

Competitive Strategy: Techniques for Analyzing Industries and Competitors
by Michael E. Porter.
In this landmark book about strategic management, Porter lets readers in on Dell's game plan and offers tools any business can use to succeed in its industry.

Learn about **translating strategy into results.**

↓

CASE:

Boston Lyric Opera
by Robert S. Kaplan.
In late 1992, the Boston Lyric Opera realized that production costs were outweighing income. Under new leadership, it reevaluated its productions and scaled them down while still focusing on quality. After seeing increased membership, the Opera leveraged that loyal community to convert members to donors and solicit volunteer workers and board members, resulting in an engaged audience and a return to profitability.

BOOK:

The Balanced Scorecard: Translating Strategy into Action
by Robert S. Kaplan and David P. Norton.
Kaplan's book reinforces the idea of how organizations profit by understanding and comparing both tangible and intangible costs and benefits.

Learn how to **use innovation to your advantage.**

↓

CASE:

Eli Lilly and Company: Innovation in Diabetes Care
by Clayton Christensen.
Eli Lilly had manufactured the highest quality of insulin available since the early 1920s. However, when competitor Novo Nordisk came out with an insulin pen in the early 1990s—a device that provided customers with incredible ease of use, Eli Lilly knew it was in trouble. It responded by creating a similar pen, but one filled with an even better product that closely matched how insulin acted in nondiabetic people.

BOOK:

The Innovator's Dilemma
by Clayton Christensen.
Christensen's book elaborates on how companies such as Eli Lilly can examine their place in the market and leverage creative ideas to move forward.

Written by Jon Mueller

Only the Paranoid Survive

ANDREW S. GROVE

Reviewed by Jack

As one of the founders and a former CEO of Intel, Andy Grove helped create a leading technology business. At first blush, *Only the Paranoid Survive* appears to be an autobiography or business narrative, but the subtitle explains the true focus of the book: *How to Exploit the Crisis Points That Challenge Every Company*. This book is an effective crusade for a method of crisis management, or perhaps crisis identification, that is well served by Grove's wealth of experience in a competitive market.

The cornerstone of Grove's book is the Strategic Inflection Point (SIP). Grove advocates the use of Michael Porter's five-forces model to help determine the competitive well-being of a business. In addition to customers, competitors, suppliers, substitutes, and barriers to entry, Grove suggests a sixth force, "complementors," which are businesses that offer complementary products, like what paper is to ink. A company experiences a strategic inflection point when one of these six forces topples its strategic plan, like a ripple becoming a tsunami, silent movies instantly antiquated by talkies, or what Wal-Mart did to Main Street America. When a monumental change like this happens, management is forced to take alternative actions. "The business responds differently to managerial actions than it did before. We have lost control and don't know how to regain it. Eventually, a new equilibrium in the industry will be reached. Some businesses will be stronger, others will be weaker."

Even in retrospect, the moment an SIP happens can be hard to recognize, but an unattended SIP can be deadly to the future of a company. Grove uses the analogy of a lost hiker. At some point along a hike, the hiker realizes that he is lost but doesn't know when he actually became lost, when his foot first veered off the path. Rarely does he at the same moment realize: " 'Things are different. Something has changed.' " Grove advocates awareness as the main weapon against being defeated by an SIP.

Just as with the hiker, how one reacts to an SIP is key to orienting oneself once an SIP has been recognized and acknowledged.

Grove then offers an example from Intel in the early 1980s, when the Japanese arrived in the memory chip market and ate Intel's lunch because the Japanese companies could make the chips cheaper and more efficiently. Grove emphasizes again just how difficult it is to identify an SIP. He uses the metaphor of "signal vs. noise" for distinguishing whether a threat or problem is the real deal or just a temporary blip on the radar. Grove states that the only way to know whether a market or internal change signals an SIP is through "the process of clarification that comes from broad and intensive debate." Grove admits that in this situation, Intel waited too long to acknowledge that they were facing a real SIP due to significant concern about how Intel's existing customers would react to any change in business as usual. What Intel ultimately did was get out of the memory chip market—which was their main business at the time—and move into making processor chips.

The author's analysis of how the computer industry went from a vertical market built with DEC, Wang, and IBM—who made the hardware and software for their own machines—to a horizontal market consisting of Microsoft, Dell, and HP is valuable. When this SIP ran through the computer business, Novell became a "first mover" in networking in the new horizontal industry. Novell, a small, vertically oriented company doing both hardware and software, literally ran out of money to pay suppliers and had to redesign itself. Within a few years, Novell became a billion-dollar business because it was able to react to the SIP quickly. As Grove points out, it is easier to be the best with a narrow focus like networking than by making the best computers with the best software in a vertical business.

"Managing, especially managing through a crisis, is an extremely personal affair."

The book business I started has had three serious Strategic Inflection Points in its lifetime. The anxiety and stress of feeling lost but not knowing how we took the wrong path, just like Grove's hiker, were low points in my career. No business or market is static, and *Only the Paranoid Survive* will convince you to "look over your shoulder" at the potential incoming train that may be a Strategic Inflection Point, and know whether to jump the track or get on at the next station. JC

Only the Paranoid Survive: How to Exploit the Crisis Points That Challenge Every Company, Currency/Doubleday, Paperback 1999, ISBN 9780385483827

WHERE TO NEXT? ◀◀ Page 77 for **more on Porter's five forces** ◀◀ Page 57 for **how to lead through an SIP** ▶▶ Page 244 for **how a company navigated through an SIP** | EVEN MORE: *Andy Grove* by Richard S. Tedlow; *Swimming Across* by Andrew S. Grove; *Direct from Dell* by Michael Dell with Catherine Fredman

Who Says Elephants Can't Dance?

LOUIS V. GERSTNER JR.

Reviewed by Todd

"This is not my autobiography," starts Lou Gerstner in *Who Says Elephants Can't Dance?* As Gerstner's retirement approached, he expected business leaders and bystanders to start asking for his thoughts on the big trends—the economy, globalization, and the like. That was the kind of book he meant to write. Instead, everyone wanted to know how he did it . . . how he turned around IBM. During his tenure from 1993 to 2001, revenues grew from $62.7 billion to $85.9 billion and IBM's stock price grew tenfold. Of course, people were curious; Gerstner believes he had no choice but to write *this* book.

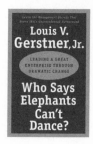

And certainly, to not document the story of how this Long Islander, after stops at McKinsey, American Express, and RJR Nabisco, orchestrated the highest profile turnaround of the twentieth century would have been a travesty. While Jack Welch may have had a tough task reenergizing the still highly successful General Electric, Lou Gerstner gets the top prize for saving Big Blue from near bankruptcy.

When the newly appointed CEO started, rather ominously, on April Fool's Day 1993, he found the company in a shambles. IBM, the pioneer that created the technology industry, had lost half its market share in fewer than ten years. Among competitors, it ranked eleventh in customer satisfaction behind some companies that no longer existed. But Gerstner's gravest concern was IBM's cost position: "On average, our competitors were spending 31 cents to produce $1 of revenue, while we were spending 42 cents for the same end."

To quickly change course, Gerstner made a series of bold decisions. At that time the personal computer was reaching its product zenith and $5 billion were committed to mainframe research and development. Nevertheless, the company-built communications grid was put up for sale. Add to that the abandonment of application development, the decision to sell competitor hardware and software, and a big move into integration services. Thirty-five thousand people were laid off in addition to

TOM WATSON SR.'S BASIC BELIEFS

• Excellence in everything we do.
• Superior customer service.
• Respect for the individual.

the forty-five thousand others who had been let go a year earlier. While these seem like obvious moves in retrospect, Gerstner reflects that, at the time, skepticism filled the pages of business magazines and the halls of IBM office buildings around the world.

But each move was based on a deep strategic view of where IBM and the technology market were headed. The communications network was sold to AT&T for $5 billion as Gerstner saw the coming ubiquity of broadband and IBM's inability to compete with the scale of the existing telecommunication companies. Doubling down on the mainframe business created $19 billion in new revenue, a direct result of hearing the anger of chief information officers and their expectation that IBM defend the role of "big iron" in their transaction-intensive retail, financial, and governmental operations. IBM Global Services went from a rogue arm of the sales function to a $30 billion business that employs one-half of IBM's total workforce.

"Fixing IBM was all about execution. We had to stop looking for people to blame, stop tweaking the internal structure and systems. I wanted no excuses."

After describing the first ten months of his tenure and explaining his strategic moves, Gerstner then digs into the culture of contentment that was pervasive at IBM. Looking back, he believes the root of IBM's problems came from its unparalleled success. The computer giant had for so long been immune to economic cycles and price wars that the company had become insular and unresponsive. Gerstner compares his job of revitalizing the culture to that of "taking a lion raised for all of its life in captivity and suddenly teaching it to survive in the jungle." From abolishing the dress code to sending his executives and their reports out to customers, it was a cultural change made successful by the willingness of hundreds of thousands of employees who believed in Big Blue and in the direction Gerstner was taking the company.

But what about that curious title of this quintessential turnaround story? I'll let Gerstner answer that with a quote that also illuminates just what Gerstner always believed was the potential for IBM:

Big matters. Size can be leveraged. Breadth and depth allow for greater investment, greater risk taking, and longer patience for future payoffs. It isn't a question of whether elephants can prevail over ants. It's a question of whether a particular elephant can dance. If it can, the ants must leave the dance floor. **TS**

Who Says Elephants Can't Dance? Leading a Great Enterprise through Dramatic Change, HarperBusiness, Paperback 2003, ISBN 9780060523800

WHERE TO NEXT? « Page 54 for **the other great corporate turnaround of the twentieth century** » Page 164 for **why one IBM executive compared reengineering to "starting a fire on your head and putting it out with a hammer"** » Page 319 for **comments from the son of IBM's founder** | EVEN MORE: *The Maverick and His Machine* by Kevin Maney; *Father, Son and Company* by Thomas J. Watson Jr. with Peter Petre; *The Future of Competition* by C.K. Prahalad and Venkat Ramaswamy; *Harvard Business Review on Turnarounds* by Harvard Business Review

Discovering the Soul of Service

LEONARD L. BERRY

Reviewed by Jack

We share our home city of operation with a gem of a company: Midwest Airlines. The airline started as a corporate jet fleet that shuttled Kimberly-Clark executives from the company's headquarters in the Fox Valley in the middle of Wisconsin to the company's R&D department in Atlanta, Georgia. When the airline industry was deregulated, the corporate fleet was converted to a passenger airline. Midwest Airlines has grown to handle 50 percent of the Milwaukee market, and it is the customer service that wins the day. Midwest regularly garners accolades as the best domestic carrier, offering flights on reclaimed Boeings with wide leather seats (i.e., room to move). Like all great companies, it creates stories for its customers to tell. The story Midwest Airlines' customers are telling is that warm chocolate chip cookies are served on every flight. There is just something special about the Midwest Airlines experience.

In *Discovering the Soul of Service*, Dr. Leonard Berry discusses fourteen companies, including Midwest, that are sustainable businesses with service at their core. Written ten years ago, the featured businesses had an average age of thirty-one years of work, an admirable amount of time in which to develop tried and true strategies. The companies Berry studied are not the usual business-media suspects and range from Charles Schwab, The Container Store, and Enterprise Rent-A-Car to the St. Paul Saints minor-league baseball team, all companies whose missions vary widely. I must admit that there is only so much new material to read about Southwest Airlines or Starbucks or Harley-Davidson or Ritz Carlton, those common elite examples of good business, no matter how fascinating their evolution. So, Berry's featured businesses offer a fresh perspective, and include those managing 120 employees to over 35,000, those that are public and those that are private, those that are local, national, or international. I find this range adds a depth to this book absent in many others that focus only on the giants of the service industry.

Despite the differences in companies represented, the one thing they have in common is that they all built their success on sustainable service. Only three of the fourteen have had more than two CEOs in their history. Even now, ten years after Berry wrote the book, most are still run by their original CEOs. Having this kind of stability at the top level allows leaders to build trust and show the integrity and authenticity needed to sustain the success.

These organizations are built on the value of humanity, of treating their employees and customers—or, as the author states, the organization and its partners—humanely, with concern for their well-being and opportunities for development. Value-driven leadership, trust-based relationships, and generosity are three of the nine drivers the author calls out as being essential when establishing a humane organization. These values are remarkably consistent among the companies.

Berry shares with us wisdom from leaders who have faced the challenge of maintaining humane organizations in the face of constant pressure. Restaurateur Drew Nieporent has been very successful in a business that can be very defeating. He has many restaurants scattered around the globe and has won every major restaurant award. He believes that building a values-based business is key to building a sustainable business. "'Restaurants are like children,' he says. 'They need your attention when they're young. You give them values and principles and hope they grow up strong.'"

"My purpose in this book is to identify, describe, and illustrate the underlying drivers of sustainable success in service businesses."

Yet there are three challenges in sustaining service success. These challenges are made worse when you are creating value for the customer with service: "The more labor-intensive the service, the greater the challenges of: operating effectively while growing rapidly, operating effectively when competing on price, [and] retaining the initial entrepreneurial spirit of the younger, smaller company." Berry then offers the selected companies as examples of successfully avoiding these pitfalls. He talks about Valujet and its rapid growth in the 1990s . . . and its equally rapid decline because of lax controls and a lack of attention to nonfinancial goals. The company that eventually returned as AirTran had not been able to operate effectively during rapid growth.

Age has taught me to lead a quiet and happy life, and has given me the knowledge that the way to achieve such a life is to live it for the right reasons, whether you follow the Ten Commandments or the Golden Rule. For my own life, I place a lot of value on karma (or, what goes around comes around). You do something because it is the right thing to do, not because you are going to get paid for it. *Discovering the Soul of Service* shows that this type of soul-inspired philosophy has been successful in a wide range of organizations, and Berry shows you how to succeed while holding on to the values around which you built your business and live your life. **JC**

Discovering the Soul of Service: The Nine Drivers of Sustainable Business Success, Free Press, Hardcover 1999, ISBN 9780684845111

WHERE TO NEXT? » Page 279 for **discovering more possibilities** « Page 50 for **the soul of leadership** » Page 207 for **another airline with soul** | EVEN MORE: *A Complaint Is a Gift* by Janelle Barlow and Claus Moller; *Minding the Store* by Stanley Marcus; *The Nordstrom Way* by Robert Spector with Patrick D. McCarthy

Execution

LARRY BOSSIDY AND RAM CHARAN

Reviewed by Jack

O ver ten years ago I worked with an MBAer who listed himself as a Mensa member on his résumé. He was meant to be the operations guy, the strategy guy, while I concentrated on what I did best: sales and service. During the six years we were partners, I would drive to the finish line on a project at the same pace with which I started it; he, on the other hand, would get all revved up at the start but end up taking the leisurely route, often not completing the project at all. Not a productive pattern for accomplishing operational changes and strategic goals. For a time I thought the problem lay with me. Perhaps I was being slipshod or missing something important. Granted, my end result wasn't always perfect and we would have to go back to review parts, but the task had been completed and the changes made were often minimal. A year after he left the company, this book, *Execution*, arrived on my desk and it revealed to me that the problem wasn't mine but his own inability to take action and follow through—to *execute* the big ideas. For me, *Execution* proved to me that action is necessary—no, paramount—to success. And this message clearly resonates with readers, because we all have experienced a failure of execution during our careers.

The value of getting things done on a personal level is a sound one, but execution is about more than personal performance; a company can surely have the same difficulties making strategic moves and acting on new initiatives. As the authors explain, "Execution is a specific set of behaviors and techniques that companies need to master in order to have competitive advantage." This book offers three perspectives on the problem. Part 1 explains the "discipline" of execution.

- Execution is a discipline, and integral to strategy.
- Execution is the major job of the business leader.
- Execution must be a core element of an organization's culture.

Part 2 presents the "building blocks"; and Part 3, the real "how-to" section of the book, emphasizes the need for action. The authors succeed in making it easy to recognize the areas in which we and our companies need to stretch past our comfort zones.

Reading the book is so thoroughly enjoyable, with its conversational style, that it opens us up to the challenges that lie within. Writing in the first person, Bossidy and Charan take turns sharing experiences, and as a result we get the full benefit of their superstar status in the business world. These first-person sections—an approach that should be used more often in business books—add a human feel to the subject. To shore up their conclusions, Bossidy tells "war stories" from Honeywell, Allied Signal, and GE, and Charan adds views from outside of Bossidy's world and from his thirty-five years of experience as an advisor. This dual perspective lends weight to their conclusions.

"Execution is not only the biggest issue facing business today; it is something nobody has explained satisfactorily."

Despite having sold over one million copies in five years, *Execution* has been criticized since it was first published in 2002. Many have cited the use of failed examples and the authors' personal aggrandizing as detrimental to the message. But the elusive skill of getting things done is an evergreen topic in business literature. Look for a better book on organizational effectiveness and you will spend a lot of time searching. I would ask those same people to suggest an alternative. Drucker's *Managing for Results* covers some of the same ground, but lacks the pointed focus of Bossidy and Charan's argument. Here, the authors map out a blueprint for how leaders can inject a healthy sense of realism into their organizations. *Execution*, no matter how readers or critics choose to interpret it, gets to the basic tenet that business doesn't get done unless things happen. JC

Execution: The Discipline of Getting Things Done, Crown Business, Hardcover 2002, ISBN 9780609610572

WHERE TO NEXT? ◄◄ Page 12 for **execution at the individual level** ◄◄ Page 54 for **GE and execution** | EVEN MORE: *Executive Intelligence* by Justin Menkes; *You're in Charge, Now What?* by Thomas J. Neff and James M. Citrin; *The Power of Alignment* by George Labovitz and Victor Rosansky

Competing for the Future

GARY HAMEL AND C. K. PRAHALAD
Reviewed by Todd

Most executives think the competitive fight takes place in the present. Look at how leaders spend the majority of their time—approving yearly budgets, taking global trips to important customers, waiting for the sales number at quarter's close. Gary Hamel and C. K. Prahalad write that the battle, or the war itself, is already lost if business leaders spend all their time on the issues of today. *Competing for the Future* is a fiery rebuke of conventional strategic wisdom, challenging short-term incrementalism as the answer to company growth.

Writing this book in 1994, Hamel and Prahalad were revolting against the vogue of reengineering and "denominator managers" who chose to slash investment and workforce to improve a company's return on investment rather than focus on generating more income with the return they had in hand. At this same time, the authors were seeing a handful of companies redefining their markets with fundamentally new strategies: Wal-Mart, Honda, Canon, Schwab. Getting smaller or better was not the strategy for these mavericks; it was about being different.

Creating strategic differences requires foresight. "If a top management team cannot clearly articulate the five or six fundamental industry trends that most threaten its firm's continued success, it is not in control of the firm's destiny." And the authors say understanding these market forces creates the foresight that allows a company to get to the future first. For those who arrive first, the rewards are plentiful: investment recouped ahead of their foes, early adopters pining for the new with their open checkbooks, and the rule book waiting to be written.

Predicting the exact nature of an industry five or ten years from now is not the end goal, but understanding the forces at play and making an educated guess about direction creates foresight. Hamel and Prahalad's example of the future of a record store illustrates that exact challenge. They write about the advantages of a retail store's knowledgeable staff, immediately available product, and reasonable proximity. However, despite these positives, they go on to describe a future (remember, this was 1994) that sounds eerily like today's iTunes: "10,000 pieces of music," "listen to a 90-second sample," "selections downloaded onto a digital recording device." While it is amazingly accurate in one aspect, completely missing from the description is the emergence of the MP3 format, the role of piracy in distribution, or other Web retailers simply selling a wider selection of product than is possible in a physical outlet. What the authors did predict would have been enough to give any record store a look into the future and time to strategize to fight against the new trend. Thus, a complete picture isn't necessary; awareness is.

A directional sense for trends sketches a picture of the skills a company will need to compete in the future. The term "core competency" was coined by Hamel and Prahalad to describe the broad basket of skills a company needs to compete. Decisions about which core competencies to pursue dictate the markets a company can compete in, and the long-time horizon for competency development can put a company in the right (or wrong) place at the right (or wrong) time. Honda has concentrated its core competencies on engine and power-train development, and this has allowed it to enter markets ranging from motorcycles to small jet aircraft. JVC started investing in the competencies needed to build video cassette recorders twenty years before the product became a mainstream consumer device, and benefited handsomely when that time came.

"[S]eeing the future first may be more about having a wide-angle lens than a crystal ball."

Each chapter in *Competing for the Future* has the thought density of a *Harvard Business Review* article, with the tone of a Sunday fire-and-brimstone sermon. Hamel and Prahalad are preaching the same thing you might hear in the pew on Sundays: consider the choices you make today, for they are the seeds of tomorrow's success.

Competing for the Future, Harvard Business School Press, Paperback 1996, ISBN 9780875847160

WHERE TO NEXT? ▸ Page 164 for the ideology the authors oppose ▸ Page 315 for the realities of market leadership ▸ Page 321 for exercising your wide-angle lens | EVEN MORE: *The Art of the Long View* by Peter Schwartz; *Fortune at the Bottom of the Pyramid* by C. K. Prahalad; *The Mind of the Strategist* by Kenichi Ohmae

SALES AND MARKETING

Peter Drucker said the singular goal of a company is to create customers. Marketing gathers information, formulates product offerings, and develops messages to attract precious prospects. Sales translates interest and intent into dollars and cents. This section covers approaches and pitfalls in the never-ending process of creating customers.

Influence

ROBERT B. CIALDINI, PHD
Reviewed by Todd

T he simple act of accepting a flower from a stranger starts a chain reaction. The recipient immediately feels compelled to reciprocate in some way. Humans are preprogrammed with a whole set of these types of innate behaviors that move us through life. If we were required to consciously consider every decision we made, we would quickly become paralyzed. As humans have evolved, we have developed a set of "mental short-cuts" that helps us deal with this onslaught of choices. Many of these mechanisms are generally positive and have served to help society function and flourish.

Social psychologist Robert Cialdini's deep understanding of human behavior is evident in the wide array of examples he uses throughout *Influence*, especially, as the subtitle tells us, in the psychology of persuasion. Here, university research is interwoven with well-known, often infamous events in U.S. history. He adds personal anecdotes from field research, ranging from busing tables at a high-end restaurant to enrolling as a sales trainee at numerous companies. His research draws together what con men and car dealers have known for a long time: unconscious reactions can also be used to exploit us. He links this phenomenon to a variety of forms of persuasion (identified here in italics).

Back to that flower. This kind of age-old compulsion for *reciprocity* allowed ancient tribes to divide tasks among members and cultures to trade goods across oceans. The Hare Krishnas maintain their sect financially by giving flowers to travelers passing through airports; most recipients automatically return the favor with a small donation. Samples at your local supermarket can create the same feeling of indebtedness; you might pick up the product just to please the salesperson who offered you the sample.

Making commitments and staying consistent with those commitments turns out to be very important to us and those around us. Once a person commits to a point of view, he often has a very hard time doing a U-turn. If you are ever elected the foreman of a jury, Cialdini recommends requiring secret ballots when voting to avoid public commitments that may later cause difficulty in reaching a unanimous verdict. Signing petitions has the same effect; people will commit to bigger and bigger supportive acts (like putting billboards for a social cause in the front yard) after agreeing to little things like a signature. To use this tendency to your advantage when setting a goal—whether quitting smoking or starting a business—the act of writing and sharing your dream activates that dual mechanism of commitment and constituency.

People are also persuaded by taking social cues from others around them. Cialdini labels this form *social proof* and says we are most susceptible under two conditions. The first is when there is uncertainty. Laugh tracks on sitcoms use this opportunity to engage viewers by giving them confirmation that the scene or line should be interpreted as funny. The second condition is when we take cues from those who are similar to us. The more similar, the more likely we are to follow. From the clothing we wear to the music we listen to, social proof is a powerful form of persuasion.

Sales professionals are specifically trained in a technique that plays on *affection*. A bag of golf clubs or baby stroller in your trunk gives the car dealer checking out your trade-in a topic of conversation in which to invoke emotion. Consultants at Tupperware understand and use this technique in a different way, organizing their parties around the host and the bond of friendship shared by the attendees. The strength of affection between attendees is a better predictor of purchase than the affection for the product itself. Our best defense, Cialdini says, is to concentrate on the transaction and not the person presenting it.

The better judgment of our conscious minds can be bypassed, prompting us to do the inexplicable, through the use of *authority*. Cialdini tells of Stanley Milgram's set of experiments conducted in response to the Nazi war crime trials, in which he attempted to determine if individuals could be put in a situation where they would willingly follow orders despite knowing those actions would cause harm to others. Test subjects were told by an authority figure, the researcher, to ask questions of an actor (collaborating with Milgram) and to press a button to send an electric shock to the actor upon each incorrect answer. The shocks increased in intensity with each incorrect answer. The final shock administered a whopping and painful 450 volts to the actor, and about two-thirds of Milgram's subjects willingly flipped all thirty switches needed to reach that point. Milgram concluded that the researcher, firmly exerting authority, created the influence necessary for the subjects to proceed.

Scarcity is probably the easiest type of persuasion to understand, and is the method of influence we are most exposed to. It is a favorite tool of marketers (e.g. "Limited time offer!!!") and salespeople ("I am not sure how much longer this car will be on the lot."), because we hate losing out on things. Lost opportunity creates a stronger desire for what can't be obtained readily. Hence, misprinted stamps and Brett Favre's rookie card carry higher value due to their limited supply.

"I can admit it freely now. All my life I've been a patsy."

There is protection against becoming a victim of manipulation, Cialdini assures readers. After explaining each type of persuasion, he offers antidotes to being fooled, tricked, and exploited. For example, if a salesman tries to employ his charms, remember to focus on the merits of the deal and not the person selling it to you. But Cialdini believes the reliability of these shortcuts must remain intact for us to function in a world that is growing ever more complicated.

After the entertaining stories and cautionary tales fade away, Cialdini leaves us with two key insights. First, our lives would be difficult without the mental shortcuts that influence our decision making, and second, those same assets leave the door open to exploitation, creating a blurry line between an innocuous recommendation and a planned deception. **TS**

Influence: The Psychology of Persuasion, Collins Business Essentials edition, Paperback 2007, ISBN 9780061241895

WHERE TO NEXT? » Page 323 for **more than you know** « Page 63 for **how stories can influence** « Page 21 for **a classic on influence** | EVEN MORE: *Nudge* by Richard H. Thaler and Cass R. Sunstein; *Sway* by Ori Brafman and Ron Brafman; *The Art of Woo* by G. Richard Shell and Mario Moussa; *Blink* by Malcolm Gladwell

Positioning:
The Battle for Your Mind

AL RIES AND JACK TROUT
Reviewed by Jack

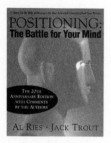

When you think of portable music, one brand rules: iPod. How Apple came to dominate this market is simply an extraordinary example of successful "positioning." Positioning is the process by which you get your product into the minds of prospective customers. In 1972, Al Ries and Jack Trout introduced their idea of positioning in a series of articles in *Advertising Age* called "The Positioning Era Cometh." In 1981, they published *Positioning: The Battle for Your Mind*. Positioning becomes necessary for a product, service, or company because overcommunication in today's world leads to what Ries and Trout call an "oversimplified mind"—a defense mechanism consumers use to deal with all the clutter companies and, subsequently, marketers throw at them. The choices available to us today can be overwhelming. For example, in the 1970s, Frito Lay offered ten chip varieties; in the 1990s, it offered seventy-eight. Running shoes? There were five choices in the 1970s, 285 varieties in the 1990s. With this kind of contemporary overload, the mind just shuts down. So, for Ries and Trout, "[p]ositioning is an organized system for finding windows in the mind."

Since advertising's effectiveness is weakened by this overload, the authors advise marketers that only a simplified message will actually make it through the clutter. One of the ways they suggest positioning a product is by "[o]wning a word in the mind. Volvo owns 'safety.' BMW owns 'driving,' FedEx owns 'overnight,' Crest owns 'cavities.' Once you own a word in the mind, you have to use it or lose it." Just how do you embed a word that symbolizes your product in a person's mind? One way is to get there first. We remember Charles Lindbergh and Roger Banister as the "first" to fly across the Atlantic Ocean and to break the four-minute mile, respectively, but we don't remember who the next person was. Another powerful way to be memorable, the authors say, is "If you can't be the first in a category, then set up a new category you can be first in." For example,

Miller Brewing certainly wasn't the first brewer, but it created Miller Lite, the first mainstream light beer.

For the twentieth anniversary of this classic, the publisher reprinted a new version in hardcover, and the authors added comments in the margins of the expanded format. What really adds value in the new edition are stories of more recent successes and failures. The authors' concise and direct writing style made this book a success when it was first published in 1981, and their clear communication of facts and opinions, continued in subsequent editions, compels readers to think about marketing in a new way.

"Positioning is an organized system for finding windows in the mind. It is based on the concept that communication can only take place at the right time and under the right circumstances"

Ries and Trout believe you can position just about anything. Their case examples range from the Catholic Church to the country of Belgium to the biotech firm Monsanto. The authors believe you can even position yourself. In each case, the end game is clarity, and the primary mission is to become the customer's first thought. **JC**

Positioning: The Battle for Your Mind, McGraw-Hill, Twentieth Anniversary Edition, Hardcover 2001, ISBN 9780071359168

WHERE TO NEXT? « Page 54 for **the power of being number 1 or number 2** » Page 241 for **the power of consistency** » Page 210 for **the power of low prices** | EVEN MORE: *Ogilvy on Advertising* by David Ogilvy; *Building Strong Brands* by David A. Aaker; *The 22 Immutable Laws of Marketing* by Al Ries and Jack Trout

A New Brand World

SCOTT BEDBURY WITH STEPHEN FENICHELL

Reviewed by Jack

Scott Bedbury was at the epicenter of the ascent of two of the most recognizable brands in the world. He was senior vice president of marketing at Starbucks from 1995 to 1998. During that period Starbucks had over 40 percent annual growth. Before Starbucks, he was head of advertising at Nike for seven years during the period in which the company changed its image radically. In *A New Brand World*, he offers insight into these classic brand creations and delivers a relevant book about brand building, brand extension, and brand loyalty. The book is heavily reliant on the Starbucks and Nike examples, but he also looks at other branding successes and failures.

Bedbury helped launch the "Bo Knows" and "Just Do It" campaigns. In rich detail, he relates stories of internal tension at Nike as it moved from its previous testosterone-heavy, "wimps need not apply" attitude to a brand with enough room for the entire family, and, ultimately, to the leading sports and fitness company. "Just Do It" became a brand that isn't about sneakers or products but about values and ethos.

Bedbury went on to help create an actual brand definition for Starbucks, which, the year after he started, opened its first outlet outside the United States, in Japan. In a role that was much different than his previous one at Nike, he worked with Howard Schultz to create a brand code that helped define who Starbucks was. To do that he needed to gather intelligence, and to procure the intelligence, he used a three-pronged approach. First, he researched the product: coffee. He found that it was "... estimated that more than 3 billion cups of coffee were brewed around the world every day. Out of this, I figured that at least 2.7 billion of those cups sucked. In short, we faced a target-rich environment." Then he learned as much as he could about the customer. Finally, he gained a clear understanding of where Starbucks stood in the marketplace by doing market research.

This rich information then allowed Starbucks to avoid brand extensions that were tempting but very wrong for the company. Bedbury explains that the "Starbucks brand's core identity was less about engineering a great cup of coffee than about providing a great coffee experience," and so they took pains to attend to that philosophy. Because Starbucks knew its brand so well, it realized that offering punch cards or volume discounts would not be in line with its commitment to the customer. "We wanted to reward our customers with consistently better service, not a sometimes cheaper cup of coffee," says Bedbury. To dismiss a strategy most coffee companies use to compel customers to come back into stores might have been a mistake for another kind of company, but Starbucks knew its brand and its customers and made a choice that was unusual.

In addition to sharing his experiences working with these powerhouse brands, Bedbury teaches that every company should have one organizing principle: brand building. As opposed to looking at the brand as a message created by your marketing department, he believes brand building is a process that every part of the company must be centered around. As part of his eight universal principles of brand building, Bedbury lays out the core values that all brands should embody: simplicity, patience, relevance, accessibility, humanity, omnipresence, and innovation. Want a quick prescription for adding some humanity to your brand? Laugh at yourself; show genuine compassion; stand for something; listen and watch; admit your mistakes; find your soul; and become a more human employer.

"Relevance, simplicity, and humanity—not technology—will distinguish brands in the future."

What I found particularly revealing about *A New Brand World* was Bedbury's championing of two important aspects of brand—love and trust. Whether of a product or service, love and trust, he says, are crucial for brand building. Since the most aggressive advertising campaign cannot make a brand when a company or product lacks a soul or heart, both are required for marketing to resonate with consumers. Bedbury makes it clear that the best brands in fact started as great products or services. They don't come out of the gate as great brands, but once a brand is chosen by the public, an opportunity exists for you to let the rest of the world know about it.

In most books written about or by entrepreneurial superstars, you can get a general feel for the leaders of world-class brands or perhaps a glimpse at an industry at one moment in time. What Scott Bedbury gives us in addition is an in-the-trenches look at brand creation. ᴊᴄ

A New Brand World: 8 Principles for Achieving Brand Leadership in the 21st Century, Penguin, Paperback 2002, ISBN 9780142001905

WHERE TO NEXT? ➠ Page 111 for **brands in black and white** ➠ Page 139 for **using data across the organization** ➠ Page 213 for **the case study in brand building** | EVEN MORE: *Lovemarks* by Kevin Roberts; *The Lovemarks Effect* by Kevin Roberts; *Pour Your Heart Into It* by Howard Schultz and Dori Jones Yang

When readers want to know which business book to buy, they reach for the *Wall Street Journal* Best Sellers list. We reached out to our friends at Nielsen BookScan for the final word on business best sellers.

Best-selling Business Books

Good to Great
1,447,000 copies

Freakonomics
1,200,000 copies

Blink
1,111,000 copies

Who Moved My Cheese?
940,000 copies

Now, Discover Your Strengths
880,000 copies

The Five Dysfunctions of a Team
652,000 copies

Winning
476,000 copies

Little Red Book of Selling
456,000 copies

Getting Things Done
446,000 copies

StrengthsFinder 2.0
443,000 copies

Data from Nielsen BookScan 1/1/04 to 7/31/08
Written by Aaron Schleicher

Selling the Invisible

HARRY BECKWITH
Reviewed by Jack

Harry Beckwith's contention is that it takes a completely different skill set to market a service versus a physical product. In his introduction, Beckwith talks about going through the Harvard Business School's catalog of marketing case studies and finding that, in 1997 when the book was written, one out of four case studies involved a service company. Looking at the Fortune 500 that included service companies, he discovered that three out of four Americans work in service companies. "In short, America is a service economy with a product marketing model. But services are not products, and service marketing is not product marketing."

With this thesis, Beckwith explains that *Selling the Invisible* is "not a how-to book, although it contains many concrete suggestions. Instead, this is a how-to-think-about book." He asserts that the key to service marketing is the *quality* of the service being provided, despite people's wrong assumption that marketing is what is *said* about a service. In fact, Beckwith concludes that you may not have to *say* anything about your service if the quality really shines. With this focus on quality in mind, Beckwith recommends taking the following fundamental steps: "defining what business you *really* are in and what people *really* are buying, positioning your service, understanding prospects and buying behavior, and communicating."

Pretty straightforward stuff, but the delivery is refreshing. His chapters are like bright flashes, some less than a page in length. In the "Getting Started" section is a chapter called "The Lake Wobegon Effect: Overestimating Yourself." Beckwith points out that we Americans have an inflated view of ourselves and, in turn, our businesses—much like in radio-host Garrison Keillor's fictitious Lake Wobegon, " 'where the women are strong, the men are good-looking, and all the children are above average.' " This type of inflated opinion does not lead to self-examination, and, as a result, the odds are that our service is, at best, average. We should assume that our service is poor, which will force us to improve.

In the "Quick Fixes" section comes the chapter "Shoot the Message, Not the Messenger: The Fastest Way to Improve Your Sales Force." Beckwith tells the story of three top-notch salespeople who are capable of selling refrigerators to Eskimos, but they are struggling at a brokerage company. Beckwith explains that the company's selling problem is in fact a marketing problem. "The company has failed to create or identify the distinction that makes a selling message powerful, and that makes the salespeople true believers." Imagine a crack sales force struggling to sell something as nebulous as "good service." This is something our book company tried to do in countering Amazon's more concrete approach of promoting their ability to discount individual books. When prospective customers would call and ask, in not so many words, "Why should we use you?" we didn't have that powerful selling message. Not until we found a distinct advantage—our ability to customize any order—did "good service" become concrete for our consumers. Only then did we have a chance to turn a consumer into a customer. To successfully market a service business, you have to clearly identify the distinction of your offering because your service isn't intuitive to the customer.

In the section entitled "Anchors, Warts, and American Express" is a chapter called "Last Impressions Last." In it is an example: Charlie Brown noticed that Linus's shoes were nicely polished on the toes but the backs were all scuffed. After Charlie told Linus about this, Linus said he cared about what people thought about him when he entered a room but didn't care what they thought when he was leaving. Beckwith says that this is wrong. Many studies have pointed out that people remember the beginning *and* the end of an encounter and often forget the middle. If you want to make an impression concentrate as always on the first impression, but don't overlook your last.

The "Marketing Is Not a Department" section contains a chapter called "What Color Is Your Company's Parachute?" From the classic career book *What Color Is Your Parachute?* by Richard Boles comes the question "What am I good at?"—a question you need to ask yourself when looking for a new career. Beckwith thinks that when businesses ask themselves that same question, however, they often paint themselves into the corner of "We are an architectural firm." That general definition statement only results in a comparison between your business and all the other similar firms, and does not allow you to look for ways to differentiate your business. Often the areas of growth are outside your current industry description. "In planning your marketing, don't just think of your business. Think of your skills."

"The central fact of service marketing is this frustrating one: It is much easier to fail in a service than to succeed."

Harry Beckwith has done what many authors have tried to do but failed. He has found a patch of blue water—a place without a lot of competing products—and he has claimed it for his own. The book explains simply and understandably what you need to do to survive and thrive when marketing a service. Whether you are a lawyer or an accountant or a dry cleaner, this book will certainly change what you think about, just as Beckwith promises. **JC**

Selling the Invisible: A Field Guide to Modern Marketing, Business Plus, Hardcover First Edition 1997, ISBN 9780446520942

WHERE TO NEXT? « Page 88 for **companies with service at their core** » Page 230 for **starting a service-based business** » Page 207 for **a story of a service-based business** | EVEN MORE: *Ted Levitt on Marketing* by Ted Levitt; *Getting Everything You Can Out of All You've Got* by Jay Abraham; *The Invisible Touch* by Harry Beckwith

Zag

MARTY NEUMEIER

Reviewed by Jack

Our first books as children are filled with pictures and very little text, allowing us to learn visually. And our ability to learn from pictures doesn't disappear after we reach a certain age. In fact, I believe the use of pictures in business books is underrated and we will see more books employing this approach in the future. Marty Neumeier's marketing books have led the way in this trend. They are short, perfect for a plane ride, but they take a subject of great importance to every business— 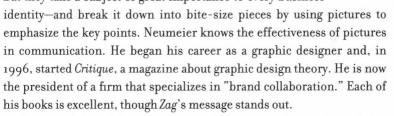 identity—and break it down into bite-size pieces by using pictures to emphasize the key points. Neumeier knows the effectiveness of pictures in communication. He began his career as a graphic designer and, in 1996, started *Critique*, a magazine about graphic design theory. He is now the president of a firm that specializes in "brand collaboration." Each of his books is excellent, though *Zag*'s message stands out.

Neumeier's broad but clear approach is conveyed even through the cover verbiage that calls the book "A Whiteboard Overview." *Zag* is high-concept and brilliant in its economy. Take Neumeier's display of six pictures, each featuring one pair of silhouettes conversing. In each picture, Neumeier conveys the most concise and effective explanation of advertising, marketing, and branding that I have seen. For example, his depiction of "Marketing" is a man telling a woman, "I am a great lover." But "Branding" is the woman saying to the man: "I understand you are a great lover." The difference is subtle but clear: branding is all about what your customer *understands* about your product or message and has nothing to do with what you are *telling* the customer.

Neumeier believes that consumers are being hammered with noise—or, using his word, clutter—about products and services. Because of all the clutter, you must differentiate—and not only differentiate, but embrace radical differentiation. As he puts it, "When everybody zigs, *zag*" (emphasis added).

Acknowledging that zagging is not instinctual for most of us, Neumeier spends the rest of the book giving you his ideas on implementation. One of the secrets to successful implementation is looking for "white space," the place nobody currently occupies. Most businesses understand the need for differentiation but struggle with the concept of radical differentiation. When Neumeier discusses radical differentiation, he means: "[If] ANYBODY'S doing it, you'd be crazy to do it yourself. You can't be a leader by following the leader. Instead, you have to find the spaces between the fielders. You have to find a zag."

"The quickest route to a zag is to look at what competitors do, then do something different. No—REALLY different."

Neumeier presents a process for differentiation by including chapters to help you find, design, build, and renew your zag. Established companies can reposition their brand or learn where to take the brand after launching it. But, Neumeier says, to do that you need to know where your company is within the "competition cycle." He uses the child's game of Rock Paper Scissors as an analogy to show the way large, medium, and small organizations go through that cycle. Start-ups are "scissor" companies and grow because of their sharp focus. They grow by taking "white space" from larger "paper" companies because they can move more quickly to market or the large business is too busy to notice. The small business eventually morphs into a "rock" or medium-sized business. Rocks thrive by crushing scissor companies that don't have the resources to compete. Eventually, rocks become paper companies that use their network and resources to smother rock companies. The Rock Paper Scissors analogy beautifully illustrates how companies of different sizes transition between cycles and how the strengths and weaknesses of those companies change over time.

In the final chapter, called "Take-Home Lessons," Neumeier summarizes each chapter with a short paragraph, describing its key points. This approach offers a helpful summary and serves as a future refresher.

He also includes a list of recommended reading, offering concise, one-paragraph descriptions along with all the information you need to find the suggested book.

Zag is an unconventional book with an unconventional message. It is a potent and enjoyable zag for business books as well. **JC**

Zag: The #1 Strategy of High-Performance Brands, New Riders, Paperback 2007, ISBN 9780321426772

WHERE TO NEXT? ❱❱ Page 265 for **another book with pretty pictures** ❱❱ Page 268 for **learning to make cool stuff** ❱❱ Page 187 for **Marty's method of client collaboration** | EVEN MORE: *The Brand Gap* by Marty Neumeier; *The 22 Immutable Laws of Branding* by Al Ries and Laura Ries; *Brand Sense* by Martin Lindstrom

Crossing the Chasm

GEOFFREY A. MOORE

Reviewed by Todd

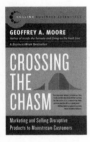

In the late 1950s, sociologists developed a bell-shaped curve to describe how farmers adopted new varieties of potatoes. In this initial study, five distinct groups were identified, each adopting the change at different degrees of acceptance. The new techniques were first enthusiastically embraced by a small group of leading-edge innovators, followed by a larger group of early adopters. As the innovation spread, the bulk of farmers, the early majority and late majority, changed their planting practices. Laggards were the last to commit to any change, and often did only when there was no other option. In 1962, Everett Rogers popularized and expanded this framework to broader trends of consumerism and change in his landmark book *Diffusion of Innovations*, and the technology sector has long used this paradigm to describe the adoption of products and services.

Geoffrey Moore published an important caveat in 1991 with *Crossing the Chasm*. The conventional marketing wisdom instructed companies to build momentum in each segment of the adoption curve and use that to energize the next group along the curve. Moore's research confirmed small acceptance gaps between each of the groups, but his true insight was the discovery of a chasm between early innovators and the early majority.

With the discovery of this chasm, Moore was finally able to explain the difficulties many early-stage technology companies experience with this discovery. Just as start-ups feel they are gaining traction due to success in the early markets, the initial revenue growth starts to flatten and the companies start to burn through cash. Firms find themselves unable to leverage the reputation and word-of-mouth they accumulated with the early groups as they sell into the early majority because the chasm that separates the two groups is one of opposing motivations.

Customers who are early adopters approach technology as an opportunity to upstage their personal competition and bring change to the companies they work for. The early majority, in contrast, wants moderate improvements with reliable components. The early adopters want revolution; the pragmatic early majority wants evolution.

The chasm is crossed only with a D-Day–style invasion, Moore says. The potential customers in the early majority are quite satisfied with what they have. Moore implores invaders to strike at a single niche and concentrate all of their efforts on a single subset of customers. Only by creating a small beachhead in the early majority will there be the needed reference point for others in the early majority to feel comfortable in adopting a new product.

Moore is quite specific in the ways companies need to plan the attack. Niches are chosen based on the industry of an existing customer or an identifiable, inefficient operating method that can be improved. As an example of the latter case, Moore introduces Silicon Graphic, a manufacturer of high-performance computing solutions which targeted Hollywood by proposing their high-end workstations as a replacement for the physical editing of film stock.

"The chasm phenomenon ... drives all emerging high-tech enterprises to a point of crisis where they must leave the relative safety of their established early market and go out in search of a new home in the mainstream."

Moore also believes you should build alliances and bring partners in to wage the war. Those of the early majority want compatibility with their existing purchases, plug-and-play accessories, and published how-to manuals waiting for them when they sign the check.

For those who read the original 1991 edition of *Crossing the Chasm*, the 1999 revised paperback may be worth a second read. Moore rewrote most of the anecdotes and introduced a new set of companies trying to cross the chasm. But even more interesting are his descriptions of how companies use this knowledge. Some companies now piggyback on the success of others' crossings; Moore points to Netscape's successful chasm crossing and Microsoft's follow-up in the Internet browser market. He even discusses companies that are building strategies to deter and foil chasm crossings.

Crossing the Chasm addresses major change events and references the experiences of many high-tech companies, so the book is laden with tech-speak and insider acronyms. I only mention it as fair warning, but in no way should that deter you. Moore's hypothesis is about change and the naturally varying receptivity to it. I'll bet there is some change you are trying to get adopted, and there are more than a few lessons in *Crossing the Chasm* for change agents and the challenges you face. TS

Crossing the Chasm: Marketing and Selling Disruptive Products to Mainstream Customers, Collins, Paperback Business Essentials Edition 2006, ISBN 9780060517120

WHERE TO NEXT? » Page 219 for **starting your high-tech company** « Page 9 for **how geeks manage their lives** » Page 201 for **the start of a great tech company** | EVEN MORE: *The Change Function* by Pip Coburn; *Dealing with Darwin* by Geoffrey A. Moore; *The Cluetrain Manifesto* by Christopher Locke, Rick Levine, Doc Searls, and David Weinberger; *The Long Tail* by Chris Anderson

Secrets of Closing the Sale

ZIG ZIGLAR

Reviewed by Jack

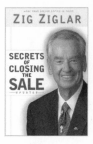

I have been a salesman all my life. I started with a newspaper route, then ran a record store, and now I've been selling books for twenty-five years. That said, I have always considered salespeople who talk about "closing" and "techniques" akin to the snake-oil salesmen of old. My approach has been more in-stinctual, perhaps even more humanistic: if people aren't in-terested in what I have to offer, the problem is with my offering, not my presentation or close. But even the greatest natural technicians (and I am not referring to me) can benefit from study and practice, and for that, Zig Ziglar's book, *Secrets of Closing the Sale*, is essen-tial reading.

Ziglar tells us that selling and closing are not mysteries to be solved; instead they are as tangible as when his wife up-sold him on a new house. Even a visit to his dentist illuminated this for Ziglar: he noticed that the dentist and his staff used predominantly positive words during that visit—words like restoration instead of filling; reception room instead of wait-ing room; discomfort or pressure instead of pain; and confirm or verify an appointment instead of remind. Words make a difference, and spin matters—so much so that Ziglar lists the twenty-four words that "sell" (like proven, health, easy, and discovery) and the twenty-four words that "unsell" (like deal, pay, contract, and sign). Just check out any late-night infomercial to see these methods in action.

Despite its name, the book unveils truths and approaches applicable to the entire sales process, with a focus on the close. Certainly the close is the key part of a sale, but in order to close, one must understand aspects like the attitude of selling, dealing with objections, and then the psychol-ogy of the closing. *Secrets of Closing the Deal* breaks the sales process into its component parts and thus is the perfect reference guide for every new salesperson.

Guides to selling are a dime a dozen, but the heart of this book lies in a series of entertaining stories Ziglar tells to demonstrate the many aspects of selling. I found one story particularly amusing. During a rainstorm, he pulled into a gas station and learned that the owner considered rainstorms to be fortuitous. The rain washed nails and other debris onto the road, which led to flat tires—and increased business. The owner had on staff a great tire changer who actually made his customers' visit pleasant. " 'There's nothing I can do about the rain falling, but there is a lot I can do about solving people's problems when that rain does fall,'" the owner explains. Ziglar shows through this story how it pays to know your customers, treat them right, and still take advantage of opportunity.

"The prospect is persuaded more by the depth of your conviction than he is by the height of your logic."

Throughout the book, Ziglar is your personal sales instructor. He asks you to get a pen and notepad in hand as you begin to read, because he wants readers to treat his book as a manual, almost an academic text. I've certainly marked up my copy with notes over the years. Yet this book is anything but an academic read. Each page is loaded with pithy sayings that might be just the nudge you need to take that next step toward improvement. Here are a few examples:

- "The prospect is persuaded more by the depth of your conviction than he is by the height of your logic."
- "You don't sell what the product is—you sell what the product does."
- "Spectacular achievement is always preceded by unspectacular preparation."
- "Your business is never really good or bad 'out there.' Your business is either good or bad right between your own two ears."

Ziglar's goal is to inspire and instruct us on how to refine our daily sales activity. The overall message in this book encourages you to stick to the basics. We sometimes overthink what is as inherently human as the sales process, and this is the book you need to stay focused on those basics. Sometimes a book's value is in its ability to get you back on track or to show you a better way to do your daily work. Zig Ziglar's classic, practical advice from an acknowledged master fits that criteria perfectly. JC

Secrets of Closing the Sale, Fleming H. Revell, Paperback 2006, ISBN 9780800759759

WHERE TO NEXT? ◄ Page 24 to **swim with a shark** ►► Page 233 to **swing with a guerrilla marketer** ►► Page 130 to **see a purple cow** | EVEN MORE: *How to Master the Art of Selling* by Tom Hopkins; *The Sales Bible* by Jeffrey Gitomer; *Cold Calling Techniques (That Really Work!)* by Stephan Schiffman

Selling

on the Silver Screen

These films capture our attention because they deal
with the very real issues of honesty, competition, and self-worth
prevalent in the sales profession.

The Big Kahuna [1999]
Anyone who has attended an industry
convention will relate to this movie.
Kevin Spacey and Danny DeVito just
need to land the hot account and the
company will be saved. Things become
complicated when a greenhorn from HQ
balks at using a personal connection to
reel this one in. Some will find the
movie slow (the entire film takes place
in the company hospitality suite with
those three characters), but the
dialogue is clever and engaging. This
movie shows how we are all selling
something.

The Boiler Room [2000]
Proponents of cold calling are going
to point to this film as proof that
it works. The main character, played
by Giovanni Ribisi, is pulled into a
stockbroker firm that uses high-pressure
sales tactics on its customers (and
employees). *Wall Street*, a celebration
of greed and ruthlessness, is considered
a training film at this company.

Death of a Salesman [1985]
This Arthur Miller play is a classic
in American theater. What we witness
through this story is the destructive
side of holding onto dreams—
dreams for yourself and dreams for
those around you. Dustin Hoffman
plays the role of Willy Loman in
this TV adaptation recorded after
its Broadway run in 1984.

Glengarry Glen Ross [1992]
A masterpiece by David Mamet, this
play is all about motivation and
what happens when you take reward
and punishment to the extreme.
The corporate sales manager rolls into
town and sets up the latest sales
contest—the winner gets a Cadillac,
the losers get fired. How's that
for motivation? The cast is peerless—
Jack Lemmon, Al Pacino, Ed Harris,
Alan Arkin, Kevin Spacey, and
Alec Baldwin.

Tin Men [1987]
Danny DeVito and Richard Dreyfuss
play competing aluminum siding
salesmen—a profession whose days are
numbered—in 1960s Baltimore. Their
less-than-ethical sales tactics have
caught the attention of the city. Neither
of these characters have the bravado
or charisma of those in the other
films listed; they are just regular folks
who you will recognize. We think it
makes this movie the most believable.

Written by Todd Sattersten

How to Become a Rainmaker

JEFFREY J. FOX
Reviewed by Jack

ow to Become a Rainmaker will help you recharge your sales force, or, as the book did for me, return your focus to the people who pay the bills: the customer. That quality—the nudge this book gives me when I stray from the most essential goals— places it very near to my heart. I wrote one of my first "Jack Covert Selects" reviews on this book when it came out in 2000. It was a fortuitous match. At the time, our business was struggling in the shadow of Amazon, which was emerging as a new powerhouse in the book business. Through Fox's book, I quickly learned that I had forgotten the basic needs of my company: happy customers who wanted to buy what we could provide. Seems obvious, but this is the kind of insight Fox presents in this book: simple but always valuable. Each of the 160 pages contains easily digestible, practical advice for the sales professional who knows that life is nothing but selling—either yourself or a commodity.

A rainmaker is a person who brings the revenue into an organization. What this book offers are strategies for maximizing your success as a rainmaker. Here's an example from the chapter on "Why Breakfast Meetings Bring Rain": You do a breakfast meeting because: (1) breakfasts are the least expensive meal—the selection is simple so a minimum of thought is needed and no alcoholic beverages are a temptation; (2) breakfast saves time—try to set up the meeting on the customer's way to work; (3) breakfast meetings are canceled less because the problems of the day are out of the picture. (Often rainmakers have two breakfast meetings per day.)

This book presents some of the best act-on-it-today advice that will immediately change the way you do business. Under the heading "Don't Drink Coffee on a Sales Call," Fox explains that because the average sales call runs only eighteen to twenty minutes, you don't want to be distracted from your presentation, and, as he says, "You can't take notes with a coffee cup in your hand." In the chapter "Be the Best-Dressed Person You Will Meet Today," Fox asserts that it is important to dress better than your client (though don't overdress) to make them feel that you are professional, confident, successful. "Dressing with care flatters your customer. . . . Your respect for your customer will show, and your customer will appreciate it; your customer will reelect you, sale after sale." It is not often that we think about how our customers see us, especially if they are people we have worked with for some time. And I would take this a step further. I would add to Fox's advice that dressing with care in the workplace shows that you respect your work. And your employees or coworkers will appreciate, and maybe even be influenced by, your effort.

"[T]he paramount job of every single employee in an organization is to, directly or indirectly, get and keep customers."

I've given a copy of this book to every newbie sales associate who begins in my company; there is no limit to its practical application. And whether you are an old-line sales manager, a C-level manager, or a college graduate looking for a job, *How to Become a Rainmaker* speaks a language of sales that will turn the oft-cited cliché "when it rains, it pours" on its head. **JC**

How to Become a Rainmaker: The Rules for Getting and Keeping Customers and Clients, Hyperion, Hardcover 2000, ISBN 9780786865956

WHERE TO NEXT? ◄ Page 15 for **how to be a star** ◄ Page 24 for **how to compete** ► Page 249 for **how corporate sales forces work** | EVEN MORE: *Hug Your Customers* by Jack Mitchell; *Secrets of Great Rainmakers* by Jeffrey J. Fox; *The Rainmaker's Toolkit* by Harry Mills

Why We Buy

PACO UNDERHILL
Reviewed by Jack

S everal careers ago, I owned a record store. Often I would sit behind the counter and watch my customers, trying to decipher their buying habits. For example, did they respond to a certain color or style of album cover to make their final choice? I did not know then that there was a "science" to my customers' interests, but I sure could have used this book, *Why We Buy*.

Twenty-five years ago, self-proclaimed urban geographer and retail anthropologist Paco Underhill founded a company called Envirosell that basically observes people shopping. His company then advises organizations, from banks to The Gap, on how to best communicate with their customers and ultimately sell more "stuff," the goal for all retail organizations. Underhill's science of shopping involves "trackers," whom he calls the field researchers of the science. These trackers stealthily follow shoppers through a store, noting on a paper form everything the shopper does. With the help of video, they personally measure "close to nine hundred different aspects of shopper-store interaction." Their findings are then factored into store design, signage, and product placement. Underhill took this rich material and wrote *Why We Buy* based on the mechanics, demographics, and, finally, the dynamics of shopping.

Underhill sets the scene by detailing the current problems in retail. Many experts agree that the marketplace is "overretailed." Retailers are opening stores not to find or to service new customers, but to directly compete with their competitors. With the decline of newspapers and the increase of information via the Web, it is becoming harder and harder to convince people to buy your product from *you*. Decisions are made with much less consideration of brand. In the past, there were Buick people, but not anymore. Now, there are "best deal" or "smartest buy" people.

While the state of retail is indeed under siege, Underhill is fundamentally concerned with what takes place once a customer is in the store. He claims compellingly that the most important way to communicate with your customer and to close the sale is to have people on the floor talking to and assisting shoppers. Underhill's studies show that the longer shoppers stay in your store, the more they buy. Engaging shoppers and listening to their needs is still the age-old solution to success.

In many ways, Underhill's message is to leave nothing to chance. Make sure there is a strategy to everything you do in your store to maximize that sale. Because the trackers are on the store floors and their observations are retold here, the book is loaded with practical advice. The author shares the following story about a Bloomingdale's store in New York that evidenced the importance of flow and merchandising. There was a rack of neckties close to one of the main entrances, and as the store got busier, people looking at the ties were jostled and bumped because the aisle was narrow. Quite quickly the shoppers moved on without choosing a tie. This phenomenon became known as the "butt brush." The trackers observed that women especially didn't like to be jostled from behind, and would abandon their quest when it happened. Sales were being lost by the placement of that rack; the same effect can happen in any narrow aisle.

"Why not take the tools of the urban anthropologist and use them to study how people interact with the retail environment?"

As much as Underhill's advice can be about opportunity lost, the right location for a product can stimulate sales. At the grocery store, dog treats are bought mostly by senior citizens and kids because these people are more likely to buy a little extra for their dog. Yet the treats are often stocked at the top of the store shelves. The trackers suggested moving the treats to a lower level and sales went way up. This is a lesson that can have broader application as retailers consider, for example, how to plan for aging baby boomers. Accurate product placement makes the buying process easier for the customer. The retail environment is about physics and mechanics, and how your customers touch things can gravely impact their desire to buy.

The real strength of *Why We Buy* is the relevance of each "Why didn't I think of that?" scenario. But the book isn't simply anecdotal; Underhill's data is meticulously gathered by Envirosell experts, and will provide you with the tools to determine what your customer really wants. One intriguing point Underhill makes is that he feels the Internet can never truly replace the experience of the physical act of shopping. Retailers must, however, listen to the customer and make even the smallest change that could keep a customer either in the store or coming back. As a brick-and-mortar retailer for many years, I immerse myself in this book time and again, and am always surprised by how many stores get the simple things so wrong. JC

Why We Buy: The Science of Shopping, Simon & Schuster, Paperback 1999, ISBN 9780684849140

WHERE TO NEXT? ▸ Page 210 for **where we buy** ▸ Page 126 for **what we buy** | EVEN MORE: *Trading Up* by Michael J. Silverstein and Neil Fiske; *Being the Shopper* by Phil Lempert; *The Culture Code* by Clotaire Rapaille

The Experience Economy

B. JOSEPH PINE II AND JAMES H. GILMORE

Reviewed by Todd

The Hard Rock Cafe, Disney World, and Starbucks all deliver more than food and drink. These establishments create theater—the script, the props, and the actors all synced to create memorable experiences. The $3 latte or $75 park admission is just a sampling of what customers will pay for help in creating memories.

Consider the evolution of the birthday party. There was a time when birthday cakes were made from scratch by mothers using flour, eggs, sugar, and milk. But I grew up in the seventies and I remember my mom making cakes from inexpensive, time-saving packaged mixes bought at the grocery store. For the couple of big gatherings in my teenage years, it was a trip to the bakery to pick up the yellow sheet cake with "Happy Birthday, Todd" in custom frosting. When my son Ethan turned four, we gathered his friends at Chuck E. Cheese's for pizza, cake, and electronic games. For the next year, whenever anyone asked him his age, he would say, "I'm four years old and I had my birthday party at Chuck E. Cheese's." Could there be a better commercial? There was no question about the dramatic effect it had on him (or the expectations it created for subsequent celebrations).

Joseph Pine and James Gilmore use the birthday party example in *The Experience Economy* to illustrate an evolution of commodities from goods to services to experiences. The cost of ingredients for a cake might be a few dollars, but purchase a birthday experience and the receipt will be twenty to fifty times that amount. And parents are willing to pay that premium because they receive huge perceived value in providing a fun and flawless party for their child. Companies are also able to maintain premium pricing because of the ease of creating experiences distinctive from their competitors'. The authors' analysis of gross domestic product and employment bears this out, showing experiences growing faster in both categories than goods or services in the overall economy.

Like all good consultants, Pine and Gilmore provide a 2 × 2 matrix for evaluating experiences. On one axis is the level of guest participation and on the other is the connection the guest has with the event or performance. *Entertainment* is the oldest and most familiar of the four "experience realms," where the audience is watching passively, absorbing the performance. A similar level of absorption but higher level of participation creates an *educational* experience, like one provided by the hands-on exhibits at a children's museum. An *escapist* experience describes a visit to a Las Vegas casino or an Internet chat room, where the participant is completely immersed and actively participating. The *esthetic* experience is also familiar, whether it's a visit to the Guggenheim or outdoor retailer Cabela's for high immersion and low physical involvement. The goal is to incorporate all four realms and eliminate activities that don't fit within any of them.

"Those businesses that relegate themselves to the diminishing world of goods and services will be rendered irrelevant. To avoid this fate, you must learn to stage a rich, compelling experience."

Creating experiences is not a new endeavor. The authors draw on the arts—in particular theater—to explore the metaphor between business and the stage. The script for a play is "the basic code of events," similar to how a firm choreographs the exchanges between sales, order entry, operations, and distribution. The performance itself is the product delivered, the value created. The metaphor grows as human resources become the casting department and the director's role resembles a more dynamic version of the typical project manager. Disney has long borrowed this language to convey to its "cast" what their role is in making memorable experiences for their "guests."

Published in 1998, the book captured early on the trend of customers demanding more experiences. Consider our industry of bookselling. Barnes & Noble's CEO Leonard Riggio is quoted in *The Experience Economy*, describing his superstores as theaters for social experiences. Amazon has experienced tremendous growth by creating its own unique experience, using personalized recommendations based on past purchases, customer participation in the form of reviews and wish lists, and unparalleled product selection impossible to replicate in retail. As we go to press, Borders is countering, according to its Web site, with a concept store in Ann Arbor, Michigan, that is "a new breakthrough shopping *experience*" (emphasis added), combining physical and digital components in one store. Maybe your business needs a new script; *The Experience Economy* will show you there is a stage waiting. TS

The Experience Economy: Work Is Theatre and Every Business a Stage, Harvard Business School Press, Hardcover 1999, ISBN 9780875848198

WHERE TO NEXT? » Page 277 for **creating experiences** » Page 213 for **a company that's all about experiences** » Page 273 for **experiences we recommend** | EVEN MORE: *Improv Wisdom* by Patricia Ryan Madson; *On Caring* by Milton Mayeroff; *Performance Theory* by Richard Schechner

Since December 2004, we have been podcasting interviews with business authors, including Dan Pink, Seth Godin, Kevin Carroll, and many more. We've built up a treasure trove of business advice and insight straight from the authors. Here are quotes from some of our favorite interviews.

Dan Pink, *A Whole New Mind,* March 2005: "These three forces—abundance, Asia, and automation—are moving us from a world where the skills that matter most are left-brain skills to a world where the abilities that matter most are the things that are more characteristic of the right hemisphere, which are intuitive, holistic, artistic, empathic."

Erika Andersen, *Growing Great Employees,* January 2007: "Just as you cannot make plants grow, you cannot make people grow. You plant them in the proper place—give them the right jobs. You take care of them, you maintain them, you nurture them. Management is, in my opinion, at its heart, a supportive process versus a creative process. You are not making the employee; you are taking an employee and helping them to thrive."

Pip Coburn, *The Change Function,* June 2006: "What is it that has a user change and use a new technology? I thought, well, that's really changing a habit. You're asking someone to do something different. There is a connection between the pain that they're in right now and their willingness to try something else. People will change their habits if their crisis is more than their total perceived pain of adopting a purported solution."

Have a listen at 800ceoread.com/podcasts.

For Your Ears Only

Written by Dylan Schleicher

Purple Cow

SETH GODIN
Reviewed by Todd

I n 2003, *Purple Cow* changed my life.

Yes, it really was that dramatic for me. At the time, I was working with my father in his sheet metal fabrication business and trying to create awareness for the company. The subtitle of the book, *Transform Your Business by Being Remarkable*, offered the insight we needed to change our thinking. The market barely knew our little four-person shop existed and we needed a way to get some attention. We focused our marketing on a single industry segment, developed a remarkable marketing kit, and doubled our customer base in twelve months. All that from a book that came in a milk carton.

To understand *Purple Cow*, you have to start with that word: "remarkable." I am not talking about the synonym of the more commonly used "incredible" or "extraordinary." Godin meant remarkable as "worthy of remark"—an adjective to describe the ability of a product or service to inspire users to spread the word to someone else. "Wow!" is not enough. "Wow! Hey, Jack, did you see that?" is the goal—just as if you had spotted a real purple cow.

People talking to other people is more important than ever given that the "tried and true" tools marketers have been using for the last fifty years are becoming ineffective. TiVo has changed the world of television advertising: when was the last time you sat through a commercial break? The Internet has altered the effectiveness of print advertisement: readership is down for almost every print medium. Advertising imagery can be found now on every surface a person might glance at, from coffee cups to airplane tray tables to bathroom stall doors. All are desperate attempts to get our attention.

Accepting word of mouth as a legitimate marketing tool, *Purple Cow* propels the tactic one step further and inspires thinking about how to optimize this method for your business. People talking to people is essential, yes. But how do you control that medium or ignite the spreading of the word? Godin suggests you concentrate on a small, specific set of people when developing your "purple cows." Cater to the early adopters in your market. These folks are willing to pay more than anyone else to say they were first to get it. You want the people who seek out a new restaurant every weekend because they want to be the first to tell their friends about it. You want the companies who believe in being the first to implement new technologies because they want to boast that they are on the cutting edge.

"My goal in *Purple Cow* is to make it clear that it is safer to be risky—to fortify your desire to make truly amazing things. Once you see that the old ways have nowhere to go other than down, it becomes even more imperative to create things worth talking about."

The marketing of *Purple* Cow itself is an outstanding example of theory put into practice. Godin printed 10,000 paperback versions of the book and put each copy inside a *Purple Cow*–themed milk carton. The nutritional information on the outside told you the serving size—the number of pages you would be consuming (152), the number of good examples (38), and the number of cow puns you would find in the book (14), among others. The final note on the carton told the real story: "Once opened, consume within seven days. And don't forget to share your copy with a co-worker."

Having been a columnist for *Fast Company* magazine for the previous four years, Godin had a built-in audience for his milk carton campaign. He offered his readers the milk carton for $5. The carton itself was designed to be sent in the mail and had a blank panel for the recipient's address. If readers wanted additional copies, the price was the same, but they had to buy them in quantities of twelve. The idea was that they would keep one or two and give the rest to friends. He sold out of the entire print run in nineteen days. The book has gone on to sell 250,000 copies since its 2003 publication.

Being remarkable doesn't come without problems. Word of mouth works only if customers talk to each other about what you do, but encouraging conversation invites both good and bad commentary. Or you may try many ideas that won't succeed, so you will need to overcome any sensitivity to failure (as will your bosses). But, there is no alternative. The only way you are going to grow your business, get the job you want, or see your cause get traction is to be remarkable, to stand out from the herd.

How many experiences did you have today that you are going to tell your five closest friends about? One? None? Now, think about the experiences your customers had today. Will they be raving to their friends? If your answer to the question is not a confident "yes," then it's time to do something remarkable. TS

Purple Cow: Transform Your Business by Being Remarkable, Portfolio, Hardcover 2002, ISBN 9781591840213

WHERE TO NEXT? ↠ Page 308 for **making marketing stick** ↠ Page 270 for **creating compelling ideas** | EVEN MORE: *The Big Moo* by Seth Godin and the Group of 33; *Creating Customer Evangelists* by Ben McConnell and Jackie Huba; *The Anatomy of Buzz* by Emanuel Rosen; *The Pursuit of WOW* by Tom Peters

The Tipping Point

MALCOLM GLADWELL

Reviewed by Jack

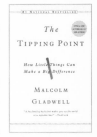

T*he Tipping Point* begins with Gladwell's story of the resurgence of Hush Puppies' shoes as a fashionable trend. The brand's renaissance took place in the early 1990s when a small group of kids in the East Village of New York City started wearing them. By late 1994, the hip fashion designers were using them in their shows. Suddenly this somewhat tired shoe brand had become all the rage just when Wolverine, the shoe's manufacturer, was considering discontinuing the line because of weak sales. How did these nondescript oxford shoes explode onto the scene? To help the reader fully understand the phenomenon of Hush Puppies and the other examples he includes, Gladwell explains that "[i]deas and products and messages and behaviors spread just like viruses do." And once we understand the concept of viruses, we can understand just such epidemics.

In his introduction, Gladwell tells us that there are three principles of epidemics: contagiousness; little causes have big effects; and change happens not gradually but at one dramatic moment. To illustrate how epidemics grow and multiply through geometric progression, Gladwell uses a simple puzzle to help us understand exponential growth. He instructs: if you take a large sheet of paper and fold it over itself fifty times, the folded paper will reach almost to the sun. This exercise shows that while people are inherently gradualists, that is not how viruses spread. "To appreciate the power of epidemics, we have to abandon this expectation about proportionality. We need to prepare ourselves for the possibility that sometimes big changes follow from small events, and that sometimes these changes can happen very quickly."

In social epidemics, Gladwell presents three essentials to the phenomenon: the Law of the Few; the Stickiness Factor, and the Power of Context. The Law of the Few introduces us to three social groups; the Mavens, the Connectors, and the Salesmen. The Mavens are the "databank," brilliant people to whom we look for answers; Connectors are the "social glue," those people who know people; and Salesmen are the people who have "the skills to persuade us when we are unconvinced of what we are hearing, and they are as critical to the tipping of word-of-mouth epidemics as the other two groups."

To explain the second essential, the Stickiness Factor, Gladwell offers examples that include my favorite about the television show *Blue's Clues*. To make sure the show resonates with the audience, researchers test every show three times before it goes on air, meeting with preschoolers every week to tweak the scripts. I just love the concept of going directly to your audience and using the data to create a product that is memorable, even if the changes are small.

The Broken Windows theory is an example of the third essential, the Power of Context, which argues that an epidemic does not occur in a vacuum. In the Broken Window theory, if a window of a building is broken and left unrepaired, people will conclude that nobody cares, nobody is in charge, and, as a result, more windows will be broken, leading to more crime in the vicinity. Gladwell uses David Gunn's work in overseeing a multibillion-dollar reclamation of the New York City subway system to show the reversal of just such a trend. In the 1980s, crime in NYC was at its highest level in history. The subway system was in a shambles, the cars were often covered with graffiti, and people were afraid to use the system. One of the first things David Gunn did was set up a plan to clean the graffiti off the subway cars and keep it off. The transit workers became almost obsessive about removing the graffiti: no car with graffiti would leave the yard. This cleaning of the cars showed riders that the system, the "broken window," was being fixed and the momentum of crime was interrupted.

"*The Tipping Point* is the biography of an idea, and the idea is very simple."

The Tipping Point is the type of book that helps us make sense of the world around us. It is a practical, nonacademic guide to the social epidemics going on around us, and perhaps to how we might take advantage of them. As people try to stay in step with a rapidly evolving business landscape, they are turning to journalistic books that bring the big picture into focus, like Thomas Friedman's *The World Is Flat*, Gladwell's next book, *Blink*, and Steven Levitt and Stephen Dubner's *Freakonomics*. Not only is the context broader, but the writing is significantly better than that in traditional business books. *The Tipping Point* is the book that started this trend, perhaps its own epidemic, and continues to carry the banner as the best. **JC**

The Tipping Point: How Little Things Can Make a Big Difference, Back Bay Books, Paperback 2002, ISBN 9780316346627

WHERE TO NEXT? ⇥ Page 304 for **another** *New Yorker* **writer** ⇥ Page 308 for **a book inspired by this one** ⇥ Page 136 for **Gladwell's trading card** | EVEN MORE: *Blink* by Malcolm Gladwell; *Collapse* by Jared Diamond; *Freakonomics* by Steven D. Levitt and Stephen J. Dubner

MALCOLM GLADWELL

SUPERPOWER:
* * * ENCHANTMENT * * *

Writes for: *New Yorker*

Famous for: An October 2000 *New Yorker* piece on Ron Popeil called "The Pitchman," which won the National Magazine Award for Profiles; *The Tipping Point*; and *Blink*.

Flash of brilliance: "We don't know where our first impressions come from or precisely what they mean, so we don't always appreciate their fragility." (*Blink*)

* * * * * * * * * *

CHARLES FISHMAN

SUPERPOWER:
* * * INVESTIGATION * * *

Writes for: *Fast Company*

Famous for: A December 2003 *Fast Company article* titled "The Wal-Mart You Don't Know," which won the 2004 Best Business Magazine Story award from the New York Press Club; *The Wal-Mart Effect*.

Flash of brilliance: "In the end, of course, it is we as shoppers who have the power, and who have given that power to Wal-Mart. Part of Wal-Mart's dominance, part of its insight, and part of its arrogance, is that it presumes to speak for American shoppers." ("The Wal-Mart You Don't Know")

* * * * * * * * * *

MICHAEL LEWIS

SUPERPOWER:
* * * INTERPRETATION * * *

Writes for: *New York Times Magazine, Portfolio,* and *Slate*.

Famous for: A December 2005 *New York Times* article, "Coach Leach Goes Deep, Very Deep"; *Moneyball*; *Liar's Poker*; and *The Blind Side*.

Flash of brilliance: "[Coach Leach] thinks the team that wins is the team that moves fastest, and the team that moves fastest is the team that wants to. He believes that both failure and success slow players down, unless they will themselves not to slow down." ("Coach Leach Goes Deep, Very Deep")

* * * * * * * * * *

DANIEL H. PINK

SUPERPOWER:
* * * FORESIGHT * * *

Writes for: *Wired*

Famous for: *A Whole New Mind* and *Free Agent Nation*.

Flash of brilliance: "We are moving from an economy and a society built on the logical, linear, computerlike capabilities of the Information Age to an economy and a society built on the inventive, empathic, big-picture capabilities of what's rising in its place, the Conceptual Age." (*A Whole New Mind*)

* * * * * * * * * *

Written by Rebecca Schlei

RULES AND SCOREKEEPING

How can you play the game if you don't know the rules?

Naked Economics

CHARLES WHEELAN
Reviewed by Todd

The most-often quoted sentence from Peter Drucker must be this one from his 1954 book, *The Practice of Management*: "There is only one valid definition of a business purpose: to create a customer." Here, Drucker found a simple way of saying what economists have said for a hundred years. In market-based economies, customers and firms are doing a dance. The former are looking to fulfill their own needs and desires, and the latter are trying to make a buck. So, if you find Drucker's insight illuminating, then Charles Wheelan's *Naked Economics* will provide your most refreshing economics lesson yet.

"Why did the chicken cross the road? Because it maximized his utility."

Many people have a hard time understanding economics, let alone finding a useful way to apply economics in their daily lives. Much of that has to do with Econ 101 courses gone bad—the supply and demand curves, anecdotes involving firearms and dairy products, the need to fill required courses in your university curriculum. But in his introduction Wheelan describes his intent to offer something different: "This book is not economics for dummies; it is economics for smart people who never studied economics (or have only a vague recollection of doing so)." You will not find graphs, equations, or incomprehensible terms in Wheelan's presentation of economics. Instead, you'll find him talking about how the The Gap determines what price to charge for its new wool sweaters. Or why Burger King has the nice note at the register that says you get a free meal if you don't get a receipt. Or what clean bathrooms, seven-days-a-week service, and consistently made hamburgers do for McDonald's restaurants. With each of these stories, Wheelan gets you thinking about concepts such as supply and demand, incentives, and information. The concepts become tangible and relevant to everyday life, and you find that economics can give us very useful information about how people and companies make decisions.

Wheelan starts his lesson with microeconomics, covering markets and incentives. Chapters 3 and 4 cover the role of government and how markets would have a hard time existing without government. There is a chapter on the economics of information as a transition to macroeconomics in the second half of the book. Productivity, financial markets, the Federal Reserve, and globalization round out the major topics. The epilogue takes a look ahead to 2050 and encourages readers to use some of their newly gained knowledge to think about potential problems that lie ahead.

This book delivers an entire college economics course, albeit an introductory one, in 228 pages. Wheelan moves quickly and covers an expanse of ground with the goal of exposing you to the not-so-dismal science and allowing you a look at the world around you through another lens. TS

Naked Economics: Undressing the Dismal Science, W.W. Norton & Company, Paperback 2002, ISBN 9780393324860

WHERE TO NEXT? » Page 259 for **application of economic theory** « Page 77 for **more application of economic theory** » Page 317 for **what the boss wants you to know** | EVEN MORE: *The Economic Naturalist* by Robert H. Frank; *New Ideas from Dead Economists* by Todd G. Buchholz; *The Undercover Economist* by Tim Harford

Financial Intelligence

KAREN BERMAN AND JOE KNIGHT WITH JOHN CASE

Reviewed by Todd

For as much press and as many op-ed columns as were dedicated to the collapse of Enron and WorldCom, the average American did not comprehend the magnitude nor the implications of those failures. If we are to truly understand business and the effects financial firms have on the world, we must understand the rules and the principles of accounting. What we need is *Financial Intelligence*.

Accounting is often likened to scorekeeping in the game of business, but that is a bad comparison. It perpetuates misconceptions about the role of bookkeeping. The 24/7/365 marketplace is much more complicated than a head-to-head matchup completed in 60 minutes of regulation time. A final score and the associated win or loss might be an able comparison to a company's net income, but net income is not the binary function of each goal line crossed or basket made. Instead, net income is more holistic, a mathematical function of costs subtracted from sales.

The underlying question always present in accounting is "When?" and the fundamental rule of accounting is the *matching principle*—the idea that sales and their associated costs should be reported together. This is where authors Karen Berman and Joe Knight, with their writing partner John Case, begin. The cash register ringing at your local bookstore records a sale and an associated expense for the book sold, the difference reported as profit. An equipment purchase like a new computer for the front counter is recorded as a series of monthly expenses, with the intention of accurately representing use over time. When companies get into trouble, their interpretation of the matching principle, the authors point out, is likely the source. In the case of WorldCom, everyday expenses like office *supplies* were being treated like office *buildings*, with their financial recognition delayed for decades.

As a manager looks over a set of financial statements, his understanding of the underlying assumptions for how a company has chosen to interpret the proper matching of sale to expense is essential. Knowing, for example, whether the revenue from an extended warranty is recognized in its entirety on the date of purchase or spread out over the subsequent months of the contract can affect everything from commissions for salespeople to calculation of product profitability to the decision to offer similar products in the future. These distinctions are not trivial concerns, and *Financial Intelligence* offers us the know-how with which to make educated decisions about the basics of business.

"Financial information is the nervous system of any business."

The authors use straightforward language throughout the book to explain income statements, balance sheets, and statements of cash flows. Terminology is defined, and common synonyms are provided, though the authors declare with pride that the words "debit" or "credit" do not appear anywhere within the pages of *Financial Intelligence*. They give the same plainspoken treatment to measurement ratios, such as return on assets and receivable days, that managers use routinely to assess the health of a firm.

The book's subtitle, *A Manager's Guide to Knowing What the Numbers Really Mean*, is the only misstep to be found in this well-constructed book. That positioning statement narrows too far the potential audience for *Financial Intelligence*. We wholeheartedly recommend this book for any employee, from service technician to shop floor manager, because it will allow every person to participate in a wider conversation about business. TS

Financial Intelligence: A Manager's Guide to Knowing What the Numbers Really Mean, Harvard Business School Press, Hardcover 2006, ISBN 9781591397649

WHERE TO NEXT? » Page 170 for **the power of sharing numbers** « Page 74 for **the strategy that creates great numbers** » Page 167 for **the knobs to turn** | EVEN MORE: *How to Read a Financial Report* by John A. Tracy; *Managing by the Numbers* by Chuck Kremer and Ron Rizzuto, with John Case

GETTING YOUR BEARINGS

The Dummies books are an invaluable resource when you want to learn about a new interest. Taking up tennis, building a deck, or brewing your own beer? There is a Dummies book for you. But Dummies books also provide an efficient way to learn about a new business subject. Here is a sampling of Dummies guides for the business person.

Six Sigma for Dummies

by Craig Gygi, Neil Decarlo, and Bruce Williams

Six Sigma practitioners have brought millions of dollars to the bottom line by removing inefficiencies from any business or manufacturing process. And yet, mention Six Sigma to most people and their eyes glaze over. Just what is Six Sigma? This *For Dummies* guide will make these valuable practices available and understandable to everyone.

IT Disaster Recovery Planning for Dummies

by Peter Gregory

Your business need not be devastated by a tsunami or an earthquake for you to need a disaster recovery plan. A power outage. A fire. Bum equipment. That's all it takes to bring down your technology systems and threaten the future of your organization. Prepare by using *IT Disaster Recovery Planning for Dummies*, which offers steps on building, writing, and testing an effective interim disaster recovery plan.

Sarbanes-Oxley for Dummies

by Jill Gilbert Welytok

Sarbanes-Oxley may sound like an Ivy League school or maybe an infectious disease, but it's really all about accounting. This legislation passed by Congress requires controls over corporate accounting practices, and, especially following the Enron disaster, its importance cannot be overstated. This book will tell you everything you need to know about the ins and outs of Sarbanes-Oxley.

Written by Aaron Schleicher with Sally Haldorson

The Balanced Scorecard

ROBERT S. KAPLAN AND DAVID P. NORTON
Reviewed by Todd

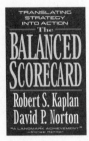

For more than a thousand years, the scientific method has served as the basis for technological advancement. Experience informs conjecture, educated guessing leads to hypothesis, and testing confirms or denies the prophecy. In business, strategy plays the part of hypothesis, as business leaders place their bets on what will work in the marketplace. Most executives fail to connect strategy and action, and when they do, they lack the measurements needed to prove success or failure. Authors Robert Kaplan and David Norton propose a more methodical metrics-based approach to link the two in their book *The Balanced Scorecard*.

The scorecard serves as a dashboard for how the company is operating, creating feedback mechanisms that align business strategy and the actions of management. First is a financial set of metrics that are common and are based on the life-cycle stage the business is in. So, growth companies focus on sales and market share while maturing firms watch unit costs and operating expenses. Customer metrics like satisfaction, retention, and share-of-wallet measure a company's value proposition. Next, a whole host of internal metrics brings focus to innovation, operations, and services—processes that provide customer and shareholder value. Finally, companies cannot deliver value without investing in the growth and development of its workers, so measurements like employee satisfaction gauge success.

"If you can't measure it, you can't manage it."

The authors report that most senior leadership teams settle on fifteen to twenty-five metrics but quickly find that 20 percent of metrics on new scorecards fail to have supporting data. "If data do not exist to support a measure, the management process for a key strategic objective is likely inadequate or nonexistent." The development process helps uncover gaps and oversights in aspects of the business that need attention.

The Balanced Scorecard is definitely the advanced class on scorekeeping. The process the authors propose must start at the top, with senior management defining an actionable strategy and vision for the company. The strategic measurements must be transferable down through the corporate hierarchy so that team goals and individual goals match the overall strategic goals. And feedback from the scorecard should provide a clear confirmation or denial of senior management's strategic hypotheses.

Poring over sales results, return-on-capital calculations, and cash flow projections is the preoccupation of almost every business leader. The appeal of *The Balanced Scorecard* is in the direct link that is created between top-level strategy and decision making at all levels of the organization. Rather than searching for unknown causes of unexpected results, executives can finally see the relationship between internal indicators, both leading and lagging, and the always-scrutinized financial results. TS

The Balanced Scorecard: Translating Strategy into Action, Harvard Business School Press, Hardcover 1996, ISBN 9780875846514

WHERE TO NEXT? ◄ Page 141 for **the basics on financials** ►► Page 160 for **fourteen key management principles** ►► Page 270 for **using data-driven marketing** | EVEN MORE: *The Strategy-Focused Organization* by Robert S. Kaplan and David P. Norton

MANAGEMENT is the punching bag of the leadership crowd. They say the discipline is boring and uninspiring. The cool kids don't like admitting how essential it is to any organization. Management is the blocking and tackling of business, and the books that we think are the best address the interpersonal dynamics of groups both big and small. It's about time that management got a little respect.

The Essential Drucker

PETER F. DRUCKER

Reviewed by Jack

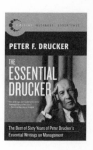

When we were choosing the books for the management section of our *100 Best* list, we both knew that Peter F. Drucker had to be represented. But which book to include? Though his name is often bandied about in business thought circles, Drucker's books are often considered too dense to tackle in order to access his invaluable ideas and observations. Since Drucker wrote thirty-nine volumes on everything from business management to entrepreneurship to nonprofits, the options can be somewhat overwhelming.

Now, as a music fan (some might say obsessed music fan), I would never recommend purchasing a "Greatest Hits" CD. The problem with these types of collections is that they miss the nuances of the complete package the artist intended when he or she created the original album. I find this to be true of iTunes and other "singles" sources too, because listeners can pick and choose the tracks they already know. Many times I have found my favorite track only after listening to an entire CD multiple times—and I highly value that opportunity for discovery. Regardless, *The Essential Drucker*, indeed a "Greatest Hits" collection of sorts, is a must-read because the entire body of Drucker's work is a tall mountain to scale. While I, as a self-described music snob, may not run out to buy *The Best of Mahler*, there is something to be said for making academic literature accessible to the common reader, and that is what *The Essential Drucker* does for this brilliant man's work.

The genesis of *The Essential Drucker* occurred when Drucker's longtime Japanese editor and good friend Atsuo Ueda, who had retired from publishing and gone into teaching, needed an abridged version for his students to read. The resulting collection was published in Japan in 2000. However, even abridged, it ran three volumes. The American edition published in 2001 was edited down to one volume. Mr. Drucker approved of the edited compilation as a good overview of his work.

The Essential Drucker is organized around the three emphases that

Drucker focused on throughout his career: Management, the Individual, and Society. He was intensely interested in the role people play in organizations. Each chapter within these sections is derived from a single Drucker book, and a curious reader will be able go back to the source book to delve more deeply into the subject. While excerpting from only ten of Drucker's thirty-nine books, the editor acknowledges that there are five other books that could have been included but which are more technical, and therefore not included in a book meant to introduce Drucker essentials.

"Business management must always, in every decision and action, put economic performance first."

Clearly, the man was prolific, but what makes the late Mr. Drucker's writings so important? I read a ton of business books, but reading Drucker is a different kind of experience. His passages require multiple readings, not because the writing is hard to understand, but because every single word is chosen with care to optimize the point he wishes to make. His sentences are sculpted, and the thoughts are read-out-loud important. If you usually read a book with a highlighter to help remember key thoughts, you might be better served to only highlight the words that you *don't* want to remember, because there are far fewer of those and you will save money on pens.

For example, Drucker says that the purpose of a business is to create a customer. Simple. He states that a business enterprise has only two basic functions: marketing and innovation. Important. In the chapter on time management, he presents a strategy I have used many times when writing reviews or other important memos, and I have found it very effective. He suggests that when you have a large writing project, you should go heads down and write a "zero draft"—which is very rough—even before the first draft. The "zero draft" will generally take much less time, and then you can edit and revise the piece in short chunks of time—which are always easier to find. Practical. Yes, these are simple concepts, but the meat is in the implementation. As managers and leaders, we realize that every business has a different way of going to market, but this little volume offers essential concepts everyone can implement in their individual organizations.

Ask those you know who have a business degree and you will be astonished by the number who say they have not read Drucker. Beginning his career as a journalist, this was a man who never stopped writing, never stopped observing, and his insights were always well-founded in industry dynamics. This is not to say his books aren't daunting, and that is why we recommend *The Essential Drucker* as an access point to a world of unparalleled reflection on this pursuit we call business. JC

The Essential Drucker: The Best of Sixty Years of Peter Drucker's Essential Writings on Management, Collins, Paperback Business Essentials Edition 2008, ISBN 9780061345012

WHERE TO NEXT? « Page 12 for **the other Drucker book on our list** » Page 196 for **the subject of Drucker's first case study** » Page 314 for **an irreverent look at management** | EVEN MORE: *The Daily Drucker* by Peter F. Drucker; *Adventures of a Bystander* by Peter F. Drucker (his autobiography); *The Last of All Possible Worlds* by Peter F. Drucker (one of his two works of fiction)

" There is only one valid definition of business purpose: to create a customer."

The Practice of Management (1954)

We no longer even understand the question whether change is by itself good or bad . . . .
We start out with the axiom that it is the norm.
We do not see change as altering the order . . . .
We see change as being order itself—indeed the only order we can comprehend today
is a dynamic, a moving, a changing one.
Landmarks of Tomorrow: A Report on the New "Post-Modern" World (1959)

An employer has no business with a man's personality.
Employment is a specific contract calling for a specific performance. . . .
Any attempt to go beyond that is usurpation.
It is immoral as well as an illegal intrusion of privacy.
It is abuse of power.
An employee owes no "loyalty," he owes no "love" and no "attitudes"—
he owes performance and nothing else.
Management: Tasks, Responsibilities, Practices (1974)

All economic activity is by definition "high risk." And defending yesterday– that is, not innovating– is far more risky than making tomorrow.

Innovation and Entrepreneurship (1985)

Morale in an organization
does not mean that
"people get along together";
the test is performance,
not conformance.
The Effective Executive (1967)

We have only one alternative:
either to build a functioning industrial society
or see freedom itself disappear in anarchy and tyranny.
The Future of Industrial Man (1942)

Large organizations cannot be versatile.
A large organization is effective through its mass
rather than through its agility.
Fleas can jump many times their own height,
but not an elephant.
The Age of Discontinuity (1969)

Once a year ask the boss,
"What do I or my people do that helps you to do your job?"
and "What do I or my people do that hampers you?"
Managing for the Future: The 1990s and Beyond (1992)

It does not matter whether the worker
wants responsibility or not. . . .
The enterprise must demand it of him.
The Practice of Management (1954)

A man should never be appointed to a managerial position if his vision focuses on people's weaknesses rather than on their strengths.

The Practice of Management (1954)

Defining the problem
may be the most important
element in making
effective decisions—
and the one executives pay
the least attention to.
A wrong answer to the
right problem can, as a rule,
be repaired and salvaged.
But the right answer
to the wrong problem,
that's very difficult to fix,
if only because it's
so difficult to diagnose.

The Effective Executive (1967)

Out of the Crisis

W. EDWARDS DEMING
Reviewed by Jack

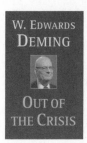

O n a summer Saturday night in 1980, in the back of a motor home in the wilds of Michigan, I watched a documentary on NBC called "If Japan Can . . . Why Can't We?" The documentary was about how Japanese manufacturing was growing at an amazing rate while U.S. firms were struggling. Despite spotty ratings, this documentary has been generally credited with sparking the quality movement in the United States. It also introduced the United States to an octogenarian mathematician, statistician, and musician: Dr. William Edwards Deming. Rumor has it that Donald Petersen, president and COO of Ford Motor Company, was also watching that show (likely *not* in the North Woods) and hired Deming to help dig the giant auto company out of a severe decline. The Ford Taurus and Mercury Sable arrived in 1985, and Deming helped change the Ford culture to "Quality Is Our Number One Priority."

Deming was eighty years old when that show was aired, but he was changing the face of business long before his contribution to Ford. During the 1940 census, the government used a sampling technique that Deming developed. As a result of this experience, after World War II, the government sent Deming to Japan to help rebuild that country's industrial infrastructure. There he found a receptive audience for new tools to improve manufacturing processes as the country tried to restart its industry. In appreciation of his work there, a prize was created to commemorate Deming's contribution and to promote the continued development of quality control in Japan. The influence of Deming's philosophy in Japan was unprecedented and continues today, though he did not get this same level of appreciation in the United States.

In the States, to help spread the word and to explain the concepts of the quality movement, Deming published *Quality, Productivity, and Competitive Position* in 1982, renamed *Out of the Crisis* in 1986. This landmark book is the culmination of over fifty years of experience. The centerpiece of the book is Deming's "14 Points," which enumerate key management principles. Though Deming's background was mathematics and statistics, over time Deming came to believe that what was important were the people in the process, and that management had incredible amounts of control over the output of an organization.

"Improvement of quality transfers waste of man-hours and of machine-time into the manufacture of good product and better service."

Take, for example, Deming's classic "Red Bead" experiment. He was known to bring audience members on stage and tell them that their task was to deliver white beads, and only white beads, to a fictitious customer. Each audience member was blindfolded and instructed to draw fifty beads from a large bowl filled with both red and white beads. Each "employee's" output was then recorded, noting the number of white and red beads drawn. With each draw, Deming would use the methods that management might try to influence results: awards for those who did well, intimidation directed at those who did poorly. Clearly, anyone who witnessed this exercise would see the futility of these managerial techniques. Though the customer will not accept any red beads, it is inevitable that some percentage of red beads will be drawn. The conclusion is that one's performance is a direct result of what one is given to work with rather than of any external influence. Thus, the people who draw more red beads are not poorer employees and should not be docked pay or receive other consequences based on their performance. The job of management is to improve the process, to increase the likelihood that an employee will draw white beads.

Red beads are the result of a bad system. "The worker is not the problem," Deming is well known to have said. "The problem is at the top! Management!" He discussed his views on the role of management in a 1993 article published by the *New Economics for Industry, Government, and Education*. Deming explains his theory of the role of management as follows: "It is management's job to direct the efforts of all components toward the aim of the system. The first step is clarification: everyone in the organization must understand the aim of the system, and how to direct his efforts toward it. Everyone must understand the damage and loss to the whole organization from a team that seeks to become a selfish, independent, profit center." With these statements, Deming makes clear how connected the concept of team is to the quality movement.

Out of the Crisis walks the tightrope between the science of statistics and process and the art of management. Within its pages, the book gives testimony to the genius of Deming, whose message began to get traction in America only after his death in the early 1990s. **JC**

Out of the Crisis, MIT Press, Paperback 2000, ISBN 9780262541152

WHERE TO NEXT? » Page 318 for **more on teams** « Page 88 for **wiring service into your group's DNA** » Page 301 for **the dark side of quality** | EVEN MORE: *The Deming Management Method* by Mary Walton; *Juran on Quality by Design* by J. M. Juran; *Understanding Statistical Process Control* by Donald J. Wheeler and David S. Chambers

Deming's 14 Points of Management

1.
Create constancy of purpose for the improvement of product and service, with the aim to become competitive and to stay in business, and provide jobs.

2.
Adopt the new philosophy. We are in a new economic age. Western management must awaken to the challenge, must learn their responsibilities, and take on leadership for change.

3.
Cease dependence on inspection to achieve quality. Eliminate the need for inspection on a mass basis by building quality into the product in the first place.

4.
End the practice of awarding business on the basis of price tag. Instead, minimize total cost. Move toward a single supplier for any one item, on a long-term relationship of loyalty and trust.

5.
Improve constantly and forever the system of production and service, to improve quality and productivity, and thus constantly decrease costs.

6.
Institute training on the job.

7.
Institute leadership. The aim of supervision should be to help people and machines and gadgets to do a better job. Supervision of management is in need of overhaul, as well as supervision of production workers.

8.
Drive out fear, so that everyone may work effectively for the company.

9.
Break down barriers between departments. People in research, design, sales, and production must work as a team, to foresee problems of production and in use that may be encountered with the product or service.

10.
Eliminate slogans, exhortations, and targets for the work force asking for zero defects and new levels of productivity. Such exhortations only create adversarial relationships, as the bulk of the causes of low quality and low productivity belong to the system and thus lie beyond the power of the work force.

11.
a. Eliminate work standards (quotas) on the factory floor. Substitute leadership.

b. Eliminate management by objective. Eliminate management by numbers, numerical goals. Substitute leadership.

12.
a. Remove barriers that rob the hourly worker of his right to pride of workmanship. The responsibility of supervisors must be changed from sheer numbers to quality.

b. Remove barriers that rob people in management and in engineering of their right to pride of workmanship. This means *inter alia*, abolishment of the annual or merit rating of management by objective.

13.
Institute a vigorous program of education and self-improvement.

14.
Put everybody in the company to work to accomplish the transformation. The transformation is everybody's job.

Toyota Production System

TAIICHI OHNO
Reviewed by Todd

TOYOTA PRODUCTION SYSTEM
Beyond Large-Scale Production

The Japanese automotive industry was in its infancy following World War II. The total market in Japan for passenger cars in 1949 was 1,008 units. Many of the industry's executives looked with envy across the Pacific. The five-million-unit U.S. market and the mass production techniques born from Henry Ford's assembly line granted their American counterparts advantageous economies of scale.

Taiichi Ohno took exception. As a machine shop supervisor at Toyota, he saw the American auto companies reducing the varieties of styles they offered and standardizing parts to gain these advantages. He saw a very different problem in his country. "Our problem was how to cut costs while producing small numbers of many types of cars," Ohno writes in *Toyota Production System*.

Toyota's rise to global automotive juggernaut came on the back of Ohno's system for shop floor coordination and was based on a deceptively simple insight: *the absolute elimination of waste*. Moving parts, waiting for parts, and even stocking parts as inventory are all forms of waste. Dealing with waste in a compartmentalized manner generates some marginal gains, but nothing compared to the quantum improvements possible when waste is dealt with on a system level.

Ohno's Toyota Production System is supported by two pillars: just-in-time and autonomation. Just-in-time is often referred to as pull production. Rather than use a centralized production schedule, each operation requests parts from upstream feeders based on their current needs, meaning engines are assembled when final production signals the need. Autonomation is the concept of giving machinery human intelligence—for example, enabling a lathe to detect faulty material or a broken tool. Smarter machinery reduces the risk of defective parts and creates a shift from craftsmen running individual machines to a team of semiskilled generalists able to handle several pieces of equipment.

The advances Ohno made were direct results of his natural curiosity and observation of the world around him. The decentralized decision making of his pull system mimicked the human body's unconscious variation of the heart and lungs based on its level of exertion. The concept of teamwork didn't really exist in Japanese culture until the import of Western sports like baseball and volleyball after World War II; traditional Japanese sports, like sumo wrestling and judo, focused on the individual. And Ohno's early years working in Toyota's textile department exposed him to operations where one worker could keep forty or fifty self-repairing looms running, leaving him shocked when he moved to the automotive individual craftsman mentality.

In the mid 1990s, I instituted a pull system for bringing raw materials into a GE plant in Columbus, Ohio, and I learned the benefits of this system firsthand. Prior to the change, purchasing and production control developed monthly schedules and ran extensive computations to determine material requirements. Purchase orders were placed and suppliers made shipments based on the initial plan. But nothing ever operated according to plan. Shifting customer demands, variable product yields, and inconsistent machine uptime all led to too much or too little of what was needed. By setting up standard ordering quantities and simple barcode tags, operators on the floor took charge of ordering the raw materials they needed. Materials were moved from a centralized warehouse to the factory floor. When completed, the project lowered the cost of purchased inventory by $2 million, or over 30 percent, but most important, the change to pull eliminated material shortages caused by the drawbacks of centralized planning.

"Industrial society must develop the courage, or rather the common sense, to procure only what is needed when it is needed and in the amount needed."

Several books have been written about Toyota and its production system, and Ohno's is the best. At 120 pages, it is a quick read, but his three decades of refining the system brings purity to the elements of his argument for a new systemic view of organizing supply chains. But there is one other advantage as well. What sounds like a completely internal effort is really about producing exactly what your customer wants when they want it. Ohno says the closer Toyota has gotten to the 100 percent elimination of waste, the "clearer [becomes] the picture of individual human beings with distinct personalities." While this conclusion is not an obvious one, it ultimately shows the elegance of the efficient system he created. **TS**

Toyota Production System: Beyond Large-Scale Production, Productivity Press, Hardcover 1988, ISBN 9780915299140

WHERE TO NEXT? ‣ Page 288 for **more on self-sustaining systems** ‣ Page 196 for **what Ohno was improving on** | EVEN MORE: *The Machine that Changed the World* by James P. Womack, Daniel T. Jones and Daniel Roos; *The Toyota Way* by Jeffrey K. Liker; *The Elegant Solution* by Matthew E. May

Reengineering the Corporation

MICHAEL HAMMER AND JAMES CHAMPY
Reviewed by Todd

Reengineering became the magic managerial term of the 1990s. Cover stories in business magazines touted Michael Hammer and Jim Champy as the strategic gurus of the moment. Companies like Deere, Ford, and Duke Power all found huge success using the concepts. Even Lou Gerstner, in his autobiography *Who Says Elephants Can't Dance?*, calls out reengineering as having played a role in his turnaround of IBM. The trouble with every fad is the ridicule that follows.

In the 1990s, the term "reengineering" became an easy substitute for the prior decade's "reorganizing," "restructuring," "delayering," "downsizing." The popularity of the term gave embattled executives needed cover when faced with media scrutiny and stock market pressure. The mere mention of a new reengineering initiative acknowledged the severity of a problem and indicated to shareholders that proper steps were being taken. But the actual results varied widely, and business leaders and journalists were quickly off to find and report on the next silver bullet. What's left is general ambivalence for one of the most important business concepts in the second half of the twentieth century.

In *Reengineering the Corporation*, Hammer and Champy center their argument on Adam Smith and his theory of the division of labor. Smith believed that the shift from a craftsman mentality—when all tasks were done by a single person—to a separation of simple, repeatable tasks among specialists was the key to economic growth. Henry Ford's assembly line and Alfred Sloan's introduction of managerial specialists are the modern embodiment of Smith's thinking.

Many organizations still model their operations on the division of labor used by their automotive forebearers. But inherent in Smith's theory are productivity issues. Handoffs between specialists create queues and introduce the opportunity for errors; ninety minutes of actual work is drawn out over several days as the work snakes its way through the organizational labyrinth. And when someone raises a hand to suggest a better way, multidepartmental finger-pointing delays any real progress in determining where the problem really lies.

Reengineering the Corporation turns that theorizing on its ear. Hammer and Champy believe it is the whole process, not the individual steps that make up the process, that should be simple. Generalists take on the responsibilities of several specialists, making the decisions about what will be done and when. Multiple processes replace standardization, and with individuals or small teams responsible, quality control checks and oversight controls are reduced or eliminated. The measurement of success in the new work flow is the satisfaction of the end customer.

COMMON ERRORS DURING REENGINEERING

- Trying to fix a process instead of changing it
- Trying to make reengineering happen from the bottom up
- Skimping on assigned resources
- Trying to make reengineering happen without making anybody unhappy
- Neglecting people's values and beliefs
- Being willing to settle for minor results

(Full list in *Reengineering the Corporation*, chapter 13)

More important, the nature of work itself changes. Workers hired as automatons become case managers, empowered to deal with situations as they see fit. Their managers shed responsibility and become coaches, monitoring performance based on how *well* something is done, rather than how *many* units are completed.

" 'Reengineering,' properly, is the fundamental rethinking and radical redesign of business processes to achieve dramatic improvements in critical, contemporary measures of performance . . ."

Hammer and Champy recommend bold moves, suggesting "starting over" as a synonym for reengineering. The blank sheet of paper may be daunting, but broken processes that directly affect the customer are the place to start. The visual evidence, whether an unaccounted-for pallet of boxes or notorious piles of paperwork, is an indicator of systemic uncertainty. E-mail trails or full voicemail boxes show overcommunication among individuals, a prime spot for process redesign. The natural evolution of a company creates these complexities as products and customers evolve. Reengineering gives leaders the opportunity to untangle these webs and simplify overgrown business processes.

Jack Welch said he always needed to be on the "lunatic fringe" to get his company to move just a little, and reengineering's extreme form of process redesign has a similar effect. *Reengineering the Corporation* has permanently added process analysis to the toolbox of every business leader, whether they know it or not. TS

Reengineering the Corporation: A Manifesto for Business Revolution, Collins Paperback Business Essentials Edition, Revised and Updated 2003, ISBN 9780060559533

WHERE TO NEXT? » Page 200 for **a primer on Adam Smith** ◀◀ Page 85 for **an ex-CEO's endorsement of reengineering** ◀◀ Page 57 for **how to implement change** | EVEN MORE: *Lean Thinking* by James P. Womack and Daniel T. Jones; *The Discipline of Market Leaders* by Michael Treacy and Fred Wiersema; *Business Process Improvement* by H. James Harrington

The Goal

ELIYAHU M. GOLDRATT AND JEFF COX

Reviewed by Jack

Eliyahu Goldratt and Jeff Cox published *The Goal* in 1984, and shortly after, a company in Milwaukee placed an order with us for ten copies of the book. I had not heard of the book before, and I was surprised to discover when I received the shipment and perused a copy that *The Goal* was a novel. While common today, writing about business in story form was striking and original at the time. What caught my eye was how the authors brought to life, using realistic, flesh-and-blood characters and fast-paced storytelling, the story of one company's struggle to turn around a failing division.

The story features Alex Rogo, a new plant manager who is leading six hundred employees in a division of UniCo. The parent company is unhappy with the UniWare division's productivity and Alex is given three months to turn the plant around. Alex must solve myriad problems, such as late shipments, soaring inventory, and unacceptable quality levels, to reverse the trend.

Flummoxed by where to start the transformation, Alex recalls a chance encounter he had with a physicist named Jonah. The two had struck up a conversation during an airport layover when Alex proudly told Jonah about his company having just installed state-of the-art robots. Alex told Jonah the robots had increased productivity 36 percent in some departments. Jonah asked Alex a series of questions about the resultant effects of the robots: Is your company making more products? Was manpower decreased? Or did you reduce inventory? When Alex answered no to all, Jonah explained to him how his perception of success was incorrect. Alex did not internalize the advice at the time, but with a deadline looming, he reconnects with Jonah.

Through a series of short meetings and phone calls, Jonah teaches Alex the metrics he *should* be looking at to match the outcomes, rather than just the output of the robots that Alex had celebrated in their earlier conversation. What should Alex track to know whether the changes he implements will help in the turnaround? First Jonah explains to Alex the results that Alex's bosses at UniCo really care about. These financial measurements are indicators of how a business is doing on the top level: net profit, ROI, and cash flow. Jonah then explains that the best internal metrics that Alex can control in the turnaround—i.e. to make factory floor decisions that will ultimately inform those top level metrics—are throughput, inventory, and operational expense. Jonah reminds Alex that " 'the goal is not to improve one measurement in isolation. The goal is to reduce operational expense and reduce inventory while simultaneously increasing throughput.' "

Alex has trouble visualizing how Jonah's ideas will work on his factory floor until he takes his son's Boy Scout troop on a long hike. He has a hard time keeping the boys together because some are faster than others. He begins to see the variations or deviations in real time. One of the really slow boys is Herbie, and Alex realizes that Herbie was being slowed up by carrying too much in his backpack. Alex removes and redistributes the heavy items, Herbie catches up, and the boys make great time. Here is where Goldratt and Cox introduce one of the most popular takeaways from *The Goal*: the Theory of Constraints. TOC is a metaphor for looking at a process—be it an assembly line or any kind of repetitive process—as a living entity and finding the bottleneck that is preventing its maximum output. By studying the actual flow of the parts through the factory and looking for and dealing with "Herbies" immediately, the plant is able to show the corporate headquarters success. Ultimately, Alex is promoted and the conglomerate incorporates the TOC into the other divisions.

"Why can't we consistently get a quality product out the door on time at the cost that can beat the competition?"

In the past twenty-plus years, *The Goal* has sold over three million copies, been translated into twenty-one languages, been taught in over two hundred colleges and universities, and was made into a movie. Goldratt, an Israeli physicist, is, of course, present in the character of Jonah and advocates that in teaching there should be more question marks and fewer exclamation points. Jonah embodies this Socratic approach, and through Jonah's questions, we are afforded the chance to learn along with Alex. *The Goal* does, however, provide plenty of answers relating to viewing a process as a whole and the need to continuously improve that process. JC

The Goal: A Process of Ongoing Improvement, North River Press, Paperback Third Revised Edition 2004, ISBN 9780884271789

WHERE TO NEXT? ↦ Page 183 for **a story about teams** ◀◀ Page 52 for **a story about leadership** ◀◀ Page 63 for **how you can use stories** | EVEN MORE: *The Toyota Way* by Jeffrey Liker; *Deming and Goldratt* by Domenico Lepore and Oded Cohen; *We All Fall Down* by Julie Wright and Russ King; *The Machine That Changed the World* by James P. Womack, Daniel T. Jones, and Daniel Roos

The Great Game of Business

JACK STACK WITH BO BURLINGHAM

Reviewed by Jack

J ack Stack is credited as the first person to have written about Open-Book Management (OBM) when he penned *The Great Game of Business* about his company, Springfield Remanufacturing Corporation (SRC), a division of International Harvester. OBM is a management policy based on sharing all of a company's financial data with employees. The theory is that if employees understand how they affect the company's health as a whole, they will work harder and more efficiently. There are, however, a few codicils that can affect the success of this approach: management has to have credibility—this cannot be another "theory/flavor of the month"—and the employees have to have some fire in their eyes.

I began sharing numbers, or using OBM, years ago, because I felt that my employees, as a group, were way smarter than I could be working alone. I have always believed that transparency is the best and most honest way to work, and, as such, allows me to sleep better at night. When times were hard (we had several lean years), the employees knew why we needed to tighten our belts and why certain perhaps unpopular decisions were made. And when the company became more prosperous, the employees understood what it took to climb the mountain and were able to genuinely celebrate their contribution to our successes. But in order for this type of management to work, education—providing employees with an understanding of the basics of business finance—is key. OBM remains an uncommon management approach because it requires constant engagement with everyone on every level of the organization. I happen to believe, and I suspect Stack would agree, that it is this engagement that makes the workday worthwhile.

Stack and a group of managers bought a division of IH that refurbished diesel truck engines; then called Springfield Renew Center, the division was in sad shape. Introducing OBM meant first committing to employee engagement. In the early days, Stack knew that you couldn't engage people unless they had pride in what they did and where they did it. He held an open house and provided employees with the equipment to paint and spruce up their work areas, and brought in finished company products to display. On the weekends, families were invited to see where their family member spent the day.

"The best, most efficient, most profitable way to operate a business is to give everybody in the company a voice in saying how the company is run *and* a stake in the financial outcome, good or bad."

Then for OBM to work, management needs to present the big picture to every member of the organization. This runs counterintuitive to old-style management practices, but as the Springfield division has proven and I have observed, it works. Employees also have to step up and speak up, become motivated by the information that has been shared, and make everyday decisions based on this knowledge. An analogy that best sums up the power behind OBM is that of "everybody pulling on the same oar." Teams and team building play a large role in the success of OBM. Stack provides a list of some of the goals that worked best for SRC:

1. Business is a team sport—choose games that build a team.
2. Be positive, build confidence.
3. Celebrate every win.
4. It's got to be a game.
5. Give everyone the same set of goals.
6. Don't use goals to tell people everything you want them to do.

This approach may seem quaint since the book was written in 1992, but currently SRC Holdings has fifteen separate companies with overall sales of $300 million. A $1 investment in SRC stock in 1983 is now worth $800. The people who work at SRC own this stock, and the company has never laid off an employee.

I firmly believe that OBM played a significant role in my company's growth and is the reason we have extremely low employee turnover. But the OBM approach Stack advocates requires a constant commitment from managers to completely share information with employees. It is a one-way trip: giving people more means that you can never take a step back, withhold information, or deny participation. **JC**

The Great Game of Business: Unlocking the Power and Profitability of Open-Book Management, Currency/Doubleday, Paperback 1994, ISBN 9780385475259

WHERE TO NEXT? ‹‹ Page 141 for **more about accounting** ›› Page 230 for **how to grow a business** ›› Page 244 for **a narrative of heavy industry** | EVEN MORE: *Open-Book Management* by John Case; *Managing by the Numbers* by Chuck Kremer and Ron Rizzuto, with John Case; *Maverick* by Ricardo Semler

First, Break All the Rules

MARCUS BUCKINGHAM AND CURT COFFMAN

Reviewed by Todd

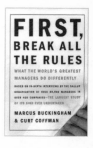

Caricatures that appear on the big (and small) screen portray managers as either tyrants or buffoons. In Pixar's *The Incredibles*, Bob Parr's manager, Gilbert Huph, exemplifies all of the prescribed attributes of a tyrant, right down to his pivotal demand, "Stop right now or you're fired!" Organizational vocabulary still draws strongly from its militaristic roots, but the "manager as major" fades as a new generation fills middle management. The business media reports on fallen leaders and inevitably points to the desire for power as their downfall when the real fall was a company's market valuation.

For a fresh idea of what a manager *should* be, *First, Break All the Rules* by Marcus Buckingham and Curt Coffman is your guide. Both authors worked for Gallup Inc., and the book was the result of a massive project to determine what good management looks like. The research starts at the logical beginning: "Do managers matter?" Managers have incredible influence over the success of a company, but Gallup wanted to prove this common wisdom analytically. And it did. When Gallup looked at individual business units within larger companies, great managers delivered greater sales, greater profitability, and lower turnover than poor managers.

Separating good management from bad came in the form of Gallup's keystone Q12 survey. Gallup's history as a polling company came in handy; it had over one million workplace interviews to draw from for this survey. The researchers looked for a set of applicable questions and found twelve that "capture the *most* information and the most *important* information." The queries linked directly to business outcomes like productivity, profitability, retention, and customer satisfaction:

1. Do I know what is expected of me at work?
2. Do I have the materials and equipment I need to do my work right?

3. At work, do I have the opportunity to do what I do best every day?
4. In the last seven days, have I received recognition or praise for doing good work?
5. Does my supervisor, or someone at work, seem to care about me as a person?
6. Is there someone at work who encourages my development?
7. At work, do my opinions seem to count?
8. Does the mission/purpose of my company make me feel my job is important?
9. Are my co-workers committed to doing quality work?
10. Do I have a best friend at work?
11. In the last six months, has someone at work talked to me about my progress?
12. This last year, have I had opportunities at work to learn and grow?

These twelve questions were given to over 105,000 employees at 2,500 business units in 24 separate companies. Employees who gave more favorable responses to the questions worked in higher-performing business units. The correlation gave Gallup the methodology to identify good managers. Gallup went ahead and interviewed 80,000 highly rated managers, generating over 120,000 hours of tape.

Over and over, in one form or another, researchers heard: "[Great managers] help each person become *more* and *more* of who he [or she] already is." The managers Gallup interviewed consistently recognized that the development of their employees came through focusing on their natural strengths as opposed to shoring up their weaknesses. This insight runs completely counter to conventional wisdom. Their research points to a change in managerial focus from making an employee fit into a position to finding the right position for the employee. Three words, "manager as coach," best describe Buckingham and Coffman's findings.

The process starts with hiring, where talent becomes the primary criterion in the selection of a new employee. Take the seven men chosen for NASA's Mercury space program, and consider how the most important human endeavor of the twentieth century missed the mark. All the candidates had the most applicable experience possible as military test pilots. The initial cadre spent two years acquiring the skills necessary for space flight. But when those astronauts were put into the capsule and shot into orbit, each performed very differently, despite the common experience. Their performances in the new environment ranged from problematic to flawless. What the hiring manager didn't consider were the individual abilities of each astronaut. Everyone has natural tendencies and reacts differently to the same stimuli. During liftoff, for example, the pulse of one topped out at 150, whereas Neil Armstrong's never got above 80, an indictor of how much each astronaut would struggle later in the mission.

Behavior-based questions ("Tell me about a time when . . . ?") during an interview can provide insight into a person's talents. Listen for quick responses that indicate the recurring use of a talent. Asking a candidate what he or she finds satisfying also can lead an interviewer toward where the person projects strength and finds fulfillment. For example, the best truck drivers will describe the constant assessment of surrounding traffic and the natural enjoyment they feel from anticipating potential problems.

"The energy for a healthy career is generated from discovering the talents that are already there, not from filling oneself up with marketable experiences."

Matching an employee's natural talents with the right job can produce remarkable results. Consider Jean P., a character in one of the authors' scenarios. This data entry clerk was averaging 560,000 keypunches a month, over 50 percent higher than the national average of 380,000. Recognizing her innate talent, the manager sat down with Jean and created a series of goals and rewards. Over the next several months, Jean improved her performance to 3.5 million keypunches, ten times the industry standard. Equally important, her manager created a talent profile for hiring, and now has Jean surrounded by people who average over a million keypunches a month. By spending time with the best people, managers learn what makes them different and how their strengths can be applied to the whole team.

Talent is not distributed equally, but everyone possesses unique skills and abilities. *First, Break All the Rules* shows the changes managers need to make in their approach to draw the greatest potential from the people who work for them. **TS**

First, Break All the Rules: What the World's Greatest Managers Do Differently, Simon & Schuster, Hardcover 1999, ISBN 9780684852867

WHERE TO NEXT? ➤ Page 295 for **how management is about more than IQ** ◀ Page 47 for **a research-based approach to leadership** ◀ Page 144 for **how metrics meet management** | EVEN MORE: *12* by Rodd Wagner and James K. Harter; *Vital Friends* by Tom Rath

Now, Discover Your Strengths

MARCUS BUCKINGHAM AND DONALD O. CLIFTON, PHD

Reviewed by Jack

We are taught at an early age to improve on our weaknesses in order to become a well-rounded person. During our school years, few of our parents and teachers celebrated our A's, and instead asked, "What is this C in math all about?" In business, these expectations continue, but Marcus Buckingham and Donald O. Clifton, along with Gallup Inc., argue that this is an ineffective approach. They assert that we can grow more quickly and get the most satisfaction in our work life when we utilize our strengths, which the authors define as a "consistent near-perfect performance in an activity." In preparing the book, Gallup asked a sampling of 1.7 million employees whether they were given an opportunity to do what they do best and found that globally only 20 percent said yes. *Now, Discover Your Strengths* aims to change this depressing reality for an entire generation of workers.

Just as the research in *First, Break All the Rules* showed that changes in a manager's approach can encourage an employee's best performance, *Now, Discover Your Strengths* resets the parameters for that employee's improvement. The previously held assumptions were that any employee could learn to be competent in almost anything, finding their "greatest room for growth is in his or her areas of greatest weakness." Instead, *Now, Discover Your Strengths* teaches managers and employees how to build on one's strengths to maximize performance. There is simply no upside to trying to fit a square peg into a round hole.

The obvious next question is, after years of worrying about our weaknesses, how do we determine our strengths? Gallup conducted over two million interviews to determine patterns of behavior and skills among successful people. Thirty-four patterns or themes prevalent in human talent consistently appeared. Now, Gallup has created an online assessment tool called StrengthsFinder to help individuals discover their strengths. When you buy the book *StrengthsFinder 2.0*, a code on the back cover allows you online access to the 180-question timed examination.

After you finish the test, you are presented with a list of five signature themes within which you have the greatest potential for strength. The book offers a one-page analysis of each theme. There are 16.7 million possible combinations, so the results are tailor-made for you.

When I took the test, I found that my first strength is harmony, which is "looking for areas of agreement," and I quickly realized that harmony may not be the best strength for a guy leading a group into the twenty-first century. While this strength *has* garnered me a fair amount of loyalty among my employees, sometimes strategic decisions must be made regardless of harmony. My coauthor's main strength is in his ability to "peer over the horizon" and ask "wouldn't it be great if . . ."—the Strengths-Finder label for this is "futuristic"—and we succeed as a team because our strengths strike a good balance. I firmly believe that our company's four years of double-digit growth in a flat industry is due to this effective partnering.

"We want to help you . . . *to capitalize on your strengths,* whatever they may be, and manage around your weaknesses, whatever they may be."

One of my shortfalls in improving the performance of my employees was indeed in trying to fit square pegs into round holes. For example, trying to get a quiet, task-oriented person to be a better salesperson when really he is an excellent support person, is a waste of his talents and my energy. Buckingham and Clifton discovered that the best managers understood two things: each employee has unique and enduring talents, and each employee's greatest room for growth is in the areas of his or her greatest strengths. They give examples of successful managers who deliver on these ideas. Phil Jackson, the famous NBA basketball coach (some would say guru), gave hand-selected personal development books to his players in order to further an inherent ability. Sam Mendes, a successful movie director, manages his movie sets through respecting the strengths of his actors, and, as a result, gets the best possible performances from them. The authors provide another treasure: a one-page bulleted list of ways to manage each of the thirty-four strength types. This online assessment is a valuable resource and well worth the price of admission.

Most of us pick up this book expecting to find answers to questions such as: "Can my themes reveal whether I am in the right career?" Certainly there are commonalities to be found among people in some careers. For example, journalists may share "adaptability" because their profession changes daily depending on the stories they are assigned that day. But generally, the authors believe that your signature themes have little to say about the field you are in and instead offer some direction for the role you play in any given field. In fact, Gallup discovered some surprising data in the number of people with similar themes who excel in very different fields. The distinction that StrengthsFinder is not a career guidance test but a performance enhancer is an important one.

Despite our tendency to focus on our shortcomings, there is great advantage in switching to a StrengthsFinder mentality. Warren Buffett is the poster child for knowing one's own strengths and staying the course. He knew he was a patient, practical man whom people trusted. The authors tell us that Buffett refrained from investing in technology because he didn't understand it, but "[h]e identified its strongest threads, wove in education and experience, and built them into the dominating strengths we see today." We might not all achieve Buffett's level of success, but if *Now, Discover Your Strengths* succeeds in making us more satisfied and confident on the job, then that will indeed be a success. **JC**

Now, Discover Your Strengths, Free Press, Hardcover 2001, ISBN 9780743201148

WHERE TO NEXT? ◀ Page 12 for **what Drucker says on strengths** ▸ Page 222 for **the strengths an entrepreneur needs** ▸ Page 259 for **how understanding strengths helped a baseball GM** | EVEN MORE: *StrengthsFinder 2.0* by Tom Rath; *Discover Your Sales Strengths* by Benson Smith and Tony Rutigliano; *What Got You Here Won't Get You There* by Marshall Goldsmith with Mark Reiter

The Knowing-Doing Gap

JEFFREY PFEFFER AND ROBERT I. SUTTON

Reviewed by Todd

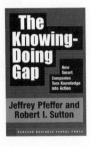

"**H**ear one, see one, do one."

That's how surgical residents learn new procedures. The final step of performing the operation proves that knowledge has been acquired and transferred. This training construct matches one used by the U.S. military during simulated drills and live-fire exercises to prepare soldiers for combat. Airline pilots, ocean freighter captains, and professional athletes follow the same strategy, but business practitioners seem to favor theory over practice.

Knowing what to do is not the problem. Over 11,000 business books, 80,000 MBAs, and $60 billion worth of corporate training each year show the wide avenues by which knowledge is dispensed and acquired. But Jeff Pfeffer and Bob Sutton, authors of *The Knowing-Doing Gap*, describe an intellectual divide, saying, "[T]here are fewer and smaller differences in *what firms know* than in their *ability to act* on that knowledge." They call that divide the "Knowing-Doing Gap."

With knowledge widely accessible, the authors' next query was "Does a Knowing-Doing gap really exist?" They cite numerous academic and industry studies to show substantial performance differences within and between companies because of the failure to adopt superior business practices within an industry, or due to the lack of sharing of best practices among plants within a single company. Rather than putting these strategies into action, organizations and their leaders choose from an array of hollow alternatives.

Pointless communication leads the list, say Pfeffer and Sutton. Talking about innovative strategy and organizational realignments with PowerPoint decks and spiral-bound planning documents resembles action in effort alone. Mission-statement development retreats consume equivalent brainpower but generate little more than frequent flier miles for the participants. Another barrier between knowing and doing are naysayers.

These individuals sound smart to their coworkers and are quick to dismiss anything new as "been done before," killing action before any momentum is reached. Naysayers are not the only impediment; strong culture, a quality of success held up by Jim Collins in *Good to Great*, can also stop action and smother needed change. History and tradition act as decision-making shorthand and can either keep the ship on course or lead it astray.

The authors further suggest that the "Knowing-Doing Gap" originates from fear. A primary by-product of action is failure, and mavericks willing to take chances fear losing their jobs, or, worse, suffering the humiliation of their peers' reactions. As Deming has famously advised, drive out fear. Pfeffer and Sutton agree. Surgeons have done this by building a culture where mistakes are shared with colleagues. Business leaders should follow the example, sharing their failures and what they learned, and bring that habit to employees. Reward the risk takers with second and third chances.

"[T]here are fewer and smaller differences in *what firms know* than in their *ability to act* on that knowledge."

The authors end the book by recounting the story of a workshop given for retail executives. A manager from Macy's came up afterward to offer thanks and to describe how none of this would work at her company. In the parking lot was a small group from Trader Joe's who also approached with thanks for the talk. They said that many of the lessons offered were already in place at their company, but there were some things they could do better. One of them was already on the phone with corporate headquarters sharing what was learned and was assured that those changes would "be implemented by Monday." The group was inspired to take action rather than consider the authors' advice as only theory. At the very least, they were willing to give it a try. As Pfeffer and Sutton say, "If you know by doing, there is no gap between what you know and what you do." TS

The Knowing-Doing Gap: How Smart Companies Turn Knowledge into Action, Harvard Business School Press, Hardcover 2000, ISBN 9781578511242

WHERE TO NEXT? « Page 9 for **doing more personally** « Page 91 for **doing more organizationally** « Page 117 for **more sales** | EVEN MORE: *Hard Facts, Dangerous Half-Truths, and Total Nonsense* by Jeffrey Pfeffer and Robert I. Sutton; *The No-Asshole Rule* by Robert I. Sutton

The Five Dysfunctions of a Team

PATRICK LENCIONI
Reviewed by Jack

Teams are a tremendously important part of modern management. But this has not always been the case. Previously a worker was given a job, shown how to do it, and then expected to do the same job over and over again until the supervisor dictated changes. Organizing individuals into a team with a common goal often results in better decision making and task completion due to diverse perspectives. However, the maintenance of a team is loaded with pitfalls because its success is dependent on the idiosyncratic nature of the people within the team—people with conflicting goals or dissimilar work habits. It can be a serious challenge to get disparate people to work together and pull on the oars at the same time and in the same direction. Herding cats comes to mind.

There have been many books written about teams: the theory of teams, managing teams, creating teams, and motivating teams. But in *The Five Dysfunctions of a Team*, Pat Lencioni has taken the subject and created a novel centered around this prevalent management approach. Lencioni's success as a storyteller lies in his ability to create believable characters and put them to work in believable companies, dealing with believable situations. Doesn't sound like much, but in the same way that some novels work and others don't—depending on how grounded they are in reality—many business novels often come off as being too pat, like a sitcom or soap opera that might reflect life in hyperbole. Lencioni's novels don't always conclude with a completely happy ending, but they are reality-based and therefore more applicable to the people who need it, the people you are training.

In *The Five Dysfunctions of a Team*, Lencioni creates a fictitious company of 150 employees located in Silicon Valley during the Internet bubble. Only two years earlier, the company was considered one of the hot new technology start-ups. But from the start, its executive team suffered from backstabbing and a lack of unity. The board asks the current CEO and cofounder to step down and hires a new CEO from outside the industry. After she observes her new company for a couple of weeks, she hosts an off-site meeting with her direct reports, saying, "We have a more experienced and talented executive team than any of our competitors. We have more cash than they do. . . . We have better core technology. And we have a powerful board of directors. Yet in spite of all that, we are behind two of our competitors in terms of both revenue and customer growth. Can anyone here tell me why that is?" In each subsequent off-site session, as the executive team struggles with turning around the company, she starts the meeting with this exact statement until the team is able to answer the question.

"Not finance. Not strategy. Not technology. It is teamwork that remains the ultimate competitive advantage, both because it is so powerful and so rare."

As the company and its new CEO deal with both internal and external issues, the different personalities of the executive team come to light and are used by the author to illustrate five common dysfunctions: absence of trust, fear of conflict, lack of commitment, avoidance of accountability, and inattention to results. The five dysfunctions are interconnected: You can't have spirited discussion without trust between team members. You can't have commitment to decisions unless you have open discussion without the fear of expressing your honest opinion. Consensus won't be reached without a little or maybe a lot of conflict. As my company has grown and we have added people with differing points of view, I have found that conflict can be positive, and is essential for a total buy-in on a new program or plan. And as Lencioni states: "All great relationships, the ones that last over time, require productive conflict in order to grow. This is true in marriage, parenthood, friendship, and certainly business."

In this case, Lencioni concludes his story with a happy ending. With a revitalized executive team, the company grows to over 200 employees and is able to draw even with the leader in its field. With a team that is working together efficiently, both morale and quality improve. But *The Five Dys-*

functions of a Team offers more than a well-told tale from which to intuit a new approach for your team or business. The fable is an effective vehicle for Lencioni's lessons, but also included are forty pages of worksheets and assessments to begin your own new team-building program or redesign of an existing team. JC

The Five Dysfunctions of a Team: A Leadership Fable, Jossey-Bass, Hardcover 2002, ISBN 9780787960759

WHERE TO NEXT? ◄ Page 47 for **stories of leadership** ►► Page 224 for **a story on starting a business** ►► Page 318 for **a practical guide to teams** | EVEN MORE: *The Five Dysfunctions of a Team: Participant Workbook* by Patrick Lencioni; *Leading Teams* by J. Richard Hackman; *Peak Performance* by Jon R. Katzenbach

Choose Your Approach

Every person learns differently; the challenge is finding the right medium for the message. Here are three ways we classify books and a few examples to show there is something for everyone.

1. Fables

Short fictional scenarios packing a punch with symbolism and analogies.

↓

2. Modern

Less than ten years old with contemporary perspectives and anecdotes.

↓

3. Classics

Business ideas that have survived the test of time.

↓

on Change

Who Moved My Cheese?
by Spencer Johnson, MD
Explores the different approaches to change taken by two mice and two people when someone moves their cheese.

Change or Die
by Alan Deutschman
A book about behavioral change, inspired by the popular *Fast Company* article.

Leading Change
by John P. Kotter
The famous Harvard professor shares eight steps for leading and guiding change.

on Motivation

Fish.
by Stephen C. Lundin, PhD, Harry Paul, John Christensen
One manager rises to the challenge of infusing motivation at Pike Place Fish Market in Seattle.

How Full Is Your Bucket?
by Tom Rath and Donald O. Clifton
Shows how to fill, with positive experiences, the metaphorical "bucket" inside each of us.

The Power of Positive Thinking
by Dr. Norman Vincent Peale
This classic book teaches how to overcome obstacles by thinking positively.

on Leadership

The Radical Leap
by Steve Farber
The guru Edg shows that love, energy, audacity, and proof are the key traits of extreme leaders.

The Leadership Challenge
by James M. Kouzes and Barry Z. Posner
Equips leaders with five usable practices to apply at every level of the company.

Leadership
by James MacGregor Burns
The original, definitive leadership text.

Written by Roy Normington

Six Thinking Hats

EDWARD DE BONO
Reviewed by Todd

I magine your company is facing a big problem. And I mean a your-biggest-client-has-left-for-your-competitor kind of problem.

The president calls a meeting to figure out what happened and each attendee enters the conference room with something different on his or her mind. The folks from research arrive with binders of pie charts detailing how well the campaign is (rather, *was*) going. The creative team has half a dozen ideas for how to improve the messaging. The account manager is wondering if he'll still be employed when the meeting is over. And the office manager walks in shaking her head, remembering how she told everyone that taking on this client was a bad idea.

The discussion becomes an argument about whose perspective has more merit. Each member's verbal commitment to his position makes considering other options difficult; however, considering a wide range of thought is the key to moving through these organizational impasses.

To move just such a discussion forward, Edward De Bono, in *Six Thinking Hats*, delineates six clear directions, or hats, that represent a particular line of human thought. To each hat he assigns a color. The metaphor of a hat is effective here because it implies that the kind of thinking one is doing can be donned, changed, or removed according to a situation. Let me use De Bono's descriptions to quickly introduce each hat:

> White is neutral and objective. The white hat is concerned with objective facts and figures.
> Red suggests anger (seeing red), rage, and emotions. The red hat gives the emotional view.
> Black is somber and serious. The black hat is cautious and careful. It points out the weaknesses in an idea.
> Yellow is sunny and positive. The yellow hat is optimistic and covers hope and positive thinking.

Green is grass, vegetation, and abundant, fertile growth. The green
  hat indicates creativity and new ideas.
Blue is cool, and it is also the color of the sky, which is above everything else. The blue hat is concerned with control, the organization of the thinking process, and the use of other hats.

In the scenario described here, each meeting attendee is coming at the
problem wearing a different hat . . . without being aware of it. Six Hats
thinking allows participants to focus their energy in a specific direction
by getting everyone to "wear" one hat at a time. During a meeting, the hats
can also be used in the order that is most appropriate to the discussion.
For example, the president may start with a red hat to gather the feelings
his employees have about the loss of this client. He may follow with a white
hat to then gather the facts about the client's defection. An intriguing conclusion to the meeting would be to have the group use some yellow-hat
thinking to consider the upside of the newly available resources.

A variety of practical benefits arise from the *Six Thinking Hats* approach. Discussions take less time because the group focuses on a particular line of thought at a given moment. Whether fear or fact, a hat exists for
those thoughts to be shared. Arguments do not dominate the meeting. Individuals who tend toward a certain line of thought are given freedom to
think more broadly under other hats. The language of colored hats itself
removes ego and allows the exploration of a topic in a natural and objective manner.

"The biggest enemy of thinking is complexity, for that leads to confusion."

De Bono's writing style is worthy of note. He frequently references
thoughts the reader would expect to hear from a group during Six Hats
thinking. A black-hat statement might sound like "I see a danger that the
competition will match our lower prices," or a red-hat confession might
be "I have the feeling that he will back down when it comes to the crunch."
This conversational treatment makes the material easier to internalize
and apply. Even when you introduce this form of thinking to a group for
the first time, the process seems familiar and you can easily anticipate
questions and concerns with the group.

De Bono is serious about thinking, as his many more academic books indicate, but *Six Thinking Hats* is the most accessible and easily applicable. Businesspeople spend a lot of time in conversation—often confrontational conversation—and this method is an effective way to organize your meetings so that they actually initiate progress. **TS**

Six Thinking Hats, Back Bay Books, Paperback Revised and Updated 1999, ISBN 9780316178310

WHERE TO NEXT? ▸ Page 268 for **a company that uses brainstorming** ▸ Page 270 for **brainstorming your marketing** ▸ Page 322 for **becoming a better brainstormer** | EVEN MORE: *Lateral Thinking* by Edward De Bono; *Tactics* by Edward De Bono; *Teach Yourself to Think* by Edward De Bono

BIOGRAPHIES

How did they do it? That is the question we all want to ask when we meet someone famous or wealthy. We want to mimic them, thinking that if we just follow their footsteps we'll arrive at the same place. But, as Mark Twain said, "History rhymes; it does not repeat." Biographies provide a direction and a context so we can better plot our own course.

Titan

RON CHERNOW
Reviewed by Jack

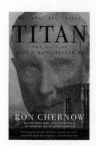

T he metal titanium was named after the Titans, a mytholog-
ical race of powerful Greek men. If we gave crude oil such a
namesake today, we would call it Rockefeller, after the first man
to transform this natural resource's power into a worldwide
commodity and wealth-amassing enterprise. John D. Rockefeller set the standard (no pun intended) for big business, and
it is his story that esteemed biographer Ron Chernow tells in
Titan.

Rockefeller was in the right place at the right time to make history:
Cleveland, Ohio, in 1853. Cleveland was home to one of five major re-
finery areas in America, and the young Rockefeller, having moved to
Cleveland with his family during his teenage years, became an expert in
converting petroleum into kerosene to be used for lighting. His career
grew spectacularly in the early days because of hard work and his ability to
cut costs and understand the big picture. Petroleum traveled on the railroads in barrels, and Rockefeller discovered he could make his own barrels cheaper than outsourcing them, thereby saving $150 per barrel: just
one small example of his thrift. He also had the unusual advantage of being able to secure loans from local bankers because of his trustworthy Pu-
ritan upbringing and his smart business sense. By 1868—just five years
after he began—his plants' refining capacity was greater than the next
three largest refineries combined. In 1870, Standard Oil was born.

Chernow makes it clear in his retelling that Rockefeller was aggressive
in his desire to maximize profits and change the industry. In 1871, the
head of the Pennsylvania Railroad proposed a consolidation of the frag-
mented refining industry that would have benefitted Rockefeller greatly.
The plan was never implemented because when word leaked out about the
estimated 100 percent increase in shipping charges—the profits from
which would be shared by Standard Oil and the railroads—some refiners
in the East protested. Things got violent in a Pennsylvania oil field, and
after the upheaval, the railroads backed off and lowered their rates. Still,

Rockefeller tried another approach and started to buy oil refineries and strengthen his hold on refining. He used aggressive tactics like selling below cost to show the other owners that they needed to sell before he put them out of business. In 1872, he bought up twenty-two of the twenty-six Cleveland competitors in a mere six weeks.

Ten years later, Rockefeller had multiple businesses in multiple states, which proved unwieldy to manage, and so the Standard Oil Trust was created to bring control to the diverse businesses. Despite the fact that the price of kerosene—the major commodity—dropped by 80 percent over the life of the company, the Trust had severe public relations issues because of Rockefeller's aggressive business practices. These business practices were not illegal since there were no laws in place to rein in this kind of big business. As a result, less than a decade later, the government ordered the breakup of Standard Oil. Very few organizations have been combated by acts of Congress, but the Sherman Antitrust legislation was created in response to the Standard Oil Trust. Today, you need only to look at the growth of Wal-Mart and Microsoft as contemporary examples of companies struggling against bad public relations and accusations of acting as a monopoly.

"He embodied all [of American life's] virtues of thrift, self-reliance, hard work, and unflagging enterprise. Yet as someone who flouted government and rode roughshod over competitors, he also personified many of its most egregious vices."

Chernow emphasizes that Rockefeller's questionable tactics and towering successes were tempered by many years of philanthropy. This dichotomy makes for an intriguing biography, and the author's passion for his subject is recognizable throughout. Chernow writes: "By the time Rockefeller died, in fact, so much good had unexpectedly flowered from so much evil that God might even have greeted him on the other side, as the titan had so confidently expected all along."

Rockefeller was a deeply religious man who believed that he was put on the earth to make money, with which he was to make others' lives better. He insisted that his greatest humanitarian accomplishment was not the philanthropic work he did in his later life, but the jobs he provided and the cheap kerosene he produced to light homes while he was making his money. But Rockefeller lived for ninety-eight years and spent more of his life giving money away than he did amassing it. While he didn't participate in philanthropy in predictable ways—building libraries or music halls as Andrew Carnegie did—he gave money to promote research that would yield widespread results. He also gave large amounts of money to schools, including Spelman College for African American women in Atlanta, the University of Chicago, and what became Rockefeller University in New York City.

This titan of oil saw opportunity and went after his vision with everything he had. Today, we have seen the same titanic ambition in revolutionaries like Bill Gates and Sam Walton. When it comes to understanding how something as innovative as the personal computer or "big box" retailing came to exist, and how their success pushed the boundaries of what we know about business, it is always informative to look to the predecessors. Ron Chernow gives readers a complete picture of this forefather of big business. JC

Titan: The Life of John D. Rockefeller Sr., Vintage Books, Paperback Second Edition 2004, ISBN 9781400077304

WHERE TO NEXT? » Page 244 for **the rebirth of an American industry** ◀◀ Page 139 for **an understanding of the rules Rockefeller was leveraging** ◀◀ Page 24 for **advice on competing with sharks like Rockefeller** | EVEN MORE: *The Prize* by Daniel Yergin; *Andrew Carnegie* by David Nasaw; *The People's Tycoon* by Steven Watts

My Years with General Motors

ALFRED P. SLOAN JR.
Reviewed by Jack

When Alfred Sloan, the longtime chairman of General Motors, contributed a management article to *Fortune* magazine in the spring of 1953, it was so comprehensive that one of the magazine's writers, John McDonald, suggested he craft it into a book. Sloan and McDonald (who would act as ghostwriter), along with a young researcher, Alfred D. Chandler Jr. (the now distinguished business historian), and Sloan's longtime assistant, pored over GM's archives to create the masterpiece *My Years with General Motors*. Because McDonald had extensive access to Sloan's files, the book is stocked with reprints of memos, detailed letters, and minutes of meetings, which, while cumbersome at times, help retell Sloan's years at GM in a uniquely comprehensive manner. In 1946, Peter Drucker published *Concept of the Corporation*, a detailed study of General Motors, a result of Sloan's invitation to Drucker to observe (while being paid) the company. Their philosophies matched well; both knew that corporations could not continue to grow unless a theory about how they should be constructed evolved.

In 1899, when GM was still headed by W. A. Durant, Sloan was the president of Hyatt Roller Bearing Company, a supplier to the nascent automobile industry. GM bought Hyatt in 1916, along with many of its other suppliers, and created a group called United Motors. Sloan was made a vice president and given some significant duties. He was also promoted to GM's board. After World War I, the auto industry faced a significant downturn, and shareholders became concerned. While Durant was regarded as a great visionary when it came to acquisitions and the automotive industry, he was not considered an effective manager. Around this same time, Sloan became head of United Motors and wrote an organization study "as a possible solution for the specific problems created by the expansion of the corporation after World War I" and submitted it to the executive committee. This study is one of the most important business documents ever written, primarily because, in those pages, Sloan revealed an organization that was so efficient, employing such processes as centralized buying and using interchangeable parts to build different GM cars, that they would ensure critical savings for GM at that time of struggle. Sloan succeeded Durant as president in 1922 and later became chairman of the board in 1937. He proved during his time at GM to be one of the management masters of the twentieth century.

During the 1920s, Ford, featuring its Model T, had captured well over 50 percent of the automobile market. Under Durant, GM had lost focus on the business at hand to pursue other sideline challenges, like the creation of a copper-cooled engine. In addition, GM had too many car brands that often cannibalized the other brands' customers. The new GM, using Sloan's organizational plan to consolidate car brands, created a concept of providing a customer with cars for a lifetime, as the slogan promoted. The first-time automotive buyer would start with the low-priced Chevrolet while the senior driver would settle back into a Cadillac. At the same time, Ford was slow to update the Model T, so when Sloan's management practices took hold, GM became the largest manufacturer of cars and trucks and remained so for decades.

"Confidence and caution formed my attitude in 1920. We could not control the environment, or predict its changes precisely, but we could seek the flexibility to survive fluctuations in business."

It would be an understatement to say that Sloan's successes were impressive during his forty-five years at GM. In 1922, Sloan captained a company of 25,000 employees; by 1962, Sloan's final year at GM, that number had grown to 600,000. During that same time, car and truck sales went from 205,000 units to 4,491,000, and total assets grew from $134 million to $9.2 billion. He accomplished this growth, in part, by being the first company to introduce new car models each year. He understood that people wanted a car that didn't reflect where they were currently, but where they wanted to be. Buyers were inclined to stretch their financial limits, so to expedite the process, he developed the General

In 2003, John McDonald wrote a book for MIT Press called *A Ghost Memoir: The Making of Alfred P. Sloan's My Years with General Motors*. Read as a follow-up to this biography, McDonald's own book provides a revealing look at the creation of this exemplary account by one of the management masters of the twentieth century. His discussion about some of the more sensitive material included in the book is fascinating. For example, Sloan's disclosure of his cornering of the market struck fear in the hearts of GM's lawyers. McDonald details how the lawyers, after they read the manuscript, wanted to stop publication of the book over concerns about antitrust issues. McDonald took the unprecedented step of suing GM so the book could be published in 1964—two years before Sloan's death.

Motors Acceptance Corporation to finance the new cars.

Sloan's management style allowed committees to make decisions, while he orchestrated debates within these committees to propel the future plans for the organization. This approach helped Sloan and GM to lead the industry for decades and with it give birth to the concept of "the professional manager," as Drucker describes Sloan in the book's introduction.

Full of lengthy excerpts from Sloan's correspondence and business documents, *My Life with General Motors* deviates from the usual biography format. The book is ideal for the student of business who wants to learn about managing both large and small groups, as Sloan offers long discourses on decision making and other key organizational issues. This book is a glimpse into the mind and actions of one of the twenty-first century's masters of business. JC

My Years with General Motors, Currency/Doubleday, Paperback 1990, ISBN 9780385042352

WHERE TO NEXT? ◀ Page 149 **for more on Sloan's consultant** ◀ Page 164 for **the revolt against Sloan's view** ◀ Page 161 for **the evolution in auto production** | EVEN MORE: *Concept of the Corporation* by Peter F. Drucker; *Guts* by Robert A. Lutz; *A Ghost's Memoir* by John McDonald

Wealth of Nations

Adam Smith's *magnum opus* of economics may not be suitable for light lunchtime reading, but its epic heft belies its accessibility. In fact, Smith, one of the greatest thinkers of his time or any other, somehow manages everyday parallels, many of which, despite an eighteenth-century viewpoint, still apply today.

Exhaustive in scope, he goes from micro to macro, globalization to taxes, never losing focus or steam. Actually, the true bulk here comes from the blow-by-blow bombardment of facts—seemingly anytime, anywhere that money has changed hands in modern capitalistic society, Smith has it in perspective.

No matter the industry, or level on the corporate totem pole, there is something here for any reader who thinks about why and where they go to work each day. Now-commonplace phrases like "invisible hand" and "self-interest" may echo from a distant high school history class, but the relevance of these, and others, is still unquestionable in everyone's nine-to-five world.

The Origin of Species

Few books throughout history continue to prove such an intellectual nuisance as *The Origin of Species*. Once highly controversial in terms of scientific thought and human nature, Darwin's masterpiece now finds its way into a discussion of business classics. In fact, much can be made of the change in the way the book has been received over time: it's almost as if the conclusions of natural selection—less complexity ceding to more—are demonstrated in the public's perception of the work.

Offering sweeping conclusions on humankind's interaction with the environment, this seminal work, when whittled down, can also act as a playbook of business push-and-pulls: "Struggle for Existence" is every start-up business; "Instinct" embodies every consumer.

Give Darwin a pass for his non-PC portions and ignore the historical baggage attached. At its core, *The Origin of Species* is a surprisingly readable, singularly keen observation of human nature.

The Prince

A classic study of power and control, this treatise by Machiavelli was written with little thought of business, or even politics. Rather, and quite ironically, his goal was to impress Lorenzo de' Medici, and, essentially, to gain back a cushy job. Somehow, within his most base and self-serving aspirations of comfort, the man crafted a pinnacle of business virtue that advocates manipulation, authority, and force, but also resiliency and the steadfast commitment to a purpose. The ends justify the means, etc., have become clichéd as terms, but in theory and practice they are still astounding in their economy and precision. Citing or abiding his work won't make you popular, and his name has become eponymous with the most feared and hated type of boss, but *The Prince* underscores a fundamental tenet: it's not personal, it's business.

The Art of War

By far the most "classic" of the classics, Sun Tzu's masterpiece is also the most concise and universally indispensable. No estimate could do justice to the role played in world history by this little "how to": memorized by Chinese fighters, revered by Napoleon, it was even studied by American forces during World War II.

Lately, though, this first of all military treatises has begun breaching the business battlefield in a big way. Spying, scheming, snaking, staying ahead by any means necessary is Sun Tzu's game. Upon reading descriptions of maintaining the offensive, the use of energy, and exploitative strategy, one gets the feeling that this is *not* the guy you'd want to have to scrapple with for the last cookie.

And this may be how competitors will feel about any who put his theories into practice.

While the book's popularity continues to mount, Tzu's delivery—simplistic, arcane, poetic—ensures every reader takes away something different and is entertained along the way.

Written in 500 BC, *The Art of War* is still the final word on all things competitive. While the weapons have changed with time, the immutable laws of human conflict never will.

Written by Todd Lazarski

The HP Way

DAVID PACKARD
Reviewed by Jack

Hewlett-Packard may be notable to you for a variety of reasons. You might have an HP printer on your desk. Maybe you're an avid fan of the history of the Silicon Valley and journeyed to the infamous garage where HP began. Perhaps you are intrigued by the rise and fall of Carly Fiorina, or maybe you watched the 2006 imbroglio involving leaks and finger-pointing in HP's boardroom. But maybe you also have heard of "the HP Way," the management approach about which Jim Collins writes, "The point is not that every company should necessarily adopt the specifics of the HP Way, but that Hewlett and Packard exemplify the power of building a company based on a framework of principles." Hewlett-Packard is an American success story, and *The HP Way* tells the story of how the company came to be and why its singular approach led to singular success.

Hewlett and Packard were unlikely partners. David Packard was born in 1912 and became an all-star basketball and track athlete. As a child he was very much interested in radio and electrical devices and later was accepted to Stanford to study electrical engineering. During his first fall at Stanford in 1930, he met Bill Hewlett, in many ways his opposite. Hewlett was dyslexic and struggled early in school. He was accepted to Stanford only because his father taught there. He joked that he chose electrical engineering because he liked electric trains.

While at Stanford, Hewlett and Packard became close friends. In 1937, they had their first "business" meeting to discuss starting a company together. Packard would manage the manufacturing tasks for the company while Hewlett would focus on the circuit technology and engineering. Their partnership was formed in 1939 (the sequence of the surnames for the company name came from a coin flip). Their first product was an audio oscillator used to create steady audio frequencies. (They called it Model 200A because that number made it seem like they had been in business awhile.) Meanwhile Hewlett, a bachelor, moved into the one-car garage behind the house Packard rented with his wife. That garage, now a landmark considered "the birthplace of Silicon Valley," became their first workshop.

By 1964, Hewlett-Packard had come a long way from its first product. The company's total sales were $125 million, and all revenue came from scientific instruments. The two innovated further, developing an automatic controller that quickly found more sales as a minicomputer, not as an accessory, and that set the trajectory for their future business. The company continued to evolve, diversifying its products. Consider that in 1994, HP's sales from computer products, service, and support were almost $20 billion, or about 78 percent of the total business.

"We thought that if we could get everybody to agree on what our objectives were and to understand what we were trying to do, then we could turn them loose and they would move in a common direction."

And while the products were enough to make HP successful and well-known, it was the management philosophy that gained the company another kind of respect. At the first off-site meeting in 1957, the company put into words what it believed was "The HP Way" of doing business. In five principles, it created a company philosophy to retain the small-business quality in a now very large company. Revolutionary management practices were enacted like "flextime" and creating small teams and letting the teams develop on their own. In 1966, the list of company objectives was expanded to seven. The seven objectives are, to this day: profit, customers, field of interest, growth, employees, organization, and citizenship. Packard explains that each can be summed up in one sentence. For example, *field of interest* is explained as: "To concentrate our efforts, continually seeking new opportunities for growth but limiting our involvement to fields in which we have capability and can make a contribution." These common objectives help set boundaries for all employees, yet allow for a certain freedom to play within those boundaries.

Hewlett and Packard were brilliant thinkers and perhaps even more effective in executing their vision, but they also seemed to do the right thing for their customers and employees when they came to a crossroads. The greatest lesson to be divined from this book isn't so much how to create a similar company but how creating a company based on a strong and clear set of values can lead to outstanding success. **JC**

The HP Way: How Bill Hewlett and I Built Our Company, Collins, Paperback Business Essentials Edition, 2005, ISBN 9780060845797

WHERE TO NEXT? ◀ Page 71 for **other firms like HP** ◀ Page 85 for **a tech turn-around** ▶ Page 204 for **a big leader with big ideals** |EVEN MORE: *Bill and Dave* by Michael S. Malone; *Tough Choices: A Memoir* by Carly Fiorina

Personal History

KATHARINE GRAHAM

Reviewed by Jack

It is unusual in contemporary business for one person to run a major business for almost thirty years. It is even more unusual if that person is a woman. Katharine Graham ran the Washington Post Company, originally her father's company, after the death of her husband in 1963, until 1991. When she took control of the company there were no women running an organization the size of the *Post*. Katharine Graham not only succeeded, but excelled, and, in *Personal History*, she tells her life story so exceptionally well that she would go on to win a Pulitzer Prize for it in 1998. But her success was not without struggle. Throughout her tenure as publisher, she had problems garnering the respect of peers and subordinates, and, in this book, she discusses her struggle to trust her own instincts. But it is indeed her obvious success as a leader and her status as a moral icon that makes this book essential reading.

Graham was born into wealth. Her father was a financier and later a public servant. Her mother was an intellectual and involved with the Republican Party. Graham acknowledges that her childhood was sheltered. Her inherent self-awareness is evidenced in this story: every other year, the family would go on a camping trip out west to see, as her mother said, that not everybody lived in large houses. Graham reflects on the lesson with wit and wisdom: "I suppose it did, but the lesson had its limits. There were five ranch hands on the trip to California, eleven saddle horses, and seventeen packhorses—not exacting roughing it." This observation is a telling example of what makes this personal history so compelling: Graham led an extraordinary life but could recognize that her experience was the exception.

Graham wasn't afraid of hard work, though, and wasn't a slave to wealth and opportunity. After a freshman year at Vassar, she transferred to the University of Chicago and got involved in labor politics during the Depression. Certainly she had a leg up through her family connections— after graduation she got a job at a San Francisco paper with help from her father—but she still got her hands dirty while covering the labor unrest at the docks and becoming close to the union leaders.

When Graham took over the Washington Post Company after her husband died, it consisted of the daily newspaper, *Newsweek* magazine, and a few TV and radio stations. As president, she oversaw all three divisions. Both fortuitously and with a number of inherent challenges, her reign began at the start of some of the major events of the century. The assassinations of John F. Kennedy, Martin Luther King Jr., and Robert F. Kennedy, and racial unrest, made the daily newspaper even more important in American everyday life. As luck would have it, just as the *Washington Post* started to expand its influence, New York City dailies were hurt by labor troubles and three papers had to close. The writers were forced out of their jobs at the weeklies, which allowed the *Post* to gain some quality writers—especially in editorial and national and international news— and elevate the standard while other dailies were reduced.

Lack of competition and an extended editorial budget allowed Graham to undertake some unconventional risks. For example, she allowed the *Post* correspondent in Vietnam to point out that the emperor in fact had no clothes even when the U.S. government had been saying otherwise. Graham also seized opportunities to develop relationships with important figures. Included in the book is her correspondence about the Vietnam War with President Johnson as the *Post* swung to an antiwar stance, especially provocative considering her husband is credited with getting Johnson on the national ticket as VP in 1960.

Surprisingly, and somewhat refreshingly, Graham's book also reveals her insecurities with the business side of the newspaper world. She acknowledges that she was way more interested in the editorial side of the *Post*, and because of that she ran afoul of the publisher. For example, when Bobby Kennedy was assassinated, she got a call in the early morning from the circulation manager asking her what to do. It was decided that they would deliver the paper that was already planned and then do a special edition and deliver it again. She made that decision on the loading dock. Her publisher was angry with her for not consulting him first.

But it should not be assumed that she wielded her power with no interest in improving her handle on the business side. She spent time at companies such as Texas Instruments, Xerox, and NCR trying to understand the basics of good management. She spent a week at an IBM course for senior executives to learn about computers. Petrified and annoyed that she was the only woman present, she discovered that the men attending the course were as apprehensive as she was to learn about technology. She was admirably willing to put herself in situations of learning, again getting dirt under her fingernails.

"I told [Phil Geyelin, a diplomatic reporter for the *Wall Street Journal*] something I have said to every editor I've worked with— that I didn't want to read anything in the paper of great importance or that represented an abrupt change which we haven't discussed; that I wanted to be in on the takeoffs as well as the landings."

Katharine Graham believed she could make a difference. She succeeded in her business by maintaining a strict moral code while being open to change and not succumbing to her insecurities. It is impossible not to be charmed by her stories, such as her account of sitting on a boat with Truman Capote, reading and critiquing the advance review copy of *In Cold Blood*. When I read *Personal History*, I am grateful for the chance to take a peek into her amazing life and to learn about one of the most prominent female figures in modern business. JC

Personal History, Vintage Books, Paperback 1998, ISBN 9780375701047

WHERE TO NEXT? » Page 313 for **coping with an unexpected career change** « Page 43 for **memorable moments of leadership** « Page 60 for **the one periodical we recommend** | EVEN MORE: *A Good Life* by Ben Bradlee; *Power, Privilege and the Post* by Carol Felsenthal; *All the President's Men* by Carl Bernstein and Bob Woodward

Moments of Truth

JAN CARLZON

Reviewed by Jack

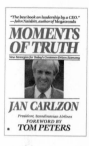

I n the 1970s, Sweden was known for ABBA, Saab, cold weather, blonds, and socialism, but not for cutting-edge leadership. That all changed when Jan Carlzon, at the age of thirty-two, was hired to run Vingresor (a vacation packager for Scandinavian Airlines—SAS). Carlzon's success with Vingresor landed him the presidency of the parent company, SAS, which was at that time in the midst of a severe loss after seventeen consecutive profitable years. During his tenure at SAS, Carlzon turned a stodgy state-run airline into a world-class airline that has become one of Europe's biggest, operating over 1,000 flights a day to 103 destinations in 34 countries. *Moments of Truth* is Carlzon's 135-page autobiography chronicling his time at the airline in a series of stories that are relevant to anyone in business.

When Carlzon became president at Vingresor (the company at which he'd been hired right out of college), he was known around the office as "Ego Boy." The promotion had caused him to act out a role of superiority he thought appropriate for a president, providing a solution for everybody's problem. An associate took him aside and pointed out to him that he had been promoted not to have all the answers, but to be a supportive presence. He reflects on that moment as a turning point of his career.

> The company was not asking me to make all the decisions on my own, only to create the right atmosphere, the right conditions for others to do their jobs better. I began to understand the difference between a traditional corporate executive, who issues instruction after instruction from the top, and the new corporate leader, who must set the tone and keep the big picture in mind.

Six years later, when he took over as COO of SAS, he used this enlightened approach to turn around the suffering airline by giving frontline employees the power to make decisions.

Carlzon determined that every customer interacts with an employee of SAS for an average of fifteen seconds. He calls these interactions "moments of truth," because whether that brief exchange is with a ticket agent or baggage handler, it is during that time that a customer makes their judgment about his organization. All the marketing and clever slogans don't mean a thing if that moment is an unsatisfactory one for the customer. So Carlzon created an organization that gave the training and the power to each of his twenty thousand employees to fix every problem. As a result, the customer is left with a positive feeling of efficacy and efficiency after every interaction.

With this change, Carlzon successfully took SAS from the traditional "production-oriented" philosophy to a "customer-driven" philosophy. But the initial challenge, before perfecting customer service, was to determine just who SAS's customer was. Carlzon decided to focus on business travelers because they are the most profitable. They shop price less often, but are also the most fickle because they want to get where they need to be with the least difficulty. In the case of business travelers, brand is seldom favored over convenience.

"An individual without information cannot take responsibility; an individual who is given information cannot help but take responsibility."

This focus on a specific customer informed each successive decision. For example, a purchase of new Airbuses to replace the older DC-9s was already in the works when Carlzon took over. The Airbuses would operate 6 percent cheaper than the DC-9s, but the planes needed to be full to realize the savings; because the Airbus had 240 seats compared to the DC-9's 110 seats, this was a considerably greater challenge. Carlzon quickly realized that his passenger base was too small to support the bigger plane; SAS would have needed to increase passengers to reduce the number of flights. But this ran counter to the needs of the business traveler, who wants and needs many flights leaving and arriving at all hours. In an unconventional decision, SAS mothballed the Airbuses. As Carlzon writes: "Our new customer-oriented perspective starts with the market instead of the product." That decision was revolutionary then, and would still be today.

The changes Carlzon brought to SAS were not made without difficulty. As he drove to reduce the management pyramid that was the existing management style, the middle managers were feeling the pinch from both ends. Upper management wanted the frontline folks to have the freedom to do extraordinary things for the customers. This decentralizing was obviously a big hit with everyone but those in the middle. After telling some amusing stories about middle managers pushing back, Carlzon clarifies to any organization that is in this flattened world that the middle needs to realize that "[t]heir authority applies to translating the overall strategies into practical guidelines that the front line can follow and then mobilizing the necessary resources for the front line to achieve its objectives."

Most business books need 250 to 300 pages to give you what this little treasure offers up in 135. Carlzon's reorganization of a European airline during the 1980s may seem distant from our current challenges, but it succinctly teaches us about great leadership and management. That, of course, is particularly relevant, considering the current expansion of resources available at consumers' fingertips when they make their purchasing decisions. Moments of truth happen to us every day as we travel and shop, but many businesses still don't get what Carlzon was talking about over twenty years ago. Reading this book will change how you make decisions as a consumer and how you do business as a service provider. JC

Moments of Truth: New Strategies for Today's Consumer-Driven Economy, HarperCollins, Paperback 1989, ISBN 9780060915803

WHERE TO NEXT? » Page 316 for **what the CEO wants you to know** ◄ Page 50 for **humanistic leadership** ◄ Page 88 for **the power of listening to your customers** | EVEN MORE: *Service America in the New Economy* by Karl Albrecht and Ron Zemke; *Customers for Life* by Carl Sewell and Paul B. Brown; *The Customer Comes Second* by Hal F. Rosenbluth and Diane McFerrin Peters

Sam Walton:
Made in America—My Story

SAM WALTON WITH JOHN HUEY
Reviewed by Jack

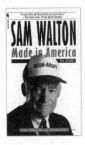

Sam Walton is the greatest merchant of the twentieth century. His legacy grew from a single five-and-dime in Newport, Arkansas, into a retail behemoth that earned $380 billion in revenue in 2007. Despite his unparalleled success, Walton couldn't understand what salacious news *Fortune* hoped to uncover when the magazine named him the richest man in America in 1985. Walton recounts in his memoir, *Sam Walton: Made in America:* "I drove an old pickup truck with cages in the back for my bird dogs, or I wore a Wal-Mart baseball cap, or I got my hair cut at the barbershop just off the town square. . . ." The book tells the tale of this self-made man in his own down-home words. Added quotes from those who knew him best give us a real sense of knowing the man personally. While the aw-shucks tone may be a little over the top, it does not diminish the story: Sam Walton was an extraordinary man and had an extraordinary tale to tell.

Walton was a very smart and ambitious guy beneath his seemingly ordinary outer façade. One needs only to look at his childhood to realize he was a leader early on. He was the youngest Eagle Scout in the history of Missouri at the time he was awarded the recognition. He was the quarterback of his high school football team when his team went undefeated. And as a basketball player (leading the team as a guard at only five feet nine), his team went undefeated as well. Walton was a young man with a serious competitive streak that served him well all through his life.

The stories about his early years could belong to many people in this country. He lived in a small town, graduated from college while working at a JC Penney, fell in love, and got married. He did his duty as an ROTC soldier during World War II and, after the war, moved to a small town in Arkansas because his wife, Helen, refused to live in a town larger than 10,000 people. In 1945, he used $5,000 of his money and $20,000 of his father-in-law's money to buy that five-and-dime in Newport.

Over the next fifteen years, Walton expanded his company to sixteen stores. He stayed under the radar in the early years by opening stores in smaller towns. Those towns were chosen because Walton would only open a new store within one day's delivery from the closest distribution center. By keeping its corporate headquarters in Arkansas, the company retained its small-town roots.

Walton was not the only entrepreneur, though, who saw potential in discount retail. In 1962, S.S. Kresge started Kmart, Dayton Hudson opened Target, and Woolworth launched Woolco. Walton's answer was Wal-Mart number 1, which he opened in Rogers, Arkansas, the same year. Within five years, Kmart had 250 stores with revenues of $800 million to Wal-Mart's 19 stores and $9 million in revenues because Walton stuck to his original plan of focusing on smaller markets. The other discounters beat each other up over the big markets. In the early years of Wal-Mart, Walton continued to run eighteen variety stores and a handful of Wal-Marts. The stories of his early accounting and distribution are amusing . . . and scary. For example, he continued using a pigeonhole method for receipts and paperwork until his responsibilities grew with over twenty stores.

"A lot of what goes on these days with high-flying companies and these overpaid CEO's [sic], who're really looting from the top and aren't watching out for anyone but themselves, really upsets me."

But it is the culture Walton created that was most notable. His early managers actually invested money in the stores they managed. Walton visited the stores continually and studied his competitors. As he traveled on business or even with his family on vacation, he would stop at any kind of retailer to study its tactics. Then he refined and improved these pilfered ideas and tried them out in his stores so that the company would be constantly innovating.

Occasionally in your life you meet someone who is so dynamic and full of boundless energy that there is no wondering how he excelled. I imagine this is what meeting Sam Walton would have been like. His communication skills and style played a significant role in how he convinced his employees to get (and stay) onboard his tight ship. There are many books written about his company, but if you want to know the origins of Wal-Mart, nothing is better than hearing from the man himself. The passion Sam Walton brought to his work is admirable, and he shares that passion in this memoir. In fact, he even advises the reader to "borrow/steal" from his successes. JC

Sam Walton: Made in America—My Story, Bantam Books, Paperback 1993, ISBN 9780553562835

WHERE TO NEXT? ▸ Page 321 for **globalization** ▸ Page 268 for **innovation** ◂ Page 91 for **execution** | EVEN MORE: *The Wal-Mart Effect* by Charles Fishman; *Direct from Dell* by Michael Dell with Catherine Fredman; *Wal-Smart* by William H. Marquardt

Losing My Virginity

RICHARD BRANSON

Reviewed by Jack

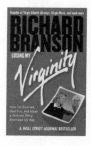

Richard Branson is arguably the most successful entrepreneur of the past half-century, creating 360 different companies and brands, from Virgin Cola to Virgin Music to Virgin Atlantic. Some failed, like Virgin Cola, and some set the industry standard, like Virgin Atlantic. But don't think that Branson is done: he calls this book Volume One of his autobiographies. It covers the first forty-three years of his life, though the first chapter begins with one of his around-the-world balloon flights that failed in 1997. The book ends in 1993, when he was forced to sell Virgin Music to save Virgin Atlantic—a move he refers to as the low point of his business life. The overall theme of the book is survival, and this book is chock full of survival stories about his life, his remarkable entrepreneurial spirit, and his successes and his failures, which offer both inspiration and caution to those who would like to follow in his footsteps.

As with most autobiographies, we begin at the beginning, and Branson recounts his childhood, telling tales about family and school. Faced with the challenges of dyslexia and a rebellious spirit, Branson had an extremely hard time with authority at school. He had ideas about reforming some of the more arcane rules, and out of this desire came the student/youth newspaper called the *Student* that he started with his friend, Nik Powell (who would be a cohort of Branson's throughout, enabling Branson to explore new ideas while Nik made them work on the front lines). The first issue was published in January 1968 when Branson was seventeen. Branson retells stories about how he and Nik called banks and large companies to get advertisers, and his methods reveal his ingeniousness. The pair called Coca-Cola, saying Pepsi was in the paper, and then reversed the tactic when calling Pepsi. Also he was fearless in pursuing the big story, and his interviews included subjects like Mick Jagger and John Lennon. Lennon almost put Branson out of business when he promised him an unreleased song to be put in the paper as a flexi-disc. Branson ramped up the print run, expecting a land rush of sales, but Lennon didn't deliver. That story reflects just one of the misfortunes that Branson did not let push him offtrack.

In 1970, the *Student* employed almost twenty people—all earning £20 per week. But by that time, Branson had identified another avenue to explore. He knew how important music was to the readers of the *Student*. He also saw that regular record shops didn't discount music, so he ran an ad in the *Student* offering cheaper mail-order records. The response was huge and a business was born. Of course, he knew they needed a clever name, and Virgin was suggested because they were all novices at business. Virgin Mail-Order Records took in bags and bags of mail orders, but the boom didn't last. In January 1971, the Union of Post Office Workers went on strike for six months.

That obstacle put Branson once again in survival mode . . . a state which seemed to stimulate his creativity. He saw an opportunity to sell music in an actual retail store. At that time, record stores were dull, formal areas owned by people who knew little about what was new or exciting. The first Virgin record shop, located on Oxford Street in London, created an environment where customers could hang out, talk, and hear new music. While Nik was running the record store on a daily basis, Branson discovered that he could save some money by selling records that were for export and therefore cheaper. The decision to sell those records caused him to spend a night in jail, and his mother had to bail him out of the pokey. He ended up having to pay a fine of £60,000. Branson had always been a worker of the angles—looking for shortcuts—but that night he vowed he would never do anything that would cause him to be jailed or embarrassed again.

"But, unlike losing your virginity, in whatever world you make for yourself, you can keep embracing the new and the different over and over again."

Branson soon realized that the margin at the retail level was small and that the real money was made behind the scenes. He found a run-down manor outside London in which to set up recording studios, and bought it for £30,000, borrowing £20,000 from a bank and the remainder from friends and family. Since mainstream recording studios were not very friendly to young bands, Branson was determined that the manor would be different. It had rooms for musicians to stay in while they recorded in the state-of-the-art studio constructed in an outbuilding. Eventually the studio would be world-famous for its state-of-the-art production facilities and ambiance. In 1992, Branson regretfully sold the Virgin label to EMI for a $1 billion to help subsidize Virgin Atlantic Airways, which he launched in 1984.

These are just a few of the stories that keep you turning the pages in *Losing My Virginity*. Branson's every decision is an example of his continual search for the next big thing. And his ability to recognize it and learn from his failures or stumbles can be a model for all readers. He tells people, when asked to describe his personal business philosophy, "It's not that simple: to be successful, you have to be out there, you have to hit the ground running, and if you have a good team around you and more than a fair share of luck, you might make something happen." **JC**

Losing My Virginity: How I've Survived, Had Fun, and Made a Fortune Doing Business My Way, Three Rivers Press, Paperback 2004, 9780812932294

WHERE TO NEXT? ▸ Page 320 for **building a compelling business** ▸ Page 279 for **envisioning a compelling life** ◂ Page 111 for **building compelling brands** | EVEN MORE: *The Rebel Rules* by Chip Conley; *Buffett* by Roger Lowenstein; *Giants of Enterprise* by Richard S. Tedlow

ENTREPRENEURSHIP

The word didn't even exist until 1950. However, blacksmiths, bakers, and candlestick makers faced the same challenges as today's organic farmers and database designers. These businesses are born out of passion but often fail in practicality. Entrepreneurship is hip, treacherous, and vital—all of which served as inspiration for our selections.

The Art of the Start

GUY KAWASAKI

Reviewed by Jack

Ⅰf you peruse the business shelves of the library or your local book emporium, you'll find a lot of books about starting a new business. So, how do you find the one that will make your idea into a reality without buying the entire shelf? Well, the author's credibility is crucial in this case. You want to learn from someone who has "been there, done that," certainly, but you also want someone who can translate what he or she knows into inspiring and applicable advice.

Guy Kawasaki is your trustworthy guide with *The Art of the Start*. In 1984, he was hired by Apple as a software evangelist to convince software manufacturers to develop programs for the yet-to-be-finished Macintosh computer, an undertaking chronicled in his first book, *Selling the Dream*. He is now a founder and managing director of garage.com, an early-stage investor in technology start-ups; he also sits on a number of boards and acts as an advisor to tech businesses. From this vast experience, Kawasaki is convinced that starting a business (or hiring the right person or building a brand—starting anything) is an art, not a science, and with this book he'll help you start your own endeavor with style.

If you have ever seen Kawasaki speak—and if you haven't, you must—you know he has a distinctive style. *The Art of the Start* is infused with this unique sensibility. For example, his use of Top Ten lists is famous, and he employs them here to great effect. But don't think you will be bullet-pointed to boredom. Kawasaki writes with a light tone, and maintains a sense of humor throughout. For example, in a list of ways to avoid hiring mistakes, he gives us the Top Ten lies job candidates use, including:

Lie: "I've never been with a company for more than a year because I get bored easily."
Truth: "It takes people about a year to figure out that I'm a bozo."

Lie: "I am a vice president, but no one reports to me."
Truth: "Any bozo can become a vice president at my company."

Kawasaki uses many of these unique devices in presenting the material. Frequently Asked Questions become Frequently Avoided Questions. Charts serve to contrast common wisdom with Guy's real-world advice. Each chapter begins with a GIST (Great Ideas for Starting Things) and often includes a "minichapter" covering everything from designing T-shirts to "The Art of Schmoozing." The final element of each chapter is a list of recommended reading.

"Working in a start-up isn't easy.... Therefore, belief in what you're doing is as important as competence and experience."

Clever organization gives way to actionable advice. In the "Pitching" chapter, he introduces the "10/20/30" rule of presentations, which states that a presentation should have only ten slides, last twenty minutes, and use a thirty-point font. Sure, most pitch meetings are scheduled to last an hour, but Kawasaki suggests twenty minutes for two reasons: one, the previous meeting may have gone long and your time will be cut; and two, you will want ample time for discussion at the end. Also in the pitch section, he tells you to set the stage for your presentation by asking the attendees three questions: "How much of your time may I have?" "What are the three most important things I can communicate to you?" and "May I quickly go through my PowerPoint presentation and handle questions at the end?" This approach may challenge you to think on your feet if their questions differ from the material you prepared, but it is worth the risk. These recommendations can change the dynamic of a presentation because it will be more transparent and considerate of the audience, which is unusual and appreciated.

When you buy *The Art of the Start*, you are investing in Kawasaki's twenty-five years of experience in Silicon Valley, his tenure at Apple, and his time as a venture capitalist. When you read *The Art of the Start*, you are experiencing his signature style. This is one of those books that is important as much for *how* he says things as for *what* he says. Starting is always the hardest part, and Kawasaki focuses on the points that need attention when you begin any kind of endeavor, business or otherwise. JC

The Art of the Start, Portfolio, Hardcover 2004, ISBN 9781591840565

WHERE TO NEXT? ⇻ Page 316 for **bytes on sales** ⇻ Page 314 for **bytes on management** ⇺ Page 130 for **bytes on marketing** | EVEN MORE: *Selling the Dream* by Guy Kawasaki; *E-Boys* by Randall E. Stross; *High-Tech Start-Up* by John L. Nesheim

The E-Myth Revisited

MICHAEL E. GERBER

Reviewed by Jack

You make the best cannoli in North Boston or the best brat-wurst in Sheboygan and you are thinking about going into business for yourself. Your friends and family, even strangers, assure you that your creation is so good it'll be a sure-fire hit. The first step toward your new venture is to take out a second mortgage on the house. Second step, leave your crappy day job.

Think I've just described the recipe for starting your own successful business? Think again! You're in danger of falling for the E-Myth, the entrepreneur's oft-made mistake of putting the cart before the horse, thinking he can succeed with simply a good idea and hard work. Before Gerber's first book on this subject, *The E-Myth*, was published, most small-business books were about honing an idea and then bootstrapping it. While he covered the nuts and bolts of running a new small business, his primary goal was to introduce some key business concepts by telling a story that every reader can relate to.

In *The E-Myth Revisited*, you'll meet Sarah. Sarah is a baker who makes the best pies in the county. She wants to open her own business, but wonders how to make the jump from expert baker to successful small-business owner. Initially she has some success because she hires a smart manager to run the business while she concentrates on what she does best—baking pies. Unfortunately, the manager leaves for a better job and Sarah has a meltdown. Through her story Gerber presents the lessons on making a new business successful without requiring the reader to decipher the abstract rules or hypothetical advice often included in other small-business books.

Gerber believes that a common cause of small-business failure lies within "The Fatal Assumption": if you understand the technical work of a business, you understand a business that does technical work. In other words, baking pies is *not* the same as running a bakery. Gerber instead shows that to be a successful small-business owner, you need three separate skills: the technical, the managerial, and the entrepreneurial. He considers a lack of understanding in one or more of these areas to be the cause of most small-business failures. The reassuring news is that Gerber believes these skills can be learned.

Gerber contends that the true product of a business is not *what* it sells but *how* it sells it. Gerber formalizes this belief in a system he calls the "Business Format Franchise." The key is to create a systems-dependent business, not a people-dependent business. To do this, you need to view your business as a potential franchise and construct your internal systems that way. Look at the way McDonald's, Disney, and FedEx do business. Their products are consistent. The model is systems-based so anybody hired can be put inside that Mickey Mouse costume or behind the counter asking, "Would you like fries with that?" The result is a business that is completely scalable and not dependant on a single person.

To take advantage of this scalability, a business needs to be able to grow. Gerber presents three distinct activities: innovation, quantification, and orchestration. He suggests changing something as simple as your in-store greeting as innovation. Instead of "Can I help you find anything?" why not try "Have you ever been here before?" You can then measure whether this new greeting increases sales, and using those results, you can then refine your presentation going forward.

"[Y]our business is a means rather than an end, a vehicle to enrich your life rather than one that drains the life you have."

Gerber ends the book with a letter to Sarah. He speaks with passion about the importance of caring, which is at the heart of entrepreneurship at its most pure form. But baking perfect pies is not enough. That same caring must infuse the entire business enterprise. *The E-Myth Revisited* takes the hope of a hobby and provides the skills to create a livelihood. **JC**

The E-Myth Revisited: Why Most Small Businesses Don't Work and What to Do About It, Harper-Collins, Paperback 1995, ISBN 9780887307287

WHERE TO NEXT? ◀ Page 213 for **lessons from the entrepreneur** ◀ Page 167 for **lessons from the technician** ◀ Page 173 for **lessons from the manager** | EVEN MORE: *You Need to Be a Little Crazy* by Barry Moltz; *No Man's Land* by Doug Tatum

The Republic of Tea

MEL ZIEGLER, PATRICIA ZIEGLER, AND BILL ROSENZWEIG

Reviewed by Todd

I love it when Jack tells stories about the beginnings of 800-CEO-READ. I always listen, rapt—wondering how three shelves in the back of a bookstore could have turned into a fifteen-person, multimillion-dollar operation, wondering what it was that Jack did that allowed us to survive as we have against big-box retailing and Internet commerce, wondering how the dynamic culture formed. I search for some meaning in our past to understand the company we have become. No definitive written history exists for the conception of 800-CEO-READ, or for most companies, for that matter. I think that is why I enjoyed *The Republic of Tea* so much. It is the genesis story of a company and its quest to change the world with tea.

Mel Ziegler, the entrepreneur behind Banana Republic, found his clothing company had over time developed "its own mind" and he was becoming increasingly at odds with his progeny. After deciding to sell the clothing retailer, and still recovering from the painful separation, the disillusioned entrepreneur serendipitously found himself on an airplane sitting next to Bill Rosenzweig. Bill was on a search to find a living he could love. The two shared one of those life-changing conversations, and *The Republic of Tea* is a record of their correspondence over twenty months. These reproductions of faxes and letters between Mel, Bill, and Mel's wife Patricia that make up *The Republic of Tea* chronicle the evolution of an idea into a business.

Rosenzweig was immediately swept up by Ziegler's zen-inspired descriptions for how tea can create a different state of mind. They both imagined the Republic as a place, physical and psychological. Patricia's illustrations, sprinkled throughout the book, bring a visual sense to the ideas brewing among the three. Stores, serving sets, tea blends for children, and water for tea bottled at the source of the Yangtze River all burst forth as potential paths of creativity in the initial weeks of their conversation.

The shared euphoria propelled both men forward, then gave way to practicality. Rosenzweig shifted his focus to understanding the mechanics of the tea market. Trips to the supermarket, conversations with tea brokers, and Lexus-Nexus searches provided a rough sketch of the world they were moving into. Imagined organizational charts and an evolving product portfolio added more concreteness. The would-be entrepreneur will appreciate Rosenzweig's thoroughness and preparation, but some of the details conveyed in his communiqués with Ziegler foreshadow problems ahead.

"As for my role, I got him pregnant."

Tension grew between the two partners. Ziegler felt that Rosenzweig was more interested in talking about the business than in starting the business. Rosenzweig was uncertain, acknowledging in added notes to the book that he needed Ziegler for direction and support. Ziegler, sensing that uncertainty, made his role clear: he was happy to mentor and possibly invest in the unformed company, but would contribute no further. Confidence wavering, Rosenzweig abandoned the Republic and took a job at a friend's design firm, vowing to bootstrap the tea business.

Rosenzweig returned to the idea with a new energy after a year had passed with no real progress. This time he would stand on his own. He needed to become an expert in tea. He spent an intense month in London at the center of the world tea trade, learning such particulars as how to identify a first-flush from a second-flush Darjeeling. He also resumed talks with Ziegler, this time with new expectations: "I stopped waiting for him to lead the way into the tea business because it was finally clear that if I didn't start it, no one else would." The Republic of Tea was incorporated by the three authors in 1992. Their idea had finally blossomed into a business.

Insights abound in *The Republic of Tea*, conveying the yin and yang of entrepreneurship. The book captures the rush of a new entrepreneurial idea, the unforgiving practicality of the marketplace, and how, in the end, the only indicator you can trust is your heart. Shortly after Rosenzweig rediscovered his passion for the project, he asked Ziegler when the right time to start a business is. Ziegler answered, in his usual thoughtful manner, "Never and always." **TS**

The Republic of Tea: The Story of the Creation of a Business, as Told Through the Personal Letters of Its Founders, Currency/Doubleday, Paperback 1994, ISBN 9780385420570

WHERE TO NEXT? ◄◄ Page 123 for **why we buy** ◄◄ Page 32 for **the magic of journeys** ◄◄ Page 126 for **the power of experiences** | EVEN MORE: *Brewing Up a Business* by Sam Calagione; *Pour Your Heart into It* by Howard Schultz and Dori Jones Yang; *Typo* by David Silverman; *The Dip* by Seth Godin

The Partnership Charter

DAVID GAGE

Reviewed by Todd

The Partnership Charter

How to Start Out Right With Your New Business Partnership

{or Fix the One You're In}

DAVID GAGE

Researchers at Marquette University studied over two thousand companies and found that 94 percent of "hypergrowth" companies were started by two or more people. Individual owners made up only 6 percent of the hypergrowth segment and almost one-half of the slow-growth companies.

Despite this evidence that a partnership can lead to success, the thought of taking on a partner makes most budding entrepreneurs cringe. *Inc.* magazine polled its readers on this very subject and two out of every three respondents felt partnerships were a bad idea. When asked why, the majority said "inevitable conflicts" and "unmet expectations" would lead to problems.

Since the data show that partnerships are either necessary or unavoidable, there is an opportunity for educators to address the unique relationships between partners, but instead business schools spend vast amounts of classroom time discussing the intricacies of manager/employee relationships. Medical professionals and lawyers, for example, after years in school, commonly join practices despite never being educated on the form of business in which most will spend their entire careers. There is also a void in the business-book canon regarding the management of partnerships, and *The Partnership Charter* is an excellent resource to bridge this oversight.

When running a business with one or two partners, any of the following scenarios may present themselves:

- One partner insists on hiring a key employee whom another partner dislikes.
- A partner is sued for sexual harassment.
- The company receives an unsolicited buyout offer from a competitor.
- The company runs out of money.

- An ongoing personal or family crisis interferes with the ability of one partner to perform.
- One partner suddenly loses interest in the business.
- A partner is caught stealing from the company.

(Full list is on page 196 of *The Partnership Charter*.)

David Gage lays out these possible trials and tribulations in *The Partnership Charter*, examining the unique relationship between partners. Business relationships generally lack the emotional ties found in personal relationships, and boundaries are drawn based on ownership stakes, salaries, and titles. But changes in the external lives of the partners or the health of the business inevitably impact the partnership. While some conditions may be governed by the legal documents that established the company, Gage suggests a written charter that addresses a broader set of needs partners have over time.

"A charter is a necessary tool because few people have been taught how to be partners."

The chartering process establishes the ground rules for how the partnership will operate. A common vision for the company is created and agreed upon. The ownership stakes are determined based on factors ranging from the amount of capital invested to the amount of control each partner assumes. Assigning roles and titles are a natural subsequent step as partners decide how active they want to be in the new firm and how decision making will take place. Most important, a plan is drawn up to allocate how money will be distributed. This process compares and contrasts the partners' values systems and expectations for how the partnership will operate. Making all of this apparent at the start, says Gage, reduces the potential for disconnects later in the life of the partnership.

Entrepreneurs are not wary of partnerships for the wrong reasons; business partnerships are complex, dynamic relationships. But it is those

nuances and synergies that bring a greater chance of success to any entrepreneurial adventure. **TS**

The Partnership Charter: How to Start Out Right with Your New Business Partnership (or Fix the One You're In), Basic Books, Paperback 2004, ISBN 9780738208985

WHERE TO NEXT? » Page 298 for **understanding our basic motives** » Page 295 for **understanding emotions** « Page 201 for **the Silicon Valley's most famous partnership** | EVEN MORE: *Start-ups That Work* by Joel Kurtzman and Glenn Rifkin; *Riding Shotgun* by Nathan Bennett and Stephen A. Miles; *Team of Rivals* by Doris Kearns Goodwin

Growing a Business

PAUL HAWKEN
Reviewed by Jack

Over twenty years ago, Paul Hawken, the cofounder of Smith & Hawken, a mail-order supplier of high-end quality gardening tools, wrote this then-unusual book. Most books about creating a business were books about raising capital, hiring the best employees, or writing a business plan. *Growing a Business* is a book about creating a good business that is sustainable and that brings you, the entrepreneur, satisfaction. It will help you become a better businessperson by showing you how to focus on the *why* of business instead of on the *how*. Hawken states his goal for his book early on: "I want to demystify, not with a set of dictums and executive summaries, but with a book that illustrates how the successful business is an extension of a person."

In 1965, there were 200,000 start-ups in the United States. In 1986, a year before this book was published, that number had swelled to over one million. This proliferation informs Hawken's belief that the future of commerce will be determined on the street by the small-business owner, not in the boardroom by corporate moguls.

Hawken also believes that business is about practice, not just about theory—no different from riding a surfboard or playing a piano. To stay grounded in practice, he suggests, "Be the customer. Go outside and look back through the window of your small business. Be a child trying to figure out how the world works. Go to a crowded park on a sunny day. Don't go into the back room to read another book about business (even this one)." No newcomer is expected to be good from the get-go, so Hawken advises, "Relax. Take your time. Work and practice and learn."

Hawken spends time discussing "tradeskill," a term coined by Michael Phillips and Salli Rasberry in their 1986 book called *Honest Business*, which he believes can make the difference between success and failure. Tradeskill is the knack for understanding what people want, how much they will pay, and how they make their decisions. The smaller the business, the more important it is to learn tradeskill. Phillips and Rasberry "break tradeskill down into four specific attributes: persistence, the ability to face facts, the ability to minimize risk, and the ability to be a hands-on learner." Hawken adds to these attributes the ability to grasp numbers.

Hawken strongly suggests that you finance a new business with your own money. You can avoid interest payments and there will be no temptation to spend money foolishly, because you know how hard it was to earn. Perhaps even more important, avoiding the temptation to borrow money from friends or family will keep you from complicating those relationships. Hawken also answers the question of how much money you will need: enough to go to market. This self-sufficiency ensures a sense of urgency and quality of product that will make you learn the business fast.

"To see the reward of commerce as money and the risk of commerce as failure is to see nothing at all."

I have discovered through writing my reviews for our book that one type of successful business book is the kind that you can pick up, open to any page, and immediately find a valuable nugget of information offering a supporting fact, an inspirational story, or a profound quotation, to get you instantly looking at your world differently. This book contains page after page of read-out-loud treasures you will want to share. For example, when Hawken discusses how one should view risk, he writes: "If you persist in seeing a situation in the terms of risk, look again. If you still see risk instead of opportunity, walk away, because you just might be right." His passion for business infuses every page, and as you read, you may just find your own passion stoked by his words. JC

Growing a Business, Simon & Schuster, Paperback 1987, ISBN 9780671671648

WHERE TO NEXT? ⇥ Page 316 for **the importance of growing a business** ⇥ Page 235 for **growing a business with a soul** ⇤ Page 50 forr **growing as a leader** | EVEN MORE: *Small Giants* by Bo Burlingham; *Let My People Go Surfing* by Yvon Chouinard; *Raising the Bar* by Gary Erickson and Lois Lorentzen; *Setting the Table* by Danny Meyer

WHERE TO . . .

. . . host a remarkable event:

CATALYST RANCH, CHICAGO

This loft space just outside the Loop is filled with vintage chairs and tables resembling the colors inside a Skittles bag, oversized dry erase boards, and stockpiled fridges. The staff is second to none. Visit the Ranch and find your muse.

. . . find a great book:

THE ELLIOT BAY BOOK COMPANY, SEATTLE

The independent bookstore of which dreams are made. Walk in, take in the smell of old books and cedar shelves, find a book, and head to the café for a cup of coffee and an organic sandwich to accompany your reading.

. . . get some shut-eye:

LIBRARY HOTEL, NEW YORK CITY

Around the corner from Grand Central Station, this boutique hotel is Dewey Decimal-inspired, with each floor decorated from philosophy and psychology 100s to geography and history 900s. Books are shelved in every room. The sixth floor is where you'll find business books.

. . . and how to get there:

MIDWEST AIRLINES

Every seat is first-class with ample leg room. Instead of pretzels and peanuts, the Milwaukee-based airline serves chocolate chip cookies, baked and served fresh.

Guerrilla Marketing

JAY CONRAD LEVINSON

Reviewed by Jack

S mall businesses have a fundamental conflict: big market- ing ideas, small marketing dollars. *Guerrilla Marketing* pro- vides the resolution. Former advertising executive Jay Conrad Levinson created the approach over twenty years ago; now, a series of books with over fifty titles bears the *Guerrilla Mark- eting* moniker. In my opinion, this is the ultimate rubber- meets-the-road, take-it-to-the-bank resource for anyone in small business.

I used the first edition of this book to grow my business in the early 1980s; we were called Schwartz Business Books then, and had an em- ployee roster of fewer than ten names. My original copy has chapters on direct marketing and catalog sales and Yellow Pages advertising. The new- est edition, published in 2007, omits those aged-out approaches and in- cludes several sections on current issues, like "new-media marketing," which addresses such new-century approaches as "e-media marketing," and "nonmedia marketing," including trade shows, PR, and community involvement. But the new edition of *Guerrilla Marketing* still retains much of what was effective in the first: the basics. For example, Levinson offers a page on how to say hello and goodbye. He suggests that customers will be more inclined to like you and continue to do business with you if you use their names in conversation. This is the kind of advice that will build your fundamental people skills.

But before you can start any kind of a marketing campaign, your busi- ness needs a predetermined, long-term goal that will get everybody within your organization on the same page. To do that, you must have a core con- cept of what your business is. Levinson believes that the concept needs to be expressed in a maximum of seven words. He gives the example of an entrepreneur whose business offers computer classes. Following Levin- son's lead, his core concept went from almost thirty words to three words: "Computers for Beginners." That new clarity led to an increase in atten- dance as people readily understood the service the company offered.

Guerrilla marketers excel in using "minimedia," which includes such things as "canvassing, writing personal letters, sending postcards, marketing by telephone, distributing circulars . . . and making business cards do double duty." At one point early on in my efforts to grow my business, I made flyers and gave them to friends to put on their companies' bulletin boards. Simple, direct, and timeless. Just look at the bulletin boards of your local coffeehouse to see this approach at work.

"Marketing is every bit of contact your company has with anyone in the outside world. Every bit of contact."

Small-business marketing strategy isn't limited to minimedia. Levinson believes that guerrilla marketers can also use mass media outlets like TV, newspapers, magazines, and radio to promote and sell their products and services. The book provides pages of suggestions on how to use "maximedia" and get the most success for your dollar spent.

Levinson concludes with a section titled, "The Nature of the Guerrilla." Here he writes about the attributes a good guerrilla marketing company needs. In particular, he describes a meme: "The instantly recognizable transmission of an idea, simple and clear, no explanation necessary" "Green Giant" and "the Michelin Man" are classic examples.

When the original edition was published in 1983, *Guerrilla Marketing* was an instant hit. The newest edition of this perennial best seller is updated for the twenty-first-century entrepreneur. Levinson shows that small businesses can use the same methods as their bigger brethren and also have a whole host of weapons that large companies could never use. This is the book that helped me build my business and it can also help you grow yours. **JC**

Guerrilla Marketing: Easy and Inexpensive Strategies for Making Big Profits from Your Small Business, Houghton Mifflin, Completely Updated and Expanded Paperback Edition 2007, ISBN 9780618785919

WHERE TO NEXT? « Read the **sales and marketing section of this book**. It starts on page 97. | EVEN MORE: *How to Make Big Money in Your Own Small Business* by Jeffrey J. Fox; *Permission Marketing* by Seth Godin; *Getting Everything You Can Out of All You've Got* by Jay Abraham

The Monk and the Riddle

RANDY KOMISAR WITH KENT LINEBACK

Reviewed by Jack

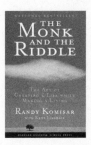

Randy Komisar graduated from Harvard Law School, then went into private practice in Boston. After pursuing a career at Apple as in-house counsel, he cofounded Claris Corporation, a spin-off of Apple, and then held a number of top roles at game development companies. In addition, Komisar helped build WebTV, TiVo, and Mondo Media. With this overflowing resume, Komisar could be considered a sage for would-be entrepreneurs.

The unconventional nature of Komisar's career is mimicked in his pseudomemoir. Most books are either fiction or nonfiction, though a handful, like *Ragtime* by E.L. Doctorow, successfully mix the two genres. In business books, it's even harder to pull off this form. But in *The Monk and the Riddle*, Randy Komisar does it beautifully. While he shares his own quest to discover the real meaning of work, he asks the readers this question: "What would you be willing to do for the rest of your life?"

Komisar opens the book with a story. During a motorcycle trip in Myanmar, Komisar gives a young monk a ride to his temple hours away; directions are given with simple gestures and shoulder taps. Upon arriving, the author meets the English-speaking abbot of the temple. After a short visit, the monk indicates he wants to return to where the author picked him up. Frustrated and tired, the author asks the abbot why the monk wants to go back. The abbot has no answer, but does offer a riddle: "Imagine I have an egg . . . and I want to drop this egg three feet without breaking it. How do I do that?" As Komisar drives through the countryside, caught up in the beautiful scenery and suddenly not so tired despite the long ride, the answer to the riddle comes to him. And the author leaves us with that provocative teaser.

We next find ourselves in a Silicon Valley office, where Komisar is speaking to a fictional entrepreneur, Lenny, who is shopping his business plan. Lenny is outrageous. He believes his payday will come selling caskets online: "We're going to put the fun back into funerals," he says. But despite this intensity and enthusiasm, Komisar is not impressed with Lenny's pitch. He helps Lenny refine his idea by advising him to shift his focus from the huge payday to what actually motivates him. "What," he asks Lenny, "would it take for you to be willing to spend the rest of your life on Funerals.com?"

Komisar points out that once you answer your own version of that question, everything changes. The excitement and passion you find allows others to become excited about your idea. "[I]t's the romance, not the finance that makes business worth pursuing," advises Komisar.

"No matter how hard we work or how smart we are, our financial success is ultimately dependent on circumstances outside our control."

The Monk and the Riddle was written during the bubble of the Internet boom. The rules were different then. Komisar rightfully points out in the "postmortem" that fronts the new paperback edition that, despite Lenny's business idea, the lessons are not bound to Internet businesses and the "better, faster, cheaper" world that Internet start-ups strived for. Instead, he explains, "In truth, *The Monk* is not primarily a business book; that is, it is not about buying low and selling high, but rather about creating a life while making a living. It is about the need to fashion a meaningful existence that engages you in the time and place in which you find yourself. It is about the purpose of work and the integration of what one does with what one believes. *The Monk* is not about *how*, but about *why*."

What appeals to me about this book is the combination of Komisar's fascinating life and the contemplative lessons he extends through Lenny's story. It is so seldom that entrepreneurial books look to the human side of enterprise. In his search to find the answer to the monk's riddle, Komisar realizes that, as it is often said, it truly is the journey, not the destination, that makes our efforts worthwhile, and we need to focus on each step and not the finish line. This simple message can wring a huge amount of stress out of our lives, even as we try to change that life with a new business endeavor or other sea change. It is a rare opportunity indeed to learn at the feet of such a master. **JC**

The Monk and the Riddle: The Art of Creating a Life While Making a Living, Harvard Business School Press, Paperback 2001, ISBN 9781578516445

WHERE TO NEXT? « Page 7 for **how to achieve another zenlike buzz** « Page 9 for **more zen vibe** « Page 224 for **the zen of start-ups** | EVEN MORE: *The Magic of Thinking Big* by David Schwartz; *Founders at Work* by Jessica Livingston

NARRATIVES

When writers visit offices and factory floors, their reporting captures the romance of what many find so compelling about the pursuit of business. They also see the organizational dysfunction, and its roots in our personal flaws. The books in this chapter capture the tales of both fortune and failure at their capitalist extremes.

McDonald's

JOHN F. LOVE

Reviewed by Jack

There are areas in most towns across America in which every brand of fast-food restaurant is located seemingly one on top of the other. The most pervasive of those brands has to be McDonald's, and in *McDonald's: Behind the Arches*, John Love tells the story of this company's remarkable rise to mega-chain status. Usually industry books are either "authorized" and vetted by legal (and therefore unrevealing) staffs, or are negative, "behind the scenes" exposés. Love is careful to tell readers his position: "This is not a corporate book, not the type of history that companies commission to commemorate some milestone. I am an independent journalist, and McDonald's Corporation had no editorial control over this work." And yet *McDonald's* is written with an even hand, succeeding in giving readers a complete picture of this omnipresent brand. Love tells the story of the fast-food industry, the changing postwar society, the visionary McDonald brothers, the strategist Ray Kroc, the decision to franchise, and other facts (and fiction) about the McDonald's Corporation as we know it.

The rise of the fast-food industry was a monumental lifestyle change for our society. As usually happens when a quantum change occurs, many factors came into play. After World War II, families had more expendable money, the automobile was available to a wider consumer base and became a preferred form of family transportation, and the baby boom had begun. Entrepreneurs all over the country were exploring the opportunities made ripe by these phenomena, but few succeeded like McDonald's. Love tells readers how Bob's Big Boy, Burger King, Tastee Freeze, Dairy Queen, and Kentucky Fried Chicken got started, and shows how McDonald's broke from the pack to become the force it is today.

Despite his prominent role in the chain's success, Ray Kroc did not dream up the concept of McDonald's. It was the McDonald brothers—Richard and Maurice—who created a tiny drive-in in San Bernardino, California, in 1937 and continued to improve the business over time.

When visiting the brothers to see why these guys were buying so many of the mixers his company sold, Ray Kroc saw the potential in the brothers' simplified diner menu, speedy process of getting food to the customer, and more family-friendly restaurant atmosphere that stood in contrast to the teen-oriented, carhop-serviced hamburger joints popular at the time. The brothers' restaurant sold a ton of product; lines would form before it opened, and it would stay busy all day. On March 2, 1955, Ray Kroc became the franchiser for the McDonald brothers and their brand.

Love tells an ample number of stories to illustrate the surprisingly common struggles that new companies, even those we know now to be dominant brands, face in their early entrepreneurial days. Readers will be fascinated by how Kroc came up with the $2.7 million in cash he needed to buy the chain from the brothers, and how angry he was when he found out that the brothers hadn't included the original restaurant in the deal (he opened a new restaurant down the block and put the old place out of business). The author also tells how most of the unique McDonald's offerings—like the Egg McMuffin and the Big Mac—came from experiments the franchisees crafted and then presented to the corporate staff.

"[Ray A. Kroc] was immortalized as the founder of a major new industry. His accomplishments in food service were likened to those of John D. Rockefeller in oil refining, Andrew Carnegie in steel manufacturing, and Henry Ford in automotive assembly."

It has been said that no matter where you buy your McDonald's french fries, they will taste the same. And certainly this was Kroc's goal. The strength of the brand depended on it, because the strong psychological appeal of fast food lies in its reliability. He believed in uniformity in every restaurant. If the owner didn't follow the rules, he would not be granted a license to operate a second store. For example, there was only one

McDonald's restaurant in the area near corporate headquarters in Oak Brook, Illinois. "It was one of [the company's] most underdeveloped markets. The reason: Joseph Sweeney, who had gotten the territory in a deal he made with Kroc in 1957, ran a store that did not live up to [the company's] tough standards. Sweeney never got a license for a second store. The company bought back his franchise in 1968, and now Sweeney's old territory boasts fifteen McDonald's [restaurants]." Kroc's strict management strategy insured the uniformity of the restaurants.

This 470-page book is loaded with insightful stories told in the straightforward style of a journalist. Readers will absorb the accidental lessons surrounding developing suppliers and new products, creating franchising, and designing specific equipment. The commitment to training at all levels of the organization, and the standardization of its product offering are ideas that are still underutilized in many businesses and industries. This is not a handbook on how to make a million dollars, but it is a revealing look at one of the most successful corporations of the twentieth century. **JC**

McDonald's: Behind the Arches, Revised Edition, Bantam, Paperback 1995, ISBN 9780553347593

WHERE TO NEXT? ◀◀ Page 210 for **another entreprenuer who created a global powerhouse** ◀◀ Page 123 for **more on understanding the retail experience** ◀◀ Page 94 for **more unexpected places to find ideas** | EVEN MORE: *The Emperors of Chocolate* by Joël Glenn Brenner; *For God, Country and Coca-Cola* by Mark Pendergrast; *The Wal-Mart Effect* by Charles Fishman; *Fast Food Nation* by Eric Schlosser

American Steel

RICHARD PRESTON

Reviewed by Jack

Ameritan Steel is a startlingly well-written story by Richard Preston about a maverick who took an age-old, declining industry—U.S. steel manufacturing—and showed that it could not only compete, but win, by employing innovative manufacturing methods and a conscientious way of treating workers. But this book's appeal goes beyond that of a conventional business book or history lesson. It reads like a romantic thriller, with Preston painting eloquent word pictures about a dangerous and desperate time in the life of the U.S. steel industry. "Long blue arcs snaked through the mountain of busted cars and smashed industry machinery. . . . The steelworkers couldn't hear their own voices screaming in terror over the noise of melting steel. The noise seemed to open sutures in their skulls, and a musky odor filled the building, the reek of a long-arc meltdown."

Since the mid-1800s and the development of the Carnegie Steel Company, the United States historically ruled the steel industry and reaped huge profits. With its comfy positioning, U.S. steel did not look for new methods to make steel more efficiently or more economically, adopting the classic "If it ain't broke, don't fix it" modus operandi. When money *was* invested, it was used to replace aged equipment, not to explore new ways to do business. Other monies went to the workforce as the unions were able to get superb contracts for their workers.

The standard production method involved using a blast furnace to turn iron into steel, but the manufacturing process was a space hog, with manufacturers such as the Gary Works in Gary, Indiana, occupying six miles of the Lake Michigan shore with a plant running a mile and a half deep. Clearly there was much wrong with Big Steel, and a perfect storm was developing—of high manufacturing costs, hubris, and growing competition from Asia and Europe.

European manufacturers developed an alternative method for creating steel. Electric arc furnaces, known as "minimills," used scrap metal as opposed to iron ore to produce steel. This manufacturing method was also beneficial because it allowed the mill to diversify its output, and it could be easily started and stopped depending on demand. In 1969, Ken Iverson, president of the Nulcraft Corporation—a steel manufacturer that would later be renamed Nucor Corporation—and the hero of Preston's *American Steel*, opened a minimill in the United States, specifically in Darlington, South Carolina, and this bold move set Big Steel back on its heels.

"[A] good businessman is hard to bruise and quick to heal."

And for years, due to this pioneering, Nucor succeeded in an industry that was failing. Iverson was innovative not only in his production methods but also in his management approach. Iverson created a company with a small hierarchy of (currently) only five levels: from janitor to CEO required only four promotions. As Nucor grew from earnings of $1.1 million in 1970 to $42 million in the late 1970s, the corporate staff was contained to under twenty people. This lean staffing allowed for quick decision making and a more autonomous work environment for the steel mills. Success did not come without some troubles, however. Attempts to unionize Nucor have failed. Though steelworkers at Nucor earn far less than their unionized compatriots, Nucor offers a bonus program that can allow workers to potentially double their earnings with success.

In 1986, Iverson saw his company's growth slowing and found new opportunity in the making of sheet steel that was in high demand in the automotive industry. He took the unprecedented step of investing in a new machine, enormous and untested, which would take the molten steel and, in one process, create rolled steel. With this new machine, Iverson believed that he could manufacture one million tons of steel with only five hundred steelworkers. In Japan—one of the most advanced steel industries in the world—2,500 steelworkers were required to do the same. The option to reduce the workforce completely changed the playing field, and Nucor significantly exceeded Iverson's original goal.

Richard Preston's tale recounts the riveting story of the building of this anomalous mill, located somewhat ironically in Crawfordsville, Indiana. But it makes sense when you consider that the mill needed scrap metal, a workforce, and good access to utilities, and these were all in plentiful supply in the Rust Belt. The cast of characters includes Iverson; the mill's colorful general manager, Keith Earl Busse; and the committed workers who manipulated the molten steel in the name of Nucor. Preston imbues the story with all the romance and thrill of a fictional drama. His retelling of an explosion as workers were using an experimental process had me reading while walking, unable to put down the book, to find out the conclusion to the accident. Here is just a taste:

> Five seconds after the ladle cleared the casting tower, there was a whining sound from the crane. Millett, standing near the control deck inside the pulpit, heard the sound and looked up. He saw that the crane cables had broken and unraveled. The ladle was falling to the ground. It was a huge object, fifteen feet high, filled nearly to the brim with liquid steel, and the bottom of it was forty feet off the floor. It seemed to pass the deck slowly as it fell, the crane cables singing in the winch. . . . There was a big, bright, yellow flash, and the lights went out.

I would be hard-pressed to find a book that I've quoted aloud to co-workers as much as *American Steel*. Richard Preston is simply a great writer of nonfiction, and I would rank him with contemporary storytellers like Malcolm Gladwell and Michael Lewis. Here he brings his talent to a tale of creativity and resurrection. The story of Ken Iverson and his success with Nucor is inspirational and educational, and demonstrates that an adoption of a new technology as well as an innovative organization that retains its humanity can succeed in business. **JC**

American Steel: Hot Metal Men and the Resurrection of the Rust Belt, Prentice-Hall Press, Hardcover First Edition 1991, ISBN 9780130296047

WHERE TO NEXT? ◀ Page 78 for **how disruptive Nucor really was** ▶ Page 301 for **how engineering is an art** ▶ Page 268 for **how innovation is an art** | EVEN MORE: *Plain Talk* by Ken Iverson; *And the Wolf Finally Came* by John Hoerr; *Making Steel* by Mark Reutter; *Andrew Carnegie* by David Nasaw

From Theodore Dreiser's 1912 *The Financier* and Sloan Wilson's *The Man in the Gray Flannel Suit* in 1955 to, more recently, *Then We Came to the End* by Joshua Ferris, the business novel is slippery to define and has had a tumultuous and confounding life cycle. Classic themes of the American work ethic and pursuit of happiness, parables of self-destructive pride, and tales of the remade man make this form useful to many types of people, from high school students to high-level executives. Many business novels address business issues directly while others are infused with subtle lessons, but only a few have stood the test of time and remain poignant reminders of the need for all readers to step outside themselves and learn from others' experiences.

Found in Fiction

The Great Gatsby
by F. Scott Fitzgerald

Largely considered the greatest American novel, *The Great Gatsby* is also perhaps the best encapsulation of the American dream: Jay Gatsby, self-made, young, and rich, gazes longingly at the more exclusive lights of East Egg from his lofty new mansion. He wants more, he wants to belong, and the book is as much a testament to this rags-to-riches possibility of American life as it is a condemnation of such self-serving morals. Gatsby doesn't contain as much Rockefeller in him as his business associates might think, but rather has a bleeding, bursting heart. Fitzgerald succeeds best at demonstrating how over-ambition robs Gatsby of this one thing that made him "Great" compared to his peers.

A Confederacy of Dunces
by John Kennedy Toole

Destined to be remembered for its tragedy of the posthumous publication, and the humor and zany embodiment of New Orleans's otherworldliness, *Dunces* also demonstrates the every-man aversion to labor and toil—that is, aside from the perks and moments of self-discovery. Flatulent, obese Ignatius Reilly finds himself at a turning point while strolling the French Quarter slinging hot dogs—more going down the hatch than to customers. In fact, everyone here seems to be in a job for a reason other than making money, from the Holiday Ham-aspiring Miss Trixie to the police-dodging Burma Jones. Even Ignatius wants little more than to keep an overbearing mother at bay. Throughout, Toole captures the lonely ridiculousness of pounding the pavement, and maintains a sharp eye for the absurdity of the people, places, hungers, and tasks that make up a working day.

American Pastoral
by Philip Roth

Seymour Levov, aka "The Swede," is Roth's 1960s Gatsby, displaced by the social upheaval of the day. Pain-stakingly detailed about the Newark-area glove-manufacturing legacy that Seymour is born into, the novel explores the tender devotion requisite of a lasting family business. Lyrical and funny at once, Roth's story sweeps generations, offering a slice of Americana both specific and general that in the end proves that being righteous, steadfast, decent, and honest can't always prevent society from tumbling the walls around everything you've built.

A Man in Full
by Tom Wolfe

In Wolfe's epic, sprawling account of intersecting business, political, and social spheres in modern-day Atlanta, the focus varies but remains sharpest on disillusioned corporate magnate Charlie Croker. His plunge from grace, paralleled with the recently laid-off warehouse employee Conrad Hensley 3,000 miles away, grants empathy to the faceless, slaving masses and emphasizes the vast distance between the have-nots and the gates of their employers' mansions. Wolfe maintains a keen eye throughout, trained sharpest on the business ego's battle between self-preserving pride, and looming, devastating debt.

Then We Came to the End
by Joshua Ferris

The next generation of the business novel, Ferris's hilarious critique of modern office life and the world of marketing acts almost as the written-word companion to the movie *Office Space* or the show *The Office*. Addictively funny, it also belongs in the same vein of rumbling satire as that employed by Toole. Ferris sheds light on all of our oft-overlooked interoffice mannerisms, inanities, and silly drama. Throughout, the prose paints a portrait that, while obviously entertaining, is also sharply revealing about that forty-hour-a-week alternative universe known as "work."

Written by Todd Lazarski
with Rebecca Schlei

The Force

DAVID DORSEY

Reviewed by Jack

he Force is a nonfiction narrative about sales and very different from the other practical sales books we chose to feature. This book is, at its core, a glimpse into the dynamics of a master sales team. But the book reveals a seedy underside of selling, and, as an extension, the aggressive business practices necessary when the goal is always driven by short-term results. The book reads like a novel and reminds me of *The Office* crossed with *Glengarry Glen Ross*. Yet, through *The Force*, we get an insider's view of the personalities and perseverance it takes to excel in the highly competitive arena of sales.

David Dorsey, a former journalist, begins his story long after the glory years of Xerox, during a time when it took a lot of work to sell their expensive copiers. Given unprecedented access to a successful Xerox sales team in Cleveland, Ohio, Dorsey spends a year following Fred Thomas, the sales manager, and his group at a time when they are significantly behind their yearly goals. Thomas, a longtime high performer for the company, is doing all he can to help himself and his team succeed while questioning his commitment to the effort it requires. *The Force* goes beyond being simply an industry book to reveal the constant personal strain that each team member, as well as his family, is under when the future relies so heavily on pulling the right strings to close an all-important sale.

Dorsey excels at drawing candid portraits of the characters, allowing us to see all the facets of these relentless achievers. Frank Pacetta, a star salesperson at Xerox and one of the most intriguing subjects in Dorsey's book, embodies both the heroic and the distasteful in the sales profession. His drive and success in taking the district from the rank of 57 out of 67 Xerox sales districts to number 1 in the country is legendary. His people would walk through walls for him. And understandably so, given his power to motivate the sales force with speeches like this: "You can have fun and call it work, gang. You can escape the dull reality of work that most human beings face, because here, with me, you can be as wild as you were in college and still earn six figures a year." The reality was that while they were having fun, they were always selling. When they succeeded at making their sales numbers, Pacetta staged celebrations that were without restriction—think renting the classic Firestone Country Club for a day. Yet he drove his people mercilessly, requiring uniformity and expecting outstanding results. Of course, the people he led were required to view the world in black and white. They were out to win. If they didn't win, they lost. There was no in-between. Over and over again, Pacetta used sports or war analogies to motivate his people. Despite Dorsey's intense portrayal of Pacetta, despite the bravado and rah-rah, I found a real sadness running through the story.

"When you sold, you took control of other people, you motivated them to do things they wouldn't otherwise have done—all the while making them feel as if *they* were in control."

The mantra of this dark side of sales—where each day revolves around the thirty-day goal, and where salespeople live and breathe the end result—is epitomized in Frank's words to Fred: "'Put your helmet on, Freddie. It's a war out there.'" The fly-on-the-wall perspective of *The Force* also allows readers to bear witness as a new salesperson, a miserable cold caller, is groomed into a successful closer. Learning ways to sweeten a deal, like baking faux charges into a deal at the start so they could be taken away during negotiations, was part of his training. These kinds of manipulations let the customer feel he was gaining the upper hand when all along the salesmen "were giving away money you never expected to get in the first place," writes Dorsey. *The Force* reveals it all, and we are privileged for—and maybe a little shocked by—the view.

I appreciate that *The Force* reveals the less-than-favorable underside of the sales profession, a reality I have battled through the years of building up my business. But the book's value is as a narrative of an industry that was in a severe transition and the struggles many salespeople faced each month to make their numbers when they had previously been very successful. Perhaps you will find *The Force* a cautionary tale about life in sales or perhaps you will read the book for inspiration, desiring to succeed in a competitive profession. Either way, *The Force* is an unparalleled look at the day-to-day reality of the fuel that powers business: sales. **JC**

The Force, Ballantine Books, Paperback 1995, ISBN 9780345376251

WHERE TO NEXT? ◀◀ Page 120 for **selling in films** ▶▶ Page 316 for **a starter book on sales** ◀◀ Page 121 for **great tips on being a better salesperson** | EVEN MORE: *Xerox: American Samurai* by Suzanne Snyder Jacobson; *SPIN Selling* by Neil Rackham; *Selling to VITO* by Anthony Parinello; *Hope Is Not a Strategy* by Rick Page

The Smartest Guys in the Room

BETHANY MCLEAN AND PETER ELKIND
Reviewed by Jack

I read crime fiction, watch English police procedurals on PBS, and wait hungrily for new books from my favorite mystery authors James Lee Burke and James W. Hall. Perhaps my natural appreciation for a good mystery story is one of the reasons the story of Enron intrigues me. If you can wipe away the haunting images of the crying employees, the victims in this story, sitting outside the headquarters on the base of the company's big "E," their careers packed away with their possessions in the banker's boxes balanced on their laps, the story of Enron's deceit and demise has the makings of the most engrossing mystery. And as with all good whodunits or whydunits, the story is populated with rich characters with questionable (or admirable) motives and all the ingredients for a perfect storm.

First, let's set the scene. Originating in Omaha, Nebraska, Enron became a holding company in 1979. The company moved to Houston and made its money in the transmission and distribution of gas and electricity. Previously the energy industry was regulated by the government, and costs and profits were controlled. During deregulation in the 1980s, opportunities to experiment and make piles of money arose. The company's CEO, Ken Lay, knew that deregulation was a good thing, but didn't have a plan to take full advantage of it going forward. Enter Jeffrey Skilling: he sure knew how, and Enron took off like a shot. In 2000, Enron became a Fortune 500 company with $60 billion in market capitalization. The time between Skilling's arrival and the day Enron declared bankruptcy comprised some of the most compelling moments in corporate history.

Now let's get to know the essential characters in this drama. First, there's the inspector who unearthed the clues and narrates our story, Bethany McLean. Two traders who got an initial whiff of Enron's decay while looking for a short position went to Ms. McLean. One of the traders told her, " 'Read the 10-K and see if you can figure out how they're making money.' " The traders went to the right person. McLean had become a writer at *Fortune* after being an investment banker/analyst for Goldman Sachs. So, when she talked with the Enron people, she was able to ask the right questions. What McLean then did was write an article in the March 5, 2001 issue of *Fortune* called "Is Enron Overpriced?" which asked, essentially, where is the money coming from?

"The tale of Enron is a story of human weakness, of hubris and greed and rampant self-delusion; of ambition run amok; of a grand experiment in the deregulated world; of a business model that didn't work; and of smart people who believed their next gamble would cover their last disaster— and who couldn't admit they were wrong."

Next, let's look at the antagonists, Jeff Skilling and Ken Lay, and the murder weapon, a form of accounting called "mark-to-market." Both Lay and Skilling were born to lower-middle-class families. Both men were smart and driven. Lay had a doctorate in economics and Skilling was a Baker Scholar—meaning one of the top 10 percent—from Harvard Business School's MBA program. Lay started at the soon-to-be called Enron in 1984 as chairman and chief executive officer. Within a year, he had merged with an Omaha company called InterNorth, and to help with that purchase, the company retained the consulting firm of McKinsey & Company. One of the consultants there was a young Jeffrey Skilling. In 1990, Skilling was hired as chairman and CEO of a new division of Enron called Enron Finance.

Despite the similarities in accomplishments and ambition, the differences between Lay and Skilling couldn't be more pronounced. Lay really wanted to be liked. He loved to socialize and was really more of a politician (he thought he had a shot at being U.S. treasury secretary in 2000) who disliked making hard business decisions. He loved the frills of being a high roller; the corporate jets were well used by Lay and his family. In the executive dining room for lunch, an assistant would take Lay's sandwich and put it on fine china while his top executives ate the sandwiches wrapped in paper.

Jeff Skilling was a brilliant man who could conceptualize new ideas very quickly and simplify complex issues, but he had poor people skills. He didn't care what people thought of him; instead, he focused on the stock price and satisfying Wall Street's next quarterly conference call. He came up with great ideas but had difficulty putting them into action. An Enron executive later explained this chasm well: "Jeff Skilling is a designer of ditches, not a digger of ditches." He also had a very hard time knowing when to pull the plug on an obviously unsuccessful idea, and as time went on this problem would lead to disaster.

Because Enron dealt in long-term contracts to supply energy to large consumers like cities and utilities, customers would often sign ten-year contracts. Normal accounting practices would have you "book" the assets and liabilities on your balance sheet over the entire period of the contract. Mark-to-market accounting allows you to book the entire estimated value of the contract on the day it is signed. In 1992, Skilling and Enron got SEC approval to use this system. The problems with this form of accounting are twofold: One, when you book the sale is not when you get the cash. This results in huge sales and often serious cash issues. And two, with this type of accounting you can show the investors huge growth well before you see revenue. What ultimately brought Enron to its knees was a lack of cash caused by the constant drive for growth at all costs in an effort to keep the stock price growing—along with all those glorious stock options. Debt is what did them in. When all was said and done, Enron was rumored to have $38 billion in debt with no cash flow.

Smart, rich, influential men do not deliberately destroy the source of their wealth and influence. In this case, they got trapped in a nightmare of their own creation, or perhaps their own egos. Enron's failure was not deliberate; it was the result of a series of interconnected events. Can this happen again? Sure, particularly, when you have hubris at the CEO level, salespeoples' compensation based on short-term success, upper-level people totally focused on growth to satisfy short-term Wall Street success, an accounting system that supports this concept, and, finally, an accounting firm that doesn't do a good job of oversight. Add to this a deregulated industry and watch what happens.

When this story first broke I devoured any information on the subject. I read the *Wall Street Journal* every day to keep up with the latest news.

And I read several of the books that came out right after the decline. However, this book came out later, intentionally, because the authors wanted to have the full story and all the facts before they published the definitive title on the subject . . . which is exactly what *The Smartest Guys in the Room* is. **JC**

The Smartest Guys in the Room: The Amazing Rise and Scandalous Fall of Enron, Portfolio, Paperback 2004, ISBN 9781591840534

WHERE TO NEXT? » Page 256 for **Hubris: The Sequel** « Page 193 for **Hubris: The Prequel** « Page 61 for **stories of hubris** » Page 141 for **all the rules they broke** | EVEN MORE: *Den of Thieves* by James B. Stewart; *The Predators' Ball* by Connie Bruck; *Barbarians at the Gate* by Bryan Burrough and John Helyar

When Genius Failed

ROGER LOWENSTEIN
Reviewed by Todd

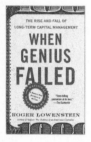

Throughout *When Genius Failed*, financial journalist Roger Lowenstein foreshadows the coming doom, and so there is no surprise in how the story of the Long-Term Capital Management fund ends. But what Lowenstein does best is show how blind arrogance brought down the company and almost the entire financial system. Building on the work of two Nobel laureates and the growing capabilities of computer technology, Long-Term Capital Management pushed academic theory further into real-world practice than had ever been done before, and it became a case study for how markets defy formulaic explanation. Lowenstein's narrative, while set in the complicated financial market of today, tells an age-old story many will recognize.

The story begins with a Midwestern kid named John Meriwether, whose penchant for gambling and stocks eventually led him from teaching math in a high school classroom to trading bonds at Salomon Brothers. In the 1970s, the bond market was being revolutionized by the instant access to pricing that new computer technology brought, and Meriwether saw favorable odds everywhere. His earliest trading concentrated on spreads between various bond interest rates. These bonds were easy to value, and Meriwether found that the market often oversold the debt instruments in reaction to unfavorable news. As the spread widened, arbitrage opportunities were created, allowing him to place bets that spreads would contract after the emotion dissipated. His calculated gambles paid off handsomely for his employer, and he was quickly given more latitude in trading, but Meriwether believed he needed an edge in this new game.

His answer was to hire the best and brightest from academia. His growing Arbitrage Group was made up of students and professors with degrees from MIT, Harvard, and the London School of Economics. These data jockeys were quick to take to Wall Street. Their models suddenly meant something more than simply accolades in obscure journals; they were playing with real money now. Meriwether managed them, encouraged them, and protected them from the fraternity of Salomon's trading floor. He also encouraged their interest in gambling, with internal wagering on everything from elections to frequent games of liar's poker.

As his career at Salomon reached an apex, Meriwether was forced to leave after a trader under his watch was found to have committed several securities violations. Meriwether wanted to quickly regain his stature on Wall Street and formed a hedge fund under the name Long-Term Capital Management (LTCM). He sought to replicate the size and scope of the operation he had at Salomon. Meriwether easily recruited most of his intensely loyal team and added to the roster Robert Merton and Byron Scholes, superstars in academic finance and who, as the story of LTCM unfolds, both win the Nobel Prize in Economics for their overall work. And for his team he provided the means: one-and-a-quarter billion dollars to work with.

The traders picked up where they left off and started placing trades on bond interest spreads. Scholes had described the small amounts of money made on each trade to investors during the fund-raising as "vacuuming up nickels that others couldn't see." The only way to make large sums of money was through leverage, through taking on incredible amounts of debt to make the thousands of trades needed to earn substantial profits. This was both the genius and, as it turned out, the flaw of the strategy.

" 'You're picking up nickels in front of bulldozers,' a friendly money manager warned."

The modeling that had been tested at Salomon and polished at the new company was working perfectly. Meriwether and his dream team had delivered a panacea: guaranteed results with little risk. In the first year, LTCM returned twenty-eight cents for every dollar their investors put in. The formulas told traders exactly what and when to buy. But as time went on, LTCM started to believe their modeling could work for other wagers. They were becoming victims of their own success: the money they were making needed someplace to go and opportunities in bonds were becoming harder to come by. It was relatively simple to predict a value of a bond; other instruments, like stocks, currencies, and interest rate swaps, carried higher risks, many of which required judgments on the part of the traders. This moved the firm dangerously further from the strategy of their success; regardless, in four years, LTCM quadrupled their capital and investors were ecstatic.

But in August 1998 everything came apart, and in a matter of five weeks, LTCM lost everything. Many of the bets they made were going the wrong way; rather than returning to historical norms, the bond spreads were widening. Meriwether's traders watched in disbelief. The incredible amount of leverage that LTCM was using exacerbated the problem. Almost every firm on Wall Street was involved somehow, most having lent huge sums to LTCM. These firms had also built similar internal operations, making similar trades and competing with LTCM in many ways. In the end, the Federal Reserve pulled together a coalition of fourteen banks, which provided $3.65 billion to keep LTCM solvent. The bailout calmed markets, money was returned to investors two years later, and a chapter closed with real-world proof that markets are more than random movements.

We read narratives on history or industry for the lessons, and Lowenstein has many to share. He argues that the Fed's intervention stopped the market from correcting itself, providing tinder for other financial recklessness. And while the fall of Enron was brought on by greed, the collapse of Long-Term Capital Management was a function of hubris: the traders believed they could predict the future. The book ends with a short note about Meriwether and his traders. They moved on two years after the collapse and formed JWM Partners with $250 million dollars of seed capital from the same people who helped start LTCM. With no consequences, was there ever a lesson learned? TS

When Genius Failed: The Rise and Fall of Long-Term Capital Management, Random House, Paperback 2001, ISBN 9780375758256

WHERE TO NEXT? » Page 259 for **a book by Meriwether's former trading colleague** « Page 252 for **another corporate failure that still reverberates** » Page 301 for **how to learn from failure** | EVEN MORE: *The Bonfire of the Vanities* by Tom Wolfe; *Liar's Poker* by Michael Lewis; *Buffett* by Roger Lowenstein

Moneyball

MICHAEL LEWIS
Reviewed by Jack

Norman Mailer, Tom Wolfe, and Joan Didion. Each is a great contemporary writer of nonfiction, and I contend that Michael Lewis is a writer of the same caliber. He and Malcolm Gladwell have taken narrative nonfiction to new heights. When you put Michael Lewis and an interesting subject together, magic happens.

In 2003, Michael Lewis wrote *Moneyball*, which details the process of Billy Beane's resurrection of the Oakland Athletics baseball organization. If you are a fan of business or a fan of baseball, or simply a sucker for a great underdog success story, this book is essential reading. First, let me tell you how the story ends: from the mid-1990s on, the A's consistently had one of the bottom five payrolls in baseball, and during the same period they were consistently one of the best teams in baseball. What's so interesting about that? Well, put yourself in Billy Beane's shoes. A very young general manager, Beane was put in an untenable position, one destined for failure. He was given no investment, a team of second-stringers, and instructions to improve the team. And he succeeded. If I wanted to use a tired cliché, I would tell you he did it by "thinking outside the box." But what he really did was approach a very traditional game with a fresh attitude and a lot of guts. These are lessons each of us can take into our business. Here's how it went down.

Beane decided that the tried and true statistics used by other teams weren't as valuable or reliable as another set of stats that he had discovered. In the mid-1970s, a baseball fanatic named Bill James had created an alternative way to look at a baseball player's performance. Instead of batting average, he used on-base percentage and slugging percentage as gauges—helpful, but not groundbreaking. James's real breakthrough was realizing that a crucial qualifier was batters with good plate discipline (in other words, they were not swinging at bad pitches). The better the batter worked the pitcher and the more often he walked, the more runs a team scored. And of course, scoring is the real job of a baseball team. Beane applied James's new metrics to the A's organization.

With this data, Beane next went about finding cheap young players or slightly over-the-hill veterans with a couple of years left. Over the course of a few seasons, once the young players reached free agency and moved to another team for big bucks, the A's would get a compensatory first-round draft pick from the acquiring team. Thus, in the 2002 draft, the A's had seven first-round picks (the most in the modern history of the baseball draft), allowing them to pick good, young players who met the radical, new performance stats.

"In what amounted to a systematic scientific investigation of their sport, the Oakland front office had reexamined everything from the market price of foot speed to the inherent difference between the average major league player and the superior Triple-A one."

In addition to using Bill James's alternative statistics, Beane also applied other contrarian ideas. Don't draft high school pitchers (college pitchers are okay, but not usually valuable), don't steal bases, don't bunt. Look at actual numbers and output, not speed and body type. Baseball is a game with a rich history and indoctrinated practices, so with each of these innovative decisions, Beane's approach was viewed as unusual, to say the least.

Beane's negotiations became legendary. Certain general managers from other major league teams would not take calls from him, because they had had their pockets picked by him in the past. Beane's staff took advantage of technology and the proliferation of stats available on the Internet, and tracked every player on every major and minor league team. Because the A's were looking for players with a different skill set than most teams, they were able to "shop the bottom" for a player that fit their profile. Beane had to be careful, however, because if other GMs heard that Beane was interested in a player they currently had on their roster, the player's stock would go through the roof, moving the player out of the A's budget.

Every expert will tell you that the keys to running a successful business are recognizing talent, retaining talent, negotiating, and budgeting. The business of baseball is no different. What Michael Lewis succeeds in doing is telling a fascinating success story that offers insight after business insight. And yet *Moneyball* is more than a tale about a shrewd businessman. Michael Lewis tells a story that will inspire any reader to think creatively and individually, and not be limited by limited resources. The monster takeaway from this book is the need for new metrics. Find a new way to conduct your business that is lean and creative. This atypical business book book belongs on every businessperson's bookshelf. **JC**

Moneyball, W. W. Norton Company, Paperback 2004, ISBN 9780393324815

WHERE TO NEXT? « Page 133 for **another great storyteller** « Page 136 for **other great writers** » Page 292 for **another way to look at your talent pool** | EVEN MORE: *Liar's Poker* by Michael Lewis; *Fooled by Randomness* by Nassim Nicholas Taleb; *Shoeless Joe* by W. P. Kinsella

INDUSTRY IN DEPTH

Industry books take a wide-lens look at the broader playing field. They show us how our work fits into the broader context while sharing the practices used in other segments of the economy, and take us behind the scenes to get the inside scoop.

The Wal-Mart Effect
by Charles Fishman

No other company has reached the size and status of Wal-Mart. Its persistent focus on cost and efficiency has made it the dominant force in the world economy, setting the standard in packaging, product design, and business practices. With *The Wal-Mart Effect,* Fishman shows how the Bentonville behemoth continues to change business as we know it.

Big Picture
by Edward Jay Epstein

Epstein shows us the seldom-seen background operations of Hollywood and the six major media companies that rule the motion-picture business. It's typical for a film's production costs to exceed revenues; top actors garner huge salaries, while media companies generate profits not through ticket sales but reproduction licenses and movie-related swag. That is the *Big Picture* Epstein encapsulates in this book.

Oil on the Brain
by Lisa Margonelli

Margonelli traces oil from refineries around the world to our gas tanks. Along the way, she shares the story of an independent gas station owner who earns more selling water than gasoline. She finds that when buying a new car, consumers are often more particular about cup holders than fuel efficiency. Each story sheds light on the complex process that goes into delivering a tank of gas.

The Travels of a T-Shirt in the Global Economy
by Pietra Rivioli

Rivioli, an economics professor at Georgetown University, set off to discover just how her cotton T-shirt came to be. From the cotton fields in West Texas to a textile factory in China, she finds that politics in Washington, D.C., dictate each step of the process—and, ultimately, that the cost of free trade is not as free as she had imagined.

For more industry books, visit 100bestbiz.com

Written by Kate Mytty and Rebecca Schlei

INNOVATION AND CREATIVITY

is about more than painting pictures. And leaving imagination to those in the art department helps no one. Though playwrights and composers have been innovating for several centuries longer than us suits, we would be wise to take some cues. Our picks focus on the inspiration and the process of developing new ideas.

Orbiting the Giant Hairball

GORDON MACKENZIE

Reviewed by Todd

W e love to ask readers if they have ever read *Orbiting the Giant Hairball*, because when we get an affirmative answer, it makes asking the question so worthwhile. Their answer starts nonverbally: over the phone, you hear the pause as they recall the experience of reading the book; in person, you can see everything in the person slow down—their shoulders drop slightly, they take a deep breath, and they smile. Only then do they answer verbally with a simple "yes." Few books create such an emotional response.

Gordon MacKenzie opens his book with a story of schoolchildren and creativity. During workshops he holds to show children how he makes his metal sculptures, MacKenzie always asks his classes how many of them are artists. The first graders eagerly raise their hands, but as the children get older fewer hands are raised. The pressure to fit in and "be normal," so common as children age, suppresses their creative genius. And with this anecdote he lays down the bad news—this same suppression of creativity happens in corporations.

MacKenzie explains that the phrase "corporate creativity" is often an oxymoron. He had an early boss who referred to Hallmark's Creative Division, in which they both worked, as "a giant hairball." The description bothered MacKenzie until he pondered the question "Where do hairballs come from?": "Well, two hairs unite. Then they're joined by another. And another. And another. Before long, where there was once nothing, this tangled, impenetrable mass has begun to form."

As the hairball grows, everyone and everything is pulled toward its core. The organizational physics of normalcy and conformity rule the day. MacKenzie admits that this is what allows many organizations to be successful. The problem, though, is that people never reach their full potential nor do the companies that employ them.

MacKenzie's stories and suggestions throughout promote ways of getting and keeping yourself and others in that creative orbit. MacKenzie's solution is not to untangle the hairball but to find a way for individuals to draw from the power of the organization and yet stay in orbit. Some of the topics are surprising. He spends a chapter talking about teasing and how it robs people of the confidence to take risks. Chapter 19 is just one sentence long: "Orville Wright did not have a pilot's license."

In another story, MacKenzie, while furnishing a new set of offices, bought a collection of antique milk cans. When he decided to use them as clever wastebaskets, he was forced to justify his purchase. Accused of procuring unapproved office supplies, he became furious. His clear-headed coworker saved the day by suggesting the items be donated to the corporate art collection and loaned back to the company. Corporate regulations were met and everyone was happy. MacKenzie reflects that letting his anger take hold robbed him of the opportunity to create a solution that worked for everyone—a skill those orbiting the giant hairball need.

"Orville Wright did not have a pilot's license."

His stories are inspirational, but more important, MacKenzie offers a map to the creativity roadblocks inherent in organizations. This is not a common approach. There are plenty of books on how you personally can become more creative or how your team can generate more ideas. The backdrop of a creative person working for a creative organization like Hallmark makes the message real and even more profound ("Wow, if Gordon had these problems, then my journey is going to be even harder").

What makes *Orbiting the Giant Hairball* truly stand apart from any other book in our collection is its perfect fusion of word and image. Many business books have tried to use graphics and pictures to enhance the message, but they often fall short. The visual treatment always seems like an afterthought. MacKenzie uses illustrations to act as signposts throughout the text rather than the usual pulled-out quotes and section headings. His riff on a proposed organizational evolution of Hallmark from pyramid to plum tree appears on yellow ruled paper as scribbled notes, and a crumpled piece of paper at the end of the chapter describes in an instant how the presentation went. MacKenzie's initial choice to self-publish also allowed the book to escape the tendency to normalize by giant publishing hairballs.

The only proper result of this review would be you picking up *Orbiting the Giant Hairball* and being able to answer "yes" when someone asks if you have read it. The inspired smile alone will be worth it. **TS**

Orbiting the Giant Hairball: A Corporate Fool's Guide to Surviving with Grace, Viking, Hardcover 1998, ISBN 9780670879830

WHERE TO NEXT? ◄◄ Page 74 for **more about hairballs** ◄◄ Page 252 for **more about dirtballs** ◄◄ Page 32 for **"the magical things you can do with that ball"** | EVEN MORE: *Rules of the Red Rubber Ball* by Kevin Carroll; *One Great Insight Is Worth a Thousand Good Ideas* by Phil Dusenberry; *Unstuck* by Keith Yamashita and Sandra Spataro

The Art of Innovation

TOM KELLEY WITH JONATHAN LITTMAN

Reviewed by Todd

IDEO, the Silicon Valley's design firm of choice, has brought to life a staggering list of groundbreaking products—the original Apple mouse, the Palm V handheld organizer, Samsung's award-winning monitors—leaving outsiders wondering what IDEO does differently to generate such memorable products and services.

The answer can be found in *The Art of Innovation*, the twenty-first century's hallmark book on how to generate new ideas. The opening pages read more like a company biography than a guide to product transformations, but by chapter 3, *The Art of Innovation* picks up speed and shows why this book is a prime example of what can make a business book so valuable. IDEO opens up its doors and takes the reader on a tour that reveals what makes the studio/firm successful. Author and IDEO general manager Tom Kelley cautions readers against thinking there is a magic formula for generating new ideas—a lesson that exemplifies the kind of honest advice infused throughout the book.

Many of the methods Kelley recommends contain a "best practices" mentality. IDEO's core belief in observation borrows from the field of anthropology. Observation leads to counterintuitive insights: bigger, thicker toothbrushes are better for smaller hands. The company ignores the myth of the individual and embraces the power of teams, pointing to the group of fourteen individuals that enabled Thomas Edison to invent the telephone, phonograph, and lightbulb as exemplars. Prototyping, an activity associated with engineers and technicians, is simply a word for doing; the models become the physical manifestations of their bias for action.

Brainstorming is an essential part of the innovation process at IDEO. Rather than a nebulous gathering over coffee and cake, says Kelley, every "brainstormer" should start a session with a clear, outwardly focused problem statement, with sixty minutes of brainstorming yielding a hundred ideas. To improve group memory, cover everything in the room with paper; it allows plenty of room for ideas and makes it easier to go back and find an idea that needs more development. Numbering each of those ideas is a simple trick IDEO learned to motivate a group and allows for quick movement between ideas without losing the group's place. Best way to prep group members? Send them to a toy store. These best practices show that brainstorming is more than just a tool at IDEO. Kelley elaborates: "It's also a pervasive cultural influence for making sure that individuals don't waste too much energy spinning their wheels. . . ."

"Publicly acknowledge a risk taker, a rule breaker, even a failure, and explain why every successful organization needs them."

The Art of Innovation teaches that the best ideas come from more than daydreaming. Observation trumps conjecture. Teams trounce individuals. And making something happen always beats imagining what it would be like. **TS**

The Art of Innovation: Lessons in Creativity from IDEO, America's Leading Design Firm, Currency/ Doubleday, Hardcover 2001, ISBN 9780385499842

WHERE TO NEXT? ➠ Page 277 for **habits that spark innovation** ◄◄ Page 180 for **what hinders "doing"** ◄◄ Page 187 for **how to keep teams talking** | EVEN MORE: *The Ten Faces of Innovation* by Thomas Kelley with Jonathan Littman; *Thoughtless Acts?* by Jane Fulton Suri and IDEO; *Everyday Engineering* by Andrew Burroughs and IDEO

Jump Start
Your Business Brain

DOUG HALL
Reviewed by Jack

You may have had the chance to see Doug Hall on television, as one of the judges on a reality show called *American Inventor*. His qualifications for appearing on that show and writing this book include becoming an inventor at age twelve, earning an engineering degree, and putting in years at Procter & Gamble as master marketing inventor, before starting his company called Eureka! Ranch—an organization whose sole purpose, according to its Web site, is to accelerate top-line growth. Hall's book, *Jump Start Your Business Brain*, shares his system of analysis developed at the Ranch; with it he believes you can markedly improve the odds of success of your next project or idea.

Hall's concepts are based on scientific analysis. Sixty thousand data points support his analytic system, along with "[o]ver 1,200,000 customer reactions to new business concepts [that] have been measured and analyzed to identify the core truths that define winning customer ideas." In the first section, "Marketing Physics," Hall asserts that there are three factors that can dramatically improve your chances of success for your next product or idea. In fact, he claims you can improve your percentage of success from the usual 20 percent to well over 40 percent by following these teachings. The three principles are: (1) Overt Benefit—or, What is in it for your customer? Hall teaches that you must be very direct with the overt benefit to break through the clutter in the marketplace; (2) Real Reason to Believe—customer confidence is at an all-time low, and because of that, it is crucial that you are credible and deliver on your promises; and (3) Dramatic Difference—"[w]ithout uniqueness, you have a commodity that sells for commodity-like profit margins." Hall believes this uniqueness, which must be ten times greater than you might think it should be, must also be a function of the Overt Benefit and the Real Reason to Believe. Building on that prior work guarantees relevance for your customer and in turn improves your chances for success. In summary, Hall says the Overt Benefit is *what* you are offering, the Real Reason to Believe is *how* you are going to make good on your promise, and the Dramatic Difference is *why* customers should get excited.

In the next section, "Capitalist Creativity," Hall introduces three fundamental laws for successful idea generation: (1) Explore Stimuli—"stimuli are the fuel that feeds business-growth thinking—or any creative thinking, for that matter"; (2) Leverage Diversity—"diversity is the fuel that turns the spark into a chain reaction of continuous idea creation"; (3) Face Fears—the previous two laws only come alive when you face your fears. The chapter on facing fears is an eye-opener, because you'll discover that while most people use other limitations, such as budget, organizational norms, or passive employees as excuses for limiting creative growth in a company, it is really fear that may be at the root of any imposed limitation. I found this statement in the book from the poet David Whyte especially insightful: " 'Creativity is about coming out of hiding and exposing yourself. Practicing creativity is about humiliating yourself in public.' " Hall makes it clear that creativity can sometimes require a person to put ego aside or go against the grain in a meeting. This is an essential, if not comfortable, challenge for most of us.

"The mission of this book is ... to help managers create products, services and advertising that persuade customers to spend money."

The inspiration for Hall's research came from the work of W. Edwards Deming. Hall recounts what Deming taught:

> [T]he only way to improve manufacturing quality was to improve the process through better systems, worker training and systemic improvement. When the process is improved, Dr. Deming maintained, a chain reaction of reduced waste, less rework and greater customer satisfaction inevitably results. Fix the system, Deming said, and you fix the factory.

Hall took this philosophy and applied it to idea-generation and business-building concepts. Hall believes that Dr. Deming's concept can be applied to any small business or simply to your department and is not limited to factory production systems. The problem may not be your competition or your employees or the marketplace. Instead, Hall believes the cause of much stagnation is the way you choose new ideas or new products. With *Jump Start Your Business Brain*, he supplies us all with the process needed to improve our chances of "winning" our next idea-generation session. JC

Jump Start Your Business Brain: The Scientific Way To Make More Money, Emmis Books, Paperback 2001, ISBN 9781578601790

WHERE TO NEXT? ◀ Page 219 for **how to jump start your start-up** ◀ Page 157 for **more from Deming** ▶ Page 308 for **how to make it memorable** | EVEN MORE: *Jump Start Your Marketing Brain* by Doug Hall; *Cracking Creativity* by Michael Michalko; *Rules for Revolutionaries* by Guy Kawasaki with Michele Moreno

CONFERENCES TO ATTEND

Continuing communication with your peers inspires progress and fosters new ideas. What better place to continue the dialogue than at conferences where you can listen to industry leaders share ideas, and talk through ideas with those around you?

SXSW Interactive

This is where hard-core geeks, serious content creators, new-media entrepreneurs, and creative people gather for five days of provocative panel content and parties. Around 400 industry experts come to Austin, Texas, to share their expertise. There is no shortage of information at this hip educational conference. Beyond the panels, there is an Interactive/Film (iF!) Trade Show + Exhibition showcasing the tools employed by digital creatives and filmmakers alike. And, of course, there's the music festival.

TED Conference

More than a thousand people attend this annual seminal event in Monterey, California. It sells out a year in advance. The content speaks to science, business, the arts, and global issues facing our world. Over four days, fifty speakers each get eighteen minutes to address attendees. Having no breakout groups insures that everyone shares the same experience. That is why it's so successful— all of the knowledge is connected and shared.

Gel

Short for "Good Experience Live," Gel covers a diverse set of topics—from cinematography to literature to business. Attendees leave feeling refreshed and inspired after touring New York City art galleries, partaking in technology experiments, and learning through workshops.

Pop!Tech

Every October, 500 visionary thinkers in the sciences, technology, business, design, arts, education, and government gather in Camden, Maine, to explore the cutting-edge ideas, technologies, and forces of change that are shaping our collective future. Attendees then share what they learn with communities throughout the world through books, television, live "satellite" events, and more. Even after the Pop!Tech conference draws to a close, the conversation continues to inspire people around the world.

Written by Aaron Schleicher

A Whack on the Side of the Head

ROGER VON OECH
Reviewed by Jack

All ideas have a life cycle. They are born, live, and die, and new ideas are needed to replace them. But we need a reliable way to generate new ideas, because, unlike good dogs, good ideas don't always come when called. The challenge of being creative is timeless, and when it comes to generating ideas, new technology doesn't necessarily make the challenge any easier. But Roger von Oech's book does. He has taken a potentially complicated issue, because of its subjectivity, and broken it down into stimulating and functional advice.

At the core of the book are ten chapters that detail what von Oech believes to be the biggest mental blocks to creativity. Each chapter addresses these hazards: be practical, follow the rules, play is frivolous, avoid ambiguity, don't be foolish. In each chapter, von Oech focuses on the fundamentals of creative thinking. For example, from the "Be Practical" chapter comes this advice: "When you judge new ideas, focus initially on their positive, interesting, and potentially useful features. This approach will not only counteract a natural negative bias, it will also enable you to develop more ideas." As a guy who has always tried to be pragmatic when it comes to new ideas, I have been accused of being negative. This fundamental approach shows that changing the lens through which you first look at an idea can open you up to compromise or even inspiration.

At the end of each chapter is a summary, like this one from "Play Is Frivolous:" If necessity is the mother of invention, play is the father. Use it to fertilize your thinking.

> **TIP:** The next time you have a problem, play with it.
> **TIP:** If you don't have a problem, take time to play anyway. You may find some new ideas."

There is often a serious disconnect in using creative thinking to solve business problems. Many of us believe that facts and research will lead to solutions before taking some time to play, thinking that playing isn't serious work.

"By changing perspective and playing with our knowledge, we can make the ordinary extraordinary."

The exercises von Oech uses to stimulate just such creative problem solving are unique. For example, he offers readers the following scenario: You are a marketer given the challenge of promoting a company's $1,000,000 overstock of ball bearings. What do you do? Creative thinking first allows you to search for ideas within your experience, but then you need to try different approaches, one then another and often not getting far. But there should be no limits. "We use crazy, foolish and impractical ideas as stepping stones to practical new ideas," says von Oech. Once you've brainstormed the scenario, he reveals the possibilities, including: use the ball bearings as level testers, sew them into a canvas vest and use them as "weight clothing" for athletes in training, or use them as filler for beanbag chairs or other furniture. The author explains that "[t]he point of this exercise is that an idea, concept, or thing—in this case a ball bearing—takes its meaning from the *context* in which you put it. If you change its context, it will take on a different meaning. For example, transferring a ball bearing from the 'things that reduce friction' context to that of 'shiny and pretty things' gives us all kinds of jewelry and art ideas." This exercise is an effective way to show how even when we are thinking creatively, we often have self-imposed boundaries that actually limit our creativity. Pushing the boundaries, sometimes literally, is a way of opening our eyes to additional possibilities.

It is difficult to convey all of the stimulating information Roger von Oech shares with us in this short review. With every page, you will feel new clarity about how creativity should play a role in your work. He distributes perspective-changing quotes throughout the book, such as, "'Discovery consists of looking at the same thing as everyone else and thinking something different'" from Albert Szent-Györgyi, and "'Every act of creation is first of all an act of destruction' " from Pablo Picasso. *A Whack on the Side of the Head* is a pragmatic guidebook to assist you in unearthing your creative self. **JC**

A Whack on the Side of the Head: How You Can Be More Creative, Business Plus, 25th Anniversary Edition, Paperback 2008, ISBN 9780446404662

WHERE TO NEXT? ▸ Page 322 for **another creativity tool kit** ◂ Page 99 for **getting into someone's head** ▸ Page 99 for **some fresh perspectives** | EVEN MORE: *One Small Step Can Change Your Life* by Robert Maurer; *The Artist's Way* by Julia Cameron; *Creativity* by Mihaly Csikszentmihalyi

The Creative Habit

TWYLA THARP
Reviewed by Todd

My love for big, crazy ideas certainly shades my view, but after reading Twyla Tharp's *The Creative Habit*, I am certain corporate innovation doesn't hold a candle to the challenges of artistic creation. And before you start listing all of the differences, I'd ask you to stop and consider the last marketing campaign or machinery upgrade you were involved with. When you were done, did you measure the results based on how much sales went up and how it compared to your competitors' results . . . or whether it was on par with a Picasso painting or Edison invention? Apple is clearly doing the latter, and maybe it is time for you to do the same.

"Scratching" is the term Tharp, one of America's greatest choreographers, assigns to the initial, exploratory steps of finding a new idea. The primordial matter in which to scratch comes from what we experience—recalling early memories, conversing with friends, observing nature. "Scratch among the best and you will automatically raise the quality of ideas you uncover." For Tharp, the music she chooses makes or breaks the dance she creates, and Mozart, Beethoven, Brahms, and Haydn are her first stops. The companions you choose to accompany you while you scratch shape the entire creative process.

Once those initial creative ideas take flight, you need some way to capture them. For Tharp, every project begins with a simple cardboard box. Everything she acquires during the process goes in the box, much as a musician might capture a melody on composition paper or an illustrator a silhouette in a sketchbook. Whatever the device, the inspirations are gathered in a place without confining the creativity itself. The first item in each of her boxes is a blue index card stating the goal for the project. For her Broadway show *Movin' Out*, one box became eleven boxes. The index cards said " 'tell a story' " and " 'make dance pay for the dancers,' " and items like Billy Joel's entire discography, a copy of the film *Saturday Night Fever*, and a macramé vest filled the boxes.

Tharp discusses creativity using a gracefulness drawn from her career as a choreographer. A natural extension of her eye for art, the book's design is elegant, with oversize text filling oversize pages. Narrative is followed by exercises—more parallels with her life as a dancer. The material throughout reveals more about the author, the creative process, and—we hope—the participating reader. Tharp ends her book with a sense of satisfaction about the life she has chosen: "When it all comes together, a creative life has the nourishing power we normally associate with food, love, and faith."

"Applying algorithms to creativity is like biochemists trying to formulate the chemistry of love. It takes some of the romance out of the enterprise."

Dan Pink, in his book *A Whole New Mind*, says "The new MBA is the MFA [Master of Fine Arts]," and he is right. Artists have long struggled with constant and consistent idea generation for centuries longer than us corporate types. It is about time we use such methods of creativity to enrich our every project. Before the next blank screen or empty page finds you, get a copy of *The Creative Habit* and keep it by your bedside long after you've devoured it the first time. TS

The Creative Habit: Learn It and Use It for Life, Simon & Schuster, Paperback 2006, ISBN 9780743235273

WHERE TO NEXT? ◄ Page 78 for **what happens to industry when inspiration is found** ◄ Page 230 for **how business needs practice too** | EVEN MORE: *The War of Art* by Steven Pressfield; *A Whole New Mind* by Daniel H. Pink; *Bird by Bird* by Anne Lamott

The Art of Possibility

ROSAMUND STONE ZANDER AND BENJAMIN ZANDER

Reviewed by Jack

About ten years ago, Harvard Business School Press had Benjamin Zander present to booksellers at its annual convention in preparation for his forthcoming book. I was there that day and he was one of the best motivators I had seen. Zander is the conductor of the Boston Philharmonic as well as a teacher, and, as I saw at the convention, he is a polished communicator. With his wife, Rosamund Stone Zander, an executive coach and a family systems therapist, he has written a book about possibility, using inspirational stories, parables, and fun personal anecdotes. Early on, they write: "Our premise is that many of the circumstances that seem to block us in our daily lives may only appear to do so based on a framework of assumptions we carry with us. Draw a different frame around the same set of circumstances and new pathways come into view." The way to internalize this transformation is, as Zander has learned through his career in music, practice.

The first "practice" in the book is called "It's All Invented." After pages of scientific research showing how animals, insects, and humans perceive their surroundings and make meaning from those sensations, the authors assert that we are confined by the constructs we create. We don't look beyond our assumptions. The practice comes from challenging those assumptions. Since reality is "all invented" anyway, inventing a story or framework of meaning that enhances our quality of life and the lives of those around us is the first step.

Benjamin Zander was teaching a graduate course at the New England Conservatory to instrumentalists and singers. After twenty-five years of teaching, he realized that every year his students so dreaded the performances they had to give for their final grade that they were fearful of taking risks with their playing. So Zander started his next course by telling everyone that they would get an A. The only requirement was that the students write Zander a letter from the future that began, "Dear Mr. Zander,

I got my A because . . ." and include in that letter what they did to deserve the grade. The letters Zander includes in his book are truly amazing in their insight and passion. When you take the pressure of a grade off the table, creativity is allowed free rein. Students discovered the freedom to take risks that they would not have had the courage to attempt if Zander had not removed the usual constraint of academic assessment.

"A shoe factory sends two marketing scouts to a region of Africa to study the prospects for expanding business. One sends back a telegram saying, SITUATION HOPELESS STOP NO ONE WEARS SHOES The other writes back triumphantly, GLORIOUS BUSINESS OPPORTUNITY STOP THEY HAVE NO SHOES"

The simple act of eradicating our rule-bound instincts can change a school classroom or a corporate culture. The Zanders refer to this as "Rule Number 6." The essence of the rule is that there are no rules, and that you should lighten up and stop taking yourself so seriously. When you lighten up, those around you naturally follow suit: "This new universe is cooperative in nature, and pulls for the realization of all our cooperative desires." Shedding self-imposed limitations allows for a deeper level of interaction, and thus new possibilities result.

You can imagine what change the rest of the twelve lessons inspire, with other "practices" like Lighting a Spark, Leading from Any Chair, and The Way Things Are. Reading this book can be revolutionary if you are open to the Zanders' ideas—if you are interested in finding more happiness and satisfaction in your job and your life. *The Art of Possibility* has taught me how to look through a different lens, one that leads to a more humane and satisfying, passion-filled life. ᴊᴄ

The Art of Possibility: Transforming Professional and Personal Life, Penguin, Paperback 2002, ISBN 9780142001103

WHERE TO NEXT? ◄ Page 268 for **the art of innovation** ◄ Page 235 for **the art in small business** ◄ Page 50 for **how leadership is an art** | EVEN MORE: *Are You Ready to Succeed?* by Srikumar S. Rao; *What Got You Here Won't Get You There* by Marshall Goldsmith with Mark Reiter; *Leadership and the New Science* by Margaret J. Wheatley

There are a number of international business titles worth a read that you won't stumble upon in your local bookstore. Each book is radically different from a traditional business book, unique in format and chock-full of pictures. If you're looking for fresh perspectives, you'll find them in these books.

Fresh Perspectives
<u>not</u> in a bookstore near you.

Creativity Today
by Igor Byttebier and Ramon Vullings, Netherlands

Byttebier and Vullings believe that creativity is important in every career, and that you are responsible for the development of your personal creativity. They help foster creativity with case studies, exercises, and various challenges such as finding solutions to traffic jams and waiting in lines.

The Idea Book
by Fredrik Härén, Sweden

A good idea is often inspired by something external. To that end, *The Idea Book* has 150 pages saturated with ways to learn about creativity through various activities, stories, and quotations from famed thinkers like Albert Einstein and IKEA founder Ingvar Kamprad, interspersed with 150 blank pages for jotting down new ideas as they come.

Life's a Pitch
by Stephen Bayley and Roger Mavity, United Kingdom

Two separate books are bound together in *Life's a Pitch.* Both are about presentation. Mavity argues that people respond more readily to emotion than to logic, and that how you pitch yourself is more important than what you're pitching. Bayley sees life itself as theater, and writes on how to be a better actor.

KaosPilot A-Z, 2nd Edition
by Uffe Elbæk and friends, Denmark

In 1991, Elbæk founded a revolutionary business university called KaosPilot, with an education program based on creativity, projects, and business design. This book embodies that education. Contributors include the late Anita Roddick of The Body Shop, Kevin Kelly of *Wired* magazine, and more. Elbæk explains, "And just so you're warned, *KaosPilot A-Z* is a book full of values, beliefs and critical orientation, full of life, references and tips, full of flashbacks, visions and jumping up and down . . . and not least full of pictures."

Written by Kate Mytty and Dylan Schleicher

BIG IDEAS These books take you to unexplored crossroads, connecting common knowledge with the most advanced understandings of the world. New insights appear at these intersections when the walls of academic discipline are removed. The future of business books lies here.

The Age of Unreason

CHARLES HANDY

Reviewed by Jack

When I ran my record store, I knew my product better than anyone who crossed the threshold because I have an innate passion for music. But when I moved on to selling business books, truth be told, I bluffed my way through conversations by detailing information about publishers or reciting an author's track record. I would talk about anything but the content of the book because I didn't have the academic background or the personal experience to discuss the merits of a particular book. *The Age of Unreason* was the first business book that spoke my language. And through it, Charles Handy offered me a way into business books.

Born and raised in Ireland, the son of an archdeacon and educated at Oxford, Handy spent over ten years with Shell International. During the 1960s, he attended the Sloan School of Business and met Warren Bennis and other cutting-edge leadership and management people who sparked in him an interest in organizations and how they work. He then taught at the London Business School for almost three decades, wrote eighteen books, and penned numerous articles. Handy calls himself a "social philosopher," and from that perspective he advocates the humanistic approach to business that first appealed to me. In *The Age of Unreason*, Handy writes about changing, living, and working—the essentials to leading our best lives.

At the time of this book's publication, in 1989, Handy declared that "the Age of Unreason is upon us," that "discontinuous" change, change that is irregular and unpredictable, had become the norm. Handy provides the following insightful example of discontinuous change. When he started working at a young age, he was expected to work 47 years, 47 weeks per year, and 47 hours per week, or a total of a little over 100,000 hours. The generation following his works half those hours, entering the workforce after graduate school and working 37 hours a week, 37 weeks a year (due to training and extended time off), equaling only 50,000 hours over a lifetime. All that changed in one generation. Imagine the sorts of effects this has had on leisure, education, family life, and generally on how society ends up spending its time.

Handy says, "Now, for the first time in the human experience, we have a chance to shape our work to suit the way we live instead of our lives to fit our work. We would be mad to miss the chance." To accomplish this we need to take the job outside the organization, because that allows us more control and we can make our work our own. With the change to 50,000 hours comes more time to take that control, and Handy reminds us to spend this time learning new talents, meeting new people, and learning new skills.

"The purpose of this book is to promote a better understanding of the changes which are already about us, in order that we may, as individuals and as a society, suffer less and profit more."

Handy is not opposed to organizations, though he sees a gradual shift to a "shamrock"-shaped organization. Within this structure, there are three distinct groups of people who are "managed differently, paid differently, organized differently," and are held to different expectations. The first of the three groups is the "core"—the qualified professionals, managers, and technicians. The second leaf of the shamrock includes the outside contractors who perform specialized but nonessential work, and the members of the third leaf are the temporary or part-time people. Handy believes that this third group is the fastest growing section as business changes to a service economy. Handy's shamrock organization, visualized almost twenty years ago, is proving to be true today.

In keeping with his self-defined role as social philosopher, he applies the "shamrock" concept to schools. In addition to the existing schools, another lobe would feature an education manager who would create an appropriate educational program for each student. And the third lobe would contain a host of minischools teaching a specialized curriculum (independent art schools, language schools, computing). This type of school would be small, flexible, and focused on the needs of the student.

It is difficult for me to express how affected I am by Handy's writing. Because there are so many books that cross my desk and populate the shelves of our warehouse, I rarely keep books on my own personal shelves. But I keep Charles Handy front and center. Tom Peters captured my feelings about Handy when, in March 2007, he wrote on his blog, "Put simply, he is one of the most decent and thoughtful and profound people-professionals I have ever known. We agree on many-most-almost all-virtually everything when it comes to the 'important stuff.'" I certainly could not have said this better myself. Many years ago, I had the real honor of sharing a dinner with Handy. Here is your opportunity to meet him through this insightful, timeless book. JC

The Age of Unreason: Reflections of a Reluctant Capitalist, Harvard Business School Press, Paperback 1990, ISBN 9780875843018

WHERE TO NEXT? ◀◀ Page 57 for **how to implement your Unreason** ◀◀ Page 63 for **how to communicate your Unreason** ◀◀ Page 244 for **a business that lived through Unreason** | EVEN MORE: *Myself and Other More Important Matters* by Charles Handy; *The Age of Discontinuity* by Peter Drucker; *Nuts!* by Kevin Freiberg and Jackie Freiberg

Out of Control

KEVIN KELLY
Reviewed by Todd

The continuing development of human civilization has been predicated on our ability to control nature. The development of agriculture and domestication of animals typify the early grasp we gained over plants and animals. Mendel's cross-pollination of peas in 1866 shows even greater control, the first step toward the bioengineering of today. Kevin Kelly, in his 1994 book *Out of Control*, challenges the very notion of control and argues that the biggest advances in science, economics, and social systems will come through letting go.

Now that is not to say that control doesn't lead to progress, just that we need to change our perception of it. Kelly believes step-function changes have come with advances in automatic controls. For example, the steam engine converted superheated water into mechanical power, but it wasn't until James Watt added a centrifugal governor that the machinery could regulate itself. The control of energy was followed by the control of materials. The feedback mechanisms available to fabricators make possible the creation of almost anything. Kelly imagines, "Cameras the size of molecules? Sure, why not? Crystals the size of buildings? As you wish. . . . Matter—in whatever shape we want—is no longer a barrier. Matter is almost 'free.'" The new regime of automatic control is that of information, a paradigm we are only beginning to understand but one that Kelly believes will usher in an era of self-evolving machines capable of making their own decisions.

In 1990, graduate students at Carnegie Mellon designed a six-legged robot named Ambler. The designers of Ambler labored to create a machine that could act autonomously with capabilities needed for a fictional trip to Mars. But the two-ton creation could barely navigate the test area. The flaw was Ambler's centralized brain and its need to consider every choice before even the smallest movement. At MIT, Rodney Brooks approached the problem differently, inspired by the construction of insects. His robot Genghis had a tiny microprocessor to run each of its six legs, mimicking the neurons ants and cockroaches have in their legs. Each leg looked at what the other legs were doing and acted accordingly, and with a little fiddling by Rodney, Genghis was scampering across the floor. Brooks slowly taught the machine how to climb and navigate over more complex environments, one simple routine built upon another.

"Complexity must be grown from simple systems that already work," Kelly writes. With the recent discovery of neurons on the heart and taste buds in the stomach, we are coming to realize that human life too is actually quite decentralized, more akin to the chaotic, swarming fields of individual agents, each playing their own small part in the manifestation of a greater whole. We seem to accept this functionality from a beehive or an ant colony, but shudder at the thought that life may be nothing more than subroutines built upon subroutines. Control resembles multifaceted reflex rather than some highly structured consciousness.

"The song goes: No one is in charge. We can't predict the future. Now hear the flip side of the album: We're all steering. And we *can* learn to anticipate what is immediately ahead. To learn is to live."

And machines, whether mechanical or biological, only begin to scratch the surface of complexity. Consider the scale of many human organizations and how individuals are now acting as the smaller subroutines. Financial markets, with their multitudes of traders, each acting independently, signal economic meaning through price while computers ironically curb their erratic behavior. The Internet is showing the first signs of intelligence as participants provide Amazon reviews, del.icio.us links, and Digg votes that filter and illuminate greater meaning to the cacophony of random bits and bytes.

I cannot come close in this review to covering everything that Kelley does in 472 pages. The author's survey is wide and deep, drawing on history to build readers' appreciation and on science fiction to feed their imagination. Though written in 1994, *Out of Control* still possesses a prescient quality, because we still struggle to accept and internalize a world that is complex and out of our control by design. Kelly writes, "What little time left in this century is rehearsal time for the chief psychological chore of the 21st century: letting go, with dignity." TS

Out of Control: The New Biology of Machines, Social Systems, and the Economic World, Basic Books, Paperback 1994, ISBN 9780201483406

WHERE TO NEXT? » Page 304 for **crowd control** ◄◄ Page 54 for **corporate control** ◄◄ Page 18 for **self-control** | EVEN MORE: *Emergence* by Steven Johnson; *Sync* by Steven H. Strogatz

In August 2004, Seth Godin and his team of interns built a distribution hub for world-changing ideas, where everyday people could find an audience for their ideas, and the audience had a say in which ideas would be published. Those fresh ideas would be ahead of the curve—they'd push people to action.

And so was born ChangeThis, a Web site that publishes four to six essays, called manifestos, monthly. Some manifestos begin as idea proposals, submitted by people from around the world. These ideas are voted on by the reading public; the most popular become published manifestos. Other manifestos are sought out and written by well-known thinkers, including Tom Peters, Donna Brazile, Malcolm Gladwell, Michael Pollan, Al Gore, and Seth himself. Topics range from corporate sustainability to creativity to nutrition. Each manifesto is free to read and distribute.

Whether it's how to better manage e-mail to free up time, or how to manage communal space to benefit the community, ChangeThis endeavors to spread ideas that make peoples' lives better.

❝ You don't know if your idea is any good the moment it's created. Neither does anyone else. The most you can hope for is a strong gut feeling that it is. And trusting your feelings is not as easy as the optimists say it is. There's a reason why feelings scare us." Hugh MacLeod, "How to Be Creative" Issue 6.05, 10/19/2004

❝ Companies that strive for a higher purpose . . . often find that customers, vendors, suppliers and employees naturally root for its success. A well-defined cause can change the world, no matter how big or small." Ben McConnell and Jackie Huba, "The Customer Evangelist Manifesto" Issue 1, 8/13/2004

❝ Henry Ford could have said, 'We're all manufacturers' and been right. Today, we can say, 'We're all marketers,' and we will be just as right." Seth Godin, "Marketing Mismatch: When New Won't Work With Old" Issue 42.01B, 1/16/2008

Go to changethis.com for more.

The Rise of the Creative Class

RICHARD FLORIDA
Reviewed by Todd

If you are reading our book, there is a good chance you are a member of Richard Florida's Creative Class. Engineers, writers, actresses, and architects make up the core of this new economic segment, and it expands further when you include occupations like lawyers, accountants, and managers, who all use creativity to solve problems. *The Rise of the Creative Class* is as much about finding out who we are as it is about hearing Florida's intriguing theories on creativity's role in economic development.

Florida's research shows that roughly 30 percent of America's workforce falls squarely in the Creative Class, rising from 20 million people in 1980 to over 38 million in 1999. The average salary of a Creative Class member is $48,750, roughly double that of those working in manufacturing or service industries, and that sum accounts for one-half of all salary and wage income in United States. But the differences appear in more than just numbers.

Florida tells us that the Creative Class shuns conformity and prefers to express its individuality. For example, during interviews, the Creative Class will ask potential employers about same-sex partner benefits, independent of their own orientation, to test a company's openness to diversity. This bohemian mind-set is not new for artisans, but these values have now been adopted by a much wider group. And yet the Creative Class believes in the rewards earned through hard work, with goal-setting and achievement among their criteria for success, which is what sets this group apart from the bohemian. The adoption of these values by the Creative Class explains a variety of worldwide trends, ranging from casual Fridays to corporate interest in employees' personal fitness and health.

The social contract between the Creative Class and its employers has changed as well. Workers expect to be treated like individuals, demanding flexible work schedules and an even more flexible dress code. Managers are left to customize their approach to each employee, but companies have also gained in this changed relationship. Because the Creative Class is intrinsically motivated by challenge, companies hook their employees with a cadence of new products and demanding release schedules, and in turn get a high level of devotion. In this arrangement, the compensation is not in dollars but recognition from peers and industry leaders.

"The best cities, like the best companies, do many things well, offering something for everybody."

If the Creative Class expects different rules in the workplace, it is because members live by different ones in their personal pursuits. "Creative work is largely intellectual and sedentary; thus Creative Class people seek to recharge through physical activity." Florida believes the meteoric rise in health-club memberships and the upswing in adventure sports, from rock climbing to snowshoeing, reveals a group of people pursuing a creative, active lifestyle. He further emphasizes that their activities come in the form of individual sports like running, biking, and swimming, pursuits that again match personal interests and flexible work schedules. This lifestyle trend drives to the core of Florida's research and conclusions.

In the past, access to water or other natural resources determined the economic potential of a region. But Florida believes that the Creative Class is the new resource for economic growth. When choosing where to live, the Creative Class looks for "thick labor markets" that allow for easy horizontal moves from one company to another. Some choose cities with easy access to outdoor recreation, allowing daily engagement to match unpredictable work schedules. As a result of Florida's conclusions and with the publication of *The Rise of the Creative Class*, regional economic development has been turned on its ear. Spending by state and city governments to attract corporations or finance professional sports arenas was proved useless by Florida's research. Instead, his 3T's—technology, talent, and tolerance—are the new blueprint many areas are using to grow creative capital.

Florida says that there is much for the Creative Class to do. To begin, its members must recognize their common values of individuality and meritocracy and shed their dated differences of artist versus engineer or liberal versus conservative. The next step is to take a leadership role in growing creative capital through investing in research and development, both public and private, and supporting multidimensional and varied forms of local culture.

The regional economic issues for business leaders make the book alone worth reading, but it is Florida's naming of a new tribe that many readers will identify with and find most encouraging: Who doesn't want to be part of the Creative Class? **TS**

The Rise of the Creative Class: And How It's Transforming Work, Leisure, Community and Every-day Life, Basic Books, Paperback 2004, ISBN 9780465024773

WHERE TO NEXT? ◄◄ Page 265 for **the tension between creativity and organizations** ◄◄ Page 173 for **the connection between management and retention** ◄◄ Page 263 for **innovation and creativity** | EVEN MORE: *The Death and Life of Great American Cities* by Jane Jacobs; *The World Is Flat* by Thomas L. Friedman; *Bowling Alone* by Robert D. Putnam

Emotional Intelligence

DANIEL GOLEMAN

Reviewed by Todd

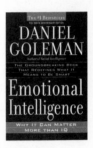

We are a society fixated on testing for intelligence. But as we lament reading about how our community or country is lagging in the latest reading and arithmetic scores, author Daniel Goleman tells us that one's Intelligence Quotient, or IQ, doesn't predict much of anything. IQ tests are a relic of World War I, when they were used by the armed forces to filter millions of recruits into the appropriate positions. Study after study since shows IQ is a poor predictor of eventual success in the real world.

Instead, Goleman asserts, it is *emotion* that plays a greater role in our ability to learn, act, and relate to others. Goleman put the term "emotional intelligence" (EI) into our collective vocabulary by popularizing the work of researchers John Mayer and Peter Salovey. Published in 1995, *Emotional Intelligence* is the broadest of Goleman's books and provides the best survey of how EI plays into all aspects of our lives.

Goleman begins with a discussion of self-awareness, the first of five competencies identified in the original research on EI. One's ability to deal with emotion falls somewhere on a continuum: from a healthy conscious ability to detect and alter one's mood, to an in-between level that brings awareness but accepts a mental state whether good or bad, to a stormy, uncontrollable cocktail of emotion that engulfs the individual. Goleman offers examples of the detriment caused when people handle emotions poorly: Gary is unable to sense his fiancée's emotions nor describe his own, while Elliot, after the removal of a brain tumor severed a neural connection that allows people to place emotional value on alternative choices, loses the ability to reach decisions. In both cases, without the ability to determine one's emotional state, it is impossible to handle the emotions themselves and managing them is no small feat.

The brain leaves us with "little or no control over *when* we are swept up by emotion, nor over *what* emotion it will be." Therefore, being able to control these emotions once they're present, the second competency, is essential. Anger, anxiety, and melancholy have all developed through human evolution to deal with danger, uncertainty, and loss. The mild forms of these emotions are what most of us struggle with on a daily basis and Goleman draws on research to suggest coping mechanisms to manage them. He suggests watching television or reading as a way to minimize anger and anxiety, and, when melancholy and withdrawn, to get out of the house to spend time with friends.

Empathy is just as important as emotional self-awareness, says Goleman, going on to describe the third competency of emotional intelligence. Many of our emotional cues come from the 90 percent of communication that is nonverbal. Babies from an early age look for cues that their expressions are being understood and will mimic the moods of their parents. One-year-olds will cry in reaction to another child's tears, and by age two, the toddler can separate his or her feelings from others, offering the appropriate consolation for upset playmates. Teenagers who develop a natural aptitude for empathy are more popular, more outgoing, and have better luck dating. Empathy is not easy to practice and requires the ability to set aside one's own emotions to perceive the feelings being transmitted by those around him or her.

"Emotional self-control—delaying gratification and stifling impulsiveness— underlies accomplishment of every sort."

The fourth competency Goleman identifies, managing relationships, is the art of managing the emotions of those around you. Actors are masters at playing with the emotions of their audiences. Politicians and business leaders use the same skills to motivate and persuade their constituents. Goleman suggests that studying children at play provides some interesting insights. Researchers find that everyone, popular and unpopular alike, gets rejected by the group at one point or another, but rather than pushing their way in and drawing attention to themselves, the popular kids observe and then imitate what the group is doing in order to be included.

Finally, harnessing emotion can also be a powerful force in the pursuit of success in relationships. This starts with our ability to control impulses that might distract us. In the 1960s, psychologist Walter Mischel developed a test in which four-year-olds were given the choice between eating one puffy treat immediately or waiting several minutes to be rewarded with two treats. The level of restraint foreshadowed social competence as the children were tracked into adolescence. The teenagers who showed restraint as youngsters embraced challenges, were self-reliant, and took initiative, while their impatient counterparts were shy, indecisive, and tended to overreact with a quick temper. Forgoing immediate gratification, reining in that emotional instinct, is a key difference between excellent and world-class performers. Goleman also suggests that optimism and creating a positive state of mind are the answers to connecting emotion to successful efforts. In fact, MetLife now uses optimism as the key determinant for new sales hires.

Emotional Intelligence presents a case that compels the reader to reconsider a whole range of situations from work to home, containing chapters on marriage, management, and ways to teach children about EI. For most, the message will be how to increase awareness of emotions, which results in making relationships healthier. For many, it will be hard not to see personal demons, past or present, in what Goleman describes. TS

Emotional Intelligence: Why It Can Matter More Than IQ, Bantam, Paperback 10th Anniversary Edition 2006, ISBN 9780553383713

WHERE TO NEXT? « Page 252 for **some folks who thought they were smart** ▸ Page 298 for **how emotions manifest from our primal drives** « Page 52 for **how love and leadership go together** | EVEN MORE: *Frames of Mind* by Howard Gardner; *Why Marriages Succeed or Fail* by John Gottman; *Executive* by Harry Levinson

Driven

PAUL R. LAWRENCE AND NITIN NOHRIA
Reviewed by Todd

My wife and I have this running joke that when we witness some human behavior we don't understand, we ask, "What would a caveman do?" We ask this question most often when observing our young children in their daily routines, but recently our reflection on behavior has widened to include our own habits and associated motives. As much as we think we have evolved into refined humans, our basic drives are the same as our ancestors from 70,000 years ago.

And Harvard Business School professors Paul Lawrence and Nitin Nohria agree. In *Driven*, the authors hypothesize that the actions of today's homo sapiens are based on a set of genetically programmed drives. If you think sex and hunger are on that list, you'd be misled by a purely biological point of view. The authors took on the role of academic outsider, trying to connect the realms of biologists and social scientists. The authors lament that the compartmentalization of knowledge within psychology, anthropology, sociology, and the popular ideologies within these disciplines makes it difficult to propose a unified theory for human behavior. But that is the quest in *Driven*.

In many ways, *Driven* is a survey of evolutionary theory proposed over the last forty years, and Lawrence and Nohria do more than an adequate job of describing the terrain. The authors begin with an idea proposed by psychologist Steven Pinker: the human mind has a wide set of preprogrammed skills ranging from basic concepts of quantity, the ability to select suitable habitats, and a moral code and sense of what's right. They continue with archeologist Steven Mithen's postulation that it was the intermingling of these skills that lead to the species' large cognition leap 50,000 years ago.

Lawrence and Nohria then hypothesize that, during this time, human behavior came to be driven by one of four sources: acquiring, bonding, learning, and defending. On the surface, these ring with truth, certainly, but the authors are careful to show these four as primary sources and other motives that we may attach instinctively to the four as just derivatives. For example, the drive to acquire is most often associated with ambition and envy, but at its most basic, this drive is for long-term survival. The drive to bond, again in evolutionary terms, led us to form tribes, further improving the likelihood of survival, but it also sits at the base of atrocities such as genocide. It is the drive to learn which best explains how humans singularly evolved beyond their primate cousins, with the persistence of religion and art in all known human cultures filling in the gaps of our understanding. The drive to defend protects possessions, relationships, even ideologies and leads to, at one end, disagreements, and at the other extreme, war.

"Humans seem to have a predisposition to be open and curious about new theories, but it also seems true that they do not abandon old theories until convinced the new ones are better—that is, more useful, compact, and accurate."

Lawrence and Nohria take the final portion of their book to apply their own expertise with organizations, using the four-driver lens. They start with an almost utopian description of workers naturally bonding with one another, the drive to acquire tempered by well-communicated company goals, and teams defending themselves both internally and externally for needed resources. Then the authors use two U.S. companies as case studies for the four-drive organizational design. First, General Motors is compared to Japanese auto companies. The authors conclude that the company's rise under Alfred Sloan came from the emphasis on the drive to acquire, pitting managers and their divisions against one another for the allocation of resources. This drive has become even more prominent in the company's relationship with suppliers and unions in recent years and contrasts with their Japanese competitors, who foster bonding through company-wide consensus and learning through their religious devotion to continuous improvement. Conversely, in the eyes of the authors, Hewlett-Packard is the exemplar company who got it right from the start. The evidence they provide shows careful consideration by founders Bill Hewlett and David Packard to embrace a set of values that allows employees to engage in all four drives. The result is an almost unparalleled ability to adapt to changes in economic climate and technological products.

In the effort to better understand human behavior, *Driven* provides an illuminating blueprint for parenting and relating for my wife and me. For example, the effectiveness of giving our children "time-outs" to correct bad behavior is explained by their temporary isolation and resulting inability to bond with the rest of the family while in the temporary isolation. The usefulness of Lawrence and Nohria's four drivers can explain the rising credit card debt in America due to the easy means by which those plastic cards fulfill our drive to acquire. Whether your application is personal or societal, appreciating and understanding these basic drives provides another view into the strengths and weakness of our species. TS

Driven: How Human Nature Shapes Our Choices, Jossey-Bass, Paperback 2002, ISBN 9780787963859

WHERE TO NEXT? ◄◄ Page 201 for **an organization that satisfied the drives** ◄◄ Page 196 for **an organization that did not satisfy the drives** ◄◄ Page 199 for **more on Darwin, who inspired the drives** | EVEN MORE: *Consilience* by Edward O. Wilson; *The Third Chimpanzee* by Jared M. Diamond; *The Origin of Wealth* by Eric D. Beinhocker; *Descartes' Error* by Antonio Damasio; *How the Mind Works* by Steven Pinker; *Survival of the Sickest* by Sharon Moalem and Jonathan Prince

To Engineer Is Human

HENRY PETROSKI

Reviewed by Todd

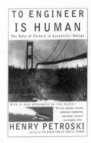

Everything fails; it is just a matter of when.
Parents forewarn their children that failure is common, even likely, through the nursery rhymes of "Humpty Dumpty" and "Jack and Jill." Our first steps and first bike rides without the training wheels give us an idea of what failure feels like, literally. As we find our balance, scraped-up knees and bruised pride happen less frequently. Henry Petroski begins his book, *To Engineer Is Human*, by revisiting these same children's tales, cautioning us again, and, with an engineer's eye, describing a world more reminiscent of London Bridge.

Due to their design, the pen on your desk is likely to last for months while your automobile will likely get you from point A to B for many years, their life spans governed by a balance between function, aesthetic, and economy. Engineers arbitrate those competing forces when bringing an idea into the material world. This arbitration, as Petroski describes it, is something closer to art than science. But sometimes, Petroski warns, art comes at the expense of sound engineering and construction.

The construction of the Hyatt Regency Hotel in Kansas City called for a grand atrium with two walkways suspended from the ceiling by a set of rods that ran through both structures. The single rod mechanism was replaced, during early planning, with two separate rods to simplify construction and utilize standard fabrication techniques. This small change left the system with barely enough strength to support the walkway; adding people proved disastrous. On July 17, 1981, the walkway collapsed, killing 114 people and injuring 200 others.

Petroski uses the Hyatt Regency story to illustrate several nuances of engineering. Many parties were simply negligent: an early ceiling collapse and comments from construction workers about instability gave engineers ample warning to reexamine the walkway plans; no changes were made. Letters to the editors of trade publications following the accident also suggested what seemed like obvious engineering alternatives.

But that is the trick. Knowing the nature of a failure provides paths to the core problem, but this is a hindsight luxury the original engineers didn't have. And there we return back to the idea of engineering as art. The unique design and construction of these walkways left engineers working in a thought space that was dangerous, more so than they realized.

As much as the field of study seems to be based in fact and formula, engineering is better described as grounded in hypothesis, a working practice of individuals developing ideas that tentatively describe phenomena but need constant reevaluation. Engineers spend enormous amounts of time studying the mistakes made by their colleagues. Petroski points to an Egyptian pyramid in Dahshur, with its sudden change to a more shallow angle midway up, as an early example of a trial and error method of construction. Flying buttresses on European cathedrals indicate a similar postconstruction epiphany. Computer-aided three-dimensional drafting and finite element analysis do not protect today's engineers from failure as new designs further strain the tensions between competing factors. While unequivocally a tragedy, the Hyatt Regency walkway collapse becomes a valuable case study from which future engineers can learn.

"Engineering, like poetry, is an attempt to approach perfection."

Petroski's expertise in failure analysis provides important lessons for those in business. Formulas for organizational success, whether self-determined or suggested, are, like design, better described as hypothesis, accurate under some conditions and always open for reexamination. What engineers call "a factor of safety" and inventory analysts call "safety stock" deals with the parallel uncertainty of real world conditions on a rope or a distribution system. Businesses have their own versions of engineering's "factor of safety," whether it concerns extra boxes of inventory under the expeditor's desk or adding a few days to a customer promise for variation in the distribution center, but they'd better make sure those safety factors don't inflate and allow sloppy business practices.

Much lip service is given to accepting failure in business as a natural phase in the learning process, yet internalizing the idea seems a little more difficult. Shareholders don't show sympathy for failed products. Customers expect their product to arrive when promised and in pristine condition. Most of the other books featured in these pages detail the workings of successful companies, while Petroski's book tells a more complicated tale of failure, one in which business practitioners can find wisdom. The most important lesson has to be appreciating failure as a learning opportunity. Failure is common. Not learning from failure forces companies to repeat the same mistakes. In engineering, that repetition can cost lives; in business, our livelihood. ᴛꜱ

To Engineer Is Human: The Role of Failure in Successful Design, Vintage Books, Paperback 1992, ISBN 9780679734161

WHERE TO NEXT? ◄◄ Page 61 for **more subtle forms of failure** ◄◄ Page 256 for **how genius can fail** ◄◄ Page 167 for **operational failure** | EVEN MORE: *The Evolution of Useful Things* by Henry Petroski; *The Logic of Failure* by Dietrich Dorner; *Mistakes Were Made (But Not By Me)* by Carol Tavris and Elliot Aronson

The Wisdom of Crowds

JAMES SUROWIECKI

Reviewed by Todd

The field of nonfiction narratives was a crowded one in 2006, with a number of books published examining varying aspects of decision making. Steven Levitt and Stephen Dubner's immensely popular *Freakonomics* takes the tools of the dismal science of economics and applies it unexpectedly to things like the housing decisions of drug dealers (many, it turns out, choose to live with their mothers). Malcolm Gladwell's sophmore effort, *Blink*, explores the subtle nuances of intuition. While the previous two books looked at decision making by individuals, James Surowiecki took a decidedly different approach in examining the decision-making power of groups in his book *The Wisdom of Crowds*.

Surowiecki offers copious examples to show when groups solve problems better than individuals. When contestants on the TV game show *Who Wants to Be a Millionaire?* use their phone-a-friend lifeline, the likelihood of a right answer stands at 65 percent, while asking the audience delivers the correct response 91 percent of the time. The Iowa Electronic Markets bring together individuals who make trades based on what they think will happen in a variety of political elections. This market-based method is more accurate than voter polls 75 percent of the time and predicts actual election outcomes within a few percentage points.

This is not to say that group decision making is superior in all instances. Surowiecki proposes three conditions that must be satisfied in order for masses to outperform their members. First, the group must be diverse, a condition that ensures a wide sourcing of ideas and perspectives. The members of the group must have a certain level of independence, a tougher constraint given our social nature and natural tendency to follow the crowd. Finally, there must be a method to aggregate the differing opinions of the group. For example, markets use price to pull together all of the opinions of buyers and sellers and determine value.

When these conditions are satisfied, groups prove well suited to tackling three categories of problems. The phone-a-friend example or making election predictions are what Surowiecki refers to as *cognitive* problems, those questions which have definitive answers. The problem of *coordination* finds a solution in the stock market, in this case matching supply with demand. Organizations do much the same in organizing individuals in the pursuit of a purpose. The toughest of the three problems requires *cooperation* to reach a solution. Individuals have a hard time looking past their own self-interests and adopting a broader view. Paying taxes or curbing pollution are among the many problems that fall into this category.

"What I think we know now is that in the long run, the crowd's judgment is going to give us the best chance of making the right decision, and in the face of that knowledge, traditional notions of power and leadership should begin to pale."

The second half of the book is devoted to cases, three of which deal specifically with business issues. "Committees, Juries, and Teams: The *Columbia* Disaster and How Small Groups Can Be Made to Work" is the best example of Surowiecki's ability to synthesize issues of economics, sociology, and psychology with real-world storytelling. In this case, the focus is on the dysfunction present in NASA's Mission Management Team during the ill-fated flight of the space shuttle *Columbia* in 2003. From the start, team leader Linda Ham worked from a preset conclusion that the foam debris that struck the shuttle on liftoff was not a risk, ignoring inquiries and statements to the contrary. The absence of questioning by Ham's team in the face of further evidence confirms studies conducted by political scientist Charlan Nemeth, who found that juries that consider a minority opinion produce more nuanced decisions and used a more rigorous process for reaching their conclusions. Transcripts of the NASA team meetings show Ham did not allow minority opinion. Surowiecki also uses social psychologist Garold Stasser's research to illustrate some of the problems of small teams like this one. In Stasser's experiment, all members of a team are given the same two pieces of information, while a few of the members are given one or two additional pieces of information. Consistently, teams deliberated on the common information, not the unique knowledge held by the minority. The *Columbia* tragedy could have been avoided with a broader decision-making process that brought all team members to the table, allowing their information to be shared and integrated into the deliberations.

Companies are already utilizing *The Wisdom of Crowds*. Companies like Hewlett-Packard, Google, and Microsoft are using internal-decision markets to predict customer demand for their products. Spanish-based clothing retailer Zara is using real-time feedback from its thousand-plus stores worldwide and its three-week concept-to-product cycle to introduce twenty thousand new products each year and produce the exact type and quantity needed for each outlet, replenishing stock twice weekly. But the widespread use of teams requires leaders to understand the pitfalls in group dynamics and ensure that the overall organization and its subcomponents are making the best decisions possible.

When next posed with the question "How do we solve this problem?" the answer should be clear—listen to the crowd. They make better decisions, period. TS

The Wisdom of Crowds, Anchor Books, Paperback 2005, ISBN 9780385721707

WHERE TO NEXT? » Page 318 for **the nuts and bolts of small groups** ‹‹ Page 187 for **working well in small groups** ‹‹ Page 288 for **complex group dynamics** | EVEN MORE: *Flavor of the Month* by Joel Best; *Super Crunchers* by Ian Ayres; *Smart Mobs* by Howard Rheingold

READERS' POLL

While writing this book, we set up a poll so readers could vote on their favorite business books of all time. Here are the Top 10:

1 *The Goal*

2 *The 7 Habits of Highly Effective People*

3 *Good to Great*

4 *The Effective Executive*

5 *How to Win Friends & Influence People*

6 *The Tipping Point*

7 *Purple Cow*

8 *Freakonomics*

9 *The World Is Flat*

10 *Flow*

Readers' Poll conducted, tabulated, and audited by Kate Mytty.

Made to Stick

CHIP HEATH AND DAN HEATH
Reviewed by Todd

Ideas are slippery. Yet each day, we are called upon to communicate our ideas to others—to our employees, our clients, our spouses, our children. Often the words and images used to communicate ideas fade, and with them the ideas' intent, as our listeners' brains filter the endless stream of fact and opinion, notion and conclusion. The challenge lies in how to get your idea not to slip, but to stick.

Your childhood home, Kennedy's challenge to put humans on the moon, a moral lesson from one of Aesop's Fables. Each of these ideas possesses identifiable qualities that make it stick in our memories. Chip Heath, a professor at Stanford, has been intrigued for over a decade by the phenomenon of how many bad ideas gain traction, many in the form of urban myths. Dan Heath cofounded a company that produces video-based textbooks, and he found while working with some of the most-loved professors in the country that they used almost identical teaching methodologies. The two brothers brought together their interests, theories, and experiences to write *Made to Stick*, a book that will help anyone with a message make it memorable and effective. Dan and Chip lay out six key principles of sticky ideas: simplicity, unexpectedness, concreteness, credibility, emotion, and stories.

Human memory excels at remembering identifiable "things" like one-room apartments or midcentury ranch houses. Concreteness trumps the abstract. This explains why it is easy to remember your childhood home. We also care about events from our childhood, associating birthday parties and broken bones with the places where they happened. Those emotions trigger strong memories and make them even stickier. Concreteness and emotion are hallmarks of a sticky idea.

Chip and Dan use President John F. Kennedy's State of the Union speech in 1961 to illustrate another principle of stickiness: unexpectedness. Kennedy covered most of what was expected for that era: the Cold War, NATO, and civil defense. The speech's conclusion, though, changed the course of American history. He declared, "This nation should commit itself to achieving the goal, before this decade is out, of landing a man on the moon and returning him safely to Earth. . . ." The declaration was unexpected, and the call for serious space exploration caught the attention of the American public. More important, the challenge created a "knowledge gap," as a nation asked itself how it would do that. That curiosity—the gap between what we know and what we want to know—is what propelled the United States to put Neil Armstrong on the moon in 1969.

THE SIX PRINCIPLES OF STICKY IDEAS:

Simplicity
Unexpectedness
Concreteness
Credibility
Emotions
Stories

Proverbs are the quintessential sticky ideas. The proverb "A bird in the hand is worth two in the bush" is full of concreteness in its reference to clearly understandable objects. A complex moral idea with wide applicability is communicated simply, with no wasted words. A similar sentiment can be found in Spanish, Polish, and medieval Latin. This idea appears to have originated in Aesop's "The Hawk and the Nightingale," written in 570 BC. Now, *that* is a sticky idea.

"We wanted to take apart sticky ideas—both natural and created—and figure out what made them stick."

Like all great books, business or otherwise, stories are the backbone of *Made to Stick*. They bring ideas—both the Heath brothers' and ours—to life. Stories, the authors say, act as flight simulators for the mind. Xerox repairmen frequently share stories with their cohorts over lunch. What at first might look like the sharing of gripes among coworkers is actually a rich learning environment. As each repairman tells his tale of some unexpected machine malfunction, the other lunchmates visualize those same problems, preparing themselves for a future encounter. These Xerox technicians' tales contain most of the Heaths' principles of stickiness. In each, you'll find concrete descriptions of copier components, unexpected problems, and emotional frustration. The trick is keeping the story simple enough that it retains its essence and its impact.

What do Fortune 500 CEOs and health-care workers in Africa have in common? Both have the formidable challenge of selling ideas to thousands of people. Whether communicating a strategic course correction or

BIG IDEAS **309**

advocating healthy behaviors that can save lives, making their ideas sticky is what will make their efforts successful. It's the same for teachers, tool-and-die makers, managers, marketers . . . and, well, you. Everybody is selling something (and I mean that in the most positive of terms). *Made to Stick* gives you the tools to find more traction for your ideas. ᴛs

Made to Stick: Why Some Ideas Survive and Others Die, Random House, Hardcover 2007, ISBN 9781400064281

WHERE TO NEXT? ◀ Page 133 for **the Heaths' inspiration** ◀ Page 102 for **becoming top of mind** ◀ Page 130 to **get people talking** | EVEN MORE: *Words That Work* by Frank Lutz; *Story* by Robert McKee; *Start-up* by Jerry Kaplan

TAKEAWAYS We've made our case: business books solve problems. The eighty-nine preceding books certainly prove that. But these eleven books have an additional advantage, a particular ability to be quickly applied to the problems you face today. It's what every busy businessperson is looking for: a good takeaway.

The First 90 Days

MICHAEL WATKINS

THE AUTHOR › Michael Watkins is a professor at Harvard Business School, doing research into leadership and negotiation. He is the author of *Right from the Start* (2005) and *Shaping the Game* (2006), in addition to a number of books on business negotiations.

THE MESSAGE › The average person will have five transitions—moving up or laterally on the career food chain—during his or her career, says Watkins. Being good at one job does not mean that you will naturally excel at another. But if you take too much time to adjust, or don't adjust enough, you'll be taking a return trip back down the ladder. Watkins has created a ten-step road map to help you in your transition. The road map has practical and instantly applicable advice summed up in directives like: promote yourself, create coalitions, and secure early wins.

WORDS ON . . . TRANSITIONS ›
"The President of the United States gets 100 days to prove himself; you get 90. The actions you take during your first three months in a new job will largely determine whether you succeed or fail. Transitions are periods of opportunity, a chance to start afresh and to make needed changes in an organization. But they are also periods of acute vulnerability, because you lack established working relationships and a detailed understanding of your new role."

The First 90 Days: Critical Success Strategies for New Leaders at All Levels, Harvard Business School Press, Hardcover 2003, ISBN 9781591391104

WHERE TO NEXT? » Pages 237-240 of *The First 90 Days* for **the solutions to five transitional challenges.**

LEADERSHIP

Up the Organization

ROBERT TOWNSEND

THE AUTHOR › Avis's bold advertising jab at the top-rated Hertz, "We're only No. 2, but we try harder," is emblematic of the style Robert C. Townsend employed to turn around the struggling car rental company when he was CEO from 1962–1965.

THE MESSAGE › *Up the Organization* is the alphabet primer for running a business. Townsend was a relatively young executive at fifty when he first wrote *Up the Organization* in 1970, and his energy infuses each chapter. Some are as short as one paragraph, but all are in alphabetical order, with headings like: Budgets, Decisions, and No-No's. The effectiveness of the book is a direct result of this commonsense handling of critical business advice. Townsend's approach to his own business was to concentrate on innovation, abolish a hierarchy, and encourage decision making from all employees up and down the line, and that philosophy is reflected here.

WORDS ON . . . TITLES ›

"Titles Are Handy Tools: There is a trade-off here. In one way, titles are a form of psychic compensation, and if too many titles are distributed, the currency is depreciated. But a title is also a tool. If our salesman is a vice president and yours is a sales rep, and both are in a waiting room, guess who gets in first and gets the most attention . . . If you find you can't get applicants for menial jobs, maybe your titles are obsolete. A restaurant cured a chronic busboy shortage by changing the title to 'logistics engineer.' "

Up the Organization: How to Stop the Corporation from Stifling People and Strangling Profits, Foreword by Warren Bennis, Jossey-Bass, Hardcover Commemorative Edition 2007, ISBN 9780787987756

WHERE TO NEXT? » Pages 141–159 in *Up the Organization* for **"Further Up the Organization."**

Beyond the Core

CHRIS ZOOK

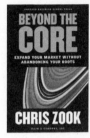

THE AUTHOR ▸ Chris Zook is a partner at Bain & Company, where he leads the company's Global Strategy Practice. He is also author of *Profit from the Core* and *Unstoppable*.

THE MESSAGE ▸ *Beyond the Core* is the middle volume of Chris Zook's business book trilogy about company growth. His early research found that only one in eight companies could sustain reasonable growth in sales and earnings over a ten-year period. In *Beyond the Core*, Zook examines how smart companies identify and expand into new growth areas outside their core business that he calls "adjacencies." His research identifies five dimensions to a growth opportunity: customers, competitors, cost structure, distribution, and brand. New growth initiatives that only changed one dimension were three times more likely to succeed than those that changed three or more.

WORDS ON . . . THE DIFFICULTY IN FINDING GROWTH ▸

"Just 25 percent of investments in growth initiatives, most of them true adjacency expansions, created value and added to growth. . . . The average success rate for new products is about 30 percent; for start-ups, below 10 percent; for joint ventures, about 20 percent; and for related acquisitions, about 30 percent. These studies span a wide range of methods and quality of data, but all show how hard it is to find and execute on new sources of growth in a company."

Beyond the Core: Expand Your Market without Abandoning Your Roots, Harvard Business School Press, Hardcover 2004, ISBN 9781578519514

WHERE TO NEXT? ↦ Read pages 73–107 in *Beyond the Core* for **evaluating adjacency moves.**

SALES AND MARKETING

Little Red Book of Selling

JEFFREY GITOMER

THE AUTHOR › Jeffrey Gitomer is a sales consultant and a force of nature. His presentations are legendary. His enthusiasm is unparalleled. His intensity is off the chart. Gitomer is a syndicated columnist and he has a huge audience for his weekly e-mail newsletter called "Sales Caffeine."

THE MESSAGE › This book offers motivation to get you jump-started on Monday morning. Here, Gitomer has collected all the great sales teachers' philosophies, added a lot of punch via his "on the street" writing style, and, as a result, offers us a sales book to inspire you when you need that extra kick.

WORDS ON . . . (WHAT ELSE?) SELLING ›
"Don't sell the product. Don't sell the service. Sell the appointment. They can't push a contract or a check through the phone—just sell the appointment."

"Networking works well when you employ the two-word secret: Show up. Networking works best when you employ the three-word secret: Show up prepared."

"It's not hard sell, it's heart sell. Good questions get to the heart of the problem/need/situation very quickly—without the buyer feeling like he or she is being pushed."

Little Red Book of Selling: 12.5 Principles of Sales Greatness, Bard Press, Hardcover 2004, ISBN 9781885167606

WHERE TO NEXT? ↠ Read pages 124-135 in *Little Red Book of Selling* for **Principle 8.**

RULES AND SCOREKEEPING

What the CEO Wants You to Know

RAM CHARAN

THE AUTHOR ▸ Ram Charan is an advisor to CEOs and senior employees in Fortune 500 companies. As an example of his heavyweight status, Charan was the first outsider Jeff Immelt turned to for advice when he took over GE following Jack Welch's departure.

THE MESSAGE ▸ This book, which runs a very readable 130 pages, offers a crash course in what Ram Charan calls "business acumen." The first half of the book serves as a manual, explaining a set of financial metrics that managers value, such as return on assets and cash flow. Charan then includes sections on international business, getting things done, as well as an eight-page action plan geared toward project implementation. New employees need two things for their first day on the job: the company handbook and a copy of *What the CEO Wants You to Know*.

WORDS ON . . . BUSINESS AND INTUITION ▸
"Use this book to learn the language of business. Then put the book aside and practice until the fundamentals of business become instinctive, as they are for the street vendor. You'll discover the commonsense of business, and you'll be on your way to developing business acumen."

"People with business acumen don't just memorize these words like terms in a textbook. They understand their real meaning, instinctively sense their relationships to one another, and use them to create a mental picture. True businesspeople combine the elements of money making to get an intuitive grasp of the total business."

What the CEO Wants You to Know: Using Business Acumen to Understand How Your Company Really Works, Crown Business, Hardcover 2001, ISBN 9780609608395

WHERE TO NEXT? ↦ Read chapter 2 of *What the CEO Wants You to Know* for more about the basics of business.

MANAGEMENT

The Team Handbook

PETER R. SCHOLTES, BRIAN L. JOINER, AND BARBARA J. STREIBEL

THE AUTHOR ▸ Brian Joiner and Peter Scholtes were early teachers of the quality movement during the 1980s and 1990s. Much of their work advocated Deming's management philosophy which, in part, touted teams as being integral to improving quality.

THE MESSAGE ▸ *The Team Handbook* sets the standard for a functional workbook that can be easily employed in the workplace, and the book has owned this category since the first edition was published in 1988. This is not a book to help you decide whether you want to start a team; instead, this is the book you need to make your next team project a success. There is ample white space on each page for notes, and many worksheets, which are available for download online, to help your team flourish.

WORDS ON . . . TEAMS AND MANAGEMENT ▸

"To succeed, organizations must rely on the knowledge, skills, experience, and perspective of a wide range of people to solve multifaceted problems, make good decisions, and deliver effective solutions. . . . Teams create environments in which members can keep up with change, learn more about the organization, and develop collaborative skills."

"Once people recognize that systems create the majority of problems, they stop blaming individual employees. They instead ask which system needs improvement, and are more likely to seek out and find the true source of improvement."

The Team Handbook, Third Edition, Öriel Incorporated, Hardcover 2003, ISBN 9781884731266

WHERE TO NEXT? ↦ Read the introduction to *The Team Handbook*.

BIOGRAPHIES

A Business and Its Beliefs

THOMAS J. WATSON JR.

THE AUTHOR ▸ Thomas J. Watson Jr. took the helm at IBM from his father in 1952. During his twenty-year tenure at IBM, he moved the company forward on several fronts, including the transition from mechanical to electronic computation.

THE MESSAGE ▸ In 1962, Watson was asked to give a number of lectures at Columbia Graduate School of Business as part of a series that featured speakers presenting on the management of large organizations. *A Business and Its Beliefs* grew out of Watson's presentation. Watson discusses the humanistic philosophy of management that has defined IBM and which revolves around three tenets: respect for the individual, giving the best customer service in the world, and the responsibility to *"pursue all tasks with the idea that they can be accomplished in a superior fashion."*

WORDS ON . . . ACTING ON BELIEF ▸

"I firmly believe that any organization, in order to survive and achieve success, must have a sound set of beliefs on which it premises all its policies and actions . . . Next, I believe that the most important single factor in corporate success is faithful adherence to those beliefs . . . And finally, I believe that if an organization is to meet the challenges of a changing world, it must be prepared to change everything about itself except those beliefs as it moves through corporate life."

A Business and Its Beliefs: The Ideas That Helped Build IBM, McGraw-Hill, Hardcover 2003, ISBN 9780071418591

WHERE TO NEXT? ↠ Read pages 11-28 in *A Business and Its Beliefs* for **IBM's three simple beliefs.**

ENTREPRENEURSHIP

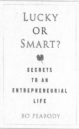

Lucky or Smart?

BO PEABODY

THE AUTHOR › Bo Peabody was the poster boy for success during the Internet boom of the 1990s. He built Tripod, a Web site hosting company with a one-million-member community, and sold it for $58 million in Lycos stock, which he turned into $600 million two years later.

THE MESSAGE › Peabody claims successful businesses are more the result of luck than smarts. The author says that besides being in the right place at the right time, there is one thing that entrepreneurs can do to improve their chances: start "fundamentally innovative, morally compelling, and philosophically positive" companies because cool people will want to work with you and customers will want to buy from you. Smart entrepreneurs recognize the role that luck plays in the outcome and ignore flattering media attention that can disguise the true reason for success.

WORDS ON . . . IF YOU SHOULD BECOME AN ENTREPRENEUR ›
"When you look up at a cloud, which of the following best describes your thoughts?

> A. Wow, that cloud would make a great painting.
> B. Hmmm, how would you describe that cloud to someone else?
> C. What a silly question. I never look up at clouds.
> D. Let's see. I wonder if I could manufacture an environmentally friendly chemical that instantaneously creates or dissolves clouds within a perfectly defined geographical area?
> E. Gee, I wonder exactly how a cloud is formed.

> "If you answered D, you are most likely an entrepreneur.
> If you answered E, read on. There is still hope."

Lucky or Smart? Secrets to an Entrepreneurial Life, Random House, Hardcover 2005, ISBN 9781400062904

WHERE TO NEXT? ❯❯ Read all fifty-eight pages of *Lucky or Smart?*

NARRATIVES

The Lexus and the Olive Tree

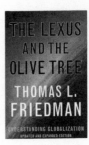

THOMAS L. FRIEDMAN

THE AUTHOR › Thomas Friedman is the foreign affairs columnist for the *New York Times* and author of four books. His 2006 book, *The World Is Flat*—a catchphrase for today's frictionless global commerce—has sold more than two million copies, at the time of this writing, and continues to influence discussion on the subject.

THE MESSAGE › Friedman asserts that in the vacuum left by the end of the Cold War, globalization entered with its own rules and logic. This globe-trotting trip of a book shows us how the effects of the trend are evident in everything from politics to the environment to the "economics of virtually every country in the world." Friedman uses vivid and wide-ranging examples, from the enormous Taco Bell in Qatar to the faceless financial traders sitting in their basements moving their money from Frankfurt to Tokyo, to highlight changes in how we communicate, how we invest, and how we learn about the world.

WORDS ON . . . THE DICHOTOMOUS STATE OF THE GLOBE ›
"It struck me then that the Lexus and the olive tree were actually pretty good symbols of this post—Cold War era: half the world seemed to be emerging from the Cold War intent on building a better Lexus, dedicated to modernizing, streamlining and privatizing their economies in order to thrive in the system of globalization. And half of the world—sometimes half the same country, sometimes half the same person—was still caught up in the fight over who owns which olive tree."

The Lexus and the Olive Tree: Understanding Globalization, Farrar, Straus and Giroux, Hardcover Updated and Expanded 2000, ISBN 9780374185527

WHERE TO NEXT? ›› Read pages 113-137 in *The Lexus and the Olive Tree* to **learn about the electronic herd.**

INNOVATION AND CREATIVITY

Thinkertoys

MICHAEL MICHALKO

THE AUTHOR › Michael Michalko is a renowned creativity specialist and frequent speaker on creativity issues to the corporate world.

THE MESSAGE › Michalko developed the ideas on creative thinking presented here while an officer in the U.S. Army assigned to NATO. He envisioned a different way of looking at the military, and its political and economic problems. To find new solutions, he organized a team of experts and collected all the known inventive-thinking methods available. After he left the military, he was asked to develop think tanks for the CIA on creative thinking. Michalko divides the book into a linear techniques section and an intuitive section for generating new ideas. Within the thirty-nine chapters, the author adds puzzles, games, and visual riddles to illustrate his points.

WORDS ON . . . DEVELOPING YOUR CREATIVITY ›
"Each one of us must affirm our own individual creativity. Although many facets of human creativity are similar, they are never identical. All pine trees are very much alike, yet none is exactly the same as another. Because of this range of similarity and difference, it is difficult to summarize the infinite variations of individual creativity. Each person has to do something different, something that is unique. The artist, after all, is not a special person; every person is a special kind of artist."
"If you act like an idea person, you will become one. It is the intention and going through the motions of being creative that counts."

Thinkertoys: A Handbook of Creative-Thinking Techniques, Ten Speed Press, Paperback Second Edition 2006, ISBN 9781580087735

WHERE TO NEXT? » Read pages 11–21 in *Thinkertoys* for **effective ways to pump your mind.**

BIG IDEAS

More Than You Know

MICHAEL J. MAUBOUSSIN

THE AUTHOR › Michael Mauboussin is chief investment strategist at Legg Mason Capital and an adjunct professor at Columbia Business School.

THE MESSAGE › The thirty-eight essays in *More Than You Know* were originally written under the newsletter column "The Consilient Observer" while Mauboussin worked at the Credit Suisse Group, a Swiss financial services company. Consilience—the idea that all knowledge can be unified into a single working system—has heavily influenced Mauboussin's investing philosophy. Each essay ties an accessible metaphor to a piece of specific research and its implication for investors. Don't be scared off by the financial angle. The essence of Mauboussin's work is understanding how humans can make better decisions—something we can all use help with.

WORDS ON . . . HONEYBEES AND STOCK MARKETS ›
"Perhaps the biggest differences between the hive and the market are incentives and the role of prices. In a colony, each bee acts not to maximize its own well-being but rather the well-being of the colony (evolution shaped this behavior). In markets, each trader seeks to maximize his own utility. This difference may make colonies more robust than markets because colonies are not as susceptible to the positive feedback that creates market fragility. . . . Also, hives do not have prices. Prices are important in a free-market economic system because they help individuals determine how to allocate resources. Bees convey information through their dances, but prices in markets often go beyond informing investors to influencing them, spurring unhealthy imitative behavior."

More Than You Know: Finding Financial Wisdom in Unconventional Places, Columbia University Press, Hardcover Updated and Expanded 2008, ISBN 9780231143721

WHERE TO NEXT? ›› Read any essay in *More Than You Know*; you'll learn something.

THE LAST WORD Thanks for reading *The 100 Best Business Books of All Time*. We wrote the book to help people find solutions to their business problems. We hope you found that and more. Visit 100bestbiz.com for more on all of the books we featured here, including chapter excerpts, interviews with the authors, videos about the books, and more.

—Jack and Todd

ACKNOWLEDGMENTS

Our first thank you goes out to Sally Haldorson. She was conspicuously hiding in our customer services group for eight years with a master's degree in creative writing. Sally's roles included editor, cheerleader, psychologist, humorist, and referee. The book would have never happened without you, Sally.

We next have to thank Joy Panos Stauber. Everything (and we mean everything) about the way this book looks is owed to Joy. She has been our designer, art director, and brand creator for several years. Joy is also our friend, which makes it even better.

Kate Mytty was our air traffic controller. This was a massive project, and there were a lot of moving parts. Imagine tracking down the permissions to use every book cover. Kate made all the little things that make all the difference happen.

Rebecca Schlei Hartman made sure everything was right. She checked quotations and page numbers. She questioned word usage. She kept an eye out for things we never would have caught. Rebecca kept us aware that details do matter.

The words of a number of our staff appear on the pages of this book. In addition to the folks above, Todd Lazarski, Jon Mueller, Roy Normington, Aaron Schleicher, and Dylan Schleicher all contributed to making this book what it is.

When we signed the contract, we told everyone that this book wasn't about Jack or Todd, but about 800-CEO-READ. We need to thank Meg Bacik, Jake Cohen, Scott Kopf, Shane Muellemann, Mel Koenig, and Shawn Quinn, along with everyone mentioned earlier, whose hard work kept the company engine running smoothly and efficiently while we were working on this project.

We need to thank Carol Grossmeyer, Rebecca Schwartz, and Daniel Goldin from our parent company, Dickens Books, for their support. The publication of this book is a big deal for the entire company.

We also need to thank the folks at Portfolio. Will Weisser read our first proposal and challenged us to go back to the drawing board. Adrian Zackheim helped us see the audience for this book. Adrienne Schultz provided the support and the guidance every book (and author) needs. There was no better cheerleader than Deb Lewis. We also want to thank Maureen Cole and Jeffrey Krames for their support through the whole process.

We send our love out to Barbara Cave Henricks and Sara Schneider, who helped get the word out for the book. Ray Bard read early drafts and helped us think about how to better market the book. Charles Fishman gets kudos for delivering the subtitle. Nick and Nikki Smith Morgan helped us hone the message for the whole book as we got out and started talking to others about it.

We need to acknowledge all the authors whose works are included in the book. We are merely summarizing your hard work. All of your thoughts and ideas have made our business better. Thank you!

And finally, we must thank our families. It was hard—much harder than either of us expected—to write this book. Jack says: "Ann, thank you for being there for the past forty years. And also thanks to my granddaughters for giving me joy and happiness. There were times during this process when your delight put this all in the right perspective." Todd says: "Amy, thanks for your patience and understanding. To Ethan, Zach, and Alexa—you *do* have a father."

Thanks for reading.

Grateful acknowledgment is made to the following for permission to reproduce the following book jackets and book covers:

Anchor Books, a division of Random House, Inc.: *The Wisdom of Crowds* by James Surowiecki. Used by permission of Anchor Books.

Bantam, a division of Random House, Inc.: *Emotional Intelligence* by Daniel Goleman; *McDonald's: Behind the Arches* by John F. Love; and *Sam Walton: Made in America* by Sam Walton and John Huey.

Bard Press: *Little Red Book of Selling* by Jeffrey Gitomer.

Basic Books, a member of the Perseus Books Group: *On Becoming a Leader* by Warren G. Bennis; *Out of Control* by Kevin Kelly; *Partnership Charter* by David Gage; *The Rise of the Creative Class* by Richard Florida; and *The Story Factor* by Annette Simmons. Used by arrangement with Basic Books. All rights reserved.

Clerisy Press: *Jump Start Your Business Brain* by Doug Hall. Courtesy of Clerisy Press Inc., Cincinnati, Ohio.

Collins Business, an imprint of HarperCollins Publishers: *Control Your Own Destiny or Someone Else Will* by Noel M. Tichy and Stratford Sherman; *Crossing the Chasm* by Geoffrey A. Moore; *The Effective Executive* by Peter F. Drucker; *The E-Myth Revisited* by Michael E. Gerber; *The Essential Drucker* by Peter F. Drucker; *Good to Great* by Jim Collins; *The HP Way* by David Packard; *In Search of Excellence* by Thomas J. Peters and Robert H. Waterman; *Influence* by Robert B. Cialdini; *The Innovator's Dilemma* by Clayton M. Christensen; *Moments of Truth* by Jan Carlzon; *Reengineering the Corporation* by Michael Hammer and James Champy; *Swim with the Sharks without Being Eaten Alive* by Harvey B. Mackay; and *Who Says Elephants Can't Dance?* by Louis V. Gerstner, Jr.

Columbia University Press: *More Than You Know* by Michael J. Mauboussin. Used with permission of Columbia University Press.

Crown Business, a division of Random House, Inc.: *Execution* by Larry Bossidy and Ram Charan; *How to Be a Star at Work* by Robert E. Kelley; *The Leadership Moment: Nine True Stories of Triumph and Disaster and Their Lessons for Us All* by Michael Useem; *Losing My Virginity* by Richard Branson; and *What the CEO Wants You to Know* by Ram Charan. Used by permission of Crown Business.

Doubleday, a division of Random House, Inc.: *The Art of Innovation* by Tom Kelley with Jonathan Littman; *The Great Game of Business* by Jack Stack with Bo Burlingham; *Leadership is An Art* by Max Depree; *My Years with General Motors* by Alfred Sloan; *Only the Paranoid Survive* by Andrew S. Grove; *The Power of Intuition* by Gary Klein; and *The Republic of Tea* by Mel Ziegler, Bill Rosenzweig, and Patricia Ziegler. Used by permission of Doubleday.

Farrar, Straus, Giroux: *The Lexus and the Olive Tree* by Thomas L. Friedman.

The Free Press, a division of Simon & Schuster Adult Publishing Group: *Discovering the Soul of Service* by Leonard L. Berry, copyright © 1999 by Simon & Schuster, Inc.; and *Now, Discover Your Strengths* by Marcus Buckingham and Donald O. Clifton, copyright © 2001 by Simon & Schuster, Inc. Used with the permission of The Free Press. All rights reserved.

Grand Central Publishing, a division of Hachette Book Group USA, Inc.: *Selling the Invisible* by Harry Beckwith and *A Whack on the Side of the Head* by Roger von Oech.

Harper Perennial, a division of HarperCollins Publishers: *Flow* by David Packard.

Harvard Business School Publishing: *The Age of Unreason* by Charles Handy, 1990; *Balanced Scorecard* by Robert S. Kaplan and David P. Norton, 1996; *Beyond the Core* by Chris Zook, 2004; *Competing for the Future* by Gary Hamel and C.K. Prahalad, 1996; *The Experience Economy* by B. Joseph Pine II and James H. Gilmore, 1999; *Financial Intelligence* by Karen Berman and Joe Knight, with John Case, 2006; *First 90 Days* by Michael Watkins, 2003; *The Knowing-Doing Gap* by Jeffrey Pfeffer and Robert I. Sutton, 2000; *Leading Change* by John P. Kotter, 1996; *The Monk and the Riddle* by Randy Komisar with Kent Lineback, 2001; and *Questions of Character* by Joseph L Badaracco, Jr., 2006. © Copyright Harvard Business School Publishing. All rights reserved.

Houghton Mifflin Company: *Guerilla Marketing, 4th Edition* by Jay Conrad Levinson.

Hyperion: *How to Become a Rainmaker* by Jeffrey J. Fox, cover copyright © 2000 Hyperion and *Never Give In!* by Winston S. Churchill, cover copyright © 2003 Hyperion.

Jossey-Bass, A Wiley Imprint: *Driven* by Paul R. Lawrence and Nitin Nohria; *The Five Dysfunctions of a Team* by Patrick Lencioni; *Leadership Challenge* by James M. Kouzes and Barry Z. Posner; and *Up the Organization* by Robert Townsend.

Kaplan Publishing, a division of Kaplan, Inc.: *The Radical Leap* by Steve Farber. Published with permission from Kaplan Publishing, a division of Kaplan, Inc.

Little, Brown and Company, a division of Hachette Book Group USA, Inc.: *Six Thinking Hats* by Edward de Bono and *The Tipping Point* by Malcolm Gladwell.

McGraw-Hill, a division of The McGraw-Hill Companies: *A Business and Its Beliefs* by Thomas J. Watson, 2003; *Chasing Daylight* by Eugene O'Kelly, 2007; and *Positioning* by Al Ries and Jack Trout, 2000. Reproduced with permission of The McGraw-Hill Companies.

The MIT Press: *Out of the Crisis* by W. Edwards Deming.

Nigel Parry/Creative Photographers inc.: *The Creative Habit* by Twyla Tharp, Simon & Schuster. Cover image reprinted with the permission of © Nigel Parry/CPi.

North River Press: *The Goal* by Eliyahu M. Goldratt and Jeff Cox.

Oriel Incorporated: *The Team Handbook, Third Edition* by Peter R. Scholtes, Brian L. Joiner and Barbara J. Streibel, © 2003 Oriel Incorporated. All rights reserved.

Pearson Education: *Zag: Number One Strategy of High-Performance Brands* by Marty Neumeier. Reproduced by permission of Pearson Education, Inc. All rights reserved.

Penguin Books, a member of Penguin Group (USA) Inc.: *The Art of Possibility* by Rosamund Stone Zander and Benjamin Zander; *Getting Things Done* by David Allen; and *A New Brand World* by Scott Bedbury and Stephen Fenichell.

Pocket Books, an imprint of Simon & Schuster Adult Publishing Group: *How to Win Friends and Influence People* by Dale Carnegie. Copyright © 1998 by Simon & Schuster, Inc. Used with the permission of Pocket Books. All rights reserved.

Portfolio, a member of Penguin Group (USA) Inc.: *The Art of the Start* by Guy Kawasaki; *Purple Cow* by Seth Godin; and *The Smartest Guys in the Room* by Bethany McLean and Peter Elkind.

Random House, Inc.: *The Force* by David Dorsey; *Lucky or Smart?* by Bo Peabody; *Made to Stick* by Chip Heath and Dan Heath; *Titan* by Ron Chernow; *What Should I Do With My Life?* by Po Bronson; and *When Genius Failed* by Roger Lowenstein. Used by permission of Random House, Inc.

Random House Children's Books, a division of Random House, Inc.: *Oh, The Places You'll Go!* by Dr. Seuss. Used by permission of Random House Children's Books.

Revell, a division of Baker Publishing Group: *Secrets of Closing the Sale* by Zig Ziglar.

Simon & Schuster Adult Publishing Group: *The 7 Habits of Highly Effective People* by Stephen Covey, copyright © 2004 by Simon & Schuster, Inc.; *American Steel* by Richard Preston, copyright © 1991 by Simon & Schuster, Inc.; *First, Break All the Rules* by Marcus Buckingham and Curt Coffman, copyright © 1999 by Simon & Schuster, Inc.; *Growing a Business* by Paul Hawken, copyright © 1988 by Simon & Schuster, Inc.; and *Why We Buy* by Paco Underhill, copyright © 2000 by Simon & Schuster, Inc. Used with the permission of Simon & Schuster Adult Publishing Group. All rights reserved.

Taylor and Francis Group, LLC, a division of Informa plc.: *Toyota Production System* by Taiichi Ohno. Reproduced by permission of Taylor and Francis Group, LLC.

Ten Speed Press: *Thinkertoys* by Michael Michalko. Used with permission of Ten Speed Press, Berkeley, CA. www.tenspeed.com.

Viking Penguin, a member of Penguin Group (USA) Inc.: *Orbiting the Giant Hairball* by Gordon MacKenzie.

Vintage Books, a division of Random House, Inc.: *Personal History* by Katharine Graham and *To Engineer is Human* by Henry Petroski. Used by permission of Vintage Books.

W.W. Norton & Company, Inc.: *Moneyball* by Michael Lewis and *Naked Economics: Undressing the Dismal Science* by Charles Wheelan. Used by permission of W. W. Norton & Company, Inc.

SIDEBARS

"Sidebars" designed by Joy Panos Stauber

Images thanks to:
The Best Route to an Idea: Sign drawn by Joy Panos Stauber
Bestselling Business Books: Cash register drawn by Dylan Schleicher
Business Books for All Ages: Image by ©iStockphoto.com/GildedCage
Classics: Image by ©iStockphoto.com/Anna Ceglinska
Conferences to Attend: Image by ©iStockphoto.com/Ingmar Wesemann